Enforcing Civil Rights

STUDIES IN GOVERNMENT
AND PUBLIC POLICY

Enforcing Civil Rights

Race Discrimination and the Department of Justice

Brian K. Landsberg

 University Press of Kansas

Published by the University Press of Kansas (Lawrence, Kansas 66049), which was organized by
the Kansas Board of Regents and is operated and funded by Emporia State University, Fort Hays
State University, Kansas State University, Pittsburg State University, the University of Kansas, and
Wichita State University

Library of Congress Cataloging-in-Publication Data

Landsberg, Brian K.
    Enforcing civil rights : race discrimination and the Department of
Justice / by Brian K. Landsberg.
        p.   cm. — (Studies in government and public policy)
    Includes bibliographical references and index.
    ISBN 0-7006-0826-5 (alk. paper)
    1. Race discrimination—Law and legislation—United States.
2. United States. Dept. of Justice. Civil Rights Division.
I. Title. II. Series.
KF4755.L36   1997   96-29501
342.73′0873—dc21

British Library Cataloguing in Publication Data is available.

Printed in the United States of America

10 9 8 7 6 5 4 3 2 1

This book is dedicated to the memory of my father,

MORRIE LANDSBERG,

a master of the art of objective, fair reporting

and my first role model

Contents

Figures and Tables

Figures

Tables

Preface

When I left the Civil Rights Division of the Department of Justice in 1986 and migrated to McGeorge School of Law in Sacramento, I told then-Dean Gordon Schaber that one of my motivations for the job change was the opportunity to write about the division. After ten years of teaching and writing law review articles, McGeorge has made it possible for me to meld the practical experience I gained during my tenure with the division and the scholarly experience of academia. McGeorge has provided generous support for this project in the form of sabbaticals, summer research grants, library resources, research assistants, and secretarial help. I would like to acknowledge the help of Dean Gerald Caplan, reference librarians Louise Roysdon, Sue Welsh, and Evelyn Posamentier, student research assistants Kristen Hoberg, Molly Mosley, Kristine Byron, Mykka Young, Maria Landeros, Eugenia Romas, and Kate Kennedy Jones, and faculty secretaries Pauline Campos, Sharleen Driver, and Paul Fuller.

I arrived in Washington, D.C., on November 22, 1963, and found at the Department of Justice a scene of indescribable sadness in the wake of the assassination of a president who symbolized high ideals and patriotism to those who came to work in his administration. By the time I began work in the Civil Rights Division in January 1964, the division was back into high gear and President Johnson had begun his successful campaign for the enactment of the Civil Rights Act of 1964. I learned so much from the men and women of the Civil Rights Division in the twenty-two years that followed. The first person to teach me that civil rights enforcement does not come easily was John Doar, who made me jump numerous hoops before hiring me and continued to do so until he left the division in 1967. My early mentor was the late David L. Norman. As the book reflects, I hold great respect for the assistant attorneys general under whom I served, despite some disagreements on issues. Career attorneys to whom I owe special thanks include three outstanding leaders who are deceased: D. Robert

Owen, Walter W. Barnett, and Thomas M. Keeling. I will not attempt to single out the living.

Portions of Chapter 9 first appeared in my article "The Role of Civil Service Attorneys and Political Appointees in Making Policy in the Civil Rights Division of the U.S. Department of Justice," 9 Journal of Law and Politics 275 (1993). Portions of the case study on school desegregation are based on my article "The Federal Government and the Promise of *Brown,*" 96 Teachers College Record 627 (1995).

Finally, I received valuable suggestions on drafts of this book from Julie Davies, Monica Gallagher, Dorothy S. Landsberg, Stephen J. Pollak, Robert Reinstein, James P. Turner, Michael Vitiello, and Stephen L. Wasby and from university press reviewers.

1

Introduction

The ancient commandment "Justice, justice shall you pursue"[1] refers not only to the ban on murder but to social justice as well. This book examines the Civil Rights Division of the U.S. Department of Justice as an agent of social justice and change. The division is an organism shaped by its own past, by internal and external influences, by the reasons for its creation, and by current needs. As Justice Oliver Wendell Holmes stated in another context, the creators of the division "called into life a being the development of which could not have been foreseen completely by the most gifted of its begetters."[2] The division has existed for forty eventful years, sufficient time to mine rich lessons from study of its evolution, its setting of priorities, policy-making, organizational structure, and relations among the relevant players—elected and appointed officials, career civil servants, courts, and private-sector interests.

From its beginning in 1870, the traditional role of the Department of Justice has been to enforce criminal laws and represent the United States in civil matters. In large measure, these traditional functions protect the status quo. Occasionally, however, the department is called on to effect changes in behavior, as in the enforcement of the antitrust laws and the failed effort to impose prohibition. Although modern civil rights enforcement began in 1957 as a narrowly focused effort, by 1964 it had assumed unprecedented breadth, and the civil rights responsibilities of the department have grown significantly since then. Deeply engrained practices of race, national origin, sex, and disability discrimination have been made unlawful, and the department has assumed a leading role in requiring major sectors of American society to change from discrimination to nondiscrimination.

The efforts to achieve nondiscrimination were inspired by civil rights leaders such as Martin Luther King, Jr., and Roy Wilkins, and the efforts were forced into the American consciousness by nonviolent direct action such as the Montgomery bus boycott, Freedom Rides, sit-ins, and voter registration drives of or-

1

ganizations such as the Student Nonviolent Coordinating Committee. The concept of using litigation to advance the civil rights agenda began with the National Association for the Advancement of Colored People and its legal offshoot, the Legal Defense and Education Fund. The story of these efforts has been often told. The Civil Rights Division of the U.S. Department of Justice was another major player in these events, but its efforts have received much less attention. Understanding how the law shapes our behavior must, however, take into account all the forces that shape the law, and I hope this book will help fill a gap in that understanding.

The attorney general today commands a force of some 500 people who are assigned to enforce the civil rights laws of the United States. This relatively small force[3] has played a disproportionately large role in securing civil rights. In 1957, when Congress and the executive created the Civil Rights Division as part of the Department of Justice, perhaps a dozen employees enforced those laws. Since that date, congressional enactments have steadily increased the scope of civil rights enforcement responsibilities of the department, so that from its initial narrow mandate to enforce a small number of Reconstruction criminal laws and to remedy racial discrimination in voting, the department has taken on a plethora of additional assignments. It brings suits to remedy many other forms of race discrimination—discrimination in employment, housing, schools, the granting of credit, public accommodations, publicly owned facilities, and federally assisted programs—and its mandate has expanded beyond race discrimination to encompass discrimination based on national origin, immigration status, religion, sex, disability, and family status. Where once the department sued only state and local governments, it now may sue private individuals and companies as well. Its responsibilities now run to prosecution of people who commit violence against abortion clinics, administrative review of submissions of proposed voting changes by jurisdictions covered by Section 4 of the Voting Rights Act, administrative determination of eligibility for redress payments to individuals of Japanese ancestry interned during World War II, and protecting the rights of institutionalized persons.

Congress's assignment of these broad enforcement responsibilities to the Department of Justice raises a host of legal and policy questions as to how they should be discharged. Issues of relief, standing, professional responsibility, and discretion abound. The government as plaintiff differs in important respects from the private individual as plaintiff. Not only are there differences of standing, relief, and the attorney-client relationship between the government and the private sector, but different considerations govern government and private priority setting and litigation policy. Differences of opinion as to the proper role of the Department of Justice can sometimes lead to disillusionment, as reflected by the wry saying of civil rights workers during the 1960s: "There's a town in Mississippi called Liberty; there's a Department in Washington called Justice."

Department of Justice lawyers represent the United States, a client that has historically displayed an institutional inability to set detailed priorities or policies. Thus, these lawyers carry on their shoulders a responsibility arguably even heavier than the one borne by private lawyers. As Sanford Levinson has pointed out, "A vibrant constitutionalism . . . requires a certain disposition on the part of *all* who participate in the work of a constitutional republic," including the attorney general.[4] Drawing on the work of Karl Llewellyn, Levinson argues that "we must be interested in the thought and behavior of *all* legal 'officials' and not only that small subset of persons called judges."[5]

The department's duties regarding civil rights are products of our nation's history and have been forged in legislation and cases extending from the Reconstruction period to the present. At the same time, new private actions, new federal agencies, and new modes of relief have been created. Although much study has been devoted to substantive issues of civil rights laws, little attention has been paid to the structure of civil rights enforcement. I wish to begin the process of study of that structure.

This book focuses primarily on the responsibilities of the Civil Rights Division to enforce laws forbidding race discrimination. It examines how those responsibilities arose and the considerations that led to entrusting the Department of Justice with enforcement of civil rights laws. It explains the impact of that history and those considerations on the department's setting of priorities and litigation positions, and it examines whether the structure of enforcement should be changed. My review of these issues concentrates on civil rather than criminal enforcement, because civil enforcement has been the primary vehicle in cases connected with the nondiscrimination principle while use of criminal enforcement has generally been limited to instances of due process violations and violent conduct based on racist views.

The book is based on a review of the legislative histories of the modern civil rights acts, case law, reports of the attorney general, Department of Justice documents, case briefs and records, and secondary sources. I write also from the perspective of my own twenty-two years of service in the Civil Rights Division. My first tasks as a Civil Rights Division lawyer took me repeatedly to rural Alabama to interview African-American citizens who wished to vote. On one memorable day my expenses included four dollars to be towed out of the mud in Bucks Chapel, seventy-five cents, paid to a local resident for guiding me to a witness's home, and money to repair the suit I ripped while climbing a barbed-wire fence and to launder clothes that got wet crossing a creek on the way to the interview. Later, I would spend much time in federal courts, trying cases and arguing appeals, and would discuss policy and law with attorneys general and solicitors general. From the red clay of Sumter County, Alabama, to the chambers of the Supreme Court the objective was always the same.

I believe the division pursues a noble mission. Congress intended that it enforce laws designed to glue together diverse individuals into a nation of equal opportunity, and the civil rights laws embody recognition by the political majority that the path of inequality leads to disaster. Nobility of mission, however, does not always lead to nobility of effort or result. In retrospect, most people would agree that the division of the 1960s was true to its mission. The division then was young, untutored, and highly motivated, and the people in it rose to meet the tasks imposed on them by the highly charged events of the time. The challenge, thirty years later, is to maintain the understanding and fidelity to mission that informed those early efforts. The danger is that the division could lose its sense of mission and increasingly become a voice, not of the public interest, but of whatever private interest is in current political ascendancy. I hope that better understanding of the role of the Civil Rights Division will diminish that danger.

Shortly after taking office as President Reagan's assistant attorney general for civil rights, William Bradford Reynolds testified before a congressional subcommittee that the department "no longer will insist upon or in any respect support the use of quotas or any other numerical or statistical formulae designed to provide to non-victims of discrimination preferential treatment based on race, sex, national origin or religion. To pursue any other course is, in our view, unsound as a matter of law and unwise as a matter of policy."[6] Fourteen years later, President Clinton's assistant attorney general for civil rights, Deval L. Patrick, told another congressional subcommittee that a proposed statutory prohibition against government preferences based on race, color, national origin, or sex "is a rejection of the compelling need to remedy the effects of past and present discrimination. It is inconsistent with principles developed by the Supreme Court and with numerous enactments of Congress and executive branch orders."[7] Both men relied on law and policy to reach these inconsistent positions, which paralleled the political stances of the presidents who had appointed them. It is worth exploring how the division forms its positions on the difficult issues it must address.

The division's policies and priorities are shaped by the external checks that characterize the allocation of responsibilities among the three branches of government and by the internal checks that characterize a multilayered department staffed by both political appointees and career civil service attorneys. The policies and priorities are part of a process that has been characterized as "law as equilibrium . . . a balance among three interacting branches."[8] Congress wrote the division's original charter and has expanded it over time. Each president has left a policy mark on the work of the division, and precedents from prior administrations affect the work of succeeding administrations. The division carries out its mission primarily through litigation, so the courts play a central role in determining how, or if, various policies are to be enforced. The attorney general, solicitor general, and other high-ranking political appointees outside the division bring differing perspectives to their oversight of division activities. The division thus is not a free agent but operates under a set of ever-changing constraints. It operates, too, in a policy arena of competing values. Ensuring nondiscrimination is the overriding purpose of the division, but it must take into account issues of fairness, efficacy, the proper role of the Department of Justice as compared to the roles of other government agencies with civil rights responsibilities, and the proper role of the national government in a federal system—issues that do not equally constrain private litigants.

Stephen J. Pollak, one of the architects of the division in the late 1960s, has observed that the spirit of that era was one of optimism.[9] That optimism reflected a belief that together government and private enforcement of antidiscrimination laws would lead to racial equality in the United States. I would add that vigorous enforcement did lead to unparalleled gains in the right of African Americans to vote and to exert real influence on the political process. It also led to African Americans gaining unprecedented access to public accommodations, jobs, schools, and housing. Yet this growth of access and opportunity has failed to reach a large minority of the African-American population and has not eliminated the two-caste system as reflected in gaps in economic and educational status and in the growth of substandard, racially impacted housing. Optimism has given way to frustration. One must wonder whether the division has a renewed role to play in confronting these conditions or whether its role should remain more narrowly confined.

Regardless of the answer to this question, the role of helping to ensure equal opportunity remains. The enforcement efforts of the past four decades have failed to deliver the desired knockout punch to racial discrimination, and it seems appropriate to reevaluate the structure of enforcement. As the division has changed from a small unit charged with enforcing a few criminal laws and eliminating voting discrimination to a large bureaucracy with wide-ranging responsibilities, its methods of operation have been significantly altered. The patchwork of antidiscrimination laws contains some gaps and some anomalies. I conclude, therefore, with suggestions for refinement of the laws governing the division and with some operational suggestions.

Key to these suggestions is the primacy of litigation as the enforcement tool of the Department of Justice. Administrative enforcement, regulation, conciliation, and education are all important pieces of the enforcement picture, but for the most part these techniques should be left to other agencies. A second key principle limits the department's litigation responsibilities to cases of public importance, leaving to private litigation and administrative enforcement individual complaints that do not raise important legal or policy issues. Finally, it should be noted that the growth of the division coincided with the growth of the civil rights injunction which Owen Fiss celebrated in his book of that name.[10] Although criminal and compensatory relief have a place in the hierarchy of civil rights remedies, department litigation should emphasize equitable relief, because that is the most effective route to systemic change. These suggestions would lead to a leaner, more focused, and more effective enforcement program.

2

The Evolution of Attorney General Authority

"NEVER"

In October 1963 Sheriff Jim Clark of Dallas County, Alabama, arrested the Reverend Benny Tucker "on provocation." In the sheriff's view, Reverend Tucker provoked the arrest when "he walked into the white rest room that was in the courthouse, that was in my presence and in the presence of a lady."[1] The Supreme Court had, of course, held that state-imposed racial segregation offended the Constitution of the United States, but Sheriff Clark was committed to maintaining a rigid racial caste system in majority black Dallas County[2] and its county seat, Selma. The arrest came during a campaign in which hundreds of African-American citizens of Dallas County were seeking to register to vote for the first time.

The Department of Justice filed suits based on this and other acts of intimidation.[3] However, the civil suits rested not on the patent violation of the right to equal access to public facilities but rather on the right to vote, for the attorney general had by then been authorized to enforce the Fifteenth Amendment's ban on race discrimination in voting[4] but lacked authority to enforce in civil litigation the equal access to public facilities[5] guaranteed by the equal protection clause of the Fourteenth Amendment.[6] Although a criminal action theoretically could have been maintained for willful deprivation of civil rights, no Southern District of Alabama grand jury would have indicted and no petit jury would have convicted on that misdemeanor charge.[7] Attorney General Robert F. Kennedy had therefore decided to concentrate the department's "greatest energies on enforcement of the [voting provisions of the Civil Rights Act], where its powers were unquestioned."[8]

Selma became a focal point in the adoption and enforcement of the first modern civil rights acts. Dallas County had long been a center of white supremacy doctrine.[9] In the 1950s and early 1960s the white minority felt impelled to mount a fierce defense of its old way of life, and the legal attack on that way of life concentrated at first on voting rights. If black citizens could secure the right to vote, they might replace hostile officials such as Sheriff Clark, District Attorney Blanchard McLeod, Circuit Judge James Hare, and Voter Registrar Victor Atkins with more responsive public officials. The newly enfranchised group then could turn their attention to remedying segregation in public schools, which persisted ten years after *Brown v. Board of Education,*[10] and to public facilities and even privately owned lunch counters, restaurants, hotels, and movie theaters, which remained rigidly segregated.

Sheriff Clark served as a tool of those who benefited from the racial caste system. He coined a one-word slogan, "Never," and he and his supporters wore buttons emblazoned with that word. Never would African Americans be allowed freely to register to vote; to enter desegregated schools, public facilities, and accommodations; to enjoy employment opportunities; to escape from white domination. Never would the guarantees of the Constitution meaningfully protect the black citizens of Dallas County. Sheriff Clark used the power of his office to harrass those who sought to register to vote,[11] and he arrested those who encouraged registration. U.S. District Judge Frank M. Johnson later noted, "This harassment, intimidation and brutal treatment has ranged from mass arrests without just cause to forced marches for several miles into the countryside, with the sheriff's deputies and members of his posse herding the Negro demonstrators at a rapid pace through the use of electrical shocking devices (designed for use on cattle) and night sticks to prod them along."[12]

On July 2, 1964, the day that the Civil Rights Act of 1964 became law, his deputies cattle-prodded and arrested two African-American students who dared to seat themselves in an ice cream parlor.[13] In March 1965, when supporters of voting rights sought to march from Selma to Montgomery, his deputies barred the way. The deputies, who were mounted on horses, tear-gassed and drove the marchers back across the Edmund Pettus Bridge, all the while swinging whips, billy clubs, and cattle prods at the fleeing protesters and sending scores to the hospital for treatment of their wounds.[14]

Sheriff Clark symbolized a clash between the law of the land and the will of a determined white minority, expressed in local law and custom and underscored by the "blunt and obscene racist jokes" that were posted in his office.[15] That such a clash was possible can only be explained by the failure of Reconstruction to eliminate the culture of slavery. Within a decade of the adoption of the Reconstruction amendments to the Constitution, such national will as existed to unify the races gave way to a national will to unify whites of North and South. Because of these social developments, the national government lost most of its powers to enforce the Reconstruction amendments to the Constitution.

Slowly, beginning in the 1950s and intensifying in the 1960s, the changing social, legal, and political climate led to restoration of those powers. Although the district attorney, circuit judge, and voter registrar joined with Sheriff Clark in barring the franchise to African Americans,[16] by 1966 the U.S. Department of Justice had restored the vote to African Americans in Dallas County. The department had brought several lawsuits, beginning in 1961, to vindicate the right to vote[17] and had sent federal examiners to Selma in 1965[18] as authorized by the Voting Rights Act of 1965.[19] Only 242 of the 15,115 black citizens of voting age were registered to vote in Dallas County when the first lawsuit was tried.[20] Department of Justice litigation and black voter registration drives brought the number to 320 by 1964. By the time the Voting Rights Act was enacted, four years of government litigation and civil rights groups' registration efforts had increased black registration to only 1,516. By May 1966, however, over 10,000 African Americans were registered to vote, and they were determined to oust Jim Clark. At the 1966 primary election, the Dallas County Democratic Executive Committee attempted to steal the election by throwing out votes from black wards. The Department of Justice brought a suit that culminated in the counting of those votes and the end of Jim Clark's tenure as sheriff.[21] More litigation followed,[22] but today Selma and Dallas County have biracial governing bodies and desegregated public facilities and accommodations. Although inequalities remain, the racial caste system has eroded markedly. The story of Selma illustrates the potential for change through law enforcement and the need to provide law enforcement officers with the legislative authority to address national problems, but it also suggests the limits of the law enforcement model as an agent of change.

The Department of Justice began with limited tools to attack the racial discrimination in Selma, but it and other agencies acquired new goals and enforcement tools through Congress's enactment of successive civil rights acts. Before examining the reasons for these laws and describing the methods of enforcing them, I want to set the stage with a brief summary of the evolution of the department's modern litigating authority.

INITIAL AUTHORITY

When Congress confronted the question of how to ensure proper treatment of the newly freed slaves, it had to decide what rights to secure, what enforcement machinery to employ, and what classes to protect. In 1866 Congress first authorized the attorney general, a cabinet position since the beginning of the Republic, to protect civil rights. In 1870 Congress created the Department of Justice, under the leadership of the attorney general, and later expanded the attorney general's enforcement authority by a series of acts culminating in the Civil Rights Act of 1875.[23] By 1875 it appeared that the newly freed slaves had broad rights to vote, own property, enter into contracts, and patronize public accommodations without discrimination and to be free from interference with the exercise of such rights. These rights could be protected by private suits, but in many instances the attorney general was also empowered to maintain a federal enforcement action.

Within a few years both the newly conferred rights and the attorney general's enforcement authority were constricted by Supreme Court decisions and legislative repeals. All that was left was "a few scattered remnants of a once grandiose scheme to nationalize the fundamental rights of the individual."[24] For the next seventy years the attorney general was limited to criminal prosecutions for denials of federal rights under color of law, conspiracy to deprive persons of federally protected rights, jury discrimination, and slavery. Moreover, since federal protections of rights were almost exclusively directed toward state action, even criminal jurisdiction over private individuals was limited. Further, the attorney general lacked statutory authority to bring civil suits to ensure civil rights.

RENEWED COMMITMENT

Executive Branch

The existence of this limited criminal enforcement authority in the Department of Justice led Attorney General Frank Murphy to create the Civil Rights Section of the Criminal Division in 1939.[25] He took this action a year after the Supreme Court had defined a set of constitutional rights it deemed worthy of heightened federal protection[26] and in the wake of the rise of totalitarian governments across the seas. Attorney General Murphy instructed the section "to make a study of the provisions of the Constitution of the United States and acts of Congress relating to civil rights with reference to present conditions, to make appropriate recommendations in respect thereto, and to direct, supervise, and conduct prosecutions of violations of the provisions of the Constitution or acts of Congress guaranteeing civil rights to individuals."[27] The creation of the Civil Rights Section in 1939 was a sort of time bomb. Inevitably, as it started investigating and prosecuting civil rights violations, the need for more effective and comprehensive machinery would become evident, and the Department of Justice would become the logical agency to develop and operate that machinery. The few other agencies dedicated to combating racial discrimination were either narrowly focused or lacked meaningful enforcement authority.[28]

In 1948 President Truman's Committee on Civil Rights recommended adoption of civil rights legislation. It proposed creation of a Civil Rights Division within the Department of Justice, arguing that "this step would give the federal civil rights enforcement program prestige, power, and efficiency that it now lacks."[29] The committee recommended that Congress grant the new division authority to use civil, as well as criminal, sanctions to protect the right to vote.[30] At the same time, a highly influential book by Robert Carr, the executive director of the committee, had developed at length the case for "comprehensive civil rights legislation," which would provide public and private rights of action to protect civil rights and would elevate the Civil Rights Section of the Criminal Division to the status of a division, with its own assistant attorney general and direct access to the attorney general.[31]

After President Truman proposed legislation pursuant to his committee's recommendations,[32] his attorney general, Tom Clark, testified in favor of creating a division "with the view of perhaps placing these prosecutions on a little higher level, giving a little more dignity to the division by having an assistant attorney general at the head of it."[33] These ideas were embraced by the Eisenhower administration. President Eisenhower's attorney general, Herbert Brownell, forwarded to Congress the president's proposal for a civil rights program, commenting that the "protection of civil rights guaranteed by the Constitution is a governmental function and responsibility of the first importance. . . . In this area . . . more emphasis should be on civil law remedies. The civil rights enforcement activities . . . should not, therefore, be confined to the Criminal Division."[34]

Congress

When Congress was finally ready to begin to renew the national commitment to civil rights, it faced the same questions as the Reconstruction Congresses: what are the reasons for civil rights legislation, what enforcement mechanisms are appropriate, and what entities should be covered? Choices made in 1957 helped shape civil rights enforcement for years to come. In the Civil Rights Act of 1957, Congress chose to target a specific form of discrimination—voting—rather than confer broad federal enforcement authority; it placed enforcement responsibility with the Department of Justice; it gave the department authority to seek injunctive relief but withheld authority to seek damages; and it created the Civil Rights Division. The 1957 act was the first in a series of laws expanding the authority of the Department of Justice to combat racial discrimination, as graphically illustrated by Figure 2.1.

Congress did not consider the full range of issues that President Truman's committee had addressed. Rather than attempt to mount a full-scale assault on racial discrimination in such areas as employment, public accommodations, and schools, Congress began with very modest, tentative steps. It created no new enforcement agency and no new rights. Even supporters of the Civil Rights Act of 1957 took care not to "reconstruct Reconstruction," as Senator Lyndon Johnson put it during the congressional debates.[35] The picture of Reconstruction that animated the desire not to repeat echoed the movie *The Birth of a Nation,* which depicted a corrupt government dominated by greedy carpetbaggers and scalawags and ignorant African Americans. The future president accordingly believed that during Reconstruction, "Basic rights were ignored. Punitive measures were voted."[36]

Congress in 1957 was willing only to enact carefully circumscribed new federal tools to enforce the Constitution. Reluctant to grant sweeping power to the

Figure 2.1. Evolution of Civil Rights Division enforcement authority

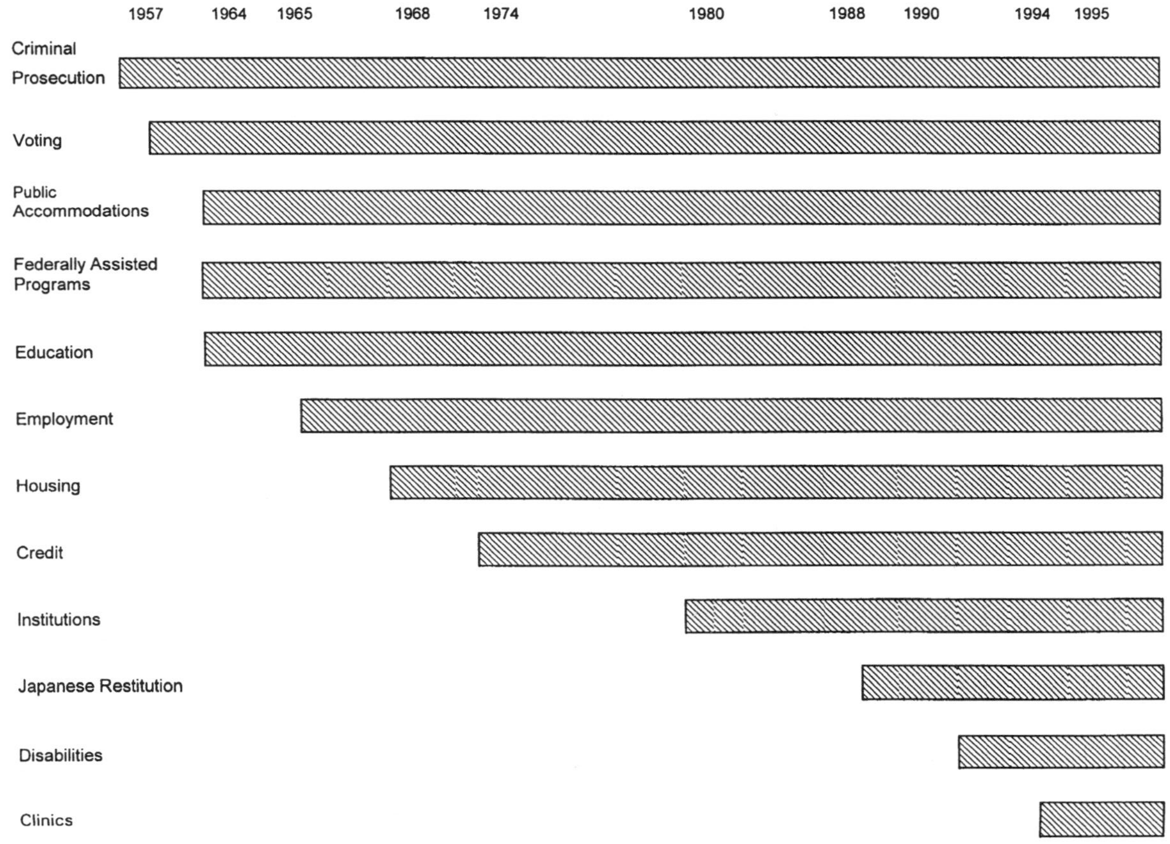

Department of Justice, it was ambivalent at best in its commitment to nondiscrimination and took a restrained view of the role of the federal government in enforcing laws against the states. It created a "temporary" commission to study civil rights issues.[37] It also elevated the Civil Rights Section to a division in the Department of Justice with authority to bring injunctive actions against race discrimination by voting authorities.[38] The 1957 act was the law that authorized the department's initial suits in Dallas County, Alabama. Voting was specifically protected by the Fifteenth Amendment to the Constitution and was viewed as the right designed to enable African Americans to secure other rights.

The Department of Justice is dependent upon Congress for its authority to bring suit.[39] Hence, perhaps the most significant choice the 1957 Congress made was to adopt only these limited measures, while refusing to authorize two others. First, Congress declined to allow the attorney general to recover damages on behalf of individuals whose rights had been infringed.[40] Second, it refused to enact Part 3 of Attorney General Brownell's proposed bill, which would have authorized the attorney general to bring civil suits against individuals involved in conspiracies to deny equal protection.[41] Had Part 3 been enacted, the attorney general could have brought cases to end racial discrimination in the schools, public facilities, and public employment. But Part 3 would have extended well beyond race discrimination to authorize such suits for sex discrimination, religious discrimination, discrimination against the disabled, or governmental discrimination against any other potentially protected group. This Part 3 (or Title III) approach reappeared in subsequent legislative proposals, but it has never been enacted.[42]

Congress's decision to eliminate Part 3 from the bill stemmed from both separation of powers and substantive concerns. It signaled Congress's intent to keep the Civil Rights Division under close control and was additionally motivated by a desire not to "approve the race-mixing decision of the Supreme Court of May 1954."[43] President Eisenhower himself disavowed an intent to empower the attorney general to require school desegregation, stating instead, "I think the voting right is something that should be emphasized."[44] The defeat of Part 3 left the attorney general with only the authority, which had survived from the Reconstruction period, to prosecute criminally for some deprivations of civil rights secured "by the Constitution or laws of the United States."[45] Thus Congress opted to remit broad and evolving constitutional rights to the criminal process and to employ civil relief only to a narrow set of constitutional violations.[46] The attorney general consequently was unable to effectively address the broad range of violations of constitutional rights in places such as Dallas County.

From the vantage point of the 1990s the Civil Rights Act of 1957 looks like a miniscule step forward. Even at the time of enactment it was recognized that it failed to address most issues of race discrimination; it fell far short of the recommendations of President Truman's Committee on Civil Rights. Nonetheless, it represents an historic moment. For the first time since Reconstruction the Congress had joined with the courts and the executive branch in recognizing nondiscrimination as an important American value, and the act passed despite the strong grip of the South on important congressional committees and the back-lash against *Brown v. Board of Education* that had engulfed much of the Deep South. Congress's recognition of the legitimate role of the federal government in combating race discrimination paved the way for the more significant acts that were to follow in 1964, 1965, and 1968.

By 1960 continued and sometimes violent southern resistance to compliance with *Brown v. Board of Education* convinced Congress to provide limited federal protection for the school desegregation process. In the Civil Rights Act of 1960, Congress enacted provisions that criminalized some interference with desegre-gation and provided for federal education of students who were dependents of military personnel in states that failed to provide a "suitable free public educa-tion."[47] A Part 3 approach was again proposed, although House Judiciary Com-mittee Chairman Emanuel Celler's bill placed limits on the provision.[48] This time, however, the Eisenhower administration withdrew its support of that ap-proach, with Attorney General William Rogers testifying against it before both House and Senate subcommittees because it "might not be wise" and might "harden the resistance."[49]

THREE-PRONGED APPROACH TO ENFORCEMENT

Deliberations on what became the Civil Rights Act of 1964[50] once again saw the rejection of the Part 3 approach, only this time it was the Kennedy administra-tion that opposed proposals to "enable the Department of Justice to seek federal court injunctions against any deprivations of federally protected rights."[51] Assis-tant Attorney General Burke Marshall argued that the broader authority would not work because of the difficulty of crafting workable injunctions to enforce ambiguously defined rights. He argued that the national problem that required attention was racial discrimination, not "the First Amendment right to protest racial discrimination." In his view the administration's bill promised to "end the discrimination itself."[52]

In the Civil Rights Act of 1964, while rejecting the uncabined breadth of Part 3, Congress broadened the responsibilities of the Department of Justice in care-fully defined and limited categories, both with respect to subject matter and pro-tected classes. Despite the rejection of Part 3, Title IX of the act did authorize the attorney general to intervene in race-based equal protection cases initiated by other parties, thus formalizing a prior practice of participating as a litigat-ing amicus curiae. The power of intervention is much more limited than the power of initiation, as it depends on other parties to file cases and is subject to more stringent timeliness requirements. Title IX has nonetheless been labeled a "sleeper" provision because if private parties filed suits regarding unsettled equal protection issues, then "the attorney general easily could assume the role of creative tactician under a constitutional clause which, like the due process clause and unlike the voting clauses, denotes a developmental principle rather than a settled norm of conduct."[53]

In addition to the existing authority to bring voting discrimination and criminal suits, the 1964 act placed authority in the Justice Department to bring suits against discrimination in public accommodations, facilities, and education as well as in employment. The statutory ban on discrimination in public accommodations and in employment expanded civil rights laws beyond protecting constitutional rights and facilitated "a massive assault on private discrimination."[54] It enabled the attorney general to bring suit against Sheriff Clark and others who sought to exclude black people from public accommodations in Selma. Furthermore, the act arguably allowed the attorney general, upon request from a program agency, to bring cases against discrimination in federally assisted programs. Adding to the authority to bring race discrimination cases, Congress included national origin, religion, and sex as some of the newly covered subject matters. Yet Congress opted for selective civil enforcement relating to perceived national problems rather than broadbrush civil enforcement relating to all manner of deprivations of constitutional rights.

The 1964 act created a three-pronged civil enforcement approach, consisting of private suits, civil suits by the Department of Justice, and nonlitigative administrative responsibilities of other federal agencies. First, private individuals were authorized to bring private suits to remedy unlawful discrimination. Second, Congress authorized the attorney general to sue to end some forms of discrimination but placed limits on that authority. It could be exercised only where a private suit was unlikely to redress the injury to the public interest, either because private plaintiffs were unable to maintain a suit or because of the broad systemic nature of the violation. These limitations were captured in several locutions. For example, authority to bring suits to desegregate public facilities or schools depended on a certificate from the attorney general attesting that the complainant was unable to maintain appropriate proceedings and that the suit would "materially further the orderly progress of desegregation."[55] Similarly, the attorney general could bring suits against discrimination in public accommodations or employment only based on "reasonable cause" to believe the discrimination was a "pattern or practice"[56] and could intervene only in cases of "general public importance."[57]

The administrative prong consisted of giving various existing and new federal agencies new administrative responsibilities to support the nondiscrimination laws; however, with one important exception—Title VI,[58] which authorized the agency to terminate federal funds to a recipient of federal financial assistance that discriminated in the program or activity—those agencies were denied enforcement powers. Thus, the Equal Employment Opportunities Commission could investigate, make probable cause findings, conciliate, and adopt procedural regulations, but lacked power to litigate or issue cease and desist orders.[59] The

Community Relations Service could investigate and conciliate public accommodations disputes but had no enforcement powers.[60] In addition to these newly created entities, the secretary of health, education, and welfare could offer technical assistance in desegregation.[61] This third prong has led to the creation of a very large civil rights enforcement structure outside the Department of Justice.[62] These additional entities compete with the attorney general for authority and add complexity to policy formulation. Moreover, the attorney general must devote resources to defending in federal court enforcement decisions of these agencies.

The 1964 three-pronged approach—with its limits on attorney general authority—may appear to deviate somewhat from the 1957 act, which granted broader authority for attorney general suits against voting discrimination and did not create responsibilities in other agencies. Congress apparently thought that the expansion of substantive authority of the attorney general should be accompanied by procedural restraints. The turn to administrative agencies may have reflected the recognition that litigation, standing alone, had been generally ineffectual in combating voting discrimination. We will see that the mix of private and public responsibility for enforcement continues to vary considerably from one statute to the next, and that later acts significantly blur the lines among these three prongs. However, the underlying reason for limiting administrative authority, to ensure that "judges, not Washington bureaucrats, would determine guilt and punish offenders,"[63] continued to shape those later acts.

This three-pronged scheme was retained in the Fair Housing Act of 1968, which authorizes private suits and attorney general suits and places investigative and rule-making authority on the secretary of housing and urban development. The attorney general may sue only to remedy "a pattern or practice of resistance to the full enjoyment of any of the rights granted by this title, or [if] any group of persons has been denied any of the rights granted by this title and such denial raises an issue of general public importance."[64]

The 1968 act also imported into the criminal area the specificity of the civil provisions. Congress added these provisions in response both to incidents of racial violence and to limitations that court decisions had placed on prosecutions under the Reconstruction criminal civil rights laws. The act made it a crime to use force or threat of force to injure, intimidate, or interfere with persons enjoying specified federal rights; or with persons because of race, color, religion, or national origin and because the person is engaging in specified activities; or with citizens aiding or encouraging others to engage in these protected activities.[65]

ADDITION OF NONLITIGATIVE RESPONSIBILITIES

Enforcement of the 1957, 1960, and 1964 Civil Rights Acts failed to eliminate voting discrimination. As the division's leader, John Doar, testified in 1965, "The fact that not all people are permitted to register and vote freely and comfortably indicates that we have not accomplished our task with the tools that we now have."[66] Congress therefore enacted the 1965 Voting Rights Act.[67] That act and its subsequent extensions not only created rigorous and highly effective protections against racial discrimination in voting but also conferred quasi-regulatory authority on the attorney general. The attorney general certification, which hitherto had simply served as a basis for the department to bring suit or enter existing litigation, then became the unchallengeable basis for bringing states and political subdivisions under the act's special coverage and for appointment of federal examiners to list voters eligible for registration and to appoint observers to monitor elections.[68] It was the presence of these federal examiners and observers that made it possible for the black citizens of Dallas County to be placed on the voter rolls and cast the votes that ended Jim Clark's law enforcement career.[69]

In addition, state and local governments could not change voting procedures or standards unless either the U.S. District Court for the District of Columbia or the attorney general had precleared the change as not having the purpose or effect of discriminating based on race. Most changes were submitted to the attorney general for administrative review rather than to the court for judicial review. These duties led the attorney general, like most administrative agencies, to "formulate and publish objective ground rules" in the form of binding regulations.[70]

The next thirty years were marked by a steady accretion of nonlitigative responsibilities. For example, in 1980 the Civil Rights of Institutionalized Persons Act gave the attorney general the quasi-regulatory responsibility of adopting standards for state grievance systems for prison inmates and of certifying those state rules that satisfied the standards.[71] The Civil Liberties Act of 1988 adds another nonlitigative responsibility by requiring the attorney general to identify individuals who were detained under the blanket Japanese exclusion orders during World War II and were therefore eligible for restitution.[72] And the Americans with Disabilities Act assigns to the attorney general several administrative responsibilities, ranging from certifying that building codes satisfy the act's standards[73] to promulgation of regulations regarding discrimination by public entities against the disabled.[74]

ADDITION OF PROTECTED CLASSES

Not only did legislation after 1960 expand the coverage of the Civil Rights Acts beyond litigation to correct voting discrimination, it also expanded the classes protected against discrimination. Race was the paradigm example of a forbidden classification, both legislatively and constitutionally. Figure 2.2 lists the federal

Figure 2.2. Federal civil rights laws enforced by the Civil Rights Division concerning race-based discrimination

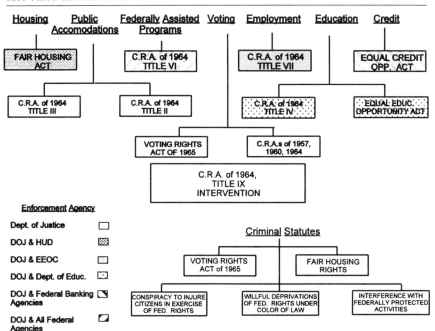

civil rights laws that currently forbid race discrimination. As shown in Table 2.1, the accretion of protected classes beyond race also continued after the 1964 act's extension of protection against discrimination based on national origin, religion, and gender. As other classifications were added, Congress (as well as the Supreme Court in constitutional cases)[75] concluded that perceived differences between race discrimination and other forms of discrimination warranted differing statutory treatment. Thus, for example, Title VII from the outset included the bona fide occupational qualification exception as to sex, national origin, and religion but not as to race. In time Title VII was amended to clarify the conditions under which it applied to sex discrimination and religious discrimination.

Similarly, when the Americans with Disabilities Act extended protections to the disabled, Congress adopted a very detailed scheme of rules.[76] This scheme stands in stark contrast to the general standards of the race discrimination ban. The same is true of the Fair Housing Act's protections against handicap discrimination.[77] Yet another protected class under the Fair Housing Act is families, and again more specific legislative definition of the proscribed discrimination was needed. The push to expand protected classes and forbidden activities continues. Congress has forbidden interference with abortion clinics, a law enforced by the

Table 2.1. Classes protected by civil rights laws enforced by the Civil Rights Division

AREA OF DISCRIMINATION

PROTECTED CLASS	RACE, COLOR, NATIONAL ORIGIN	SEX	AGE	DISABLED	OTHER
HOUSING	•Fair Housing Act	•Fair Housing Act		•Fair Housing Act	•Fair Housing Act Religion, familial status
VOTING	•Civil Rts. Act, 1957 •Civil Rts. Act, 1960 •Civil Rts. Act, 1964 Title 1 •Voting Rights Act		•Voting Accessibility for the elderly and Handicapped Act	•Voting Accessibility for the elderly and Handicapped Act	•Overseas Voting Rights Act •Motor Voter Act
EMPLOYMENT	•Civil Rts. Act, 1964 Title VII	•Civil Rights Act, 1964 Title VII		•Americans With Disabilities Act	•Civil Rights Act, 1964 Title VII Religion
EDUCATION	•Civil Rts Act, 1964 Title IV	•Educ. Amend. 1972 Title IX		•Rehabilitation Act •Educ. of Handicapped Children Act	
FEDERALLY ASSISTED PROGRAMS	•Civil Rts. Act, 1964 Title VI			•Rehabilitation Act Sec. 504	
CREDIT	•Equal Credit Opportunity Act	•Equal Credit Opportunity Act	•Equal Credit Opportunity Act		•Equal Credit Opportunity Act, Religion, Marital status
PUBLIC ACCOMMODATIONS	•Civil Rights Act, 1964 Title II, Title III			•Americans With Disabilities Act	•Civil Rights Act, 1964 Title II, Religion •Title III, Religion
OTHER	•Civil Liberties Act Japanese Restitution	•Freedom of Access to Clinics Act		•Americans w/Disab. Act, Pub. services transportation, telecommunication	•Civil Rights, Institutionalized Persons

division along with other Department of Justice components.[78] Proposals to enhance penalties for violence against women, to ensure environmental justice,[79] and to forbid discrimination based on sexual orientation are coming to the fore.

DILUTING THE THREE-PRONGED APPROACH

Dilution of the three-pronged approach to civil enforcement began with passage of the 1972 amendments to Title VII. The amendments corrected a perceived void in the 1964 act by conferring on the Equal Employment Opportunities Commission authority under Section 706 of the act to bring suits to remedy discrimination against an individual. However, the amendments also radically restructured the responsibilities of the Department of Justice. First, the department's existing authority to bring "pattern-or-practice" cases against private employers was transferred to the Equal Employment Opportunities Commission. Second, the department received new authority to enforce Title VII against state and local government employers, so that not only could it bring pattern-or-practice cases against them, but the commission could refer to the attorney general individual Section 706 cases against state and local government employers. The 1972 amendments, in addition to reshuffling and adding responsibilities, also created new ambiguities. Section 706, unlike the pattern-or-practice provision, contained no standards to guide the commission or the attorney general as to when the government, rather than the aggrieved individual, should bring suit. Nor did the amendments specify what the attorney general's responsibilities would be upon receiving a referral from the commission.

These changes were relatively minor compared with the far-reaching changes in the Fair Housing Amendments Act of 1988,[80] which fulfilled civil rights groups' long-denied wish for federal agency authority to issue cease and desist orders against discrimination. The changes also granted another wish: not only could the secretary of housing and urban development issue cease and desist orders, but the secretary could also order the payment of money damages. Since the Supreme Court had previously found a Seventh Amendment right to jury trial in fair housing suits for damages, Congress was unsure that the naked grant of such authority to the secretary could survive constitutional scrutiny. Congress therefore granted both the complainant and respondent in HUD administrative proceedings the right to opt for court resolution of the case.[81] Where such a choice is made, the statute provides that "the Secretary shall authorize and not later than 30 days after the election is made the Attorney General shall commence and maintain, a civil action on behalf of the aggrieved person."[82] Thus, in contrast with the norm of attorney general prosecutorial discretion, suit by the attorney general in such cases seems to be mandatory.

In 1991 Congress also amended the Equal Credit Opportunity Act and Title VII to allow the attorney general to recover compensatory and punitive damages on behalf of victims of credit discrimination and employment discrimination. These amendments build on the Fair Housing Act amendments in emphasizing the federal government as advocate for individuals. The equitable relief to which the government was previously confined had been primarily forward-looking, forbidding future discrimination, although decrees designed to address the effects of past discrimination necessarily looked back. However, the addition of authority to seek damages—especially punitive damages—provides emphasis on retrospective relief, although they may also have a deterrent effect.

EVOLVING MILIEU OF CIVIL RIGHTS ENFORCEMENT

The above developments did not, of course, occur in a vacuum. The period from 1957 to the present has been marked by social, economic, and political change. Some of that change, such as the growth of the African-American middle class or the rising antipathy to affirmative action, resulted at least in part from the legislative measures detailed above. And the legislative measures in turn were affected by these changes. For example, the success of the Voting Rights Act led to the adoption of extensions of the act and inclusion of ever more stringent measures, as southern politicians whose elections depended on African-American votes began backing laws that their predecessors would have abhorred.

Partisan politics also played a role in shaping legislation and enforcement. The early laws had been enacted by coalitions of Republicans and northern and western Democrats, under Republican presidents Eisenhower and Nixon and Democrat Lyndon Johnson. But later years saw changes in the coalition, with many Republicans turning away from measures imposed by the courts and the growing civil rights enforcement bureaucracy. For example, President Jimmy Carter's call for enactment of amendments to the Fair Housing Act foundered on partisan disagreements, and it was not until the Reagan administration had markedly altered the proposal that the 1988 amendments were enacted.

Although President Nixon's administration had substantially reinforced affirmative action requirements, the Reagan-Bush administration staunchly opposed them. Presidents Reagan and Bush also embraced President Nixon's earlier opposition to school busing to achieve desegregation. These positions partially reflected traditional conservative opposition to federal government intervention and partially reflected a calculated political appeal to the white majority. The story of these changes in American society is beyond the scope of this book, but full understanding of the forces that influence the Civil Rights Division's evolution, policies, and priorities requires that we appreciate the changing milieu within which the division operates.[83]

The notion of limited government has influenced civil rights enforcement, especially in its early years. The history of civil rights legislation since 1957 began with a modest foundation of highly focused authorization for the attorney general to sue to remedy discrimination in voting, based on race. Throughout this modern period Congress chose to confine the legislation to specified activities and to protect only specified classifications. Congress eschewed alternatives such as Title III that would have granted the attorney general carte blanche discretion to enforce the broad protections of the equal protection and due process clauses of the Constitution. Private suits to enforce the surviving Reconstruction civil rights acts remained the primary method for asserting broader claims. The unheralded and undebated enactment in 1994 of a partial Part 3 approach, limited to violations by law enforcement officials, added a wild card, which the division has yet to play.[84] Not only could the attorney general seek relief against a pattern or practice of racial discrimination by a police department, but she could also seek such relief as to a general pattern of police brutality or unlawful arrests or interferences with free speech.

As evidence of need mounted and as political circumstances dictated, Congress gradually added to the protections. The division's experience under its initially very limited authority helped lay the foundation for a national assault on the racial caste system.

> The laws of 1957 and 1960 protecting the right to vote were *not* aimed at the caste system—but rather at what the majority understood at the time to be necessary—that is, the protection of the right of certain extraordinary, intelligent Negro citizens who, under any standard, were entitled to vote. Some time during 1960 and 1961—it didn't happen all at once, nor did it happen to each member of the Division at the same time—the Civil Rights Division seized these statutes as their weapon against the [racial] caste system.[85]

Beginning with the 1957 act's coverage of voting rights, Congress expanded protections against various other manifestations of the caste system: discrimination in schools, public accommodations, housing, employment, credit, and federally assisted programs. It also added protections, based on the due process clause, relating to conditions of involuntary confinement and the right to an abortion. Although race has continued as the paradigm protected class, Congress expanded the protected classes as to some activities, including national origin, gender, religion, age, disability, and familial status.

Congress has generally preferred that civil rights claims be resolved by courts rather than by administrative tribunals. This preference has led to much of the enforcement responsibility being placed in the Department of Justice. However, Congress has not acted consistently in choosing between courts and administrative enforcement. Congress has shown similar inconsistency on the relationship between private and public enforcement. Moreover, it has scattered administrative enforcement among a legion of federal agencies—for example, all federal agencies are responsible for ensuring that they do not extend federal financial assistance to racially discriminatory programs or activities[86]—with the Department of Justice being only one of those.[87]

The modern civil rights laws generally employ civil rather than criminal mechanisms insofar as nonviolent deprivations of rights are concerned. The evolution of these laws has led to different enforcement approaches for different activities and to considerable overlap of responsibilities. As practice has revealed flaws in early legislation, subsequent laws addressing other civil rights issues have been written in a manner that takes those flaws into account, but inertia has left some flaws in place. Finally, the growth of enforcement responsibilities requires reexamination of priorities, since numerous needs compete for limited resources.

3

Reasons for Federal Role

The policies and priorities of the Civil Rights Division are or should be grounded in the underlying reasons that support establishing a federal role in civil rights litigation and assigning a major part of that role to the division. The division's authority stems from a series of congressional and Supreme Court decisions regarding the perniciousness and illegality of racial discrimination and from Congress's choices as to the appropriate means for combating discrimination. The division's authority was forged in light of understandings regarding the role of national law enforcement in a federal system and the role of the executive branch in a system governed by separation of powers.

In determining what reasons support the division's mandate to remedy unlawful racial discrimination, one might proceed by examining the historical and political forces that inexorably led to the modern civil rights laws. At times the battle was led by Republicans, at times by Democrats. The leadership shifted among the federal courts, the president, and the Congress. Civil rights groups provided increasingly intense pressure, perpetrators of racial discrimination exposed their emptiness and excess, the media began to pay attention, and the American people responded with moral outrage.

In a sense, the reason for the federal role was summed up by Senator Everett Dirksen's famous invocation of Victor Hugo: "No army is stronger than an idea whose time has come."[1] So it is important to reach beyond the personalities and political maneuvers and recognize that underlying the force of history are the premises and arguments which support ideas. The following discussion does not attempt to describe historical forces or what motivated Congress.[2] Rather, it surveys the ideological foundation of the modern civil rights acts.

* * * * *

AUTHORITY FOR FEDERAL CIVIL RIGHTS LAWS

The U.S. Constitution is the foundation upon which civil rights legislation rests, and it has always provided that Congress may regulate interstate commerce.[3] Therefore, "our economic unit is the Nation,"[4] and Congress may ensure that individuals are not excluded from the national market because of race.[5] Congress's power was greatly expanded by the Reconstruction amendments, which created rights designed to afford liberty, citizenship, equal treatment at the hands of the state, and political equality to the newly freed slaves. Given the history of slavery and the states' enactment of the Black Codes following the Civil War, the need for federal legislation was clear, and these amendments confer on Congress the power to enact appropriate legislation.

Prior to enactment of the Reconstruction amendments the federal system was marked by autonomy for each constituent state, thus allowing wide variations in the treatment of African Americans, from slavery to freedom, from discrimination to equality. The national government's power to require the states or private individuals to abandon racial discrimination was limited. The amendments radically changed the relationship of the federal and state governments in three ways, giving a new face and meaning to federalism.

First, Congress could regulate state practices.[6] The enforcement clauses of the Reconstruction amendments provided a firmer basis for such legislation than, for example, the Commerce Clause.[7] As the Court said of the 1957 and 1960 Civil Rights Acts, "There is the highest public interest in the due observance of all the constitutional guarantees, including those that bear the most directly on private rights, and we think it perfectly competent for Congress to authorize the United States to be the guardian of that public interest in a suit for injunctive relief."[8]

Second, the Thirteenth Amendment[9] applied not only to state action but to private action as well, creating a direct relationship between the federal government and private individuals.[10] Finally, the Supreme Court recognized in *Carolene Products*[11] that certain types of issues, including race discrimination, warranted the application of a higher standard of review when passing on the constitutionality of some state laws. The reasons, the Court noted, would justify special congressional treatment of those issues.

WHY ENACT FEDERAL CIVIL RIGHTS LAWS?

The Constitution provides strong grounds for Congress to enact civil rights legislation. However, the constitutional authority would justify legislation extending well beyond race discrimination to such matters as, for example, violations of the First Amendment right of free speech. The rationale expressed by the *Carolene Products* footnote is not limited to race discrimination but would also warrant special protection for first amendment freedoms. The fact that authority exists does not mean it should be used. Reliance on the Constitution as the sole reason for enacting civil rights legislation would set virtually limitless bounds on the scope of such legislation. Yet, as the history of the ill-fated Part 3 proposals demonstrates, Congress has, at least until recently, declined to provide the same protection for due process violations as for equal protection violations and has even limited the federal role as to equal protection. In addition, not only has Congress generally failed to require private actors to comply with the due process clause, it also has limited the scope of the nondiscrimination laws insofar as private action is concerned. Thus, in order to explain why some civil rights are protected and others are not, we must look past formal authority and examine the underlying reasons for civil rights legislation: community, commerce, morality, order, the legacy of history, and the need for structural change.

First, however, let me briefly discuss another rationale that has been mentioned: preservation of our international standing. Today that rationale seems like a makeweight justification because the United States generally has not allowed world opinion to dictate domestic policy. However, in the 1960s it received much serious credence and was closely related to our international posture of support for democracy. Once the United States supported decolonization in Africa and elsewhere, the continued colonization of our own undercaste became difficult to sustain. In 1952 the United States noted in its brief in *Brown v. Board of Education*[12] that "the existence of discrimination against minority groups in the United States has an adverse effect upon our relations with other countries." Ten years later, President Kennedy, in his first State of the Union message, declared, "The denial of constitutional rights to some of our fellow Americans on account of race . . . disturbs the national conscience, and subjects us to the charge of world opinion that our democracy is not equal to the high promise of our heritage."[13]

Some historians, noting such statements, ascribe great significance to "the Cold War imperative as a force for racial change in this country; its importance is difficult to overstate."[14] President Truman's Committee on Civil Rights had included this rationale among the three it listed for urging national action against discrimination: "We have a moral reason, an economic reason, and an international reason for believing that the time for action is now."[15] Even in the absence of a foreign relations rationale many reasons would have supported requiring special legislative measures to prevent the perpetuation of the racial caste system, in addition to the general protections that Reconstruction amendments and laws already provided.

Divisions over race had plagued the nation since our earliest days.[16] Although the Declaration of Independence had proclaimed the equality of all men, the racial issue led to the omission of that ideal from the Constitution. Instead, the drafters of the Constitution employed circumlocution to sanction the continuation of slavery. The question of slavery provoked recurring national crises. Once the Civil War decided that question, the country showed similar division as to the fate of the former slaves, and the existence of a racial caste system continued to divide the nation geographically, economically, and politically. The modern legislation was designed to overcome this unique history.

Moral Reasons

In part the legislation hearkened back to the abolitionists and vindicated moral values. These values were best articulated by Martin Luther King, Jr. To Dr. King, morality and justice were intertwined: an "unjust law is a code that a numerical or power majority group compels a minority group to obey but does not make binding on itself." He noted that "throughout Alabama all sorts of devious methods are used to prevent Negroes from becoming registered voters, and there are some counties in which, even though Negroes constitute a majority of the population, not a single Negro is registered. Can any law enacted under such circumstances be considered democratically structured?"[17] This formulation echoes all three themes from the *Carolene Products* footnote: racial prejudice, skewing of political processes, and subordination of discrete and insular minorities.

President Kennedy concurred: "We are confronted primarily with a moral issue. It is as old as the scriptures and is as clear as the American Constitution."[18] More recently, in his inaugural address as assistant attorney general for civil rights, Deval Patrick referred to civil rights as a "great moral imperative" and stated: "This nation, as I see it, has a creed. That creed is deeply rooted in the concepts of equality, opportunity, and fair play."[19] Of course, not all shared these views of morality. Thus, Senator Sam Ervin (D-N.C.), arguing against the Fair Housing Act of 1968, said that "there is nothing iniquitous in men of one race preferring to sell or rent their residential property to men of their own race. Such conduct is in perfect harmony with the natural law that operates in all areas and decrees that people prefer to reside in residential neighborhoods inhabited by others of their race. Like instinctively seeks like."[20]

Those who question the moral underpinnings of antidiscrimination law point primarily to a perceived clash between liberty and equality.[21] They claim that to forbid an individual to discriminate is to deprive that individual of liberty. This claim harks back to the age of social Darwinism, when William Graham Sumner wrote:

> Let it be understood that we cannot go outside of this alternative: liberty, inequality, survival of the fittest; not-liberty, equality, survival of the unfittest. The former carries society forward and favors all its best members; the latter carries society downwards and favors all its worst members.[22]

However, as de Tocqueville noted, "men cannot become absolutely equal unless they are entirely free,"[23] and there is common recognition today that discrimination itself deprives its victims of liberty. Thus, the question is not whether the law should impinge on liberty, but whose liberty it should favor: that of the discriminator or of the discriminatee. In a society founded on opportunity and merit, the right of an individual to deprive another person of an opportunity for reasons unrelated to merit is a less valuable liberty than the right to be free from such discrimination.

National unity and morality are connected by the Declaration of Independence, which holds that "all men are created equal" and endowed with "certain unalienable rights" including "Life, Liberty, and the pursuit of Happiness" and that "to secure these rights governments are instituted among men."[24] The Civil Rights Act of 1866 and the Fourteenth Amendment were meant to incorporate these ideals, which had deliberately been omitted from the original Constitution because they clashed with slavery.[25] The strength of various rationales differs as applied to different rights; for example, the right to vote without regard to race can be tied to Lockean ideals,[26] while the right to private employment without regard to race cannot. But the recognition that certain acts of one person toward another may constitute offenses which deserve sanctions from the community is ancient, as illustrated by the biblical injunction: "When anyone, man or woman, wrongs another and thereby breaks faith with the Lord, that person has incurred guilt which demands reparation."[27]

Pragmatic Reasons

It is not clear whether morality alone would have led Congress to enact the legislation. Pragmatic reasons, however, provided powerful additional impetus. First, the racial caste system, under which a large racial group was permanently consigned to an underclass, undermined national unity; there could be no sense that all Americans were part of one community. Thus, the caste system prolonged the reign of the *Dred Scott* ruling that African Americans could not be citizens. As President Kennedy stated, in proposing the Civil Rights Act in 1963: "This is one country. It has become one country because all of us and all the people who came here had an equal chance to develop their talents."[28]

A second rationale for enacting civil rights legislation was economic. It was believed that racial discrimination sapped the nation's economic strength by excluding 10 percent of the potential market for jobs, housing, and public accommodations.[29] Third, public order was undermined by the massive resistance of southern states to the constitutional mandate.[30] Unlike most other constitutional violations, massive resistance was systemic, deliberate, and widespread. As Dr. King noted, the southern states were employing the tools of the law to promote a reign of lawless behavior.[31] In addition, he prophetically noted that "law and order exist for the purpose of establishing justice and that when they fail in this purpose they become the dangerously structured dams that block the flow of social progress."[32]

The challenge to public order was increased by the nonviolent public disobedience campaign of the civil rights groups in the 1960s and by later violent public disorders in urban centers in the north and in the south. The Kerner Commission found that the disorders in 1967 manifested national problems which "threaten democratic values fundamental to our progress as a free society."[33] Enactment of civil rights laws channeled protests against segregation into the courts.[34] Finally, the independence of former colonies in the third world, the Cold War, and the ideals of the United Nations charter heightened the embarassment of the world's leading democracy failing to follow its putative ideals. These considerations differed in kind from the justifications for state or local legislation; they all pointed to a federal role.

National Unity. President Lincoln understood the strains that race placed on national unity, and he taught that the United States could not survive half slave and half free. That same lesson applies to a nation divided by discrimination, both official and unofficial. In 1964, the official racial caste system prevailed in the southern states but not in the northern states. By 1960 seventeen northern states had adopted fair employment statutes.[35] The laws respecting race increasingly diverged in the two regions, and unofficial discrimination, especially in the private sector, was common throughout the nation.

Discrimination of both types, official and unofficial, sustained a society that in many respects continued to be part slave and part free. Black people were primarily relegated to an underclass, without the freedom to live or to patronize public accommodations where they wished, to attend integrated schools, or to obtain decent jobs.[36] White persons by and large enjoyed all those freedoms. The strains of maintaining opportunity for one race and denying opportunity to the other were untenable. Our nation could not survive without a common set of basic values, and the caste system was at odds with the long-stated core value, equality.

Two conceivable solutions existed for President Lincoln's predicament: the states could become all slave or all free. The first solution, however, solved only the regional problem and not the caste problem. Moreover, the Fourteenth Amendment's solution to the problems of racial discrimination was not to equalize rights by constricting them, because the citizenship, due process, and privileges and immunities clauses protect against the diminution of some rights.

It was not until 1948 that President Truman returned to the theme of national unity and linked it to national ideals. He argued to Congress:

We shall not . . . finally achieve the ideals for which this Nation was founded so long as any American suffers discrimination as a result of his race, or religion, or color, or the land of origin of his forefathers. . . . The Federal Government has a clear duty to see that constitutional guaranties of individual liberties and of equal protection under the laws are not denied or abridged anywhere in our Union.[37]

The racial caste system was shredding the fabric of national life, as race and national origin discrimination posed the greatest threats to the goal of national unity.

An opposing view holds that national unity is best preserved by according the states great latitude as guarantors of individual rights. This view, sometimes characterized as federalism, stresses the harm of extensive federal encroachment into state preserves. For example, Justice Felix Frankfurter, an advocate of racial justice, thought federal civil rights legislation raised troubling issues. His dissent in *Screws v. United States* relied in part on a historically inaccurate myth that Reconstruction "was born of that vengeful spirit which to no small degree envenomed the Reconstruction era. Legislative respect for constitutional limitations was not at its height and Congress passed laws clearly unconstitutional."[38] These limitations to which Justice Frankfurter referred confine Congress's power to legislate, and Frankfurter seems to have been expressing agreement with precedents such as the *Civil Rights Cases*,[39] which found an absence of congressional power to forbid private discrimination in public accommodations. The thrust of those cases is that in a federal system such matters are for the state to regulate. Although modern scholarship paints it in a more favorable light,[40] the unflattering view of Reconstruction was widely held in the first half of the twentieth century and continued during much of the deliberation leading to the civil rights acts.[41] It was initially shared by President Kennedy, a lifelong student of American history who eventually changed his mind.[42]

This reliance on "federalism" results from a particular vision of the relationship between federal and state government. Federalism, strictly speaking, simply refers to the Constitution's system of sharing power between the state and federal governments. As Madison argued, the Constitution establishes neither a wholly national government nor a wholly federal one, but one "of a mixed character, presenting at least as many *federal* as *national* features."[43] Federalism reflects, as well, a political theory that dividing power places restraints on the ability of both levels of government to abuse power. The framers believed that the national government's power should extend to legislating "in all cases for the general interests of the Union, and also in those to which the States are separately incompetent, or in which the harmony of the U. States may be interrupted by the exercise of individual Legislation."[44] The federal system thus refers to allocation of power to the state or national government based on which level was most suitable to exercise that power.

The sense in which Justice Frankfurter used the term, however, seems to connote a series of severe restrictions on federal power over states. It stems from a historical view that the federal government was formed by the states.[45] Such a view distorts federalism into a state's rights doctrine, without recognizing the restrictions on the states contained in the Constitution and underscored by the Fourteenth Amendment. Chief Justice John Marshall's seminal opinion in *McCulloch v. Maryland* authoritatively established that the national government "proceeds directly from the people," not the states, and "is supreme within its sphere of action."[46]

Since the enforcement clauses of the Reconstruction amendments join with the Constitution's original grants of legislative power to authorize Congress to legislate against racial discrimination, civil rights legislation is perfectly compatible with the notion of federalism. Nonetheless, Justice Frankfurter viewed *Screws,* in which a sheriff who had beaten to death a handcuffed African-American prisoner was convicted in federal court of willfully depriving the prisoner of the right to due process of law, as involving a renegade sheriff whose action did not represent state policy but in fact violated state homicide laws. He believed that a prosecution by the United States for such a crime undermined federalism, and he characterized the "practical question" as "whether the States should be relieved from responsibility to bring their law officers to book for homicide, by allowing prosecutions in the federal courts for a relatively minor offense carrying a short sentence."[47]

Thus, one concern expressed was that federal law enforcement would displace the ordinary operation of local law enforcement. Justice Frankfurter opined that the Court's construction of a criminal statute that is now 18 USC §242 "fails . . . to leave to the States the province of local crime enforcement, that the proper balance of political forces in our federalism requires."[48] Because Sheriff Screws's brutal killing of a prisoner violated state law as well as federal law, Justice Frankfurter believed federal action was not only unnecessary but dangerous. He argued that to allow the prosecution here would effect "a revolutionary change in the balance of the political relations between the National Government and the States without reason."[49] Frankfurter was concerned about "abuse of the broad powers of prosecution" that the federal government sought.[50] He worried that "this shapeless and all-embracing statute can serve as a dangerous instrument of political intimidation and coercion in the hands of those so inclined."[51] Finally, he argued that if "local authorities cannot be relied upon for courageous and prompt action," "the cure is a re-invigoration of State responsibility. It is not an undue incursion of remote federal authority into local duties with consequent debilitation of local responsibility."[52]

Justice Frankfurter seemed primarily concerned that federal duplication of state law undermines federalism. Where the state practices race discrimination, encourages discrimination, or fails to outlaw discrimination, adherence to federalism would not preclude federal legislation. Federalism is a two-way street, imposing powers and limitations on both the federal and state governments. Where state law violates the constitutional protections against discrimination, federalism is advanced by federal antidiscrimination legislation; the federal plan imposes on the states the obligation to follow the Constitution. Thus, the justices who argued in dissent in *EEOC v. Wyoming*[53] that extension of the Age Discrimination Act to the states offended constitutional principles of federalism nonetheless agreed that Congress could extend Title VII's ban on race discrimination to the states.[54] The difference, in their view, was that the Constitution banned race discrimination in state employment but did not ban the age discrimination at issue.

Justice Hugo Black also relied on federalism in his dissent in *South Carolina v. Katzenbach,* where he argued that Section 5 of the Voting Rights Act treated covered states as "little more than conquered provinces."[55] The answer to Justice Black's concern is found in the opinion of another great southern federal judge, John Minor Wisdom of the Fifth Circuit Court of Appeals, who explained the constitutional basis of the 1957 act:

> When the alleged wrongdoing is based on a State law which is contrary to the superior authority of the United States Constitution, the Nation, as well as the aggrieved individuals, is injured. In such a conflict with the State the power of the Nation to protect itself and to go into its own courts to prevent the States from destroying federally protected rights of citizens derived from the Constitution would seem to be implicit in the Supremacy Clause and inherent in our federal system.[56]

The case for federal action had been strengthened by the time Attorney General Katzenbach urged Congress to adopt the Voting Rights Act. He argued that the "whole Federal system really depends upon" the states voluntarily complying with valid federal laws. However, since the southern states had not complied with the 1957, 1960, and 1964 Civil Rights Acts, "we really can no longer rely on good faith."[57]

Note that even though Attorney General Katzenbach rested his case for enactment of the Voting Rights Act on the covered states' lack of good faith, once the act took effect he appealed once more for good faith compliance. Although the act arguably authorized wholesale assignment of federal voting examiners to most of the covered counties in the South, the attorney general did not do so. He sent examiners to the few counties with the most egregious history of noncompliance but also sent letters to the remaining counties urging voter registrars to voluntarily comply. Warning that examiners would be appointed "where it is clear that past denials of the right to vote justify it or where present compliance with federal law . . . is insufficient to assure prompt registration of all eligible citizens," the letter stressed that the "primary responsibility for registration remains with state and county officials" and promised to withdraw examiners from any county where "the prospect of discrimination is gone."[58] The department, in other words, continued to prefer compliance by local officials rather than performance of local duties by federal officials. Although this policy attracted much criticism at the time, ten years later the Civil Rights Commission noted that over a million new minority voters had registered since enactment of the 1965 act, of whom only 155,000 were registered through federal listing.[59] The policy of seeking local compliance before assigning federal examiners had worked. Federalism, in other words, did not require the federal government to continue to tolerate state deprivations of voting rights but instead led to a particular manner of enforcement, designed to maximize local responsibility and to encourage local compliance.

In the wake of *Brown v. Board of Education,* southern states revived another concept of federalism: that the states were sovereign and could lawfully "interpose" their authority against that of the Supreme Court, and that *Brown* would not be valid until a constitutional amendment decided the contest of power between the southern states and the Court.[60] This theory conflicted both with Supreme Court doctrine[61] and with the Civil War amendments and was defeated by superior federal force when Governors Orval Faubus of Arkansas and Ross Barnett of Mississippi attempted to carry out interposition by excluding nine African-American students from Central High School in Little Rock and excluding James Meredith from the University of Mississippi.[62]

National unity remains an important governmental goal, but one which coexists with a belief that the states continue to stand as a counterweight to overly centralized government. Federalism reflects both of these values. The Reconstruction amendments, however, reject state racial discrimination as a permissible value, opting instead for complete national unity on the issue. This view does not mean that the value of state autonomy should be ignored. Enforcement policies may defer to state autonomy where two methods exist for enforcing the nondiscrimination principle, one of which is more compatible with state autonomy. Finally, when the federal government enforces the nondiscrimination laws, state governments that formerly excluded African Americans from equal participation become more fully representative and therefore hold a stronger claim to legitimacy and autonomy. In short, nondiscrimination laws properly understood and enforced promote the values of federalism in several ways.

Early in the Reagan administration a talented young lawyer who had recently been hired for a noncareer position in the Civil Rights Division visited me in my office on the fifth floor of the Department of Justice building. His gaze fixed on two framed documents on my wall: attractively printed copies of the Fourteenth and Fifteenth Amendments that had been given to me by my colleagues in recognition of my work in helping to enforce these constitutional bans on race discrimination. We discussed our business and he left. A few weeks later there appeared on the office wall of this budding civil rights lawyer a framed copy of the Tenth Amendment to the Constitution:

> The powers not delegated to the United States by the Constitution, nor prohibited by it to the States, are reserved to the States respectively, or to the people.

Much of the federalism debate, at least in a formal sense, has turned on a perceived tension between the ban on state racial discrimination found in the Reconstruction amendments and the truism found in the Tenth Amendment. In my view, this is a false tension; under the Reconstruction amendments discrimination is, in the words of the Tenth Amendment, "prohibited by [the Constitution] to the States." Rather, the underlying value suggested by the Tenth Amendment is that the federal government, even when enforcing other provisions of the Constitution, should recognize the dignity and distinct interests of the states and intrude no more than the situation requires.

Economic Strength. National unity is closely linked not only with morality but with commerce: "Our economic unit is the Nation."[63] As Michael J. Klarman has noted, "once the [other] forces . . . fostered a national climate conducive to racial change, the South would find maintenance of its outlier racial status increasingly difficult because of national economic and social integration."[64] Just as unity may require a moral consensus as to what business practices are permissible, so also the free flow of commerce may be impeded if some businesses are allowed to discriminate while their competitors are not. Even a primarily economic community such as the original European Economic Community saw fit in 1957 to ban sex discrimination in employment.[65]

The economic rationale for nondiscrimination laws posits that race and sex discrimination place undue burdens on commerce. Commerce is enhanced by a free market, but a market in which arbitrary discrimination reigns is not free; we tend to equate a free market with merit and to view race, gender, and certain other characteristics as unrelated to merit. Not all agree. For example, Senator Sam Ervin (D-N.C.), arguing against the 1964 act, said: "The best way to increase employment is to allow the free enterprise system to work rather than to have the Government come in and take control of private employment. . . . I think this bill, instead of making more jobs, is going to result in decreasing jobs."[66] The economic critique of the antidiscrimination laws, however, gives insufficient weight to the gravity of the personal costs of discrimination.

President Kennedy used the forum of his economic report to Congress to make the point about the negative economic effects of discrimination: "An end to racial and religious discrimination—which not only affronts our basic ideals but burdens our economy with its waste—offers an imperative contribution to growth."[67] Similarly, in 1974 Congress stated, "Economic stabilization would be enhanced and competition among the various financial institutions and other firms engaged in the extension of credit would be strengthened by an absence of discrimination on the basis of sex or marital status."[68]

The point was graphically illustrated in the report of President Truman's Committee on Civil Rights, which depicted the results of discrimination in employment as leading to inefficient use of our labor force, resulting in less purchasing power and less consumer demand, and thence to less production and "a lower living standard for *all.*" By contrast the report depicted fair employment practices as helping establish full and efficient use of all our workers, resulting in greater purchasing power, which in turn leads to greater consumer demand, full production, and "a higher living standard for all."[69] Although the committee's analysis may seem relatively unsophisticated, especially in light of its failure to discuss the costs flowing from enforcement of nondiscrimination laws, the essential point seems consistent with the country's general suspicion of artificial restraints on economic markets.

The committee's view was no doubt influenced by the theories supporting federal antitrust legislation. Just as the antitrust laws attempt to reduce disparities of power that stifle competition, the civil rights laws disfavor arbitrary uses of power to deprive protected classes of the free opportunity to compete.[70] Restrictions on the use of power constrict the liberty of those who hold the power. Both the discrimination laws and the Sherman Antitrust Act have been criticized as impinging on liberty. However, the Supreme Court noted in a Sherman Act case that "liberty of contract did not involve a right to deprive the public of the advantages of free competition. . . . Liberty of contract does not imply liberty . . . to defy the national will, when legally expressed."[71] Moreover, the civil rights laws arguably intrude less than the antitrust laws and not only protect potential victims of discrimination but also free employers, public accommodations, and sellers from the constraints of laws or customs requiring discrimination.

Just as the antitrust laws were meant to address structural barriers to the free market, the civil rights laws tend to address structural barriers to equal opportunity in that market, which is part of the message of the *Carolene Products* footnote and of John Hart Ely's approach to the equal protection of the laws.[72] However, both the antitrust laws and the civil rights laws have been criticized as flawed means of economic reform. The validity of these critiques depends in part on one's characterization of the economic goals that these laws are to advance. Three possible goals that have been suggested for the antitrust laws might also apply to the civil rights laws.[73] One is a wealth maximization rationale, described in the preceding pages. The political and cultural rationale emphasizes the unfair economic structure of the racial caste system. And for some commentators, redistribution of wealth is the objective of the civil rights laws.

Neither piece of legislation was based on sophisticated economic analysis. However, the civil rights laws share strengths attributed to the Sherman Act: "The goals of the Sherman Act . . . are multidimensional. . . . [It] is an organic document. . . . That interpretations of the Sherman Act have not been 'frozen in time' or mired in ideology as the country has grown and matured is the continuing strength of the document."[74] Although weighty economic arguments support antidiscrimination laws, reliance on them alone would not do justice to the multiple grounds for Congress's adoption of the civil rights laws. Indeed, many objected to the 1964 act's tie to the commerce clause, arguing that the act addressed a moral problem, not an economic one.[75]

Public Order. Open and notorious lawlessness undermines government. As Willard Hurst has noted, we assign to law "the legitimate monopoly of violence," and we use law "to define and to implement an idea of constitutionalism as the norm of all secular power."[76] Although maintenance of public order normally falls to the state governments, the Constitution recognizes an overarching federal role. The Preamble includes the following among the purposes of the Constitution: "in Order to form a more perfect Union, establish Justice, insure domestic Tranquility." Article 1, Section 8, authorizes Congress to "provide for calling forth the Militia to execute the Laws of the Union, suppress Insurrections." Article 4, Section 4, requires the United States to "guarantee to every State in this Union a Republican Form of Government . . . and on Application of the Legislature, or of the Executive (when the Legislature cannot be convened), against domestic Violence." Article 6 makes the Constitution and laws of the United States "the supreme Law of the Land; and the Judges in every State shall be bound thereby, any Thing in the Constitution or Laws of any State to the Contrary notwithstanding."

The federal government is the ultimate guarantor of public order where state government either is unable to maintain order or is itself acting in a lawless manner.[77] The Civil War and Reconstruction arguably exemplify this principle. The Reconstruction constitutional amendments and laws also created new norms against which to judge issues of public order. In place of the authority of states to permit slavery[78] and the rights of slaveowners as protected by the fugitive slave clause,[79] these amendments protected the ex-slaves from the state and from their former owners. In cases such as *Screws v. United States,*[80] the United States attempted to remedy state lawlessness.

Public order can be breached in numerous ways, and the civil rights legislation responded primarily to four types of breach. First, some states not only asserted the authority to "interpose" state law against the constitutional ban on discrimination[81] but engaged in or tolerated violent state and private action against the exercise of rights of nondiscrimination,[82] as the events in Selma illustrated. Individuals seeking to secure the right to vote were arrested or harassed by local law enforcement officers,[83] as were those seeking to travel in interstate commerce on nonsegregated buses, as evidenced by the arrests of freedom riders in Birmingham, Alabama, and Jackson, Mississippi, and the failure to protect freedom riders in Anniston and Montgomery, Alabama.[84] President Kennedy observed that official acts seeking to deny the rights of African Americans "can result only in a decreased respect for the law and increased violations of the law."[85] In the summer of 1964 Attorney General Robert F. Kennedy reported to President Johnson:

> The unique difficulty that seems to me to be presented by the situation in Mississippi (which is duplicated in parts of Alabama and Louisiana at least) is in gathering information on fundamentally lawless activities which have the sanction of local law enforcement agencies, political officials and a substantial segment of the white population.[86]

A second, and related, breach of public order occurred when public officials disobeyed or interfered with federal court orders to desegregate schools, as when Governor Barnett failed to comply with orders to admit James Meredith to the University of Mississippi or when Governor Faubus interfered with school desegregation in Little Rock.[87] These breaches threatened the administration of justice. As the court in *Faubus* stated, "[The Attorney General, who had sought an injunction against interference with the school desegregation order, was] acting under the authority and direction of the court to take such action as was necessary to prevent its orders and judgments from being frustrated and to represent the public interest in the due administration of justice."[88] Southern officials challenged the basic concept of *Marbury v. Madison* that "it is, emphatically, the province and duty of the judicial department, to say what the law is."[89] Senator Ervin of North Carolina, for example, took the position that no law authorized a federal court school desegregation order, which was therefore not encompassed within the phrase "laws of the United States" in 10 U.S.C. §332, so that President Eisenhower lacked authority to use troops to combat obstruction of the Little Rock school desegregation order. Congress and the executive reacted slowly to the states' failure to comply with *Brown*.[90]

The failure of the Department of Justice to fully employ the few tools it possessed to combat violence emboldened state officials to continue their resistance. For example, in 1957 the head of the Civil Rights Section, A. B. Caldwell, told Governor Faubus that disturbances over school desegregation in Little Rock would not of themselves warrant federal intervention. Faubus therefore went ahead with his plans and barred the African-American students from Central High School.[91] Indeed, Faubus later said that he thought the department's failure to send marshals to maintain order was " 'an absolute default' of what was 'clearly its responsibility.' "[92] During this same period the Justice Department also "instructed local U.S. attorneys not to have integration disturbances investigated as possible violations of the civil rights statutes."[93]

The power wielded by the white minority in places such as Selma combined with the official violence and official disregard for law to promote an overall atmosphere of official corruption. One small incident brought this home to me: while working on a case against Sheriff Clark, two young women who were paralegal employees of the Civil Rights Division were invited by a sheriff's deputy to go to an after-hours drinking and gambling club allegedly owned by the sheriff himself.[94] Either the deputy was oblivious to the impropriety of inviting employees of a federal law enforcement agency to an illegal club, or he was trying to set them up. The inappropriateness of the invitation was heightened by Sheriff Clark's involvement in the club and his stake in the outcome of the lawsuit on which the employees were working. Ten years of state defiance was undermining respect for law, and so finally in 1964 Congress enacted legislation to enforce *Brown*.

Third, private individuals opposed to racial equality interfered with state efforts to comply with the Constitution[95] or federal court orders.[96] The Justice Department found that from 1953 to 1957 there had been "six racially motivated killings in the South; twenty-nine other shootings; forty-four beatings; five stabbings; forty-one bombings of homes, churches, and schools; and seven burnings of similar buildings."[97] Congress acted more quickly to address interference with court orders by providing in the Civil Rights Act of 1960 that obstruction of federal court orders was a crime.[98] The same act partially responded to interference with state efforts to comply with the Constitution by criminalizing possession, transportation, or threats regarding the use of explosives to damage school buildings.[99]

The final threat to public order came from the rising demands of black citizens for equality in the private sector. Sit-ins, marches, and demonstrations demanding jobs and equal treatment in public accommodations led to more state violence, whether in the form of police dogs and fire hoses in Birmingham, Alabama, or of arrest and imprisonment in Albany, Georgia, and many other cities. The nation was faced with a choice: condone private sector discrimination and its accompanying public sector violence or forbid private sector discrimination and thereby eliminate the causes of civil unrest and state violence. The 1964 act opted for the latter solution. President Kennedy argued that without such legislation "Negroes ... can be expected to continue increasingly to seek the vindication of these rights through organized direct action, with all its potentially explosive consequences."[100]

The following year, violence at the Edmund Pettus Bridge in Selma, Alabama, was the state's response to black demands for the vote; that incident became a powerful catalyst for Congress to pass the Voting Rights Act of 1965. In brief, according to Michael J. Klarman:

> The Kennedy and Johnson administrations were spurred into action when the nation—including, most significantly, northern whites—was appalled to witness the spectacle of southern law enforcement officials brutally suppressing generally nonviolent civil rights demonstrations. The nation was made painfully aware, through the immediacy of television coverage, of the cruel excesses of Jim Crow; the response was a wave of indignation that such behavior could be tolerated in mid-twentieth-century America.[101]

Klarman points out that southern businesspeople, while generally satisfied initially with the racial status quo, "were not prepared ... to permit civil disorder detrimental to a stable investment environment to ruin their hard-fought efforts to bring economic growth to the South."[102] As Derrick Bell has argued, *Brown* was of value to those "whites who realized that the South could make the transition from a rural, plantation society to the sunbelt with all its potential and profit only when it ended its struggle to remain divided by state-sponsored segregation. Thus, segregation was viewed as a barrier to further industrialization in the South."[103]

Ivan Allen, Jr., the mayor of Atlanta, supported the proposal to ban discrimination in public accommodations for both moral and economic reasons. Atlanta needed this law, he said, "to see that ... business is preserved and at the same time see that the rights that the Court says that the 200,000 Negroes in Atlanta

are entitled to [are given to them]." Mayor Allen argued that "we need definition," because "this thing builds up day by day. People's tempers get worse.
People's excuses and reasons in this situation, in the matter of race, are becoming stronger, both white and Negro."[104] He argued that failure to enact the law
would cause cities like Atlanta to "slip backward" because congressional inaction "would amount to an endorsement of private business setting up an entirely
new status of discrimination throughout the Nation."[105] Michal Belknap characterizes the change in the attitudes of southern leaders thus: "Prior to 1964 the
vast majority of white southerners, although taking no part in anti–civil rights
violence, found it difficult to condemn those who did. Gradually, many of them
came to realize that toleration of racist terrorism could lead only to anarchy."[106]

The protests that spurred Congress to enact the 1960, 1964, and 1965 acts were
governed by Dr. Martin Luther King's principles of nonviolent resistance. As
Hanes Walton has pointed out,

> King . . . decided to create so much tension, conflict, and struggle between
> blacks and whites through nonviolent marches, demonstrations, and protests
> that the federal government would be forced to step away from the sidelines
> and take sides with the movement and against those who used violence and
> fraud to deny individuals their basic human rights.[107]

Most of the violence had come from supporters of white supremacy. Violence of
another kind disrupted public order in 1967 in nearly 150 cities, culminating in
large-scale disorders in Newark and Detroit.[108] Some believe that the rioting after King's assassination in 1968 led to passage of the Fair Housing Act.[109] Certainly the disorders of 1967 and 1968 were responsible for the inclusion of anti-
rioting laws in the 1968 act.[110] Thus, the 1968 act embodies the two possible
reactions to civil disorder: attempt to address the root causes of the dissatisfaction that prompted the rioting or attempt to control the rioters. The attempt to
address the root causes of dissatisfaction focused on eradicating racial discrimination. Nondiscrimination might give people of color more of a stake in the economic system. Legally mandating at least formal equality has partially removed
an ideological cause of dissatisfaction, but many of the underlying conditions
that led to dissatisfaction persist.[111]

The Centrality of Race in the Civil Rights Laws. Ending the racial caste system
meant, first, eliminating laws and government actions that separated or discriminated between the races. In addition, societal custom and practice reinforced the
racial caste system, and Congress recognized and addressed this interconnection
by extending the discrimination ban to the private sector.

Despite the similarity of some reasons for banning both public and private
discrimination, other reasons for creating rights against public action may differ
from the reasons for creating rights against private action. As Judge Friendly has
said, "It is hard to conceive a task more appropriate for federal courts than
to protect civil rights guaranteed by the Constitution against invasion by the

states."[112] Perhaps Thirteenth Amendment rights, which exist as against both state and private actors, are equally appropriate for federal protection. However, most other rights as against private parties are not directly guaranteed by the Constitution. Rather, Congress has relied on the commerce clause to create and protect other rights such as freedom from private discrimination based on gender or disability.

Not only did elimination of the racial caste system constitute the core of the modern civil rights legislation, it also became the paradigm for expansion of civil rights protections. This use of race discrimination as paradigm is most marked in Supreme Court decisions interpreting the equal protection clause of the Fourteenth Amendment.[113] However, the Court has been far more cautious than has Congress in extending race discrimination principles to other classifications.[114] The public acceptance and moral authority of the ban on race discrimination has emboldened Congress to protect the elderly, the disabled, families with children, and institutionalized persons against various forms of discrimination. This expansion raises new questions: to what extent do these new protections fit the race paradigm, and has the growth of these new protections benefited or harmed the core goal of ending the racial caste system?

The passage of time also raises questions about the racial caste system paradigm. The civil rights laws were originally enacted to achieve "the breaking of a pattern."[115] As those patterns are broken, the purpose will become protecting against the reemergence of discrimination; the policies and practices that were needed to accomplish the former are not necessarily appropriate to accomplish the latter. In addition, Richard Epstein argues that although Title VII initially was warranted, its costs now outweigh its benefits.[116] However, it has proven more difficult than anticipated to break the racial caste system insofar as the continued existence of a vast race-based underclass is a remnant of that system. The solution may lie elsewhere, but until it is identified and successfully employed, nondiscrimination laws will be deemed necessary.

Albert O. Hirschman has written that "conservative attacks on existing or proposed progressive policies" commonly rely on three reactive theses: the perversity thesis, the futility thesis, and the jeopardy thesis.[117] The attacks on antidiscrimination legislation predictably invoke all three theses by arguing that antidiscrimination law exacerbates the societal problems it seeks to solve, that it is ineffectual, and that the cost of antidiscrimination law is too high. This "rhetorics of intransigence"[118] forms the tenor of the claims of Senator Ervin and Richard Epstein, for example. Those claims tend to undervalue the harm of racial discrimination and overstate the extent to which antidiscrimination law intrudes on liberty, and they both ignore the progress that has flowed from enforcement of the antidiscrimination laws and reflect a willingness to proclaim futility too soon. As Hirschman argues, there is "a rush to judgment and no allowance is made for social learning or for incremental, corrective policy-making."[119] Moreover, like Hirschman's example of the minimum wage laws, they confuse "the undoubted possibility of a perverse outcome" with the certainty of a perverse outcome.[120] His conclusion—that both action and inaction carry risks, which should be "canvassed, assessed, and guarded against to the extent possible" and that the baneful consequences of either action or inaction can never be known with certainty—provides a more balanced method for assessing nondiscrimination legislation.[121]

An unusual variant on the futility thesis, which Hirschman associates with the epigram *plus ça change plus c'est la même chose*,[122] is found in Derrick Bell's analysis, which argues that the foundations of the American nation are rooted in racism and that African Americans gain legal rights only when white self-interest dictates. He reduces his argument to this formula:

$$\text{White Racism v. Justice} = \text{White Racism}$$
$$\text{White Racism v. White Self-Interest} = \text{Justice}^{123}$$

The formula suggests that where white racism conflicts with justice, white racism will prevail. Only where white racism conflicts with white self-interest and white self-interest coincides with justice will justice prevail. In one sense Professor Bell simply states the obvious regarding our majoritarian system of government. It is not that a white majority will inevitably exercise dominion over a minority of persons of color. Racial dominion is inevitable only where race is thought to make a difference, and white racism depends on that perceived difference. Bell is reacting, in part, to the political forces that throughout American history have appealed to a narrow interest in racial dominion by the white majority. A less pessimistic evaluation would point to the growing recognition of the broader interests that nondiscrimination policies serve.

It is not possible to quantify the extent of white racism. As Drew Days has observed about the attitudinal evidence, "one generalizes at some peril."[124] Measurement of racism is difficult because so much depends on the question asked. By the 1980s, for example, most Americans had "adopted the rhetoric of formal racial equality . . . [but] expressed anti-Black opinions and attitudes when questions were directed towards specific issues such as housing integration and miscegenation."[125] Measurement of racism also depends on a common definition of the term. Derrick Bell characterizes as racist the failure to attack the root causes of African-American poverty, and he concludes that racism is a permanent fixture of American life because oppression of African Americans serves the economic interests of America's economic elite. His definition depends not on the invidious intent of whites but on the depressed economic status of the African-American underclass.[126] There is some evidence white racism is receding, though far from extinct.[127]

What is more important, if one accepts Professor Bell's premise, is the quantification of white self-interest. Professor Bell himself notes that "the elimination of racism as a policy factor in public and private decisions would seem in the interest of every American, white as well as black."[128] On the other hand, some adherents to the law and economics school argue that once state laws requiring or encouraging racial discrimination disappeared, no further civil rights legislation was necessary. They reason that free market forces disfavor discrimination and that self-interest of sellers and employers dictates nondiscrimination.[129]

Presumably Bell would agree that the factors discussed above, such as national unity, morality, public order, and commerce, all support that view of white self-interest. Nonetheless he is concerned that "white dominance over blacks is not only profitable, it is also . . . comforting, and because of the ancestral fears of inundation, essential."[130] Hence arises his fear that "the first Reconstruction experience, as bitter as it was, did not enable avoidance of what could become a quite similar withdrawal of the rights and opportunities granted during the second Reconstruction of the 1960s."[131] The evolution of the modern civil rights laws provides grounds for cautious optimism, notwithstanding the interests Professor Bell identifies and the setbacks and shortcomings that many have chronicled.[132]

The first Reconstruction lasted less than twenty years. The second Reconstruction arguably began with *Brown* in 1954 and has lasted twice that long. There is no sign of widespread retrenchment from the ideal of nondiscrimination, although individual doctrines have inevitably risen and fallen during the past four decades. The ongoing task of civil rights advocates is to appeal to the law and to enlightened national self-interest. In sum, both pragmatic and moral reasons combine with oft-noted political and historical forces to support the federal ban on discrimination. Once having decided that discrimination should be outlawed, Congress then faced the task of creating an enforcement mechanism.

4

Enforcement Roles of Individuals, States, and Federal Government

Enforcement responsibility could be placed with private individuals, the federal government, the state government, or some combination of the three. The factors influencing placement of enforcement responsibility include history, whether the rights to be enforced are considered public or private rights, the nature of the sanctions available, the relative effectiveness of the possible enforcers, and considerations of federalism and its opposing pulls of centralization and diffusion. Congress did not consciously or carefully examine all these factors and then reach a reasoned judgment allocating enforcement responsibility. It undoubtedly reacted to various political and transitory considerations. Nonetheless, we enhance our own understanding of the current enforcement scheme, and our ability to formulate proposals for improving it, if we examine these factors.

THE SPECTRUM OF POSSIBILITIES

Private Enforcement

Most civil litigation is initiated by private parties; this is as true of litigation to secure statutory rights as it is of common law litigation. Litigation, however, costs the parties money, and potential civil rights litigants tend to be persons without sufficient financial resources. Large, systemic cases are very expensive—attorney's fees and costs for plaintiffs in some northern school desegregation cases have run into seven figures.[1] American law creates no general right to free legal services for civil cases.[2] Under the traditional American rule each party bears its own attorney's fee costs and such costs as investigation and expert witnesses.[3]

For the above reasons, absent some alternate mechanism, private civil rights would have to be financed by private plaintiffs or civil rights organizations.[4] Indeed, the few civil rights cases preceding passage of the modern civil rights acts were primarily sponsored by organizations such as the National Association for the Advancement of Colored People (NAACP) and the American Civil Liberties Union (ACLU).[5] Such organizations are able to sponsor litigation only selectively; they lack the resources to bring a large number of suits on behalf of individual plaintiffs.[6] Moreover, their ability to bring suit generally depends on the existence of an aggrieved person who wishes suit brought on his or her behalf. Therefore, even if an organization were ready and willing to bring suit to vindicate public values, the suit could not be brought unless a private individual whose private interest was at stake were also ready and willing to sue.[7]

Unlike the American rule, another alternative, the English rule, awards attorney's fees to the prevailing party. This rule, too, may discourage filing cases that are not sure winners. A plaintiff who cannot afford to pay his or her own attorney will surely lack resources to pay the defendant's attorney. One solution is to give an edge to plaintiffs with respect to the awarding of fees, in essence what occurs under the Civil Rights Attorney's Fees Award Act of 1976, which created a presumption in favor of an attorney fee award for prevailing civil rights plaintiffs and a presumption against attorney's fees for prevailing defendants.[8] Payment of fees for experts was added by Congress in the Civil Rights Act of 1991.[9] Although the attorney's fee award statutes have enhanced the ability of civil rights organizations[10] and large law firms to bring civil rights cases, many smaller firms cannot survive the cash flow delays and contingencies associated with discrimination litigation, even if they ultimately obtain attorney's fees.[11]

Another method of enhancing the ability of private parties to bring litigation is government assistance. Such assistance can be indirect, as in a tax subsidy. The costs of civil rights litigation often will be deductible from income as an ordinary and necessary business expense,[12] a deduction normally more helpful to deep pocket defendants than to penurious plaintiffs. The government also endows charitable organizations with tax-exempt status.[13] Some organizations that litigate civil rights suits may take advantage of this subsidy, but they must still depend primarily on private donations or attorney fee awards for their resources. Charitable foundations have provided some assistance for civil rights litigation—up to 16 percent of the NAACP Legal Defense Fund budget, for example—but this assistance is not dependable and often comes with strings attached.[14]

Government subsidy may be direct. The Legal Services Corporation, which Congress created in 1974,[15] provides federal funds for civil legal assistance for poor persons. A recent estimate that current funding meets "less than a fifth of the perceived needs of eligible clients"[16] preceded even more drastic cuts in the FY 1996 budget. Moreover, a backlash toward law reform suits that the Legal Services Program and Legal Services Corporation offices[17] litigated in the 1970s led to statutory restrictions[18] and "Corporation guidelines that prohibited attorneys from engaging in . . . representation in certain controversial areas such as school desegregation."[19] With rare exceptions, government has proved unwilling to grant direct subsidies to private parties who bring public interest litigation.[20]

Finally, the class action suit is a tool used by private litigants to enforce civil rights. This option allows victims of discrimination to pool resources and theoretically enhances their ability to protect their individual rights. Although the class action remains a useful tool in some situations, decisions regarding notice, representation, and scope of class have significantly limited its availability in many civil rights cases.

Public Enforcement

With respect to public enforcement, the basic question is whether it should be vested in the federal government, the state governments, or both. Even before passage of the modern federal civil rights acts, a significant minority of states had created agencies to enforce state civil rights laws.[21] However, other states aggressively encouraged racial discrimination. Where state mechanisms adequately protect civil rights, there is arguably no need for federal protection. However, state enforcement is sometimes ineffective. It is true, as Michal Belknap has pointed out, that by the time Congress strengthened criminal civil rights laws in the 1968 act a "growing fear among white southerners about a breakdown of law and order" had led to stronger state prosecutions of violence directed against civil rights.[22] However, the annual reports of the attorney general are full of examples of federal prosecutions brought for actions that would have violated state laws as well. Either the state did not prosecute or the standards for a dual prosecution were met in these cases.[23]

Even where state enforcement is effective, federal civil rights laws advance some national values that Congress might conclude should not depend on the states to enforce. Conversely, no local peculiarities exist to suggest that different standards of discrimination should exist in different states. Regulated industries, moreover, may prefer the uniformity of national rules and enforcement standards. Finally, some civil rights laws protect individuals from discriminatory state action, and the Reconstruction amendments depend on federal enforcement against the states.

In sum, state law enforcement provides some protection for civil rights but would not suffice as an exclusive protector of federal rights, which requires the active presence of the federal government as the ultimate enforcer of rights. In addition to criminal laws, the federal government has long enforced the antitrust laws, food and drug laws, labor laws, and other laws that promote the national interest. The federal government serves as the ultimate protector of individuals against abuse of state authority. In modern times Congress has also empowered the federal government to protect individuals against private abuses that offend national policy.

Because each of the possible enforcers of the civil rights laws brings strengths and weaknesses to the task, it should come as no surprise that modern civil rights laws have tended to adopt a system of mixed enforcement, assigning roles to private parties, states, and the federal government. As Assistant Attorney General J. Stanley Pottinger observed:

> The history of effective civil rights legislation in the Nation has almost universally included statutes which had a wide variety of remedies, including both class actions (often implicitly) and lawsuits by the Department of Justice. Action by private individuals and groups, as well as governmental agencies, have been of great importance in moving toward equal rights for all our citizens.[24]

This insight seems to have broad application throughout the modern world. It echoes Mauro Cappelletti's conclusion that the "needs of our time are so complex and demanding that it would be foolish to rely upon any single governmental institution to solve them. The state itself, let alone one of its institutions, is unable to meet all of those needs."[25] The question then becomes how to define the various roles.

FACTORS TO BE CONSIDERED IN ASSIGNING ENFORCEMENT ROLES

The traditional enforcement model differentiates between private and public rights, consigning the enforcement of private rights to private persons, whose ultimate recourse is litigation.[26] For example, if a private contract is breached, no legal consequences ensue unless the injured party brings suit. "To enforce a contract for a party who is willing to leave it unenforced is just as absurd as making the contract for him in the first place."[27] The enforcement of public rights normally falls to the government.[28] The dichotomy between private and public rights is not rigid, both because the two terms lack definitional clarity and because there is overlap between the categories.[29] Moreover the growth of "public law" litigation, in which "the object of litigation is the vindication of constitutional or statutory policies," has further blurred the dichotomy.[30] A doctrine known as *parens patriae* sometimes allows the government to enforce private rights,[31] and private individuals may sometimes enforce public rights in what is referred to as a *qui tam* action[32] or as an incident to a suit enforcing private rights. A party's litigative authority is also determined by the doctrine of standing, which denies uninjured parties the right to bring suit. The Congress may give standing to sue to private individuals, the government, or both as to particular issues.[33] The question is what criteria should govern the decision to entrust litigative authority to private individuals, to the government, or to both.

Public Policy

On one hand, suits to remedy unlawful race discrimination affect private rights because the relief benefits individual victims or potential victims of discrimination.[34] On the other, one could argue that what is at stake in discrimination litigation is the public right to a discrimination-free society as well as "securing broad compliance with the law," as the Supreme Court has put it.[35] The Court concluded that private suits to remedy racial discrimination by a place of public accomodation are "private in form only,"[36] and that a plaintiff who obtains an injunction "does so not for himself alone but also as a 'private attorney general,' vindicating a policy that Congress considered of the highest priority."[37]

Some racial discrimination violates the Constitution, and it might be thought that the executive, who is sworn to "preserve, protect and defend the Constitution of the United States,"[38] should play a role in enforcing the Fourteenth Amendment. At times the notion of a personal right to be free from discrimination has been merged with the notion of the United States as the chief enforcer.[39] The Supreme Court has noted that Congress authorized the EEOC to bring suits to enforce Title VII "to implement the public interest as well as to bring about more effective enforcement of private rights."[40] Congress addressed the distinctive role of the attorney general when it considered the Civil Rights of Institutionalized Persons Act:

> The Attorney General's authority extends to initiating suit "for or in the name of the United States," in order to represent the national interest in securing constitutionally adequate care for institutionalized citizens. As a representative of the United States, the Attorney General does not directly represent any institutionalized plaintiffs, and the authority granted him is in no way intended to preclude, delay or prejudice private litigants from enforcing any cause of action they may have under existing or future law.[41]

It has been argued that "there is a general presumption against executive power to litigate constitutional rights," and that such litigation should be remitted to private individuals.[42] That sentiment is based on fear of excessive executive and judicial power. Congress has several times rejected proposals to allow the attorney general broad-based authority to sue for constitutional or statutory violations.[43]

We might usefully compare those civil rights that Congress has chosen to be protected by the executive branch and those that it has rejected for such an executive branch role. For example, Congress's reservations over the Part 3 proposal reflect a distinction between specified forms of racial discrimination and other violations of the Fourteenth Amendment. Perhaps it is where national unity and national economy loom most prominently that the case for government enforcement is the strongest. Contrast, for example, discrete state action depriving free speech and a pattern of race discrimination. The former poses little danger to national unity even though it violates the Constitution, while a pattern of private racial discrimination undermines the cohesiveness of the nation. Of course, a pattern of repression of speech would present a more compelling case for national protection, but at the time Congress was considering the 1957 act, the national government itself was still pursuing prosecutions of members of the American Communist party and resisting the defendants' free speech claims.[44] So for a variety of reasons, the civil rights laws of the 1960s through the 1980s granted only a private right of action to remedy First Amendment deprivations while creating a government enforcement apparatus to combat racial discrimination.

Note, however, that Congress has not provided the same elements of federal enforcement against all forms of race discrimination. For example, Congress in 1968—at the same time as it was enacting the far-reaching Fair Housing Act—failed to adopt the proposal to authorize the attorney general to sue for reform of state jury discrimination.[45] A factual record of jury discrimination was presented to Congress, but the record of widespread harm to the national interest was not as complete as it had been as to voting, schools, housing, and employment. Apparently Congress was satisfied with the status quo: the attorney general could already prosecute criminally any official who excludes a person from jury service on account of race,[46] and private remedies for jury discrimination existed not only under the Fourteenth Amendment but also under the Sixth Amendment guarantee of an impartial jury.[47]

Another criterion for allocation of litigative authority is the relief sought. The central role of the division developed at a time when the courts held to a rigid public–private right distinction, which has somewhat eroded, under which private litigants could obtain individual relief for wrongs that specifically affected them, such as the denial of the right to vote, but could not obtain structural relief for public wrongs.[48] An injunction against racial discrimination benefits the public at large as well as the victim of discrimination. By contrast, the most common form of monetary relief compensates the victim alone. Although some large awards of compensatory relief may have an incidental deterrent effect, most compensatory relief for individual victims of discrimination confers no direct benefit upon the public at large.

The history and structure of the civil rights laws betrays some legislative ambivalence as to which rationale, public good or private rights, supports them. For example, the requirement in Title IV of the 1964 act that the attorney general receive a written complaint before suing for school desegregation suggests that the suit is to vindicate the right of the complainant, but the law then requires the attorney general to certify that the suit will "materially further the orderly achievement of desegregation," which suggests that the suit is to vindicate a broader public interest.[49] It should therefore come as no surprise that the proponents of the modern civil rights acts have sometimes blurred the distinction. Thus, the Eisenhower administration's proposed civil rights legislation would have authorized the attorney general to sue on behalf of the United States "or in the name of the United States but for the benefit of the real party in interest."[50] However, Attorney General Brownell stressed that the department would not be representing the private individual. As he put it,

> By and large, the actions which the Attorney General would bring would be for the benefit of a specific segment. There might be an individual named or involved who was the chief witness or something of that sort. But the benefits of any such decree would go far beyond 1 or 2 individuals in the ordinary case.[51]

There is a clearer basis for federal executive intervention where the violation directly impinges on federal programs or personnel.[52]

The matter is further complicated by the question of what practical consequences might flow from any distinction between the federal government as litigant and private plaintiffs as litigants. The question can be framed as whether the civil rights laws should designate federal attorneys as counsel for private grievants. The answer depends in part on the rationale for entrusting enforcement responsibility to the government. For example, when the defendants in an early private suit under the Voting Rights Act argued that the authorization of attorney general suits to enforce the act excluded private enforcement actions, the Supreme Court said that "the achievement of the Act's laudable goal could be severely hampered . . . if each citizen were required to depend solely on litigation instituted at the discretion of the Attorney General."[53] The Court here saw the United States as supplementing, not supplanting, private enforcement.

Similarly, the Court allowed white tenants of an apartment complex to file suit against the owner for racial discrimination against potential African-American tenants. In finding the white tenants were "persons aggrieved" within the meaning of the Fair Housing Act, the Court relied in part on HUD's lack of enforcement authority and the limited capacity of the Department of Justice to ensure nationwide compliance.[54] It agreed with the solicitor general that "complaints by private persons are the primary method of obtaining compliance with the Act."[55]

The rationale for authorizing the government to bring suits leads to differing rules regarding the time within which suits must be brought. The Court has ruled that the statute of limitations under Title VII does not apply to suits by the government but to private suits only.[56] The Court held in the same case that state statutes of limitations also do not apply to suits by the government, reasoning that the EEOC not only litigates on behalf of private parties but is also a federal administrative agency

> charged with the responsibility of investigating claims of employment discrimination and settling disputes, if possible, in an informal, noncoercive fashion. Unlike the typical litigant against whom a statute of limitations

might appropriately run, the EEOC is required by law to refrain from commencing a civil action until it has discharged its administrative duties.[57]

Because the EEOC sought relief for all victims of discrimination, an employer contended that such a case should be treated as a class action and that the commission should be required to comply with Rule 23 of the Federal Rules of Civil Procedure. The Court rejected that contention, stating:

> Unlike the Rule 23 class representative, the EEOC is authorized to proceed in a unified action and to obtain the most satisfactory overall relief even though competing interests are involved and particular groups may appear to be disadvantaged. The individual victim is given his right to intervene for this very reason. The EEOC exists to advance the public interest in preventing and remedying employment discrimination, and it does so in part by making the hard choices where conflicts of interest exist.[58]

The same rationale would, of course, apply to a Department of Justice suit to enforce a civil rights statute.[59]

The rationale for government authority may also determine whether private litigants are allowed to intervene in government litigation. Thus, in an environmental enforcement suit brought by the United States, private groups were allowed to intervene as plaintiffs because "the United States is charged with representing a broad public interest, and, as the Government of the people, must represent varying interests, industry as well as individuals."[60] Maimon Schwarzschild notes that "when the federal government brings a Title VII suit and negotiates a consent decree, . . . the minority 'beneficiaries' are often given no opportunity to be heard on the adequacy of the remedy."[61] His concern that "courts frequently deny white third parties any opportunity to be heard before a consent decree is approved"[62] was addressed in *Martin v. Wilks*[63] (decree not binding on nonparty whites) and the Civil Rights Act of 1991,[64] which provides that consent decrees bind nonparties who had notice and opportunity to object or whose interests were adequately represented by other objectors.[65]

The distinction between public and private rights and enforcement affects abstention doctrine as well. For example, in *United States v. Wood*[66] the United States sought to enjoin a state court prosecution of John Hardy, a civil rights worker, on the ground that the prosecution was intended to intimidate African Americans in Walthall County, Mississippi, from registering to vote. Judge Richard Rives, for the court of appeals, noted that "the rights the Government asserts are not the rights of Hardy" but "the rights of all those Negro citizens in Walthall County who are qualified to register and vote."[67] The court further stressed that the government was seeking to "stay irreparable injury to a national interest"[68] and also noted that the Civil Rights Act of 1957 conferred authority on the United States to bring such suits and on U.S. district courts to hear them.[69] The court therefore held that abstention doctrine, which normally disallows private suits to enjoin pending prosecutions, did not bar the government's suit.

The notion that public rights are at issue in civil rights cases also has given rise to the concept of a "private attorney general." The Court treated the rights created by the 1964 act as public in nature, saying that when the act was passed, "it was evident that enforcement would . . . have to rely in part upon private litigation as a means of securing broad compliance with the law."[70] The Court noted that the plaintiff in a Title II suit could not obtain damages and concluded that "if he obtains an injunction, he does so not for himself alone but also as a 'private attorney general,' vindicating a policy that Congress considered of the highest priority."[71] The Court has applied the private attorney general concept to other race discrimination contexts, such as school desegregation,[72] and to employment discrimination,[73] because as with Title II these suits are "private in form only."[74]

Congress later extended the notion of the private attorney general even to the types of cases covered by the rejected Part 3 approach.[75] Thus, there may now be a private attorney general in cases where the U.S. attorney general is powerless to act. As Justice William Brennan has explained, "Congress could, of course, have provided public funds or Government attorneys for litigating private civil rights claims, but it chose to 'limi[t] the growth of the enforcement bureaucracy,' . . . by continuing to rely on the private bar and by making defendants bear the full burden of paying for enforcement of their civil rights obligations."[76]

Effectiveness

The United States as enforcer provides some strengths not provided by private parties. Generally it can bring greater resources to enforcement, and, if need be, its enforcement actions are backed by brute force. The use of federal troops at Little Rock in 1957 and the University of Mississippi in 1962 underscores a principle that is of central importance but normally left unsaid: "In the end only power can check power—and the opportunity to do so must be a secure resource in every moral community."[77] The United States also can "provide the continuity and staying power that are frequently necessary to insure compliance following complex civil litigation."[78]

The power of the United States may be contrasted with that of private litigants. Most dramatically, Justice Holmes's denial of equitable relief in a voting discrimination case relied in part on the Court's inability to control the white citizens of Alabama, who were allegedly intent on denying the vote to African Americans. He concluded:

> Unless we are prepared to supervise the voting in that State by officers of the court, it seems to us that all that the plaintiff could get from equity would be an empty form. Apart from damages to the individual, relief from

a great political wrong, if done, as alleged, by the people of a State and the State itself, must be given by them or by the legislative and political department of the government of the United States.[79]

In the intervening years, as Burke Marshall has pointed out, few voting rights "suits were brought, and no progress at all was made on the problem in some areas, until the Justice Department was authorized to bring suit itself in 1957."[80]

Commenting on proposals that became the Civil Rights Act of 1964, Alexander Bickel suggested that the greater effectiveness of government litigation could raise "serious problems on several levels."[81] He believed that even if the attorney general were authorized to sue for school desegregation, "it is still out of the question that desegregation can be achieved wholly or even chiefly through litigation."[82] Yet he feared that empowering the attorney general "to enforce all existing constitutional rights, and to seek from the courts declaration of new rights" would significantly alter "the delicate balance between authoritarian judicialism and government by consent."[83] At the same time, he also feared that "private initiative is bound to be chilled and the flow of private funds is bound to be discouraged and diverted elsewhere, where the help of the federal government is not available."[84]

Hindsight validates the congressional rejection of Bickel's concerns. From the Supreme Court's Decision in *Brown* in 1954 until the adoption of the 1964 act, the schools of the Deep South remained almost entirely segregated, despite the efforts of brave African-American parents and children and of civil rights attorneys. The courts and private litigants could not enforce *Brown* without federal help. The 1964 act's manifestation of federal determination, at both the legislative and executive levels, to end unlawful segregation played a major role in making Brown *a reality.* It took a combination of private and federal government litigation, coupled with administrative enforcement of Title VI and financial assistance to desegregating systems, to bring about significant compliance with *Brown.*[85] Government by consent suffered only at the local level, and there only temporarily. With the department's positions in school desegregation cases influenced by the state of national political consensus, private litigators did not fully trust the government to represent the interests of the African-American community and therefore continued to play a role in school desegregation litigation.

From the beginning, the limited efficacy of private actions has been invoked as a reason for federal intervention. Thus, in commenting on a proposal to amend the bill that became the Civil Rights Act of 1866 by substituting a private right of action for federal criminal prosecution, Rep. James Wilson argued:

This bill proposes that the humblest citizen shall have full and ample protection at the cost of the Government, whose duty it is to protect him. The amendment of the gentleman recognizes the principle involved, but it says that the citizen despoiled of his rights, instead of being properly protected by the Government, must press his own way through the courts and pay the bills attendant thereon. This may do for the rich, but to the poor, who need protection, it is mockery. The highest obligation which the Government owes to the citizen in return for the allegiance exacted of him is to secure him in the protection of his rights. Under the amendment of the gentleman the citizen can only receive that protection in the form of a few dollars in the way of damages, if he shall be so fortunate as to recover a verdict against a solvent wrong-doer.[86]

Congress recognized that retaliation and intimidation also might inhibit private efforts to obtain redress. During the heyday of the racial caste system, challengers to it faced violence, loss of jobs, eviction from their homes, and criminal prosecution.[87] Congress not only strengthened legal protections against retaliation and intimidation[88] but also assigned the attorney general to bring suit when such activities hampered private litigation.[89]

Violence and threats were also directed toward lawyers for private litigants, discouraging many local counsel from representing plaintiffs in discrimination suits and placing obstacles in the path of northern lawyers seeking to litigate on their behalf.[90] Federal lawyers were much less likely to be subjected to violence. With the exception of Attorney General Kennedy's assistant John Seigenthaler, who was seriously injured by mob violence in Montgomery, Alabama, during the Freedom Rides,[91] Justice Department lawyers faced only minor and occasional harassment. I discovered on my first trip to Alabama, in January 1964, that local residents seemed to be able to recognize Civil Rights Division lawyers from our coats and ties, our rental cars, and our itineraries. Motel desk clerks and even county telephone operators listened to our conversations. Yet we rarely felt threatened.

In the rare instance when a real threat was made, we could count on immediate FBI attention, as I discovered when a Phenix City, Alabama, man threatened to "whip my ass" if I continued to interview African Americans in the area. Indeed, our presence was sometimes used to protect civil rights workers. For example, in 1965, after a civil rights worker was arrested for leading a group of African Americans who wanted to swim in a public swimming pool in the tiny town of Crawfordsville, Georgia, his colleagues were concerned that the sheriff would not protect him from the angry whites gathered outside the county courthouse, where his jail cell was located. I was sent to Crawfordsville to interview the sheriff regarding the steps being taken to ensure the prisoner's safety. The white roughnecks outside the courthouse hurled verbal insults at me, but the federal presence was established and no harm came to the civil rights worker. This episode dramatically illustrated to me the protective shield that ordinarily surrounded federal officials, enabling us to intervene in circumstances when private intervention might have been much more risky.

Often the government has greater credibility, both because of its resources and availability of force if necessary and because it may be perceived as representing the public interest rather than narrow concerns.[92] As Owen Fiss has pointed out, "In many of these [civil rights] cases, Judge [Frank] Johnson just invited the Department of Justice in because he wanted a lawyer in that case he could have total confidence in."[93]

The issue of efficacy is, however, not entirely one-sided. Techniques such as class actions, government-funded legal services, and attorneys fee award statutes all are methods of evening the balance of litigative resources. Each of these techniques has limitations, but they do enhance the efficacy of private suits.[94] The recent extension of compensatory and punitive damages to Title VII actions may also create a financial incentive for victims of employment discrimination to bring suit,[95] and the removal of the $1,000 cap on punitive damages for violation of the Fair Housing Act may encourage the filing of more fair housing suits.[96]

Another strength of allowing private actions is that there are many possible plaintiffs; we need not depend on one central government entity. The efficacy of government enforcement depends on budgets, priorities, and policies, all of which are changeable. The resources available and positions taken depend on public backing. It is unrealistic to expect the executive to ignore long-term public sentiment. For example, public opposition to busing and quotas has undoubtedly influenced both Congress and the executive branch through both Republican and Democratic administrations.

The most we can realistically expect is that the executive might resist short-range swings of public opinion. At times, however, the executive succumbs, as with the Nixon administration's effort to delay desegregation in Mississippi in 1969, and it falls to the private litigants to take up the mantle of the law. The Reconstruction amendments protect against the tyranny of state majorities, and they authorize Congress to enforce those protections. But the protections against tyranny of the majority at the federal level are flimsier because they depend on the efficacy of the checks and balances of the three branches.[97] So private enforcement remains important, even where federal agencies bear much of the enforcement load. On the other hand, if we rely entirely on private suits, whether public values are adequately protected depends on the short-range perspective of potential clients. Occasionally the private sector produces a long-range strategy for enforcing civil rights,[98] but most private suits reflect ad hoc decision making.

If one is confident that a statute clearly articulates the public interest, one might find an advantage in private enforcement, where the issues are not filtered through the bureaucratic process. Joseph Sax, referring to another area of enforcement, argues that "the citizen does not need a bureaucratic middleman to identify, prosecute, and vindicate his interest in environmental quality" and complains that "the administrative process tends to produce not the voice of the people, but the voice of the bureaucrat—the administrative perspective posing as the public interest."[99] However, it is not so clear that the individual who brings a "public interest" suit can be relied on to represent the public interest. In some areas of the law, defining the public interest requires balancing competing considerations. Individual plaintiffs are unlikely to engage in such a balancing.

It was early understood that entrusting the attorney general with authority to protect public rights might lead to more sweeping relief than in a suit on behalf of an individual. For example, in the hearings on the 1957 act, Senator Ervin suggested to Attorney General Brownell that where a voting registrar discriminated on account of race, "it is conceivable that the Attorney General would have to prosecute thousands of cases." Brownell responded that he "would hope . . . that in a case like that by an injunction action brought against the proper officials, that that could all be done at one time. That is one of the real arguments in favor of the legislation which we propose."[100]

Neither the private nor the public sector holds a monopoly in relative effectiveness. The public sector provides resources, credibility, representation of the public interest, relatively centralized policy-making. The private sector promotes private interests that often correspond with public interest, and it does so in a decentralized fashion that is less susceptible to swings of public opinion.

Criminal-Civil Factors

Thus far I have been speaking primarily of civil enforcement. The modern civil rights acts emphasize civil remedies, but one must note that this represents a departure from the Reconstruction civil rights acts. The basic structure of those laws was to allow private civil suits and to authorize criminal prosecutions to be brought by the attorney general for deprivations of civil rights. Section 2 of the 1866 act, for example, criminalized the imposition of different penalties on nonwhites than on whites. Section 4 authorized federal prosecution for violating any provision of the 1866 act. Similarly, the 1870 act authorized criminal prosecutions for unlawful deprivations of the right to vote, and the 1875 act criminalized discrimination by public accommodations. Vestiges of the criminal provisions in the Reconstruction acts survive in 18 U.S.C. §§241, 242, and 243 and in the antislavery laws.[101] Moreover, some limited criminal protections appear in modern civil rights laws.[102] However, the basic bans on discrimination today are civil, not criminal, in nature.

Both tradition and functional grounds support entrusting to the government sole enforcement responsibility against criminal conduct. The federal government long ago criminalized some transactions between private persons.[103] If Henry M. Hart, Jr., is correct in describing criminal conduct as "conduct which . . . will incur a formal and solemn pronouncement of the moral condemnation of the community,"[104] the question must arise whether the criminal civil rights laws should cover private discrimination, as did the 1875 Civil Rights Act. Why, for example, should criminal penalties be assessed for anticompetitive behavior but not for discriminatory behavior? Thus far, the solution to that question when defendants have engaged in intentional discrimination has been to assess civil penalties or punitive damages that resemble criminal relief but arguably without the same degree of moral condemnation.[105]

It seems likely that the paucity of modern criminal sanctions for civil rights violations stems largely from the timing of the enactment of the first few modern civil rights laws, when jury trial and the requirement of proof beyond a reasonable doubt would effectively have nullified criminal liability for discrimination. In providing primarily for injunctive relief, the Civil Rights Acts of 1957, 1960, and 1964 avoided the need for jury trials of cases brought under them.

The difficulties of criminal prosecutions in civil rights cases had been obvious for years. For example, in the 1940s the Civil Rights Section several times commenced criminal prosecutions of voting officials for race discrimination, but aside from two nolo contendere pleas, it prevailed in none of them.[106] In 1959 the acting assistant attorney general for civil rights reported that the department had been unable even to obtain indictments when over 6,000 African Americans were illegally purged from the voting rolls of six Louisiana parishes.[107] He opined that the prosecutive difficulties encountered in routine civil rights prosecutions were "compounded in cases of nonviolent racial discrimination."[108] Also in 1959, "despite persuasive evidence presented by the Government attorneys, the grand jury refused to indict" persons charged with lynching Mack Charles Parker in Poplarville, Mississippi, three police brutality prosecutions resulted in acquittals, and a conviction in a fourth police brutality case yielded a $500 fine and sixty-day suspended sentence.[109]

Senator Ervin, objecting to President Kennedy's proposed civil rights act, noted that criminal sanctions under §242 were already available when an election official willfully denies the right to vote based on race,[110] but Attorney General Kennedy responded that "it would be virtually impossible to successfully prosecute [such] a criminal case [in Mississippi or Alabama]."[111] Earlier, Attorney General Brownell, testifying in favor of the 1957 act, had also observed, "Jurors are reluctant to indict and convict local officials in a criminal prosecution even though they recognize the illegality of what has been done."[112] Today, the rise of result-based violations, in which discriminatory intent need not be shown, has arguably rendered broad criminal liability for discrimination inappropriate. However, those few cases in which discriminatory intent can be shown beyond a reasonable doubt would seem to be prime candidates for criminal liability.

Attorney General Brownell, arguing for passage of the 1957 act, gave two other reasons for preferring civil sanctions. First, criminal sanctions are retrospective and therefore "can never be used until after the harm has been actually done," while injunctive relief can prevent threatened harm in advance. Second, he observed that criminally prosecuting state officers for civil rights violations would "stir up an immense amount of ill feeling in the community and inevitably tend to cause very bad relations between State and local officials on the one hand, and the Federal officials responsible for the investigation and prosecution on the other." He believed that injunctive relief would avoid "a great deal" of that ill feeling.[113] Although his testimony the following year adhered to these arguments, he further clarified the point. In his later testimony, he argued not against criminal sanctions but in favor of giving the attorney general flexibility in choosing between civil and criminal remedies. He also argued it would be unfair to subject to criminal prosecution local officials who are "responding to a system which is there and to perhaps pressure in the community."[114] He pointed to antitrust as a parallel where "the Department has had experience in the coordinated use of civil and criminal remedies."[115]

The use of civil remedies as punitive measures has crept into some of the recent civil rights laws. As noted above, punitive damages are now available under some statutes, and in other instances the attorney general is authorized to seek civil penalties.[116] As both punitive damages and civil penalties exact punishment,[117] concern has been expressed that this blurring of the line between civil and criminal sanctions may lead to confusion as to the role of the government attorney responsible for such litigation.

Diffusion-Centralization

Allowing only private parties to bring suit diffuses enforcement. This is the pattern, for example, under 42 U.S.C. §1983, that authorizes only private suits to remedy deprivations of federal rights under color of state law. James Madison believed that diffusion of power would ensure individual rights by controlling the effects of faction.[118] The Constitution diffused power in part by conferring on the two levels of government, state and federal, some different and some mutual powers. Madison posited that the two levels of government would check one another. The national government would be largely immune from faction because of the diversity of its components.

The Civil War amendments represent the concentration in the federal government of power to ensure individual rights as against state action. Under those amendments, Congress now may confer enormous enforcement power on the federal government. However, the potential for unrestrained infringement of individual liberty increases as the central government increases direct relations with individuals. Attorney General Robert F. Kennedy, speaking of the call for federal intervention against police abuse and private violence against civil rights demonstrators, worried that conferring too much enforcement power on the Department of Justice "would lead inevitably to the creation of a national police force."[119] He also opposed undue expansion of the limited authority of the Federal Bureau of Investigation. Carl Brauer has observed,

> Robert Kennedy and Burke Marshall believed that Negro rights had in the long run failed to survive after the Civil War because they had been established by an alien federal force; when that force was removed, the Negroes' rights rapidly withered and died. They hoped to see civil rights take root this time and were therefore determined to make the absolute minimal use of federal force.[120]

However, the Kennedy administration recognized that "the legal right of Negroes to be free from official and systematic discrimination cannot be left to trial by combat between private citizens and the states, but must be made real through federal law enforcement."[121]

Alexander M. Bickel believed that the "process of private litigation . . . is in its totality something of a political process of measuring the intensity and strength of interests affected by a judicial rule."[122] He believed that when in some southern communities lawyers had decided to delay pushing their school desegregation suits,[123] this was all to the good. He thought creating attorney general authority to bring school desegregation cases would circumvent the "imprecise safeguards that are implicit in our present reliance on private litigating initiative,"[124] although he differentiated school desegregation from voting and public accommodations rights and the criminal civil rights laws, which could appropriately be enforced by the federal executive because they laid down more precise rules. In the field of criminal law, said Bickel, the attorney general's authority had been "most cautiously and circumspectly limited by the courts, so as to encompass only well-defined and thoroughly established rules of constitutional law."[125]

Voting rights, Bickel believed, were "almost certainly beyond any private resources," while public accommodations law is statutory, not constitutional, in nature, and sufficient incentives were unlikely to exist to support private enforcement suits against public accommodations discrimination.[126] Thus the benefits of diffusion would not exist as to voting and public accommodations cases and the dangers of centralization would be minimized. In short, Bickel thought diffusion necessary in enforcing general constitutional commands but not in enforcing statutory requirements or more narrowly defined constitutional requirements.

There is, of course, an alternative to Bickel's proposed division of labor between the private and public sector. He failed to consider the possibility of an enforcement structure that simultaneously draws on both private and public enforcement. He also overstated the danger of centralized enforcement, failing to take into account the moderating influences that lead the federal government, and especially the Department of Justice, to take account of competing interests when establishing positions.

Federalism

The third possible enforcer of rights, in addition to private persons and the federal government, is the state government. The original constitutional scheme contemplated so-called police power being exercised at the state level. The problems of concentrated federal power alluded to above were to be avoided by diffusing power among the states. However, where the state is the abuser of power, diffusion localizes tyranny but does not eliminate it. This is the situation that the Reconstruction amendments were meant to rectify, a situation that still prevailed when the initial modern civil rights laws were adopted. Those laws made the federal government the watchdog over the states with respect to official racial discrimination, with the state able to avoid federal enforcement action by policing itself.

An early argument against broad federal authority to sue the states rested on fear of noncompliance. After all, enforcement of the Reconstruction civil rights laws and amendments had engendered violent and ultimately successful resistance in the nineteenth century. Moreover, the failed experiment of Prohibition—when the nation had unsuccessfully attempted to impose on itself the perceived moral imperative of abstinence from alcohol—had ended only three decades earlier, at the beginning of the public life of those who were considering civil rights legislation. Perhaps we should not be surprised, therefore, that Attorney General Rogers, arguing against Part 3 in 1959, contended, "The image of the Federal Government attempting to dominate the States . . . is apt to harden their resistance to the point where it makes any reasonable solution difficult."[127] In his view, "you have to gear your law enforcement pretty thoughtfully in with the development of public opinion."[128] Although this argument refers to restraint of federal power over the states, it is not a federalism argument. It seems of a piece with the "all deliberate speed" doctrine: both arguments sound hopeful and avoid immediate confrontation yet are ultimately unrealistic. Moreover, both arguments would reward those who resist complying with the law. In any event, hindsight reveals that resistance can be overcome where there is the national will.

With respect to private discrimination, the picture is slightly different. When the 1964 act was adopted, racial discrimination in public accommodations and employment was forbidden in some states and tolerated in others; in the Deep South, the vestiges of Jim Crow laws left public accommodations and the workplace as segregated as the public schools. Thus, the need for federal protections fell along a broad spectrum. If a state was effectively enforcing its antidiscrimination laws, federal protections would be duplicative and unnecessary. If a state had required private discrimination in the past and was arguably still encouraging it, federal protections were clearly necessary. If a state had no history of discrimination but also no protections against it, the facts might warrant a federal role. Congress was aware of these considerations and in some instances adjusted the enforcement mechanisms to require victims of discrimination to resort initially to state remedies prior to seeking federal relief.[129] Thus state authority was not completely bypassed, although the strict time limits of these provisions resulted in many cases becoming federalized.

The interplay of these issues—public policy, effectiveness, diffusion/centralization, federalism, and criminal/civil enforcement—suggests a framework for dividing responsibility. Ordinarily private interests should be entrusted to private enforcement and public interest to public enforcement. Where the general rule proves ineffective, exceptions should be carved out. The inevitable overlap between public and private interest may lead to concurrent enforcement power. Concurrent power also promotes the dual values of diffusion and centralization. Federalism is promoted by strong federal enforcement where states violate the Constitution or laws of the United States or where states fail to ensure nondiscrimination in the private sector. Conversely, the federal government should seek voluntary compliance from the states and should give them the first opportunity to enforce their nondiscrimination laws.

5

Enforcement Roles Within
the Executive Branch

Federal authority to enforce laws has been placed in various agencies. Initially all law enforcement was carried out by executive agencies, and the litigation of the United States was entrusted to the attorney general and U.S. attorneys.[1] In 1870 the Department of Justice Act created the department and placed the attorney general in charge of it and of the U.S. attorneys.[2] In the Sherman Act of 1890, Congress authorized the department to obtain injunctive relief as well as bring criminal actions to protect specified public values.[3] In 1895 the attorney general gained some authority to seek injunctive relief even in the absence of express statutory authorization when the Supreme Court sustained his right to an injunction to overcome a perceived threat to public order arising out of the Pullman strike.[4]

Beginning in that same era, independent regulatory agencies were created with enforcement powers and the ability to go to court where agency orders were not followed. Similarly, some executive agencies were granted enforcement authority and authority to go to court.[5] Thus, civil rights enforcement could be lodged in the Department of Justice, other executive agencies, or an independent regulatory agency. Broadly speaking, if the primary enforcement technique was to be criminal prosecution or civil suit, authority would normally be vested in the attorney general.[6] Sen. Everett Dirksen (R-Ill.), discussing the proposed 1964 act, observed, "People shout about the powers of the Attorney General. I wish someone would tell me who in our form of government is to enforce the Constitution and the laws if it is not the Attorney General. Will someone point to a law officer or to an administrator who is going to do it except the Attorney General?"[7] If the primary enforcement technique was to be administrative action, authority would be vested in an executive or independent regulatory agency.

EXPERTISE

Enforcement power is normally placed in an agency with expertise in the subject matter to be regulated. Congress could have created a separate agency to enforce all the civil rights laws such as exists in some states—for example, California's Department of Fair Employment and Housing, with responsibility for enforcing both its fair housing and its fair employment laws—and in the United Kingdom—which created a Race Relations Board to enforce all its laws against race discrimination and another agency to enforce its sex discrimination laws.[8] However, Congress has never seriously entertained creating an umbrella civil rights enforcement agency. Its consistent defeat of the Part 3 proposal to authorize the Department of Justice to bring a broad range of equal protection cases reflects hostility to the concentration of enforcement power in one agency. Although the diffusion that resulted from what Congress did enact may undermine uniformity, it may also enhance the institutional equilibrium of civil rights enforcement.[9] The department has nonetheless become the repository of great power and great expertise in enforcing the antidiscrimination laws.

Placement of enforcement responsibility in the Department of Justice entrusts development of legal principles to the case method. Placement in an administrative agency tends to favor the development of regulatory standards. Thus, Hugh Davis Graham remarked that an EEOC without cease and desist powers "gravitated quickly toward the new model of wholesale rule-making."[10] Since the attorney general had had civil rights enforcement responsibilities since Reconstruction and had also participated as amicus curiae in other civil rights cases, the Department of Justice was the agency with the most expertise when the 1957 act passed, having through its accretion of experience in these actions become "a focal point for continuity in civil rights development and acquire[d] a virtual leadership role."[11] Moreover, the 1957 act narrowly focused on voting rights, and the department had experience in prosecuting criminal voting rights cases while no other agency possessed expertise in enforcing voting rights. Other reasons pointed to placing responsibility in the Department of Justice. Thus, one observer writing about the Mansfield-Dirksen compromise in 1964 regarding Title VII noted:

> Dirksen well knew that the Justice Department was a relatively small, elite cabinet agency, in comparison with the more typical and large program-running departments like HEW or Defense, and so prided itself on enforcement through key case selection rather than through massive litigation. As a result the Justice Department posed a smaller threat of potential harassment to employers than would a new mission agency like the EEOC, which reminded Dirksen and his more conservative colleagues uncomfortably of its crusading early model: the NLRB.[12]

The Justice Department's new responsibilities paved the way for broader ones. As a veteran civil rights litigator notes, "The lessons we learned in preparing the voting rights cases carried over to our new responsibilities under the Civil Rights Act of 1964."[13] The expertise that division lawyers developed in voting rights law related to both substantive antidiscrimination law and to litigation. As Rosenberg points out, the expertise gained in civil litigation carried over to criminal prosecutions, enabling the division to prevail in civil rights conspiracy and police brutality cases.[14]

The creation of the EEOC in 1964 led to another center of expertise, so that it was possible in 1972 to transfer to the EEOC much of the attorney general's authority to litigate Title VII cases.[15] The two agencies possessed different kinds of expertise. The EEOC employed a very large staff whose energies were all directed to employment discrimination issues, and until 1972 those efforts were concentrated in rule making, investigation, and conciliation. The Department of Justice staff assigned to the Civil Rights Division was relatively small and addressed a broad range of civil rights issues, primarily through litigation. This led Senator Roman Hruska (R-Nebr.), in arguing that the Department of Justice should retain its pattern-or-practice authority over employment discrimination cases, to note that

> with the Department of Justice it is possible to develop in an orderly way and in a logical way case law which will serve as a valuable precedent. They can do that because they see the picture as a whole; they see civil rights, not consisting of separate segments, but consisting of many aspects, including voting, education, housing, and so on, which require a rounding out of precedents that can be logically developed in the litigation of pattern and practice cases.[16]

In 1988 a similar effort to transfer to the Department of Housing and Urban Development litigating authority under the Fair Housing Act failed. HUD had developed expertise under the 1968 act, but this time litigating authority was kept at Justice because, as Senator Orrin Hatch (R-Utah) explained:

> The Department of Justice is the litigating arm of the executive branch. Over the years since the 1968 act was first placed into effect, the Department of Justice has always had litigating authority in fair housing cases and has developed the expertise necessary to pursue these matters. The House compromise would have fragmented the Federal litigating authority and thereby promoted interference and confusion.[17]

Although litigation of housing cases is concentrated in the Justice Department, enforcement responsibility is divided between it and the Department of Housing and Urban Development. Indeed, Representative F. James Sensenbrenner, Jr. (R-Wisc.) objected in 1988 that the division of responsibility between the two agencies was "nothing but a mishmash that will get the wheels to fall off adequate enforcement of fair housing complaints."[18] This problem is even more pronounced as to discrimination in mortgage lending practices, where enforcement responsibility is diffused among the banking regulatory agencies, HUD, and the Department of Justice, and no single agency bears ultimate responsibility.

It is unclear what reasons led to diffusing litigation authority with respect to employment discrimination in 1972 while concentrating in one agency the litigation authority with respect to housing in 1968. The debates do not provide insight into Congress's thinking. Perhaps the track records of the agencies involved explain it; perhaps political factors do. The issue whether litigating authority should be placed with the specialized agency or with the Department of Justice reflects a tug of war that has continued for over a century. The idea behind both the 1870 creation of the Department of Justice and the 1933 Executive Order no. 6616 placing control of government litigation in the department was to "make[] the Justice Department the gatekeeper to the courts for federal officials and agencies."[19] Agencies tend to want to litigate their own cases rather than refer them to the Department of Justice,[20] but with a norm of Justice Department control of litigation, it usually takes congressional action to assign litigating authority to executive agencies.

Finally, one should note that today the great preponderance of federal enforcement authority with respect to civil rights lies outside court litigation. Litigation lawyers at the Department of Justice and EEOC constitute a small part of the federal resources committed to enforcing the civil rights laws.[21] Administrative enforcement may end up in court, but most administrative efforts do not. Investigation, conciliation, fund-termination administrative proceedings, contract debarment proceedings, and HUD proceedings asking adminstrative law judges to issue orders under the Fair Housing Act cumulatively represent a diffuse and large nonjudicial enforcement structure. In 1957 the judicial branch played the ascendant role in enforcing civil rights. Congress's gradual shift toward administrative enforcement has affected the separation of powers because of the deference the courts are required to pay to executive branch decisions.

POLITICAL DECISION-MAKING

Concentration of responsibility in one agency centralizes decision-making, which on the one hand enhances uniformity and accountability and on the other increases susceptibility to political manipulation. Uniformity of enforcement is an important value for several reasons. Uniform enforcement sends a clear message to potential violators and to protected classes without which it would be difficult for either to know their rights or obligations. Nonuniform enforcement can lead agencies of the same government to operate at cross-purposes, which would not only be inefficient but would also undermine respect for the law. Accountability, too, is a central tenet of good government because it protects against buck-passing. Accountability enhances the opportunity of the people to change policy or to demand improved policy implementation.

Counterbalanced against the importance of uniformity and accountability are the dangers of concentration of power. The tension between diffusion and centralization that informs the division of enforcement authority between private and government sectors also exists within the government sector. Concentration of power enhances the potential for so-called political decision making. Concerns about political decision making have often been expressed in debates over proposals to confer authority on the attorney general or to place all employment discrimination enforcement in the EEOC. Thus, in the debates on the 1957 act one of the primary objections to attorney general authority was that, as Senator Richard Russell (D-Ga.) averred, "This law will be administered by a politically minded Attorney General."[22] Similarly, in the debate on the 1964 act, Sen. Ervin argued against the discretion vested in the attorney general: "Any Attorney General, who happened to be a pragmatic politician, could pervert the avowed purposes of this measure and use it to curry favor with some groups or to browbeat into submission to his will State officials or private individuals covered by it."[23]

This position was not limited to opponents of the act. Sen. Joseph Clark (D-Pa.), a proponent, regretted that the Mansfield-Dirksen substitute withdrew the right to sue from the EEOC and gave it to the attorney general. He was concerned that under Section 706, after investigating and conciliating "there its power stops, and all it can do is to report its findings and conclusions to the Attorney General who, in his infinite wisdom, may or may not, in due course, bring proceedings to enforce the equal job opportunity denied the complainant."[24] In the debate on the 1972 act, Representative David Martin (R-Nebr.) argued against giving the EEOC cease and desist powers, asserting that such a proposal would give the commission powers comparable to those of the NLRB and that experience had shown that the board routinely reversed its own decisions each time a new administration appointed new members. Moreover, the commission should not have "the power of being investigator, prosecutor, judge and jury."[25]

It is not always clear what is meant by political decision making. In a democracy, the executive should normally be responsive to the people. The real questions are what we mean by such responsiveness and whether it is ever inappropriate. In theory, the Constitution and, to a lesser extent, the laws of the United States express the will of the people. That will may be distinguished from the normal erratic swings of public opinion that characterize the polity. Nondiscrimination provisions of the Constitution and laws are meant to be enforced even if that requires disregarding the public sentiment of the moment. Often complaints of "political decision-making" simply mask substantive disagreements with a decision.[26] The test of propriety of political decision making in enforcing the civil rights laws should focus on whether the decision is fairly calculated to enhance enforcement and is based on fairly reasoned considerations.

Two techniques exist to minimize improper political decision making. One is to insulate enforcers from political interference, which can be done by government subsidization of private litigation, but the experience of the Legal Services Corporation shows that the greater the autonomy, the greater the vulnerability to budget cuts and restrictions on authorized activity. The corporation exercised minimal control over independent legal services providers who received federal assistance from the corporation. The providers brought politically unpopular cases, and the result was a backlash that seriously endangered the very existence of federal assistance to legal services. The corporation survived only after substantial limits were placed on activities of the providers.

Insulation might also take the form of creation of independent regulatory agencies, but Congress has been unwilling to create such agencies to administer civil rights legislation. The Civil Rights Commission may be an independent agency, but it has no regulatory power. The EEOC as initially created had no enforcement power. Congress did grant it the right to bring suit in 1972, but denied it the right to issue cease and desist orders and left the Department of Justice as an enforcer of Title VII with respect to some employers. Whether the EEOC became an independent regulatory agency at that point is unclear. In any event, the Carter administration transferred additional authority from two executive agencies, the Department of Justice and the Department of Labor, to the EEOC. Subsequently, the Office of Legal Counsel issued an opinion during the Reagan administration that this transfer made the EEOC an executive agency.[27] Thus it never was an "independent" agency in a legal sense.

Independent regulatory agencies have not in practice proved consistently politically independent, at least of the Congress. Judge Frank Easterbrook has pointed out that the Federal Trade Commission, an independent regulatory agency with antitrust enforcement responsibilities, has done "more to protect producers and the Antitrust Division [has done] more to protect consumers."[28] He attributes this action to the greater responsiveness of independent regulatory agencies to congressional committees, which he says represent the force of faction. By contrast, executive agencies such as the Justice Department are responsible to the president, who "may resist claims by factions in the way Madison envisioned: by adding other items to the agenda."[29]

The civil rights enforcement authority of the executive branch depends upon another branch, the judiciary, to sanction enforcement efforts. The courts react cautiously to sudden changes in policy that accompany changes in administration.[30] Moreover, Congress may also legislatively overrule such changes.[31] Dispersal of responsibility among several agencies encourages experimentation and diffuses the risk of error. For example, the Reagan-Bush Department of Justice disagreed with the Federal Communications Commission and the EEOC regarding affirmative action issues, and the competing views were presented to the Supreme Court.[32] This presentation of conflicting positions weakens the authority with which the executive speaks.[33]

Reconstruction legislation had diffused enforcement by placing authority with the attorney general and the Freedmen's Bureau, created in 1865 to "distribute clothing, food, and fuel to destitute freedmen and oversee 'all subjects' relating to their condition in the South."[34] The bureau's responsibilities included "introducing a workable system of free labor in the South, establishing schools for freedmen, providing aid to the destitute, aged, ill, and insane, adjudicating disputes among blacks and between the races, and attempting to secure for blacks and white Unionists equal justice from the state and local governments."[35] It was dismantled after Reconstruction. After a period of almost exclusive Justice Department control, in 1964 Congress and President Johnson opted for a mixed system, with lead responsibility in the Department of Justice but with other agencies undertaking various aspects of the job of civil rights enforcement. This initial system has served as the basic model under successive civil rights laws.[36]

METHOD OF ENFORCEMENT

Agency enforcement can follow two models: a litigation model or an administrative model. Historically, the courts had been the prime protector of civil rights. Congress did virtually nothing to protect civil rights between 1876 and 1957; not until 1939 did the executive branch take vigorous though limited action. Not only did most executive agencies acquiesce in violations of the equal protection clause in their programs, but some actively discriminated. When the Supreme Court failed to protect civil rights, as in *Plessy v. Ferguson*[37] and *Giles v. Harris,*[38] there was nowhere else for African-American citizens to turn. However, in a series of private civil rights actions, advocates of racial equality persisted in pressing the Supreme Court, which eventually took the lead in enforcing the equal protection clause.[39] Thus, when Congress wrote the modern civil rights acts, court litigation was the natural model to adopt, which is another reason for the early primacy of the Department of Justice as the agency to enforce the civil rights laws.

Today, litigation is the primary method of enforcement employed by the Department of Justice and the EEOC, although Congress initially gave the EEOC only investigative and conciliation functions[40] and the department's responsibilities under Section 5 of the Voting Rights Act more closely resemble the administrative model. Government enforcement of Title VI's proscription of racial discrimination in federally assisted programs follows the administrative model, with judicial review.[41] The same is true of Executive Order 11246,[42] which imposes nondiscrimination and affirmative action obligations as to the employment practices of federal government contractors.[43] Until passage of the Fair Housing Act amendments in 1988, the administrative model applied only to claims of governmental discrimination and to government contractors. Although the Fair Housing Act now allows administrative enforcement against private respondents, its provisions to elect litigation provide an escape hatch that has been used in most cases.[44]

From the outset there has been controversy as to what is the best model for Title VII enforcement. In 1964 and 1972 civil rights groups and many members of Congress favored modeling Title VII on the National Labor Relations Act (NLRA), under which an independent regulatory agency, the National Labor Relations Board (NLRB), is authorized to issue cease and desist orders against violations.[45] In the debates on the amendments to Title VII the argument for cease and desist powers centered on the nature of the tribunal. An administrative tribunal was thought to have greater expertise, and removal from the courts would alleviate perceived judicial overload of Title VII cases. In addition, the more relaxed procedural and evidentiary rules of administrative tribunals were seen as an advantage. Proponents of cease and desist powers also argued that this scheme would lead to more consistency in the development of Title VII law.[46] "Among liberal Democrats this demand [for cease-and-desist authority for the EEOC] had become a test of seriousness in civil rights."[47]

Although some features of the EEOC organization resemble the NLRB, Congress decided on a litigative model rather than administrative enforcement power, as proponents of court enforcement argued that courts would be more impartial, provide more direct and therefore more expeditious relief, and bring greater prestige (and therefore public acceptance) to Title VII enforcement.[48] Even when Congress transferred authority over private employers from the Department of Justice to the EEOC in 1972, it retained the litigation model and rejected the administrative model.[49] Sen. Edward Kennedy (D-Mass.) noted his "serious concern" over the transfer of authority to EEOC from the Department of Labor, Department of Justice, and Civil Service Commission, because it "may impose an unmanageable burden on that already overworked and underfunded agency. Moreover, this transfer may place all of the equal employment eggs in one basket."[50] However, in the Immigration Reform and Control Act of 1986, Congress took the unusual step of granting the Department of Justice power to issue cease and desist orders against employers who discriminate based on national origin.[51]

Those who favored cease and desist powers relied on the need for agency expertise[52] and uniformity[53] and on the prospect of federal courts being overwhelmed by Title VII litigation. "Sorting out of the complexities surrounding employment discrimination can give rise to enormous expenditure of judicial resources in already heavily overburdened Federal district courts."[54] Those opposed argued that the EEOC was biased, that the NLRB cease and desist system operated unfairly, and that the courts were more efficient than the EEOC.[55] The extension of Title VII coverage to state and local governments in 1972 led to an added argument by the opponents of cease and desist orders who maintained that it "would be inconsistent with our system of division of governmental powers to subject state and local authorities to the cease-and-desist power of a federal commission."[56]

The issue of cease and desist authority persists. A tentative report of the Federal Courts Study Committee in 1989 recommended "that the EEOC be authorized on an experimental basis for a five-year period to adjudicate wrongful discharge cases," with a right of election by the claimant (but not the respondent) to proceed in federal court.[57] However, the final report changed the test program to one that would "allow the Equal Employment Opportunity Commission to arbitrate employment discrimination cases with the consent of both parties."[58] A dissent by four of the fifteen committee members argues that "adjudication of private disputes has always been a core function of courts" and that the EEOC plays "an affirmative role to act against discrimination, rather than to act as a neutral adjudicator."[59] Ironically, both Title VII and the Fair Housing Act require that issues of state and local government discrimination be litigated by the Department of Justice while allowing the EEOC to litigate and HUD to bring administrative enforcement proceedings against private actors. This allocation of responsibility is based on comity and an apparent belief that the Department of Justice is more likely to show proper deference to state and local governments. For example, a Senate committee considering the 1972 amendments to Title VII argued that responsibility for cases against state and local governments should be assigned to the attorney general:

> This enforcement scheme provides the necessary power to achieve results without the needless friction that might be created by a Federal executive agency issuing orders to sovereign States and their localities. In short, the committee believes that the objective of equal employment opportunity can best be achieved by providing this particular means of enforcement where State or local governmental units fail to comply with the law.[60]

So the private-public dichotomy exerts somewhat contradictory pulls on the allocation of enforcement responsibility. By contrast, when Congress two years later amended the Age Discrimination in Employment Act to make it apply to state and local governments, it left enforcement in the hands of the EEOC.[61]

EVOLUTION OF ENFORCEMENT STRUCTURE

As we have already seen, the role of the Department of Justice has evolved. Originally the department was limited to criminal law enforcement, then it began participating as amicus in some seminal civil cases. Its entry into civil litigation as a party began when federal agencies were accused of unlawful racial discrimination, and in some early cases the department supported the accusers rather than the federal agency.[62] This marginal role slowly expanded, and the 1957 and 1960 Civil Rights Acts conferred on the department authority to bring injunctive suits to address violations of the Fifteenth Amendment, although Congress refused to enact the broader Part 3 authority. That refusal was reiterated in 1964, and since then there have been no more serious efforts to provide Part 3 authority against all state officials, though Congress added limited authority against law enforcement officials in 1994.

The 1960 act also marked Congress's first consideration of the use of administrative remedies for racial discrimination. The Civil Rights Commission had proposed that it be authorized to investigate complaints of voting discrimination and that upon a finding that the complaints were well-founded "the President . . . shall designate an existing Federal officer or employee in the area from which complaints are received, to act as a temporary registrar."[63] However, Congress placed the responsibility for appointing federal voting referees on the federal courts, who were to appoint them if the Department of Justice proved a pattern or practice of discrimination. Jack Peltason characterizes the 1960 act as "another futile attempt to sweep political issues under judicial rugs by an effort to avoid disagreeable tasks by assigning them to judges."[64] Peltason correctly predicted that federal judges would not aggressively employ the voting referee provision, arguing that "the federal executive must enter the battle" because federal officials would be able to register Negro voters and then leave, while federal judges who were permanently stationed in the South were unlikely to enforce the Civil Rights Act "in such a fashion as to arouse the ire of southerners."[65] Congress adopted his position in the 1965 Voting Rights Act, as discussed below.

In 1964, when the department's authority was expanded to encompass suits against discrimination in public accommodations and facilities, public schools, and private employment, Congress viewed the department as the litigator of last resort. And Congress made it clear that the department was not to function as attorney for private parties; it represented the public interest, not private interests. Government intervention was to be a matter of the attorney general's discretion, subject to the limitations of the act. Ordinarily, private suits were to be the vehicle for combating private racial discrimination as well as state and local governments' denials of equal protection of the laws. Departmental authority to sue was contingent on a variety of prerequisites: receipt of a written complaint, inability of private parties or organizations to bring suitable litigation, filing of a private suit of public importance, existence of a pattern or practice of discrimination, failure of the state to remedy the violation, signature of the attorney general on a complaint, certificate of the attorney general. Although these types of restrictions have been retained in some later laws, the Fair Housing Act amendments of 1988 come close to treating the department as attorney for private interests; not only need there not be a pattern or practice of discrimination, but the department is *required* to sue in certain cases, for example, on behalf of a fair

Figure 5.1. Enforcement options under the Fair Housing Act

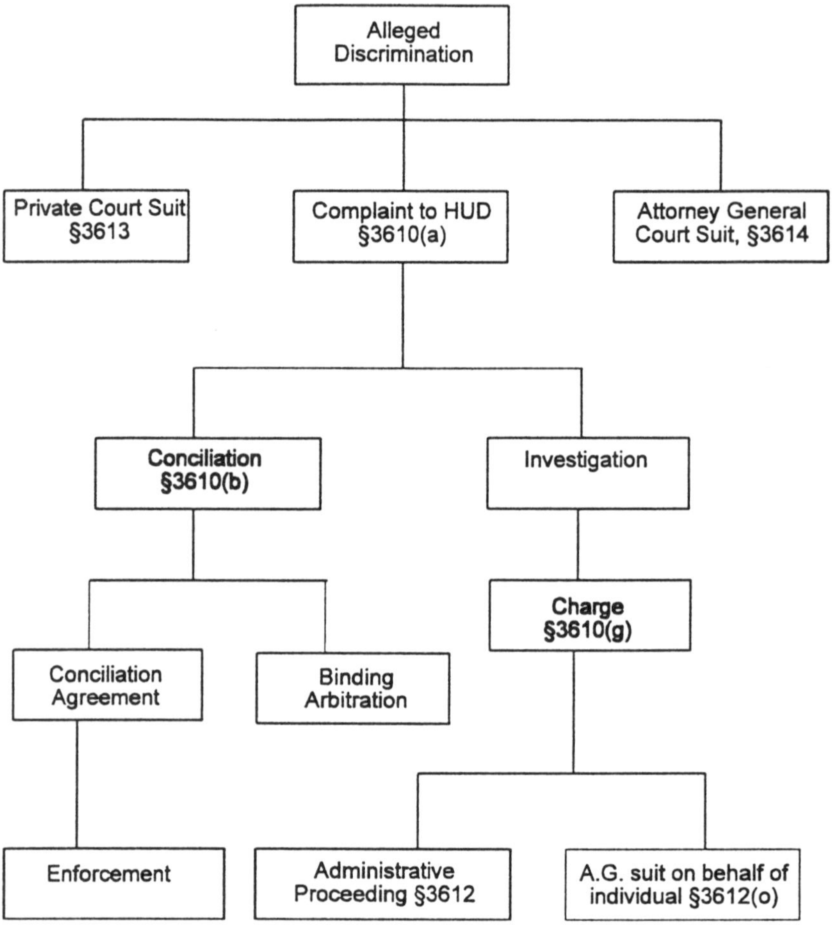

housing complainant if HUD has found probable cause and either the complainant or respondent has elected to have the case heard in court rather than before an administrative tribunal. See Figure 5.1 for a summary.

The enforcement mechanisms available to the department also evolved. Prior to 1957, criminal penalties, after trial by jury, were practically the sole remedy, but the 1957 act granted the department the right to seek injunctive relief. The proponents of the 1960 act's referee provision[66] presented it as a traditional adjunct to remedial powers, citing the special master as an analogy. The 1964 act slightly expanded the department's remedial authority, allowing it to recover back pay as part of its equitable relief.

Table 5.1. Bases for attorney general suits

AREA OF DISCRIMINATION

	Prerequisites Written Complaints	Referrals	Pattern or Practice	Reasonable Grounds	Intervention	Mandatory Suits
HOUSING		•Fair Housing Act §814	•Fair Housing Act §814		•Civil Rights Act, 1964 Title IX §903 •Fair Housing Act §813	•Fair Housing Act §812
VOTING				•Civil Rights Acts •Voting Rts Act §12 •Overseas Voting Rights Act §105 •Voting Access of Elderly & Handicapped Act §6	•Civil Rights Act, 1994 Title IX §903	•Voting Rights Act Poll Tax Challenges §10
EMPLOYMENT		•Civil Rights Act, 1964 Title VII §706	•Civil Rights Act, 1964 Title VII §707		•Civil Rights Act, 1964 Title VII §706 •Title IX §903	
EDUCATION	•Civil Rights Act, 1964 Title IV §407	•Equal Educ. Opp. Act §207 •Civil Rights Act, 1964 Title VI		•Equal Educational Opportunities Act §213	•Civil Rights Act, 1964 Title IX §903 •Equal Educ. Opp. Act §207	
FEDERALLY ASSISTED PROGRAMS		•Civil Rights Act 1964 Title VI			•Civil Rights Act, 1964 Title IX §903	
CREDIT		•Equal Credit Opportunity Act §706	•Equal Credit Opportunity Act §706		•Civil Rights Act, 1964 Title IX §903	
PUBLIC ACCOMMODATIONS	•Civil Rights Act, 1964 Title III Public Facilities §301		•Civil Rights Act, 1964 Title II §206		•Civil Rights Act, 1964 Title II §204 •Title IX §903	
OTHER			•Civil Rts. Institutionalized Persons Act §3	•Freedom of Access to Clinics Act §3	•Civil Rights Act, 1964 Title II §204 •Civil Rts. Institutionalized Persons Act §3	

The first radical departure from traditional equitable remedies came with the 1965 Voting Rights Act, which authorized the attorney general to grant relief directly, bypassing the federal courts. The attorney general could designate political subdivisions to receive federal examiners who could enroll applicants for registration, and local election officials were required to treat those persons as registered voters; the attorney general could also send federal observers into polling places. Finally, Section 5 of the act reversed the ordinary burdens of proof in injunctive cases by providing that covered political subdivisions could not change voting standards, practices, or procedures unless they could prove the change was not discriminatory. Although no other civil rights statute grants the attorney general authority comparable to that provided in the Voting Rights Act, subsequent laws have further expanded the available enforcement mechanisms to include money damages for victims of discrimination and civil penalties, as reflected in Figure 5.2.[67]

The next major departure from the equitable relief model came with the Fair Housing Act of 1968. Unlike the Civil Rights Acts of 1957, 1960, and 1964 or the Voting Rights Act of 1965, the 1968 act authorized private litigants to recover

Figure 5.2. Remedies in Civil Rights Division suits. Remedies under the Americans with Disabilities Act are the same as under the corresponding provisions of Titles II and VII of the Civil Rights Act of 1964, as amended.

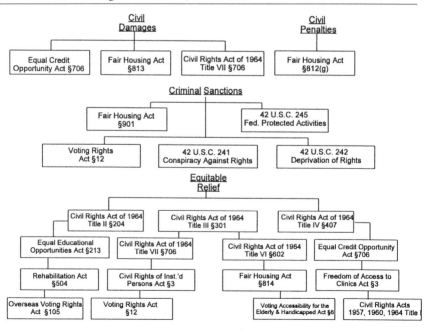

money damages.[68] Although it did not authorize the attorney general to recover money damages,[69] Congress amended the act in 1988 to include for the first time attorney general recovery of money damages for individual victims of housing discrimination and civil penalties to vindicate the public interest.[70] The Civil Rights Act of 1991 extended to both private plaintiffs and the enforcement agencies (EEOC and Justice) authority to recover compensatory and punitive damages under some circumstances in Title VII suits.[71]

The current structure of enforcement does not result from a master plan. Instead, it flows from an evolutionary process that adapts variations in response to changes in the political and situational environment. The Department of Justice and the EEOC share responsibility for litigating employment discrimination cases. The EEOC has substantive rule-making powers under some statutes but not under Title VII, and it lacks administrative enforcement authority. Housing discrimination is governed by a much different scheme. HUD has strong administrative enforcement authority and substantive rule-making authority, but all government fair housing litigation is conducted solely by the attorney general. School desegregation law is enforced by the Department of Education, which has rule-making and administrative enforcement authority, and by the Department of Justice, which litigates school desegregation suits. The Department of Justice is the sole federal agency enforcing voting rights, public accommodations law, the criminal civil rights laws, the Civil Rights of Institutionalized Persons Act, and the Freedom of Access to Clinics Act. It shares with banking regulatory agencies the enforcement of the Equal Credit Opportunity Act. All federal agencies have enforcement obligations under Title VI of the Civil Rights Act of 1964. The primary enforcement authority under Executive Order 11246, which bans employment discrimination by federal contractors, falls to the Department of Labor.

The complexity of this existing enforcement structure arguably traces back in part to Congress's decision not to enact Part 3 authority for the Department of Justice but instead to allocate enforcement responsibility separately as to each possible form of discrimination. This decision led to great variations in the circumstances under which the department could bring suit to enforce the equal protection clause and in the relief it could seek. The variations are even more marked as to private sector defendants. Although Congress concentrated in the Department of Justice the power to enforce the Constitution and most antidiscrimination laws against public sector defendants, it conferred private sector enforcement authority on a broad spectrum of agencies, from the EEOC to HUD to the banking regulatory agencies and the Department of Health and Human Services. One can point to no single statement providing a rationale for this structure, but the desire to diffuse authority surely undergirds it.

The subtle change in the department's approach to the Equal Credit Opportunity Act gives some explanation of the forces affecting enforcement structure under the various civil rights acts. Testifying on the original act in 1974, which did not contain explicit enforcement authority for the department, Assistant Attorney General Pottinger said:

> The Department supports, in particular, the breadth and diversity of the enforcement machinery embodied in H. R. 14856. This bill contains, in addition to individual remedies, both administrative and litigative enforcement powers in the Federal Government. I think history has shown, as for example, with the Civil Rights Acts of 1964 and 1968, that the problems of discrimination are such that a multiplicity of remedies—private, administrative, and judicial—are necessary to effectuate the purposes of the legislation.[72]

In 1975 Congress took up proposed amendments to protect additional groups against credit discrimination and to strengthen the enforcement provisions. Representative Leonor K. Sullivan (D-Mo.) supported pattern-or-practice authority for the attorney general because "it protects the public in those instances where a government agency with enforcement powers under the Act is lackadaisical in investigating possible violations." She also supported a provision allowing the banking regulatory agencies to refer cases of violation of the act to the attorney general, because under the 1974 act "that is implied rather than explicit."[73]

Assistant Attorney General Pottinger gave a somewhat different rationale. First, litigation by the department would allow "for the development of law in the appropriate forum, namely the courts." Second, referral authority would help the administrative agencies:

> If they know that they cannot refer the unusual, novel legal issues to the Attorney General for resolution in court, there is pressure on the administrative agencies either not to enforce the action at all because it is not an appropriate forum, or to do so with a kind of broad brush approach that is unfair, frankly, to both creditors and credit applicants.[74]

Pottinger argued, "Administrative proceedings ought to be reserved for those kinds of enforcements that are clear, that are fairly widespread, subject to administrative regulation, can be handled through hearings on a quick, expeditious basis, and do not involve the highly novel issues."[75] He also argued that the attorney general should be able not only to seek injunctive relief but also compensatory relief on behalf of victims of discrimination. Although not requesting authority for the attorney general to seek punitive damages, Pottinger supported punitive damages in private actions, with a maximum cap of $100,000 for large creditors.[76]

In 1975 Congress did not give the department explicit authority to seek damages for victims of credit discrimination. The department's attempt to secure damages was rebuffed by the courts,[77] but in 1991 Congress finally did confer authority on the attorney general to seek actual and punitive damages.[78] In addition, the 1991 legislation *requires* the banking regulatory agencies to refer to the attorney general cases in which they have reason to believe a creditor has engaged in a pattern or practice of unlawful credit discrimination.[79] This latter provision reflects a return to a division of responsibility for the attorney general and the regulatory agencies, with the attorney general being responsible for systemic cases and the agencies being responsible for individual cases. If the agency believes a complaint of credit discrimination would violate the Fair Housing Act, it must notify the Department of Housing and Urban Development of the violation if it has not referred the matter to the Justice Department.[80] It thus appears that Congress believes that HUD should serve as a backstop on nonsystemic cases, somewhat paralleling the Justice Department's role in systemic cases. The withdrawal of agency discretion as to whether to refer systemic cases reflects congressional dissatisfaction with the regulatory agencies, which "showed great reluctance to take strong action against any depository institution found to be discriminating."[81] Implicit as well, however, is congressional belief that the Department of Justice does not share the reluctance to take enforcement action.

THE ENFORCEMENT STRUCTURE TODAY

The Constitution provides ample formal basis for Congress to enact laws forbidding race discrimination. The convergence of moral and pragmatic reasons creates legislation against race discrimination and places it in the core of our federal legal code. Analogies to race discrimination have led to expansion of protected classes that share some but not all of the characteristics of race.

Once Congress determined to forbid race discrimination it was faced with the question of enforcement techniques. It wisely opted for mixed enforcement, making use of the resources of private individuals and the federal and state governments. The role of each should flow from the particular interests each represents. Within the federal government, Congress has relied on a variety of enforcement techniques and agencies. A somewhat chaotic enforcement structure has emerged, which in Chapter 10 I suggest should be made more coherent.

The civil rights laws affirmed Supreme Court decisions establishing the nondiscrimination principle as the central meaning of the Reconstruction amendments, and they extended that principle to the private sector. The resultant civil rights enforcement agencies were to be guided in their activities by the national values of the nondiscrimination principle while recognizing that enforcement methods should also consider other interests, such as state and private autonomy. Although political forces might intrude, the overriding principles and purposes of the statutes should provide the primary guide to enforcement. The distribution of enforcement responsibility also stems not only from political considerations but from the broader values of federalism, separation of powers, and individual rights. The calculus of these factors changes over time, as the enforcement of the civil rights laws changes old habits of discrimination. Enforcement agencies then face the challenge of adjusting to changed circumstances while continuing to promote the overall values of the antidiscrimination laws. The next chapters examine the application of these principles in the setting of priorities and fashioning of litigation positions and in the relations between civil servants and political appointees.

6

Setting Priorities

A successful organization musters its resources to achieve its mission. For the Department of Justice to enforce the civil rights laws successfully requires it to develop a clear understanding of mission and then to establish priorities and litigation policies calculated to most effectively advance the mission.

Some guidance comes from the various considerations that shaped the civil rights laws. It is clear enough that the department should direct its resources to combat systemic practices and egregious acts of racial discrimination. But that does not answer the question of how to deploy limited resources. As we will see, priorities must not only respond to these broad, overarching considerations but also be shaped by exigencies of the moment, by political and social forces, and by the evolution of the law itself. Priorities are sometimes created by an ad hoc process and are sometimes carefully planned. They are ever-changing, sometimes imposed from above by the president, attorney general, or assistant attorney general, sometimes from other branches through legislation or court decision, and they may also be influenced by de facto exercise of power of career civil servants.

THE NEED TO SET PRIORITIES

The staff of the Civil Rights Division has never been sufficiently large to redress every alleged act of unlawful discrimination that falls within its authority, a limitation that has long been recognized.[1] Its size over time is shown in Figure 6.1. Slightly over four attorneys per state serve in the division, and no trial section in the division has more than one attorney per state. As of December 29, 1993, there were 238 attorneys in the Civil Rights Division. The largest trial section, Housing and Civil Enforcement, had forty attorneys; the smallest, Educational Opportunities, had fourteen.[2] This paucity of attorney resources places significant limits on the ability of the department to enforce the law.

Figure 6.1. Number of Civil Rights Division attorneys, 1958–1996

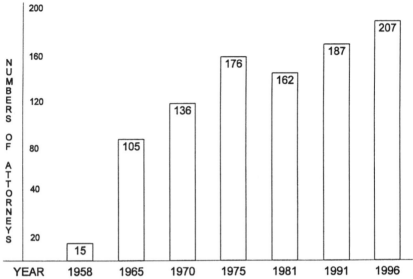

The department may respond to those limits by seeking more resources, but it has not sought large staff increases for the Civil Rights Division. The budget has at times reflected a work ethic philosophy, best captured by John Doar's testimony at the hearing on his nomination as assistant attorney general:

> I am not a big staff man, Senator, and I like to see the attorneys have a full day's work. I think if you get the right attorneys and the attorneys work hard, relatively few attorneys can accomplish a great deal of litigation; and so it is not so much numbers as it is caliber, dedication, and performance, which measure the effectiveness of a legal division in the Department of Justice.[3]

Nonetheless, it is probably true that one hundred hardworking attorneys can accomplish more litigation than fifty of similar caliber.

Implicit in the budget and arguably in the civil rights laws themselves is the notion that not every case requires the attorney general's intervention and that the division, like other divisions, must adopt priorities.[4] One might argue that the role of the executive branch is simply to carry out Congress's wishes as displayed through the legislative process. In this argument, every law that Congress has enacted holds equal dignity and an equal place in the firmament of enforcement priorities. William Bradford Reynolds, responding to questions in connection with his nomination to be President Reagan's assistant attorney general for civil rights, articulated this position when he said:

> My first priority as head of the Civil Rights Division will be to ensure that all civil rights protected by the Constitution or federal statutes receive energetic enforcement. . . . To this end, the Division's resource allocation will necessarily depend on the frequency and gravity of violations detected in the various areas of civil rights enforcement that are within the Division's responsibility.[5]

Reynolds seems to have been suggesting that all areas of enforcement stood on an equal footing. However, this argument ignores both the role of the executive in the separation of powers and the practicalities of enforcement. Those responsible for enforcement must exercise some discretion; moreover, the budget process and congressional oversight provide Congress an opportunity to influence priorities. It is doubtful that Reynolds ever fully subscribed to the equal footing notion. He did elevate the priority of some matters, such as his fight for deregulation and his fight against affirmative action, while giving low priority to cases seeking systemic relief.

Although all executive agencies may exercise some degree of discretion, the discretion of the Department of Justice is enhanced by the additional tradition of prosecutorial discretion. Early in the history of the Civil Rights Division, civil rights workers attempted to obtain a federal court injunction ordering the attorney general to arrest and prosecute state and local officials who were violently interfering with civil rights. The federal court dismissed the suit, observing that arrest and prosecution "are clearly discretionary, and decisions respecting such actions are committed to the Executive branch of the Government, not to the courts."[6] And, the court added, "such considerations of judgment and discretion apply with special strength to the area of civil rights, where the Executive Department must be largely free to exercise its considered judgment on questions of whether to proceed by means of prosecution, injunction, varying forms of persuasion, or other types of action."[7] The court granted far less discretion to the Department of Health, Education, and Welfare's civil rights enforcement program, distinguishing it from the Department of Justice's prosecutorial discretion on the ground that "Title VI not only requires the agency to enforce the Act, but also sets forth specific enforcement procedures."[8] In sum, the Department of Justice has discretion as to how, when, and perhaps even whether to bring a miscreant before a court.

Reasoned exercise of discretion is enhanced where the department has developed a set of priorities. In 1957 setting priorities was relatively simple: the department had authority only to bring criminal prosecutions or civil voting rights suits. Since Congress had determined that criminal prosecution was not effective in advancing compliance with the Fifteenth Amendment, the department nominally focused the efforts of its small staff (fourteen attorneys in 1958, twenty-seven in 1959)[9] on suits against racially discriminatory voting practices. This selection of priorities was reflected in the organization of the division, which lumped all responsibilities except voting into the General Litigation Section[10] and established a separate Voting and Elections Section;[11] other sections (Administrative, Appeals and Research, and Trial Staff) supported those two enforcement sections.[12]

The department naturally concentrated on those geographic areas where official racial discrimination was most prevalent. However, Judge Harold Greene, who was one of the original members of the division, recalls that Attorney General William Rogers called "the division together, saying, 'Let's not bring too many cases. What we want to do is bring just a few cases so that we establish the law solidly from the beginning.' "[13] Until Harold Tyler became assistant attorney general in 1960, the division brought very few race discrimination cases and was criticized by the U.S. Commission on Civil Rights for its slow start in enforcing the 1957 act.[14] Instead it devoted most of its resources to federal custody cases, election fraud cases, and criminal prosecutions for police brutality and deprivation of civil rights.[15] The gap between performance and the congressional mandate revealed that more than lip service to priorities would be needed.

On the surface it appeared in 1957 that little in the way of priority setting would be required, given the very limited jurisdiction of the division. Since then, the division has been awarded authority to enforce a proliferation of modern civil rights statutes.[16] Today the department more clearly needs to adopt priorities among its duties.[17] Long-term uniform allocation of resources to the Voting Rights Act and the so-called Motor Voter law,[18] for example, would not give proper weight to the relative importance of these two laws. One scholar has suggested that lack of priorities contributed to the failure of Reconstruction: "Pushing out in all directions, the federal government could advance but little in any one of them; concentration upon a few basic situations amenable to control through law might have promoted minority group interests more intensively and enduringly."[19] Similarly, failure to prioritize today would lead to meager resources being ineffectually deployed.

The period after passage of the 1964 Civil Rights Act and 1965 Voting Rights Act presented particularly difficult prioritization issues. The division's responsibilities had vastly multiplied, and it was busy absorbing a large number of new attorneys into its staff.[20] Schools, employment, and voting were all important issues, and as a result compromises, although perhaps not explicitly articulated, occurred. For example, first priority in enforcement of the Voting Rights Act went to ensuring that all African Americans who wished to register and vote were able to do so; emphasis was placed on the examiner and observer programs, while enforcement of Section 5's rule that covered jurisdictions could not change their voting practices until they had established that the changes were not discriminatory initially took a backseat.[21] The lower priority of Section 5 enforcement reflected Assistant Attorney General Doar's view that the preclearance requirement was not a good idea.[22] Not until 1971 did the division adopt regulations putting teeth into Section 5 enforcement.[23]

Development of priorities must proceed along two concurrent lines. First, the division must determine—from statutes, court decisions, administrative practice, and administration policy—its overall role in civil rights enforcement. Second, it must set priorities among the various elements of its law enforcement missions. Priority setting is not a science but an art, and the shifting winds of litigation place limits on the implementation of priorities. A study of priority setting and implementation by private sector civil rights litigators concludes with words that might also be applied to the Department of Justice:

> Litigation for social change, then, is often reflexive and far from completely planned, with many constraints on the planning of litigation campaigns, many detours along the road to organizational goals, and much flexibility of action by both the litigating organizations and individual staff attorneys.[24]

Finally, it should be noted that priority setting is rendered more difficult by the existence of nondiscretionary duties and unanticipated crises. When a jurisdiction subject to the special coverage of the Voting Rights Act brings suit to bail out from coverage or to preclear a voting change, the attorney general is the named defendant and the department must participate in the litigation. Similarly, the department represents other agencies sued over their civil rights policies or activities, for example defending suits to enjoin the actual or threatened termination of federal contracts or funds under Executive Order 11246, Title VI, or a revenue-sharing statute.[25] The Fair Housing Act "election" cases described later in this chapter constitute a new form of nondiscretionary duty. Unanticipated crises have somewhat abated since the tumultuous 1960s, but urban disturbances and other unpredictable events, such as the arsons of black churches and bombings of abortion clinics, still occur, placing a responsibility on the department to divert resources in order to enforce the law.

ROLE OF CIVIL RIGHTS DIVISION

Institutional Change

In 1957 the machinery of state and local government in the South was dedicated to maintaining the racial caste system. The original purpose of establishing the Civil Rights Division was to attack that systemic violation of the rights of African Americans. True, the caste system was often advanced by private discrimination and violence, but these private sector deeds were enabled and encouraged by the public sector. The philosophy underlying Burke Marshall's approach to civil rights enforcement in the early 1960s was to turn the state and local governments from engines of discrimination to responsible democratic institutions—to force them to face up to their obligations under the Fourteenth Amendment.[26] An example of this philosophy in operation is found in John Doar's marching orders to division lawyers assigned to ensure that Alabama's first elections under the Voting Rights Act complied with the act:

> One final and most important word—we cannot run these elections. We do not have the authority, the budget, or the manpower. In any event, we would not best eliminate the caste system that way. Our goal can best be achieved through local officials who recognize and meet their responsibilities, and through Negro individuals and groups who are influential enough to have a significant impact in changing the conditions which have perpetuated the system. Your assignment, then, is to insure that local officials recognize and meet their responsibilities under the law.[27]

Enforcement of the Voting Rights Act, the school desegregation decision, and Titles VI and VII have substantially transformed state and local governments. They are no longer the primary agents affirmatively encouraging and perpetuating the racial caste system, though their record is far from spotless. Where institutional discrimination or its vestiges continue to exist, one responsible view of the division's mission would require that the division give its highest priority to institutional corrective action.

The size of many private sector enterprises and the parallel activities of smaller enterprises create another soil in which institutional discrimination takes root. Widespread use of similar selection criteria for employment or loan eligibility, for example, may perpetuate patterns of racial division. Widespread failure to provide access to facilities may place the physically disabled in a disfavored caste. Eradicating patterns of private sector institutional discrimination also warrants a high priority in division enforcement.

Atmosphere of Compliance

The discussion above of reasons for assigning the enforcement role to the division suggests that it does not exist primarily to represent private grievants but to further the public interest in nondiscrimination. It fulfills this function in part by seeking to create an atmosphere of general compliance, which requires prompt redress of highly visible insults to the rule of law. For example, in the late 1950s the department assigned a high priority to addressing the unavoidable issue of massive resistance to the *Brown* decision. As one author has noted, "the government was more active in the field of public education in the late 1950s *without* statutory authorization than it was in the field of voting rights, where it had received *specific* authorization in the Civil Rights Act of 1957 to initate voting suits in its own right."[28] Most recently, several states deliberately and openly refused to comply with the Motor Voter Act, and the department had no choice but to temporarily shift to this issue resources that might otherwise have been allocated to enforcement of the Voting Rights Act.[29]

Congress's rejection of Part 3 poses a dilemma when widespread violations of the Constitution undermine respect for the law. On the one hand, the department is a creation of Congress, whose continued viability depends on observance of jurisdictional limits. On the other hand, the attorney general must faithfully execute the law, and the foundation of American law is the Constitution. The dilemma was most acute before the adoption of the 1964 act, when the attorney general resolved it in part by claiming implicit authorization to bring suit to remedy a limited category of flagrant violations of the law. In the 1960s the department relied on its role as protector of federal military or federal employees when it sued for prompt desegregation of schools so that children of members of the armed services could attend,[30] as protector of interstate commerce by attempting to desegregate travel facilities,[31] and even as protector of Fourteenth Amendment rights.[32]

These cases were products of necessity and fertile legal imagination. Although they have not left a lasting legacy of authority to bring suits not authorized by federal statutes, they stand as precedents to be employed in case of future flagrant violations of established constitutional rights. Where the courts have thought that Congress's silence denoted an intent to withhold from the attorney general authority to bring a particular kind of case, they have ruled against the suit.[33] The department therefore must take congressional action or inaction into account in setting priorities, even with respect to egregious constitutional violations.

Aside from attacking open and notorious unlawful discrimination, the department normally best promotes an atmosphere of compliance when it emphasizes remedying systemic rather than isolated violations. Congress and the executive have shown some ambivalence as to the respective roles of individuals and the attorney general in establishing department policy. The statutes that require the existence of a pattern or practice of discrimination[34] or an issue of general public importance[35] or "that the institution of an action will materially further the orderly accomplishment of desegregation"[36] point toward attorney general control of priorities.

One statute *directed* the Attorney General to sue for relief against the poll tax.[37] Here Congress set an overriding but limited priority: the attorney general was required to devote high priority to the issue, but four statewide suits sufficed to resolve it.[38] Other statutes simply authorize the attorney general to sue to redress violations of law;[39] these statutes vest the attorney general with absolute discretion.[40] Yet another category of statute allows the attorney general to sue only upon receipt of a written complaint from an aggrieved individual. This type formally places initial control over priorities in the hands of private individuals. Once the attorney general receives the complaint, control passes to her hands and she has absolute discretion. A final type of statute places in the hands of the private parties the decision whether the attorney general must sue. Only the election section of the Fair Housing Act belongs to this category.

Private litigants are authorized to bring both individual and class action cases. This private right of action is thought to "vindicate[] both the deterrence and the compensation objectives" of the civil rights laws.[41] The Supreme Court has also noted that the private civil rights litigant "vindicates the important congressional policy against discriminatory . . . practices."[42] The need for attorney general litigation against individual, nonsystemic discrimination is thus lessened by the availability of private suits.

The department enhances an atmosphere of compliance by litigating high visibility cases. Public awareness of enforcement will tend to lead prospective discriminators to reform their behavior so as to avoid judicial sanctions. High visibility cases fall into several categories. Some involve well publicized incidents, such as the killings of civil rights workers Chaney, Goodman, and Schwerner in Philadelphia, Mississippi, in 1964 and the more recent police beating of Rodney King in Los Angeles. Some become high visibility because of the number of victims or defendants or because of the amount of money at stake. For example, the statewide school desegregation cases brought in the early 1970s affected many thousands of children and hundreds of school systems across the South. In early civil rights acts Congress withheld from the attorney general the authority to obtain money damages but more recently has thought it important to authorize her to seek money damages for victims of discrimination.[43]

The predecessor of the Civil Rights Division, the Civil Rights Section of the Criminal Division, had, at least for a time, required a verified complaint from the victim prior to initiating a criminal investigation.[44] Attorney General Brownell, testifying in support of the 1957 act, stressed that at the Department of Justice "we do not start with a statute and then go out and try and find a violation of it. We have instances of prima facie violation of the statutes reported to us."[45] However, he also characterized the rights at stake as "public rights" and stated that "here the public law enforcement officer has a duty to go ahead and enforce the Constitution and the laws even though the individual who might be directly affected by it doesn't want him to do so."[46]

The initial policy of the Civil Rights Division seemed to rely heavily on citizen complaints even though the 1957 act contained no such requirement.[47] This attitude is reflected in Attorney General Rogers's testimony during consideration of the 1960 act. Representative Peter Rodino (D-N.J.) asked him to explain the disparity between the prevalence of voting discrimination and the low number of suits brought by the government. Rogers's response stressed that "we have not had as many complaints as you might expect in this area."[48] However, he acknowledged that the government sues on its own behalf, not on behalf of the complainant.[49]

Later the department deemphasized the citizen complaint. Assistant Attorney General Harold Tyler, who took office in 1960, eliminated his predecessor's requirement of a formal written complaint as a prerequisite to a voting discrimination investigation.[50] His successor, Burke Marshall, testified that he would investigate and file voting discrimination suits without a complaint from an aggrieved party if the evidence reflected a violation of the law, noting that this was consistent with the practice of the Antitrust Division.[51]

The department skirted the requirement that it receive an individual complaint before bringing a school desegregation case. Rather than wait for a complaint from each segregated school system within the state, it used a complaint against one school system as the basis for a statewide suit.[52] And former Assistant Attorney General Burke Marshall, appearing on behalf of Attorney General Katzenbach in hearings on the proposed Voting Rights Act, testified that "there are serious objections to creating a procedure whereby one citizen can force the United States to bring a lawsuit that it does not believe that it should bring,"[53] adding that "it would be a mistake to remove from the Department of Justice the decision as to whether or not it thinks a case is a good case to bring."[54]

Development of Legal Standards

The department also furthers the public interest in nondiscrimination by assisting in the development of governing legal standards, so that the protected class and the potential defendants will have a common understanding to guide their decisions and conduct. Unlawful racial discrimination is more likely to occur when the legal standards are unclear. For example, although there was widespread compliance with the core mandates of the 1964 act's ban on racial discrimination in public accommodations, racial discrimination continued in those arguably covered places "for which coverage under Title II previously had not been clearly enunciated by federal courts."[55]

The Eisenhower administration advised Congress that its proposed Civil Rights Division "probably also would be responsible for the formulation of legal and policy approaches involving constitutional and civil rights within the Department of Justice."[56] Given the case-oriented approach of law enforcement, legal and policy approaches would be advanced in litigation. The department has undertaken such development not only in its own litigation but also as amicus curiae in important federal court cases, even where the case did not directly implicate the department's enforcement authority.

This "public interest" approach dates back to President Theodore Roosevelt's attorney general, Charles Bonaparte (1906–1909). Under Bonaparte and his successor, Attorney General George Wickersham, the United States as amicus played a leading role in clarifying the legal standards for determining what is involuntary servitude forbidden by the Thirteenth Amendment. The government helped convince the Supreme Court to overturn Alabama's peonage law in 1911,[57] filing briefs that furthered the statutory responsibility of the attorney general to enforce the criminal law against peonage.[58] But in 1947, long before the department had authority to bring suit to remedy housing discrimination, it filed a brief in the seminal case of *Shelley v. Kraemer*,[59] successfully urging the Supreme Court to hold that state courts could not enforce racially restrictive covenants, a ruling that advanced understanding of what comprised unconstitutional state action within the meaning of the equal protection clause of the Fourteenth Amendment. In the early 1950s, long before the department had authority to bring suits to remedy discrimination in public education, it filed amicus briefs in *Sweatt v. Painter*[60] and *Brown v. Board of Education,* arguing that the plaintiffs were victims of unlawful racial discrimination. Those cases established that state-imposed racial segregation violates the Fourteenth Amendment.

It has been suggested that it is inappropriate for the department to seek to influence the course of the law:

> Private lawyers define and litigate the critical civil-rights questions. At best, the Government leaves them alone. At worst . . . it seeks to undermine them. Only after the courts have settled an issue, and made it politically safe, will the Government use its many resources for the comparatively routine, though important, task of enforcement.[61]

This argument is wrong for several reasons. First, even where the department lacks direct authority to bring suit, the president may legitimately decide that the attorney general should advance the national interest by promoting the equal protection of the law. Second, where unresolved issues do concern the department's law enforcement authority, the agency cannot carry out its duty without taking positions on them. When Congress enacts a law forbidding discrimination, a host of interpretive issues must be answered. After the 1957 act, for example, such questions included:

> What kind of statistics would do? Did state legislation freezing the voting roles by tightening registration requirements constitute discrimination? Could a state order re-registration of all persons under a stricter literacy test if the effect was to discriminate against Negroes? Should the Division ask the court to order registration of specific Negroes who were qualified? How could the court check on compliance with a broad injunction against discriminatory practices?[62]

If the department had followed the above advice it would never have advocated the overruling of the separate-but-equal doctrine,[63] it would never have developed the significant remedial principle that civil rights remedies must overcome the effects of past discrimination,[64] and it would never have prosecuted the killers of Colonel Lemuel Penn, a case where the indictment alleged that the defendants killed the African-American victim on a highway in Georgia in order to intimidate African Americans in their right to "travel freely to and from the State of Georgia."[65] One can say in retrospect and in light of the decisions in those cases that failure to assert those positions would have led to failure to enforce the law. When the Civil Rights Division has limited itself to enforcing only the clearest provisions of the law,[66] it has filed few cases and developed little law.

Congress has at times expressed in the strongest possible terms the desire for the department to initiate cases to clarify the law. For example, in 1937 the Supreme Court held that the imposition of the poll tax as a prerequisite for voting in state elections did not violate the equal protection clause of the Fourteenth Amendment.[67] In 1965 Congress expressed its view that such use of the poll tax was unconstitutional and "directed" the attorney general "to institute forthwith" necessary litigation to implement that view.[68] The attorney general responded by filing suits which resulted in district court determinations that the Alabama and Texas poll taxes were unconstitutional[69] and participating as amicus curiae in the Supreme Court case which led to the demise of the poll tax in state elections.[70]

Third, Congress has enabled the department to bring to litigation the advantages of "repeat player," one that litigates often and develops institutional competence on the issues it litigates. A repeat player may also develop a litigation strategy in pursuit of a goal and may be able to choose appropriate litigation vehicles for carrying out the strategy.[71] Most repeat players represent the "haves" of society, but the division was created to help the "have nots."[72]

Finally, the department's administrative duties under laws such as the Voting Rights Act mesh with its litigative authority. Its exercise of administrative responsibilities lends support to its litigative positions, because the Supreme Court accords the same deference to the "interpretation followed by the Attorney General in his administration of the statute" as to interpretations by other administrative agencies interpreting the statutes that they enforce.[73] Since the attorney general typically plays an important role in Congress's consideration of civil rights legislation, the Court has said that the department's "contemporaneous administrative construction of the Act is persuasive evidence of the original understanding."[74] The Court accorded such deference not only to attorney general regulations[75] and legal interpretations[76] but also to factual determinations by the attorney general in the exercise of her administrative responsibilities.[77]

Education About Discrimination

Closely related to the need to develop the law has been the creation of factual records that educate the courts and public about the nature and extent of discrimination and the options for remedying it. The factual records sometimes educate the public directly when a high-visibility trial receives extensive media coverage, as occurred, for example, in the trial of the officers who beat Rodney King. The records educate the public indirectly as well when the courts write opinions explaining their decisions. Judicial findings of fact enjoy a high level of credibility. It has often been noted, too, that the painstaking factual development, through litigation, of the record of voting discrimination and the need for far-reaching remedies laid the foundation for the 1965 Voting Rights Act.[78] Although Congress has cited orderly development of the law as a priority, it has sometimes displayed impatience with the department's failure to bring large numbers of cases.

Litigation is, of course, not the only tool available to educate the American public. Attorney General Janet Reno has argued that in addition "we have a responsibility to explain to the American people why civil rights enforcement is in their best interest. We have got to explain to them in terms that they will understand."[79] This speechifying function, while appropriate especially at the attorney general level, could detract from the prime function of the Civil Rights Division—to enforce the law—unless given an appropriately subordinate priority. Attorney General Edwin Meese, perhaps understanding the need for the Civil Rights Division to focus on litigation, assigned a portion of the educational function to the department's Office of Legal Policy. The result was a series of anonymously authored advocacy pieces in the guise of "reports" to the attorney general; these publications have rightly received little attention.[80] They suffer from a lack of the discipline that litigation and the rendering of binding opinions imposes on legal writing. The Civil Rights Commission, also created in the 1957 act and charged with the responsibility of investigating the state of civil rights in the country, would seem to be the better entity to issue reports on civil rights concerns.

Enforcement of Decrees

In most of the department's civil rights cases, the division seeks injunctive relief and has therefore built up a large docket of cases in which injunctions have been entered. Table 6.1, for example, shows that although the number of school desegregation cases brought peaked at 58 in 1970, the number of active cases steadily rose, reaching 253 by 1974, the last year this tabulation appeared in the department's annual reports,[81] and the number of school systems involved was even higher, 480. The department proposed to allocate almost a half million dollars to enforce the court orders in fiscal year 1976,[82] which raises the question as to the relative priority of continued Department of Justice monitoring of compliance with these decrees. It also raises the question of the duration of the decrees.

On the one hand, the federal enforcement effort should continue for a sufficiently long period of time to lock in the initial gains from federal litigation. Institutional inertia operates here to promote civil rights, because once the department has obtained relief against a defendant, monitoring of the defendant's performance will occur automatically. On the other hand, the decrees become a detailed code of action and subsequent issues arising under them may not rise to the same level of importance as the initial violation that led the United States to bring suit. For example, a school desegregation decree may approve a plan for drawing school boundary lines and for school utilization. The initial plan is of great importance, but minor adjustments typically must be made periodically in

Table 6.1. Comparative summary of school litigation, 1959–1974

Source of Jurisdiction	1959	1961	1963	1964	1965	1966	1967	1968	1969	1970	1971	1972	1973	1974
CRA 1964, Title IX (intervention)					5	35	10	1	3	1	3	1	0	0
Title IV (school desegregation)					2	12	42	12	21	15	19	1	2	2
Title VI (federal funds)					0	0	2	1	2	14	4	0	0	0
U.S. defendant					1	3	2	5	7	11	4	7	4	9
Amicus Curiae	1	5	4	5	2	8	0	5	2	16	6	7	9	4
Other	0	2	7	3	1	0	0	1	1	1	0	0	4	3*
Total	1	7	11	8	11	58	56	25	36	58	36	16	19	18
Number closed	1	5	11	6	0	9	3	1	0	22	8	15	7	28
Number still active at close of year	0	2	2	4	15	64	117	141	177	214	150	251	263	253

*Two of these cases are Title VII employment discrimination: one is a case involving constitutional rights.

Source: Annual report of the attorney general for fiscal year 1974, p. 79.

light of changes within the district, and often the issues raised by those adjustments would not have warranted suit by the government in the first instance.

The department could respond to the duration issue in several ways. It could
establish small enforcement units to monitor compliance and separate the enforcement of court orders from initial enforcement of the law. This approach
would provide control over resource allocation but could lead to shortchanging
the monitoring of compliance with statutes and regulations. It could rely in the
first instance on other agencies to monitor compliance with court orders. For example, the Department of Education could monitor compliance with school desegregation decrees, which would require a degree of cooperation among agencies that does not always exist. The department could also seek to terminate
decrees once the defendants have complied for some period of years. Termination may occur in some cases with or without the department's consent, under
standards the Supreme Court recently established.[83] If pursued too soon, such a
course amounts to abandonment of responsibility, but some cases undoubtedly
are ripe for dissolution of the decree.

Filling Gaps in Enforcing the Law

The question arises whether the United States should attempt to fill the gaps in
law enforcement arguably created by the doctrine of standing, which impedes
private individuals and classes from remedying some deprivations of rights. For
example, private plaintiffs have been denied standing to challenge zoning laws
that forbade the building of low-cost multifamily dwellings where they were unable to show that the zoning authorities had barred any particular project in
which they could live.[84] Similarly, private plaintiffs have been denied standing to
sue for redress of a racially discriminatory pattern of police abuse[85] or law enforcement.[86] Cases such as these evince a reluctance to allow individual citizens
to invoke federal jurisdiction to obtain sweeping remedies against government
officials. One might argue that the danger of irresponsible litigation is less if the
suit is brought by the attorney general than if any citizen may initiate it. That
argument assumes, of course, that we generally can rely on the attorney general
to act responsibly. Moreover, if the standing of the United States is viewed as
stemming from private rights, failure of private standing would lead to failure of
government standing as well.

In practice, the Congress has at times conferred broader standing on the attorney general than on individuals and at other times has declined to do so. For
example, Joel Selig has pointed out that there is a strong argument that *Warth*
does not limit the attorney general's ability to bring non–site-specific cases under
the Fair Housing Act.[87] On the other hand, when the United States attempted to
remedy racially discriminatory police practices after a private suit alleging those
practices failed,[88] the courts held that it lacked authority to bring the suit. The

Court of Appeals for the Third Circuit noted in particular the repeated refusals of Congress to adopt Part 3:

> Congress had three opportunities between 1957 and 1964 to authorize the Attorney General to bring lawsuits of the type that we now consider. It refused on each occasion because this authority would permit a dramatic and unnecessary shift of power from state and local governments to the Attorney General.... We conclude ... that the ... modern history demonstrates an explicit intent, to deny the government the right of action asserted here.[89]

Congress in 1994 finally provided that statutory authority, allowing the attorney general to seek equitable and declaratory relief to eliminate a pattern or practice of deprivation of constitutional or statutory rights by law enforcement officials.[90] In short, the influence of gaps in private enforcement on the priorities of the Civil Rights Division varies depending on the statutory scheme.

Cases on Behalf of Individuals

Congress has authorized the department to sue to remedy discrimination against various classes and to bring suits of general public importance. In addition, however, several statutes authorize or even require the department to sue to remedy discrimination directed at one individual. If the primary objectives of the division are to create an atmosphere of compliance, develop legal standards, educate, and enforce decrees, these objectives, along with the department's limited resources, suggest that so-called "one-on-one" cases should receive a low priority. Yet some such cases could deserve higher priority because they could decide important legal questions, affect more than the immediate parties, or otherwise satisfy one of the above objectives.

For example, the Bush administration thought it important to bring suit on behalf of a white teacher whom the Piscataway, New Jersey, school district had laid off for racial reasons.[91] The case raised novel issues as to whether Supreme Court case law banning race-conscious layoffs[92] applies where the employer deems both the white and the minority teacher equally qualified and there are few minority teachers in the school system. Even if the department were to follow a policy of redressing only "the particular wrong that is addressed in the litigation" rather than "effectuate class relief for an individual wrong,"[93] the suit had the potential of clarifying an important point of discrimination law. However, most individual cases simply require a factual determination and neither raise a novel legal issue nor lead to significant relief for others.

In some statutes Congress has gone further, directly authorizing or even requiring the attorney general to bring suits on behalf of individuals. For example, the attorney general must bring fair housing cases on behalf of individuals where after a HUD finding of probable cause, either party elects to have the matter heard in federal court rather than before an administrative tribunal. Although earlier proposals authorized HUD to bring such cases,[94] the normal primacy of the attorney general as the litigator for the United States appears to have influenced Congress to adopt the current arrangement. The difficult question for the department is what priority to assign to such congressionally authorized or mandated litigation on behalf of individuals and how to cope with the twin dangers created by these provisions. First is the danger that individual litigation might rob resources better devoted to cases that more broadly advance the public interest,[95] especially since the rate of "elections" to federal court has been unexpectedly high—over 60 percent.[96] The opposing danger is that by failing to accord proper deference to Congress's express wishes, the department might leave victims of unlawful discrimination without a remedy and undermine the enforcement efforts of agencies such as the EEOC and HUD.

The requirement to bring suit on behalf of private complainants is not only inconsistent with the normal discretion vested in the attorney general but also places the attorney general in an untenable litigating position. It seems doubtful that the law creates an attorney-client relationship between the attorney general and the complainant. The complainant will have little incentive to settle and will wish to direct the litigation. Indeed, cases may reach court because the complainant has rejected a reasonable settlement offer. Must the attorney general litigate such a case, or may she impose a settlement on the complainant? Must she pursue claims she deems of little merit?

Other federal agencies are assigned to provide more extensive help to individual complainants. Congress has effectively distinguished between retail enforcement, assisting individual victims of discrimination, and wholesale enforcement involving the pattern-and-practice cases and cases of general public importance. It has assigned retail enforcement primarily to litigation by private individuals and agencies such as the EEOC and HUD and has assigned wholesale enforcement primarily to the Civil Rights Division.[97]

Congress has, as a safety valve, provided for agency referral of some retail cases to the division, but referral has not automatically led the Department of Justice to file suit. Assistant Attorney General Pottinger pointed out that when a matter is referred to the department, "each case must be carefully reviewed at various levels of the Department to insure that only appropriate cases are filed."[98] Assistant Attorney General Reynolds's emphasis was slightly different. He reported:

> Consistent with the Division's policy of seeking to vindicate the rights of individual victims, and of supporting the efforts of the Equal Employment Opportunity Commission to obtain voluntary compliance, several suits filed during 1984 were based upon referrals from the Equal Employment Opportunity Commission and involve allegations of discriminatory practices by relatively small public employers. While the number of jobs covered by such suits is small, the cases are important because they enhance the Equal Em-

ployment Opportunity Commission's ability to obtain relief through negotiations with other discriminatory employers.[99]

Reynolds was correct that so long as the EEOC lacks authority to bring individual cases under Section 706 against state and local governments, referral suits brought by the Department of Justice are needed to maintain the EEOC's credibility. However, his statement also reflects the Reagan administration's antipathy to large structural remedies. If one believes that the primary task of the Civil Rights Division is wholesale relief, which often requires dismantling structural discrimination, undue stress on individual suits tends to sap resources away from that task.

One answer is to seek congressional modification of the referral statutes, especially the provision of the Fair Housing Act amendments that seemingly requires the department to sue when either side to an administrative charge elects to have the case heard by the federal courts rather than by a hearing examiner. Under existing law, complainants have an incentive to elect judicial proceedings because they may be awarded punitive damages in judicial proceedings but not in administrative proceedings. Respondents probably elect judicial proceedings because of lack of confidence in the fairness of the administrative proceedings.

A legislative solution might focus on eliminating these incentives to elect judicial proceedings. Congress might also reconsider the rationale for granting the election option to complainants as well as respondents. The option is granted to respondents because of fear that an administrative order for damages might deprive the respondent of the right to jury trial.[100] No such deprivation will occur with respect to complainants, however, because they retain the option to bring a private suit. The rationale for granting them the election option must be grounded in concern for parity, but the existence of the private right of action goes a long way toward ensuring parity.

Another answer might be more aggressive efforts to settle individual cases. The difficulty with settlement is that individuals with virtually free legal representation often have little incentive to compromise. Moreover, the government attorney is not the lawyer for the individual but is suing in the government's name on the individual's behalf. The individual neither has reason to trust the advice of the government attorney nor to distrust the zealousness of the government attorney's advocacy. The individual is paying no attorney's fees or costs, and the consequences of a litigation loss may not be great.

The dilemma of the government attorney is that the duty of representing the government's interest requires him or her to base settlement on an assessment of the value of the litigation to the government, but that assessment in all likelihood will not coincide with the individual's assessment of settlement value.[101] The dilemma is deepened by the government's obligation of fairness to the defendant, an obligation arguably different from that of the private attorney.[102] The dilemma can be resolved by informing the individual complainant that even though the attorney general will bring suit on his or her behalf, the attorney general represents the United States in the case and is not the complainant's attorney. Therefore the attorney general is at liberty to settle the case on the government's own terms, and the complainant may wish to engage private counsel.[103]

The department could also pursue resource-shifting solutions and create a unit devoted solely to bringing cases on behalf of individuals. The existence of such a unit might protect the section that tries public interest cases from resource raids, which would probably result in a degradation of quality or the buildup of a backlog of individual cases. In 1994 the attorney general directed U.S. attorneys to handle housing discrimination "election" cases assigned to them by the Civil Rights Division.[104] This action "raises concerns about ensuring quality and about the commitment that U.S. Attorneys . . . will make to these cases" because of their traditional focus on criminal matters,[105] and the traditional reliance on the division to conduct most civil rights civil cases for the government. It is too early to assess the results of that experiment. Finally, the department could delegate the responsibility for litigating the election cases to the Department of Housing and Urban Development; individual employment cases could be turned over to the EEOC. Such a delegation seems at odds with Congress's initial assignment of litigating responsibility, but similar delegations do exist. Moreover, Congress has at times authorized the president to reorganize executive branch responsibilities, and he has done so several times with respect to civil rights enforcement.[106]

The growing emphasis on money damages in administrative enforcement and in cases brought by the Department of Justice threatens to further shift emphasis from systemic cases to individual cases. This emphasis provided Congress the impetus to require the attorney general to bring individual Fair Housing Act cases when a party to the matter so elects rather than commit the matter to an administrative agency. The department can find no mooring for settling systemic cases, where damages are available, and is unable to determine if the sky should be the limit or whether the department should settle for nominal damages.

Arguably the 1988 amendments to the Fair Housing Act and the 1991 amendments to Title VII provide individuals with the necessary tools to combat disparate treatment. This change strengthens the argument for leaving to the private sector suits for damages, allowing private plaintiffs to rely on the collateral estoppel effect of findings of discrimination in cases brought by the department. A Department of Justice suit for structural or criminal relief followed by private suits for damages is the model employed in antitrust cases.

CATEGORIZING DISCRIMINATION CLAIMS

Setting priorities among the enforcement responsibilities of the division requires analysis of interrelated issues, an analysis that takes place in the context of evolving social and political pressures. One must consider the subject matter of the discrimination, the injury to individuals, the protected classes, whether the discriminator is private or public, the impact on public order, the ability of private individuals to obtain redress, the effectiveness of the enforcement mechanism, and the scope and historical context of the discrimination. For example, discrimination against African Americans in state voting systems implicates all the *Carolene Products* factors. Attorney General Brownell relied on *Carolene Products* reasoning in urging passage of the 1957 act: "The right to vote is one of our most precious rights, in fact, it is the cornerstone of our Government, and it affords protection to all of our other civil rights, and accordingly, because of its importance it must be zealously safeguarded."[107] Such discrimination involves a public discriminator, weakens public order by undermining the legitimacy of laws enacted by an unrepresentative legislature, is statewide in application, and is part of the historical tradition of a state-imposed racial caste system. Although such discrimination theoretically could be redressed by private litigation, experience teaches that many voting rights violations are beyond the resources of private plaintiffs. Addressing such discrimination should be a very high priority until it has been decisively and permanently exterminated.

Contrast the voting example with another example: discrimination against families with children by a mobile home park operator. The injury to the victims of discrimination is large, but all the other factors point against giving such discrimination a high priority in Department of Justice litigation. None of the *Carolene Products* factors apply: the discriminator is private, a violation by one private landowner has minimal impact on public order, it is not statewide, and a private suit could easily remedy the violation; moreover there is help available from HUD in investigating and there are attorney's fees for the prevailing plaintiff. Further, although there is a history of discrimination by some landlords against families with children, the United States imposes no antifamily caste system.

One might argue that the familial status discrimination is more important than the voting discrimination because Congress requires the attorney general to bring suit in such a fair housing case in some circumstance while Congress leaves to the discretion of the attorney general whether to bring a voting rights case. Such an argument betrays the poverty of an approach that draws expansive conclusions from legislative experiments while ignoring the underlying reasons for the particular laws.

Subject Matter

As we have seen, the modern civil rights acts cover a plethora of subject matters, from voting to employment, from public accommodations to fair housing and equal credit, from conditions of confinement of prisoners to school segregation. Although it seems logical to assign highest priority to those subject matters deemed of greatest importance, assigning relative ranks of importance is no easy task. Moreover, the relative importance of various subject matters is subject to change. For example, Title VII of the Civil Rights Act of 1964 became effective on July 2, 1965. A month later the Voting Rights Act was passed. At the end of the fiscal year that began on July 1, 1965, the division reported that the "commitments by the Division with respect to the enforcement of statutes covering voting, schools, juries and rights-intimidation precluded a broader scope of activity in the field of equal employment opportunity during this year."[108]

The following year John Doar testified before a congressional committee that "the trend in our work is moving from voting to employment." Doar explained: "The results of the 1965 Voting Rights Act have demonstrated a remarkable amount of compliance by local officials, and registration of Negro citizens in the area covered by the act increased to just over 50 percent, approximately. We do not have very many voting complaints any more. We are getting more and more employment complaints."[109] Two years later the Division reported that "the decision to give priority to the enforcement of Title VII of the Civil Rights Act of 1964 . . . was based on the judgment that if minority groups are to break out of the cycle of poverty, welfare and despair in which many find themselves, they must have access to a job market unrestricted by racial discrimination."[110]

The decision as to what priority should be given to employment discrimination evolved slowly in light of the need for the department both to satisfy Congress and to mount a credible litigation program, dual goals that placed the department in a precarious position. For example, the department's initial response to its Title VII responsibilities was to bring a small number of very important cases, with the department filing its first pattern-or-practice referral from the EEOC in December 1966.[111] Although the department elevated the priority of employment discrimination cases, the House committee report on the 1972 amendments noted that "the size of the [Civil Rights] Division has not kept pace with its vastly increased responsibilities. As a consequence the division has been highly selective and very limited in the number and the nature of suits which it has filed."[112] The department's lack of activity "was one reason given for the transfer of authority to sue private employers to the EEOC in 1972."[113] Responding to Congress's display of impatience, the department rapidly brought new cases against state and local governments newly covered by the 1972 amendments to Title VII.[114] The rapidity of these filings brought problems of proof in cases such as the government's suit filed in 1973 against the Hazelwood, Missouri, school district for employment discrimination. Much of the proof necessarily involved pre-1972 activities of the school system, and the Supreme Court ruled that the court of appeals had erred in ruling for the United States because the "prima facie statistical proof in the record might at the trial court level be rebutted by statistics dealing with Hazelwood's hiring after it became subject to Title VII."[115]

Despite the difficulties, the division has made efforts to adopt subject matter priorities, and the outcome of those efforts will be explained later. What follows here is a brief discussion of the need for flexibility and responsiveness to changed conditions. Unforeseen events have often stymied the effort to set and follow priorities in an orderly way. Even before the 1957 act authorized the attorney general to bring civil suits to enforce voting rights, and long before Congress expanded this authority to include other civil actions, unanticipated interference with federal court orders led the department to enter civil suits. Attorney General Brownell explained in 1956 that "recently the Justice Department has been obliged to engage in activity in the civil rights field which is noncriminal in character."[116]

During the early years of the Civil Rights Division, the department devoted substantial resources to enforcement of privately obtained court orders against state officials and to the maintainance of public order in the face of state resistance. The federal government intervened, for example, when Governor Faubus of Arkansas called out the national guard to prevent court-ordered desegregation of Central High School in Little Rock in 1957 and when governors of other states sought to defy federal court orders to desegregate the Universities of Alabama and Mississippi and public schools in Alabama in the early 1960s. Although the department had focused its priorities on enforcing the voting discrimination provisions of the 1957 and 1960 acts, events made it imperative that some resources be redirected to these crises. "The issue was no longer segregation or desegregation, but the integrity of the courts and, indeed, as in the Civil War, when the status of blacks was also the focus, whether the Union would hang together."[117]

All this federal involvement preceded the 1964 Civil Rights Act, which authorized attorney general intervention to ensure that public school authorities did not unlawfully discriminate based on race. When the department lacked statutory authorization to sue, its use of amicus participation was common. "Sometimes the law didn't authorize Justice to file certain kinds of suits; sometimes it wasn't clear. Often, powerful Southern Democrats might object, or retaliate, if Justice were to file such a case. Often inhibited by such jurisdictional and political factors, in a pattern that continued through the Kennedy administration and beyond, Justice frequently piggybacked on our [NAACP Legal Defense Fund] cases."[118]

After 1964 many new and unforeseeable crises arose. For example, the killing of the three civil rights workers in Mississippi, the state-sponsored violence that led to deaths at Kent State, Jackson State, and Orangeburg State Colleges, and the televised beating of Rodney King in Los Angeles elevated the priority of criminal enforcement. Priorities change not only as crises arise but also as they are overcome. When the Civil Rights Act became law in July 1964, it was thought that the new public accommodations law would engender the most resistance. Prior to the act's effective date attorneys from the Civil Rights Division were deployed to potential trouble spots in the South to gather information that could be used if public accommodations refused to comply or if violence broke out. As a new lawyer in the division, I was sent to Birmingham in June 1964, where I roamed restaurants and coffee shops, ordering Coca-Colas and taking copious notes about the items on the menu and the nature of the restaurant facilities.

Happily, none of the information was ever needed. Once the law was held constitutional,[119] the resistance largely melted away, along with the anticipated need for massive federal enforcement of Title II.[120] Many businesspersons gladly complied: "Once all businessmen were required to open their doors to all customers they could desegregate, yet reply to white critics that they were doing so only because of Federal coercion," and "with the business community in the main sanctioning compliance, since it was in its economic self-interest to do so, the potential mobs were lulled into acquiescence."[121]

Rather than massive noncompliance, the division was faced with scattered resistance by small establishments and with the need to resolve definitional issues regarding the coverage of Title II.[122] Similarly, in 1969 most of the schools of the South were segregated, and court decisions demanded prompt desegregation. Ten years later almost all southern school systems had desegregated, owing to private and Department of Justice suits and Department of Education pressure, and the priority issues became ensuring compliance with the decrees and desegregating systems of higher education.

Voting rights law, too, was the subject of shifting needs and therefore shifting activities. The priority under the 1957 and 1960 acts was to end discrimination in the registration of voters. The 1965 act's examiner provisions and its suspension of tests or devices quickly accomplished that goal.[123] Next, the priority was to ensure that election machinery operated without discrimination, and the department devoted its resources to monitoring elections, using federal observers, and establishing a litigating presence where the observers uncovered abuses.[124] The department then turned to enforcement of Section 5, the preclearance provision of the act, adopting formal procedures and litigating definitional issues.[125] Having established in regulations and case law the operative principles under Section 5, the department today gives top priority to remedying racial discrimination in the drawing of electoral districts and in the use of at-large forms of election. Perhaps it would have been best to move on all these fronts at once. However, not only were the available resources inadequate to do so, but many issues that loom as important today were only dimly if at all perceived when enforcement of the Voting Rights Act began in August 1965.

Prohibited Classifications

One might pose the question of priorities in terms of the various forbidden classifications. What priority should be given to eradicating discrimination based on race, gender, national origin, religion, or disability? Initially Congress answered that question by narrowly defining the forbidden classifications under the 1957 act as "race, color or previous condition of servitude."[126] A proposal to include sex discrimination among the matters to be studied by the Civil Rights Commission met opposition from Attorney General Brownell, who felt sex discrimination was "not germane to the purpose of the legislation" and should "be dealt with separately from discriminations based on color, race, religion, or national origin."[127] However, Congress's subsequent broadening of the forbidden classifications beyond the initial core of race discrimination shifted the priority-setting issue to the attorney general.[128] When the department began enforcing Title VII it initially placed all its resources into the race cases;[129] early division policy memoranda relating to criteria for filing employment discrimination cases had referred only to discrimination against "Negroes." No sex discrimination pattern-and-practice cases were brought until 1970,[130] and not until about 1973 did sex discrimination in employment receive priority from the department.[131]

Many compelling reasons supported the adoption of federal laws against race discrimination. Although strong or even compelling reasons support the later bans on other forms of discrimination, major differences have been found between race discrimination and other categories. The formal support for protections against race discrimination includes the Thirteenth, Fourteenth, and Fifteenth Amendments. Of these, only the Fourteenth would support protections against gender discrimination and perhaps discrimination based on age or disability. The Supreme Court has found state discrimination based on race subject to the highest level of judicial scrutiny, while gender discrimination is subject only to midlevel scrutiny and age or disability discrimination is subject to relaxed scrutiny. The only bases for federal law forbidding private discrimination based on gender, age, disability, or familial status are the commerce clause and the spending clause. Although those authorities are broad, they are not unlimited.

Although weighty moral grounds support the discrimination prohibitions added later, important distinctions provide more weight to the moral grounds for banning race discrimination. Gender, age, disability, and familial status, unlike race, may embody some real differences that may warrant some variety in treatment, ranging from such trivial matters as sex-segregated bathrooms to fundamental ones such as denying children the right to vote. As the Supreme Court has recognized, valid distinctions based on gender are rare, but valid distinctions based on age or disability are more common. Moreover, while other categories have also been marked by past discrimination, race is marked by the unique history of slavery, the Black Codes, and Jim Crow, resulting in an official racial caste system whose effects continue to manifest themselves today. The history of discrimination based on gender, age, disability, and family status differs in important ways from the history of race discrimination. For example, nothing remotely approaching the racially impacted urban ghetto exists with respect to these other groups, even though they may share some examples of physical separation. This difference suggests that national unity, while threatened by many forms of discrimination, is most threatened by race discrimination.

Race discrimination and the other forms of prohibited discrimination may also have similar impacts on the national economy. Freeing the market from discrimination should generally enlarge it. Finally, public order is more greatly endangered by race discrimination than by other forms of discrimination. State defiance of the Constitution's guarantee against official race discrimination was official policy in much of the Deep South. Major racial disorders in this country seemingly have not yet ended. There is simply no national parallel with respect to gender, age, disability, or familial status.

It would seem to follow from the above discussion that the national enforcement effort should give highest priority to combating race discrimination. Speaking of housing discrimination against families, James A. Kushner reached a similar conclusion, noting that "expanding the mission of fair housing enforcement to . . . family discrimination may dilute the primary, racial equality mission. . . . The overt nature of these violations may lead authorities to allocate scarce enforcement resources to such cases rather than the harder to uncover, sophisticated forms of racial and ethnic discrimination [and] . . . the primary mission of fair housing laws might be thwarted."[132]

Groups Within Classification

Within a particular classification, one could also ask what priority should be accorded to different groups.[133] For example, the ban on race discrimination was enacted because of widespread discrimination against African Americans, but it also applies to discrimination against whites. Although the department has traditionally acknowledged that whites as well as nonwhites are protected, until the Reagan administration the department did not divert substantial resources to litigation on behalf of whites.

The allocation of priorities among various groups could be very divisive. Where particular groups do not feel oppressed, they will not demand high priority attention from the department. However, several groups do feel oppressed, and so the department must take care that priorities fairly reflect the realities. Many criticized the Reagan administration for raising the priority given to combating discrimination against white males. Those criticisms stem from a perception that race and gender discrimination have not appreciably hindered opportunities of white males. However, in a period of rising unemployment, white males have often attributed their employment problems to discrimination in favor of minorities and women. Ideally the Department of Justice would examine this question objectively, but this is one area where political considerations could easily intrude into priority setting, a charge often levied against the Reagan Justice Department.[134] Hanes Walton, Jr., points out that treating civil rights as the special concern of a racial minority rather than as a fundamental right places them at the mercy of political and electoral majorities and imports interest group politics into civil rights enforcement.[135]

Geography

Finally, geography could also be considered in setting priorities. The 1957 and 1960 acts were often characterized as regional legislation aimed at the southern states. The 1964 act addressed some primarily southern issues, such as discrimination in public accommodations, and some national issues, such as employment discrimination. The 1965 Voting Rights Act and its subsequent amendments fell most heavily on the South although it also applied to the North; amendments to the act were more national in scope. The Fair Housing Act of 1968 and other acts since 1965 have been national in scope. Nonetheless, it has on occasion been charged that the department failed to shift its priorities quickly enough from a regional to a national focus. For example, Senator Jeremiah Denton (R-Ala.) complained that "certain preconceptions held by Division staff resulted in the targeting of specific regions of the country even after many of these locales had made ample demonstration of a good-faith effort to bring about corrective measures. What occurred seemed to border on vindictiveness, an effort to punish those geographic regions for alleged prior transgressions."[136]

Priorities have at times focused on those geographic areas where statistics reflect the greatest probability of racial discrimination. For example, Assistant Attorney General Burke Marshall is quoted as telling the chair of the Senate Judiciary Committee that the Civil Rights Division would begin voting rights investigations "if statistics on registration and voting in a particular area showed a heavy imbalance."[137] Early enforcement of the Fair Housing Act was "directed at 'target cities' offering the greatest potential for affecting minority groups."[138] Similarly, the *Hazelwood* case was one of several Title VII cases brought in the St. Louis metropolitan area based on statistical data reflecting an enormous disparity between employment of African-American teachers in St. Louis and in surrounding predominantly white school systems. The use of statistical disparity as a trigger for investigation is based on the assumption that disproportionately low rates of African-American voter registration, residential occupancy, or employment are more likely the result of racial discrimination than of choice by African Americans. The number of successful suits that such investigations have spawned suggests that the assumption is well-founded.

7

Following Priorities

DIRECTING RESOURCES TO PRIORITIES

Once priorities are identified, it becomes necessary to direct resources to those priorities. Conversely, effective allocation of resources to priorities is enhanced if the priorities have been fully developed and articulated. An administration with a clear vision can be more effective than one whose vision is blurred.

The Reagan administration developed priorities and litigation policies for the Civil Rights Division early. By May 1981, Attorney General William French Smith had delivered a major speech announcing that the department intended to shift away from the busing remedy for school segregation.[1] Even before Assistant Attorney General William Bradford Reynolds had been confirmed, he had written a detailed memorandum to the attorney general suggesting a policy with respect to affirmative action,[2] and that memorandum laid the foundation for the policies and priorities of the next eleven years of the Reagan-Bush era. Six months later Attorney General Smith published an article in the *American Bar Association Journal* describing and defending the administration's new litigation emphases: strict adherence to limits on justiciability, resistance to creation of new fundamental rights or suspect classes, and advocacy for judicial restraint in the fashioning of judicial decrees.[3] In essence, the attorney general publicly embraced judicial restraint as a high priority. When Assistant Attorney General Reynolds subsequently testified against reliance on busing as a remedy for unlawful school segregation, that testimony built on the judicial restraint theme of the attorney general's article.[4] To a marked extent, the resources of the division were reallocated according to these early expressions of administration policy.

The critical control points that the attorney general may employ to assure that resources are directed to priorities are budget, investigation, and the decision to file suit. In terms of overall priorities, the strongest control point is the budget: if the attorney general allocates a large proportion of appropriated funds to a particular area of concern, the Civil Rights Division will do more in that area; conversely, allocation of a small amount will lead to less enforcement activity.

Budget, however, is only a rough tool, because within the area of concern many priority issues will remain. The initiation of an investigation is a critical control point. If no investigation is undertaken, the department will not face the question of initiating suit. Once a full investigation has begun, however, it may well reveal a violation of the law. After a violation has been discovered, it becomes more difficult to decide not to bring suit, but the recommendation to bring suit is nonetheless also an important control point. Indeed, Congress in several statutes insisted that the decision to prosecute be made by the Attorney General.[5] Thus the attorney general has discretion to decline to file suit even though she believes a violation of the law has occurred.[6]

Organizing Around the Priorities

Allocation of Responsibilities Between the Civil Rights Division and Other Units of the Department. A threshold organizational issue for the Department of Justice stems from the fragmented nature of the department and how responsibilities should be shared among and within its three main branches: a U.S. attorney in each of the ninety-five federal judicial districts, the legal divisions in Washington, and the Federal Bureau of Investigation.[7] Traditionally, in other areas of law enforcement most litigation has been conducted by the U.S. attorneys[8] and most investigation by the Federal Bureau of Investigation.[9] Many of the legal divisions primarily supervised cases and investigations and provided legal assistance in difficult or important cases. This arrangement was true of the Criminal Division, in which the Civil Rights Section was located from its creation in 1939 until the creation of the Civil Rights Division in 1957.

Experience in the Criminal Division reflected that placing civil rights litigation in the hands of the U.S. attorneys led to pallid, ineffectual enforcement, for several reasons. U.S. attorneys are political appointees, selected by the senators representing their state. Although they are often able and dedicated, most U.S. attorneys in the Deep South belonged to the political structure that segregation and voting discrimination had nurtured.[10] Second, the need for a national program of civil rights law enforcement would be thwarted by placing civil rights under the U.S. attorneys. Third, the developing nature of the law of discrimination required uniform approaches to the government's antidiscrimination cases. The latter two reasons for assigning cases to the division rather than to U.S. attorneys are supported by a Department of Justice study that advocates assigning to the legal divisions in Washington "(1) multidistrict cases; (2) cases requiring national uniformity; (3) cases involving complex issues; and (4) cases requiring specialized expertise."[11]

These last two reasons have continued to influence division leadership. For example, in 1977 Assistant Attorney General Drew S. Days III argued:

Figure 7.1. Department of Justice organization chart

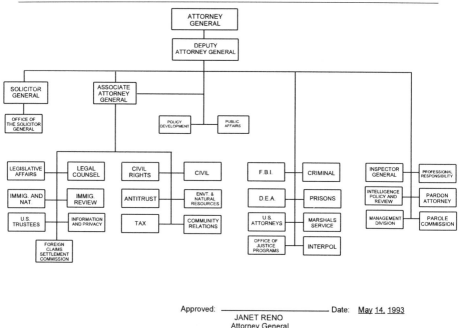

Approved: ———————— Date: May 14, 1993
JANET RENO
Attorney General

Civil rights enforcement is a peculiarly sensitive function. It requires a cen-
trally directed approach which is consistent on a nationwide basis, and
which reflects careful attention to various policy concerns. The Department's approach to difficult issues of federalism, its efforts at conciliation
and voluntary compliance, and its interpretation of subtle factual situations
and policy-oriented legal principles, must be uniform. In most instances, this
objective is best achieved through direct operational implementation by our
national headquarters office.[12]

The Civil Rights Division attorneys initially "operated primarily as desk lawyers."[13] The division became a litigating unit, similar to the Antitrust Division,
when Harold Tyler and John Doar became its leaders in 1960.[14] The story of voting discrimination in Forrest County, Mississippi, provides dramatic evidence of
the effect of the change from a supervisory to a litigative role.[15] In 1952 Thurgood Marshall, special counsel to the National Association for the Advancement
of Colored People, requested that the department investigate and take action
against allegations of discrimination by the Forrest County voter registrar. He
submitted affidavits from African-American applicants for registration who

were rejected for failure to correctly answer such questions as "How many bubbles in a bar of soap?"

The Criminal Division requested an FBI investigation, which corroborated many of the allegations. The division wrote to Joseph Brown, the U.S. attorney in Jackson, Mississippi:

> In our opinion, the report plainly reflects that the subject Cox and his deputies follow and have followed over several years a practice of refusing to permit qualified Negro citizens to register and, thus, become eligible to vote. There can be no doubt that this practice is in violation of 18 U.S.C. 242.

The U.S. attorney requested an opportunity to seek voluntary compliance. There followed a period of ineffectual negotiations, during which the African-American citizens of Forrest County were unable to vote in the presidential election. The U.S. attorney then assured the Criminal Division that the registrar would "henceforth follow the law in considering applications for voting registration," and the department so advised Thurgood Marshall.

Two months later Marshall supplied twenty-four affidavits of African Americans who had recently been denied registration. Another investigation ensued, and the Criminal Division wrote to the U.S. attorney that "an indictment should be sought against the subject Cox, charging him with violations of 18 U.S.C. 242." Almost a year later, the U.S. attorney presented the matter to the grand jury, which declined to indict. No transcript was made of the grand jury proceeding. Over the next five years further complaints, investigations, and U.S. attorney negotiations led to renewed vague promises to comply with the law,[16] but Voter Registrar Cox continued to discriminate, denying registration to almost all African-American applicants.

In 1959 Cox died and was replaced by Theron Lynd. In 1960 Assistant Attorney General Harold Tyler began dealing directly with Registrar Lynd and his attorney regarding the division's demands for voter registration records, although the U.S. attorney was still providing advice to be patient. Tyler wrote to the U.S. attorney, "It seems to me that we have been abundantly patient in trying to work out an amicable solution to this problem." The following month, January 1961, Tyler ordered the U.S. attorney to file court papers. On July 6, 1961, over nine years after Thurgood Marshall's initial complaint, the Civil Rights Division filed a discrimination suit against Theron Lynd.

When suit was filed in 1961, 56 percent of Forrest County's 22,000 white citizens of voting age and fourteen (0.2 percent) of the eligible African-American citizens were registered to vote.[17] It seems clear that had the division not taken over control of the matter, the U.S. attorney would have continued to negotiate ad infinitum and would remain satisfied with vague and incomplete promises. Even so, the filing of the suit did not bring immediate relief. It led to a series of remarkable legal battles including, finally, a court of appeals injunction and sub-

sequent contempt proceedings against the registrar. After three years of litigation, African-American registration in Forrest County had risen from 12 to 236
persons, but over a thousand African Americans were denied registration during
that three-year period.[18] Within two years of the passage of the Voting Rights
Act and the assignment of federal examiners to Forrest County, over 4,000 more
African Americans were registered to vote.[19]

In theory, the FBI is an investigative agency and the litigative divisions only
litigate, but the distinction between the two is not always clear. In describing the
preparation of a voting rights case, former Civil Rights Division officials noted
that "instead of using the Bureau to shape up the proof, we went into the field
ourselves."[20] Under a "treaty" between the FBI and the Civil Rights Division

> the Bureau would not have to analyze the records, but it would conduct all
> the interviews we requested, do it thoroughly, and if, in our judgment, nec-
> essary, on an expedited basis. For its part, the Division would analyze the
> records and would operate in parallel as an investigative agency in voting
> matters across the South.[21]

In short, the fact-gathering and analysis work of division personnel further distinguished them from the "desk lawyer" model. Going into the field, seeing conditions firsthand, analyzing records, and then litigating cases in courts throughout the country force division lawyers to understand the real world and to
transcend theoretical constructs or internal bureaucratic concerns that may hold
greater sway over desk lawyers.

The decision to concentrate enforcement of the civil rights laws in the Civil
Rights Division rendered it easier to exercise the budgetary technique of ensuring adherence to priorities. Diffusing responsibility among the U.S. attorney
offices would have defeated the budgetary technique, because the size of most
U.S. attorney offices would require the civil rights function to be one of many
responsibilities assigned to attorneys in the office.

Perhaps it is inevitable that the central office (the division) and the branch
offices (the U.S. attorneys' offices) would experience friction. The division has
often wanted to make use of U.S. attorneys but has been uncertain about how to
do so. This perspective is captured by the statement of David L. Norman, who
later became assistant attorney general: "The attitudes of the United States Attorneys' offices toward civil rights matters have run the gamut from antipathy
and apathy through interested helpfulness and heavy-handed enthusiasm. How
to make their potential effectiveness actual has been and is a high priority question."[22] Similarly, the U.S. attorneys have undoubtedly been frustrated by the
control exercised from Washington.

Several reasons suggest that U.S. attorneys should now play a larger role in
civil rights enforcement. Primary among these reasons is the vastly larger resources available to them. In 1994 the U.S. attorneys' offices employed 4,370 attorneys, compared with 229 in the Civil Rights Division.[23] Second, the division

is located in Washington, while U.S. attorneys are located where the cases are litigated, making them more familiar with local conditions and local federal courts. This situation was a disadvantage in Mississippi in the 1950s and 1960s, and local political conditions could render it a disadvantage in other places and times, but ordinarily it should not serve as a barrier to U.S. attorneys handling routine, noncontroversial cases.

Beginning in the late 1960s, some authority has been returned to the U.S. attorneys, and the division has experimented with ways to collaborate with them. For example, in 1968 the division "instituted a program for each U.S. Attorney to designate an assistant to have special responsibility for Title VII matters."[24] In 1978 the department assigned primary responsibility for enforcing the language minority provisions of the Voting Rights Act to U.S. attorneys, and in 1994 the attorney general, on the division's suggestion, also assigned some fair housing matters to U.S. attorneys. These attorneys have always had substantial responsibility for criminal civil rights matters.[25] Some important cases, such as prosecution of the police officers who beat Rodney King, have been jointly and successfully handled by the division and the U.S. attorney.

At times it has been thought that priorities should be reflected by assigning special responsibility for civil rights matters to persons in the attorney general's office. For example, in the 1960s it was proposed that responsibility for enforcement of Title VI be transferred to the attorney general's office, apparently for "cosmetic" reasons. John Doar, however, prevailed in his argument that Title VI enforcement would be more effective if housed in the Civil Rights Division.[26] During the Carter administration, when human rights were said to occupy a high priority, it was proposed that Attorney General Griffin Bell appoint a special assistant for civil liberties, who would be assigned "to act as contact point and liaison with civil liberties and related organizations, to receive their complaints about positions taken by the federal government which affect civil liberties, and to advise the Attorney General on civil liberties issues."[27] Three years later Attorney General Benjamin Civiletti responded by creating the office of civil liberties coordinator in the office of the associate attorney general.[28] That office seems to have fallen into desuetude in 1981 when William French Smith became attorney general, probably because creating such offices outside of the litigating divisions has little long-term impact.

Allocation of Responsibilities Within the Civil Rights Division. Within the Civil Rights Division, the budgetary technique involves various methods of organizing around the priorities, either geographically, functionally, or by protected class. Authorized personnel can be allocated in varying numbers to geographic regions, to specified subject matter areas, or to specified protected classes. Reorganization can be a very low-profile way of implementing policies that might be controversial if addressed more directly. As a former assistant attorney general of the Civil Division relates, "The difficulties and delights of reorganization do not make good copy. When I told reporters my reorganization stories, their eyes glazed over and soon they stopped calling altogether."[29] At the beginning of the Johnson administration in 1963, the division's organization remained functional, with most lawyers assigned to the Voting and Elections Section. The division was so small and its duties so limited that there were only four sections: Voting and Elections, General Litigation, Trial Staff, and Appeals and Research.[30]

According to Hugh Davis Graham, geographic organization "was a common form of internal organization among the federal mission agencies, and it offered the advantage of facilitating both intra-agency coordination between Washington headquarters and the field, and also interagency cooperation between different agencies serving the same region."[31] If the Justice Department's priorities are defined geographically, the department might not need to make conscious geographic decisions: all it need do is go where the violations are. Although the division was originally organized into nominally functional sections, the sections placed most of their resources into enforcement in the southern states.[32] In 1964 the functional organization gave way to a nominally national geographic one, with some southern states in each geographic section—eastern, western, southeastern, and southwestern. The department's administrative history reports that "with the addition of new enforcement responsibilities, assignment of responsibility along functional, subject-matter lines was no longer feasible. For example, attorneys working on voting communities were gaining experience which could prove useful in handling other civil rights problems in the area."[33]

In 1965, when Title VII took effect, the attention of the division was focused overwhelmingly on voting and school discrimination in the South. In 1967 Assistant Attorney General Doar reorganized the division "to permit increased emphasis upon enforcement of Title VII."[34] The change in priorities was accomplished by the "shifting of a substantial number of personnel from the Southeastern and Southwestern Sections to sections covering the northeast, midwest and western portions of the United States."[35] The congruence of geography and type of discrimination thus led to a geographic shift in order to accomplish a programmatic objective.

Functional organization—Criminal, Education, Housing, Employment, Public Accommodations and Voting Sections, and a catchall office for Title VI, legislation, and special appeals—replaced the geographic sections in 1969.[36] By this time the duties of the division had become quite diverse, as reflected in the organizational chart from the 1973 annual report of the attorney general (see Figure 7.2).[37] A former division attorney speculates that the division reorganized "probably in part to placate Southern opposition to school desegregation by shifting some of the better known lawyers in the Division from school desegregation to other matters." Other reasons he lists seem more likely: "The Department gave priority to employment discrimination . . . encouraged specialization, the development of expertise in certain areas, and planning along functional

Figure 7.2. Civil Rights Division

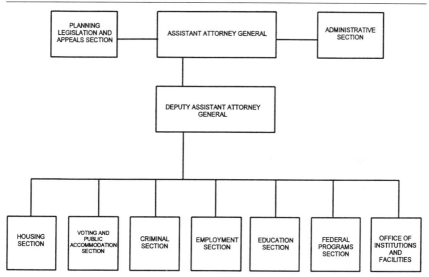

lines."[38] With minor exceptions the division has retained the functional organization since 1969.

A functional organization permits specialization. It also leads to uniformity of approach to particular subject matters and facilitates relations with counterpart federal agencies. The Education Section developed close relations with the Office of Civil Rights at the Department of Health, Education, and Welfare and later at the Department of Education. The Housing Section developed relations with the Department of Housing and Urban Development, and the Employment Section developed relations with the EEOC, the Department of Labor, and the Civil Service Commission. Finally, functional organization allows precise calibration of resources assigned to each subject matter. Functional organization does, however, sacrifice some of the advantages of geographic organization and the familiarity geographic sections develop with regional problems and with local leaders and local courts. The lawyers in them also become well-rounded, with the added depth of the generalist, and thus are more likely to draw on analogous court decisions under various civil rights laws.

Subject matter organization may be manipulated to reflect administration priorities. For example, Assistant Attorney General Drew S. Days III criticized the organizational structure that was in place when he took office because "the tendency was to litigate civil-rights cases by [subject-matter] area: housing, voting rights, etc."[39] He believed "that discrimination is not compartmentalized but that one area pours into another."[40] He therefore merged two subject matter sections into one very large "General Litigation" Section "in order to approach more effectively the interrelated problems of residential segregation and segregation in public schools,"[41] a reorganization that led to the filing of a case combining claims of housing and school discrimination.[42] His successor, William Bradford Reynolds, in an action that was consistent with the Reagan administration's antipathy to cases seeking extensive structural relief, dismantled the General Litigation Section in 1983 to "reduce[] the diversity of litigation within any one section, allowing the two new Sections to concentrate their efforts."[43]

The exceptions to a functional basis of organization have consisted of the occasional creation of units based on protected class. After passage of the Indian Bill of Rights in the 1968 act, an Office of Indian Rights was established although the Indian Bill of Rights grants no enforcement authority to the attorney general.[44] Later came a task force to look into issues affecting Hispanic Americans and a task force on sex discrimination in the U.S. Code.[45] None of those entities presently exists, but there are other units now to enforce the rights of disabled persons and to provide redress payments to persons of Japanese ancestry whom the government interned during World War II.[46] Organization of sections based on protected class favors the creation of strong links to various advocacy groups and enhances understanding of the unique issues surrounding discrimination against the class. However, there are significant corollary dangers—of creating sections that are captive to interest groups and of heightening competition among protected groups. Such an organizational plan seems inconsistent with the goal of national unity, and it has generally been reserved for exceptional circumstances such as a statute protecting only one group. Congress itself has not favored creation of specialized organizations devoted to particular protected classes. For example, unlike the United Kingdom, which has established separate enforcement mechanisms under its Race Relations Act and its Sex Discrimination Act, Congress gave the Department of Justice and EEOC the power to enforce Title VII as to all protected classes.[47]

Direct Managers to Adhere to Priorities

As a supplement or replacement for organizing around priorities, the agency may dictate to managers that they follow set priorities or meet defined goals. This technique burgeoned during the Johnson administration and has been employed in varying degrees since that time. For example, as part of the 1967 reorganization of the Civil Rights Division, Assistant Attorney General John Doar created an Office of Planning and Coordination,[48] which was to "serve as the program planning staff for the five geographic areas . . . [,] submit enforcement programs for one or two years duration for schools, northern and southern, voting, employment, etc." This office would also "supervise and coordinate litigation in each section . . . review the appellate briefs [and] . . . synthesize policy studies."[49]

Doar's successor, Stephen J. Pollak, defined the office's duties as including "planning the litigation program" and "assuring that the work of the Division is making progress toward the goals and priorities established by its program." The 1967 reorganization's "retention of the geographic form of organization" was said to make "coordination of the litigation program . . . imperative," and the department's adoption of the Planned Program Budgeting System was said to create "a need for detailed and systematic planning and preparation of the Program Memorandum."[50]

In another set of directives, in 1967 and 1968 the sections were told to devote 35 percent of their resources to employment, 20 percent to schools, 15 percent to voting, 15 percent to criminal, 10 percent to Title VI, and 5 percent to public accommodations and facilities.[51] When Attorney General Ramsey Clark and Commissioner of Education Harold Howe agreed that urban school desegregation outside the Deep South should be a high priority, the Office of Planning and Coordination worked with the geographic sections to stress school desegregation in northern and border states, with the result that new suits or interventions were brought in Indianapolis, Indiana, Pasadena, California, Tulsa, Oklahoma, and East St. Louis and South Holland, Illinois.[52]

Even after the adoption of functional organization, the division continued this sort of prioritization. The 1974 program objective submission for fiscal year 1976, based on "mission elements," listed twenty separate program objectives and allocated stated amounts of resources to each.[53] For example, the Education Section proposed four program objectives, with the first, promoting elimination of discrimination in public elementary and secondary schools, allocated twenty-one "man-years" for 1976. Objective 3, to which twenty-two "man-years" were allocated, was to enforce Title VII against educational institutions; objective 4 (seventeen "man-years") was to promote compliance with court orders in education cases; and objective 5 (eighteen "man-years") was to promote nondiscrimination in higher education.[54] The program objective statement also contained milestones by which to gauge the success of the program managers in meeting the objective.[55]

The section chiefs, normally selected based on their abilities as litigators and managers and who in turn report to deputy assistant attorneys general, are in a position to exert great influence on the line attorneys. Like Antitrust Division section chiefs, they "wield an authority of expertise rather than only the authority of office."[56] They decide on initial assignments and review investigative requests, recommendations to file suit, proposed briefs and pleadings, and litigative strategies.

The deputy assistant attorney general position at one time was apolitical. For example, John Doar began his career in that position under a Republican administration and was retained by the Kennedy administration; during the Nixon administration, several career lawyers were advanced to deputy assistant attorneys general. However, a majority of the deputy assistant attorneys general in the Reagan, Bush, and Clinton administrations have been political appointees, which may put them in a position to speak more authoritatively about administration policies. Those individuals, while normally able and sometimes having some background in civil rights law, tend to wield the authority of office rather than of expertise. Their effectiveness depends in part on the length of their tenure; many view the job as a stepping-stone to higher office and therefore do not stay long enough to leave a lasting mark.

Priorities within the division may be enforced by use of the justification memorandum (referred to as the J-memo), which has been the primary instrument for making individual litigation decisions; at times a J-memo is also required prior to commencing a full investigation. The J-memo typically outlines the factual and legal case, potential defenses, and also addresses how the proposed investigation or litigation fits within the department's priorities. The lawyer assigned to the matter initially drafts the J-memo, and the section chief or deputy section chief decides whether to forward a recommendation to the supervising deputy assistant attorney general. The J-memo may go through several layers of review and revision before being presented to the assistant attorney general. In some cases the assistant attorney general may sign off on the case, in others the attorney general signs off. At every step of the way, the decision maker may consider priorities, the factual and legal merits, and litigation policy.

The relation of the J-memo to priorities was explicit in a directive of Assistant Attorney General Pollak relating to southern school desegregation cases. He had instructed that normally the Department of Health, Education, and Welfare's administrative enforcement of Title VI of the Civil Rights Act of 1964 should be preferred over the filing of suit under Title IV of the act.[57] He required attorneys recommending the filing of such a suit to "include in the justification memorandum a paragraph setting forth the present status of HEW proceedings, if any, and discussing any problems that may exist under our coordination policies by the initiation of a suit."[58]

A supplemental control point comes at the appellate stage of litigation. In order for the division to take an appeal or participate as amicus curiae, it must obtain authorization from the solicitor general. The memorandum from the assistant attorney general to the solicitor general (the S.G. memo) recommending appeal or amicus participation is, in effect, an appellate J-memo. Not only does this mechanism ensure that appeals conform with departmental objectives, but the assistant attorney general's review of the S.G. memo allows for honing of legal and policy points.

The solicitor general normally defers to the program objectives of the division but takes an independent look at the legal issues. If the assistant attorney general and the solicitor general have divergent policy views, the solicitor general has authority to overrule the assistant attorney general's recommendation. For example, at the very end of the Bush administration, the assistant attorney general of the Civil Rights Division, John Dunne, recommended supporting African-

American litigants in two cases under the Voting Rights Act. Solicitor General Kenneth Starr not only refused to follow this recommendation but filed briefs supporting the substantive arguments of the southern political subdivisions that were defending the cases. Dunne commented: "We fought our battle, and the decision has been made. You can't win them all."[59]

The solicitor general does not, however, have the last word. In a very few instances the division has successfully asked the attorney general to overrule the solicitor general's tentative decision. For example, in 1975 Assistant Attorney General J. Stanley Pottinger proposed filing an amicus curiae brief in the U.S. Court of Appeals for the Fifth Circuit, arguing that juveniles confined as delinquents have a constitutional right to rehabilitative treatment. This was a controversial position, potentially affecting many components of the criminal justice system, and Solicitor General Robert Bork concluded that he should not authorize the filing. Assistant Attorney General Pottinger appealed to Attorney General Edward Levi, who convened a meeting of all interested department entities and concluded that the filing should be authorized. Solicitor General Bork then signed the requisite authorization slip and the brief was filed.[60] Such intervention by the attorney general, however, is rare.

For most of the life of the division—its first ten years, from 1957 to 1967, and from 1974 to the present—an Appellate Section has supervised its appellate work. Close review of the work of the Appellate Section provides another point of control for the assistant attorney general, to whom the chief of the Appellate Section reported for several years rather than following the command structure that applied to the other litigating sections whose chiefs reported to a deputy assistant attorney general.[61] Assistant Attorney General Reynolds reorganized the division, adding more political deputies and having the chief of the Appellate Section report through one of them.[62]

It is difficult to gauge the effectiveness of the efforts to articulate and impose precise priorities in a law enforcement agency. No doubt the effort devoted to developing the priorities serves to inculcate an increased consciousness in program managers. The priorities typically are developed cooperatively by the political appointees (assistant attorney general and staff) and the civil service managers and staff. I am unaware of any evidence that the division has systematically judged manager performance in accordance with the program objectives; nonetheless, no good reason appears to bar such evaluation.

LITIGATION VERSUS OTHER DUTIES

As mentioned above, Congress and the president have assigned a variety of non-litigative duties to the Civil Rights Division. The various duties under the Voting Rights Act, of preclearance of voting changes and appointment of federal examiners and observers, have received a high priority. Preclearance is a nondiscretionary duty, and the workload is largely a function of decisions of persons outside the department—the decisions of covered states and subdivisions to change voting standards, practices, or procedures. A cadre of paraprofessionals performs much of the initial analysis of preclearance submissions, but review of proposed objections under Section 5 requires attention at the highest levels of the division. Paraprofessionals also make initial determinations of eligibility for redress for persons who were confined during World War II, but some high-level attention must be paid to resolution of legal ambiguities regarding eligibility. The coordination of enforcement of various civil rights statutes is assigned to a staff composed primarily of paraprofessionals, as are many of the nonlitigative duties under the Americans with Disabilities Act.

It is unrealistic to suppose that most nonlitigative responsibilities will receive a high priority in the Civil Rights Division. Because litigation involves concrete, immediate, and often high-profile issues demanding time-consuming efforts, the leadership of the division has little choice but to devote substantial time to it. Although some nonlitigation duties, such as administering Section 5 of the Voting Rights Act, are similarly concrete, important, and time-bound, others, such as coordination of enforcement by other agencies, are not. The Voting Rights responsibilities arguably are closely related to the litigation program, but the other nonlitigative duties bear a more remote relationship to litigation. Historically, the leadership of the division has been willing to seek resources for the nonlitigative duties but not to devote significant high-level review to their implementation.[63]

EMERGENCIES

Ordinary organizational lines have proved inadequate during times of emergency, which have been of two varieties. The common usage of the word applies to unforeseen crises that tax normal government resources, such as the violent reaction to the Freedom Rides, the violence that accompanied desegregation of the University of Mississippi and Central High School in Little Rock, and the killing of civil rights workers in Mississippi in the summer of 1964. Another usage refers to any large-scale, temporary need that cannot be met with normal resources, such as the passage of the Civil Rights Act of 1964 and the Voting Rights Act of 1965 or the first elections held under the Voting Rights Act in 1966.

The ability to respond to an emergency requires a willingness to cross organizational lines. Attorney General Kennedy's management style enabled "the *ad hoc* dispatch of an army of free-lance pragmatists," employing the best attorneys from the tax, antitrust, civil, and criminal divisions to apply their expertise to civil rights emergencies.[64] Similarly, after the attack on marchers at the Edmund Pettus Bridge in Selma, President Johnson sent "more than seventy United States Government officials, including FBI agents, Justice Department lawyers, Gover-

nor Collins [head of the Community Relations Service], [and] the Assistant Attorney General Mr. John Doar."[65]

Within the Civil Rights Division emergencies have also led to the relaxation
of organizational lines. For example, in May 1966, Alabama for the first time
in this century conducted elections in which substantial numbers of African
Americans were registered to vote. Assistant Attorney General John Doar deployed his troops in a way that gave new meaning to the word "general" in his
title. He decided to "use these elections as a pilot project for programming and
accomplishing effective enforcement of the Voting Rights Act of 1965."[66] To that
end he mobilized lawyers from throughout the division, ignoring the geographic
organization that was then in place. Each lawyer was assigned to a designated
county and was told that "in the event that legal proceedings are required in the
county to which you are assigned, you will be expected to handle them" with the
support of the geographic section normally assigned to Alabama. The lawyers
were told to give this assignment priority over their normal work and to "keep
your Section Chief advised of the time that you are spending on this project, so
that he may properly compensate for this through the use of other attorneys."

Not only did Doar breach the division's organizational lines, but he also expected the attorneys to perform essentially investigative work—to "use your
eyes and your ears. You will be expected to know the details of how local elections are conducted. . . . With respect to the Negro interviewees, you should try
to see the election process through the eyes of the local Black Belt Negro who
will be voting for the first time. . . . You will need to look at the various polling
places in the county." Attorneys were told to "leave on Thursday, March 3rd, and
spend from Friday through Tuesday in your assigned counties,"[67] where they
were to interview the probate judge and other local officials and examine voting
records.

Doar moved his troops around for the duration of the project as different
needs arose. For example, although I was assigned to monitor Birmingham elections, I spent the week prior to the election in Selma and Montgomery. Around
midnight, after the polls had closed, I was called to come to Selma to help draft
the complaint in *United States v. Executive Committee of the Democratic Party of
Dallas County.*[68] Also working on the complaint was Lou Kauder, who had not
been one of the twenty-five attorneys initially assigned to the election project.
Our supervisor was the assistant attorney general for the Civil Division, John
Douglas, who slept on the office floor so that we could awaken him as we completed drafts for his review. The next morning we applied for and received an
order preserving the election records, and the following day our complaint was
filed. A trial team was immediately assembled, headed by John Rosenberg, a lawyer normally assigned to Mississippi. The favorable court ruling, after a two-day
trial, was rendered on May 24, 1966, twenty days after the election.

Strict adherence to organizational lines would have led to a far different sce-
nario in Alabama in 1966. Fewer attorneys would have been available to attend

to the election issues. Less experienced attorneys would have been assigned to some responsibilities. Only one assistant attorney general would have been available instead of the four who covered that election. The division's ability to move quickly when irregularities occurred in Dallas County would have been impaired. The division undoubtedly paid a price for breaching organizational lines. Although John Doar's memorandum instructed the attorneys that "you should be able to keep up with your regular work as well," that instruction seems overly optimistic. Inevitably other meritorious suits would at least have been delayed. But Doar's perception that the Alabama elections were the "Division's most important project in the immediate future" was probably correct, and the temporary shuffling of personnel served that high priority well.

The Civil Rights Division has always been a relatively small enforcement agency. The growth of its budget has not kept pace with the growth of its responsibilities. The division works most efficiently if its leadership articulates priorities. Those priorities reflect both the law, which is relatively stable, and the policies of each administration, which are changeable. Race must continue to rank at the top of the division's enforcement priorities. External events, such as broad compliance or noncompliance with a law, affect priorities. The leadership of the department has employed a variety of techniques to ensure that the division's performance is consistent with priorities. A combination of organizational structure, leadership, and flexibility can lead to the successful execution of priorities.

8

Litigation Policy

Litigation policy refers to the selection of cases to litigate and the establishment of substantive positions. Thousands of potential cases could be brought by the Civil Rights Division. What leads the division to bring one case and not another? Often substantive positions are established by case law or statute; however, just as often the case law and statute are ambiguous. What considerations should guide the department in resolving those ambiguities? What role should be played by the pursuit of core values, precedent, desires of interest groups, practicality, other federal agencies, comity to state government?

Litigation policy in the division is shaped by a complex and changeable calculus. The core value of nondiscrimination should be and normally is the starting point. Prior division positions and case and statutory law strongly influence policy decisions. Litigants and their supporters lobby the attorney general, solicitor general, and assistant attorney general for civil rights, and sometimes even the president, to take positions favoring particular sides. They may be joined in that effort by members of Congress or by other federal agencies. The Civil Rights Commission writes reports on civil rights issues and recommends that various enforcement measures be taken. Overarching administration policies are articulated by presidents and their subordinates, and the division is expected to pay heed to them. Obviously the weight of each of these possible influences may vary from issue to issue and from one administration to the next.

The existence of these competing influences is one of several factors that necessarily lead the department to formulate positions in a manner different from private litigants, states as litigants, or the federal courts. The department's client is the United States. It is a law enforcement organization, so that its starting place in any litigation is how best to enforce the law. Therefore, it must look for violations of the law and does so within the context of the priorities it has set. Other lawyers take as their starting point the litigation objectives of their clients, and those objectives may or may not correspond with law enforcement. The lawyer for a private litigant is most concerned with the question of whether the chances of success in the litigation outweigh the probable monetary costs. Although the department also considers costs and chances of success, neither factor is likely to weigh as heavily as it might to a private litigant.

The department differs as well from federal courts, which are meant only to apply the law in a neutral fashion. The courts often do not give the same weight to priorities or to costs of litigation as the litigants. Although neither the department nor the courts are to close their eyes to violations of the law, only the department is meant to seek them out. The courts have been called the least dangerous branch,[1] primarily because they lack the power to initiate litigation.

The department is an institution expected to pursue the public interest, while private litigants pursue private and often narrow agendas. With an attorney general appointed by the president with the advice and consent of the Senate, as is the assistant attorney general for civil rights, the department is in that sense majoritarian. State governments as litigants represent the majority views within the state; when their positions collide with federal law or the Constitution they are, in a national sense, countermajoritarian. Federal judges hold lifetime tenure and are accountable only to the Constitution and laws of the United States. When they hold a law of the United States unconstitutional, their action is countermajoritarian.

The majoritarian feature of federal civil rights enforcement is at once a strength and a weakness. The views of the United States as a litigator carry great moral force in part because of the belief that they are grounded in the will of the majority. Perhaps this is one reason why the Supreme Court often requests the views of the United States in discrimination cases and frequently also relies on those views in reaching decisions. For example, the Court sought the views of the United States on reargument in *Brown v. Board of Education* and again at the remedy stage of that case.[2] In the first major private Voting Rights Act case, both the Court and the dissent referred explicitly to the amicus curiae brief of the United States.[3] Although it would be unrealistic to expect the department not to respond affirmatively in some degree to majority sentiment, the Constitution itself restrains shifting majorities, and a Department of Justice that is overly responsive to the majority of the moment may fail in its broader mission.

Federal courts traditionally have relied on the Department of Justice because of its overall credibility, which depends on its careful selection of cases and maintenance of high standards of legal analysis, fact development, and probity. The internal standard for initiating litigation is unstated but is undoubtedly more stringent than "probable cause."[4] Errors, whether legal or tactical, may inflict political costs in addition to the loss of credibility in the courts. For example, the unauthorized loan of a rental car by a department attorney to Dr. Martin Luther King in 1963 led to a temporary setback in the level of public trust of the department during a racially tense period in Alabama.[5] The last-minute delay in school desegregation that the department sought and received in Mississippi in

1969, many years after *Brown v. Board of Education,* may have damaged the department's credibility in the Supreme Court[6] and courts of the Fifth Circuit as well as in the civil rights community. Because more is expected of the Department of Justice, error by the department is more costly than error by other litigants. The costs of significant errors by the department are seen in the diminution of its credibility after episodes such as the *Bob Jones* case, where early in the Reagan administration, the department abandoned its defense of an Internal Revenue Service nondiscrimination requirement after the Supreme Court agreed to hear the case.[7]

The desire to avoid error could lead the department into an overabundance of caution. If the department is to advance broad national policies of nondiscrimination, it must continually address the new issues of the day and must risk losing cases in doing so. Owen Fiss has suggested that in the 1960s the Civil Rights Division "was not just receiving the decisions of the 1950's, but it was also formulating new principles and ideas to realize the ambition and aspirations of racial justice."[8] To lose a case differs from the errors described above; the *Bob Jones* and *Alexander* errors stemmed precisely from the failure to give sufficient weight to the "ambition and aspirations of racial justice." As is developed in the case histories below, the division's exploration of frontiers abated in the 1970s. A question for the future is whether the department should try to reverse the direction taken by some of the case law rather than simply accepting it.

Statutory and constitutional ambiguity pose for the department the question of how to frame positions in cases arising under such ambiguous laws. Should the department routinely resolve ambiguity in favor of the racial minority? Should it adopt one of the theoretical approaches and pursue that approach in all cases? If so, which approach should it adopt? Should the department seek to find some middle ground? To what extent should political winds determine the direction of department positions? The difficulty, as Burke Marshall has pointed out, is that "the position of the Department of Justice on such matters as busing, school district consolidation, and affirmative action plans does not flow from neutral principles."[9]

Congress enacted the civil rights laws to address a compelling national problem—the racial caste system—yet while embracing nondiscrimination as a national value, it failed to provide a clear definition of discrimination and failed to choose between competing theories of equality. Those theories have variously been characterized as pitting results versus opportunity, impact versus intent, class versus classification, group rights versus individual rights, and color-conscious remediation versus color blindness. Congress did self-consciously choose the results approach in the Voting Rights Act, and the Supreme Court has inferred a similar approach in Title VII. However, Congress carefully avoided taking a position on the results approach in fair housing cases, and the Court has inferred an intent approach under the Reconstruction civil rights laws[10] and Title VI, although allowing effects regulations to enforce Title VI.[11] Looming over these statutory issues are parallel issues under the equal protection clause of the Fourteenth Amendment to the Constitution.

Some methods for approaching the task of answering the questions that must be answered in dealing with statutory and constitutional ambiguity are needed. First, the department should remember that both the Civil War amendments to the Constitution and the civil rights laws were enacted primarily to guarantee African Americans an equal place in American society. In *Strauder v. West Virginia,* the Supreme Court noted that the Fourteenth Amendment was designed to ensure "in regard to the colored race, for whose protection the amendment was primarily designed, that no discrimination shall be made against them by law because of their color."[12] The Court later reached a similar conclusion about the Civil Rights Act of 1964: "Congress' primary concern in enacting the prohibition against racial discrimination in Title VII [of the Civil Rights Act of 1964] was with the plight of the Negro in our economy."[13] Although the Constitution and statutes are phrased largely in classification terms (e.g., "on account of race"), they were enacted in response to a demonstrated need to protect the class whose rights were being denied (e.g., African Americans). The Civil Rights Division was established to further those rights. These facts suggest that as a starting principle, ambiguity should be resolved in favor of the traditionally disfavored race.

Where congressional intent is clear, the division should normally abide by it, no matter where the chips may fall. However, in addition, Congress selected the department for an enforcement role in part because it perceived that the department could be trusted to understand and weigh competing considerations. The choice of court enforcement by the Department of Justice rather than administrative enforcement by an independent agency evinces a preference for the exercise of discretion rather than the application of "one size fits all" rules.

Administration policy should also play a role in setting positions but not at the expense of the primary mission of the division. An administration might, as was the case under President Reagan, believe that some forms of affirmative action are inconsistent with the objectives of the civil rights laws. It might therefore resolve genuine ambiguities to take that policy into account. However, it should not invent ambiguities to suit its agenda. For example, although Section 706(g) of the fair employment law authorizes the district court "to order such affirmative action as may be appropriate" in cases where an employer has unlawfully discriminated, the Reagan administration thought the phrase sufficiently ambiguous to justify arguing that the relief must be limited to identified victims of discrimination.[14] The Supreme Court later rejected this position.[15]

Finally, procedural regularity should attend the department's decision making, because, as Justice Frankfurter has noted, it generates "the feeling, so important to a popular government, that justice has been done."[16] Procedural regularity in the department includes both internal and external regularity. Internal regularity requires department procedures to be followed and assures that both the political appointees and the civil servants are appropriately involved in decision making, as described in Chapter 9. External regularity allows competing interests to make their views known to the department through proper direct channels and excludes the use of improper back channels, because real or perceived favoritism undermines the department's credibility.

In an important example of perceived external irregularity, the District Court in the recent Georgia congressional redistricting case believed that the department "was more accessible—and amenable—to the opinions of the ACLU than to those of the Attorney General of the State of Georgia" during Section 5 review of the redistricting and also found the testimony of Justice Department lawyers regarding their contacts with the ACLU "less than credible."[17] The court may also have been influenced by an additional, though not expressed, belief that partisan politics tainted the attorney general's position. The Section 5 review occurred during the Bush administration, which despite its general opposition to race-based decision making evidently insisted that the legislature draw three majority African-American congressional districts. Similar objections were lodged in several other southern states. It has been noted that creating such districts has the incidental effect of enhancing Republican voting strength in many of the remaining districts.[18] The Supreme Court noted the district court's "sharp criticism of the Justice Department for its use of partisan advocates in its dealings with state officials and for its close cooperation with the ACLU's vigorous advocacy of minority district maximization."[19] The perception that the department engaged in improper favoritism seems likely to have influenced the Supreme Court to credit the district court's characterization of department policy as one of "maximizing majority-black districts," even though the department, insisting that "the Section 5 process is tailored to the specifics of each case, and no general requirement of maximization—or of proportionality—is imposed,"[20] explicitly disavowed the "max-black" policy.[21]

SELECTING APPROPRIATE CASES

Once priorities are set, case selection should further them. Under most civil rights statutes, the department exercises discretion in deciding which cases to pursue.[22] The department relies on several obvious sources for its presuit investigations: complaints from individuals or organizations, news articles, statistics, and referrals from other federal agencies. In addition, beginning with a policy initated by John Doar soon after he was hired as the first deputy to the assistant attorney general in July 1960, the Civil Rights Division developed cases through intensive field investigation by division attorneys who became intimately familiar with conditions in the southern counties and parishes they visited.[23] This technique was compatible with the style of the Kennedy administration, which brought "a new emphasis on action. Civil Rights Division attorneys abandoned their Washington offices for the field, heading South to enforce voting rights legislation."[24]

Complaints are an important stimulus for cases, but they do not automatically result in department action because they may not match priorities. Whether complaints received correspond with priorities depends on a number of factors, including the extent to which potential complainants are aware that the department may be able to help them and are willing to seek that help, with their willingness in turn depending on their feelings of vulnerability and on their perception that the department will be responsive. Often private civil rights organizations may be the source of complaints, and their priorities do not always correspond with those of the department. Moreover, many complaints either do not raise issues over which the division has jurisdiction, are facially without merit, or prove meritless upon investigation.[25]

A large volume of complaints regarding one alleged law violator may be suggestive of systemic discrimination.[26] News articles are also a useful but sporadic source of investigative leads, because it is often the systemic or high-impact nature of the discrimination that rendered it newsworthy.[27] Statistics are extremely helpful in pinpointing high-impact potential investigations. For example, after Congress amended Title VII to cover employment practices of school systems, the department reviewed census reports and EEOC statistical reports in metropolitan areas with large African-American populations. It found that in the St. Louis area half the teachers in the largest school system were African American, while several of the surrounding systems employed almost no African-American teachers. It investigated several of those systems and found substantial evidence of racial discrimination and then sued the Hazelwood, Ladue, and Ferguson school systems based on that information, ultimately obtaining relief in all three cases.

The department continues to employ this methodology. However, appropriate statistics are not easily obtainable as to some types of discrimination. For example, although the fair employment laws require employers to "make and keep such records relevant to the determinations of whether unlawful employment practices have been or are being committed,"[28] no such provision appears in the Fair Housing Act. A constant thrust of the department's legislative efforts has been to obtain better access to information regarding possible violations of the civil rights laws.[29] The department's range of discretion is limited by the lack of information regarding possible violations.[30]

Referrals to the Department of Justice from other agencies cover a spectrum. At one end are Section 706 cases referred by the EEOC, which involve individual claims that a state or local government has discriminated. Their place in the division's priorities is not much different from that of complaints received directly from individuals. In the middle are referrals of systemic cases by agencies with authority to investigate housing and credit discrimination and the like. Ideally the department works with those agencies to ensure that the referrals will correspond with jointly established priorities. The department also receives referrals of cases under Title VI of the 1964 act and Title IX of the education amendments. These are cases that client agencies are requesting the department to bring on their behalf; therefore, something akin to an attorney-client relationship may be said to exist. Finally, the so-called housing election cases, in which individuals elect to have the case heard in federal court rather than in an administrative proceeding, are referrals under the Fair Housing Act amendments. Although few of these housing election cases correspond with the priorities of the department, it is apparently required to file them, and to date the department has not challenged this requirement as to arguably meritorious cases, although it *has* returned a few cases to the Department of Housing and Urban Development for additional investigation.[31]

At times the department may find it difficult to develop cases that correspond with priorities. For example, after the passage of the Civil Rights Act of 1964, the Department of Health, Education, and Welfare terminated federal funds for some school systems because they refused to desegregate. The federal interest would be best served by desegregation, not fund termination, so litigation to desegregate those systems assumed a high priority. However, under the act the department could not sue without a written complaint from the parent of a child in the system, a requirement that stood as a barrier to carrying out this priority. Perhaps Congress imposed the complaint requirement for a reason, and the department should not have adopted a priority that ignored that requirement, but few persons would believe that Congress intended for school systems to operate both without federal funds and in violation of the Constitution.

A similar problem confronted the Reagan administration when it first took office. It was concerned that its desire to deregulate was thwarted by the perceived tendency of federal agencies to adopt regulations that went much further than the law. Searching for a vehicle to carry the deregulation position, it discovered that the Supreme Court had already granted certiorari in *Bob Jones University v. United States,* in which the university was challenging a regulation of the Internal Revenue Service that denied tax-exempt status to racially discriminatory educational institutions.[32] Although the United States had previously supported the Internal Revenue Service's antidiscrimination regulation in the case, the desire for a vehicle to advance deregulation overcame the prior policy of nondiscrimination as well as the unanimous advice of career attorneys throughout the government, including the Treasury Department, the Tax Division of the Department of Justice, the Civil Rights Division's Appellate Section, and the solicitor general's office. In what has been rightly characterized as "a public policy debacle," the department filed a brief reversing position.[33] The Supreme Court ruled against the administration's position by upholding the government regulation.

Selection of appropriate cases for amicus participation raises some distinct questions, and the division has sporadically adopted and followed general guidelines for such participation. They provide that "our participation will be limited" to cases "where the Court requests our participation" and those raising issues related to the department's enforcement authority or some other "special federal interest."[34] A later memorandum repeating these criteria adds, "There will, of course, be instances not fitting the above criteria where *amicus* participation should nevertheless be considered."[35] Implicit in those criteria is a judgment that the United States will participate as amicus in some cases in which it has no statutory interest, especially if requested by the court to do so.

The Civil Rights Division may not participate as amicus unless authorized to do so by the solicitor general. Participation both as an amicus and as a party is primarily conducted by the solicitor general when cases reach the Supreme Court. The above criteria for amicus participation are internal to the Civil Rights Division but probably state fairly the considerations that the solicitor general applies to requests for authorization to participate as amicus.[36] The government's second brief in *Brown* was filed at the request of the Supreme Court, and the Civil Rights Division has participated as amicus in numerous cases at the request of U.S. district courts, despite the lack of clear-cut statutory interest. For example, the department became a "litigating" amicus, with the rights of a party in several school desegregation cases, at the request of federal district courts.[37]

The solicitor general, or S.G., controls not only the decision whether to participate but also the final shape of the government's argument. The S.G. receives recommendations from litigating divisions in the department as well as from affected government agencies and pays deference to these recommendations, especially those from within the Department of Justice. However, the solicitor general, who has the last word, also considers the legal analyses of the career staff within the solicitor's office and the policy views of the president and attorney general. In any administration it would not be out of the ordinary to find the S.G. overruling the litigating division.

The process that the S.G. follows is well described in Solicitor General Wade McCree's motion seeking leave for the United States to file an amicus curiae brief in the *Bakke* case. As soon as the Court decided to hear the case, "the Department promptly solicited the views of the many federal agencies whose programs and enforcement responsibilities might be affected." After receiving the views of the agencies, the Civil Rights Division recommended participation, and the S.G.'s staff agreed with that recommendation. Only after "a series of discussions concerning the case" did McCree authorize the drafting of a brief. The Civil Rights Division prepared a draft brief, and McCree's assistants "made suggestions and revisions in that draft" and gave McCree a new draft, which was then circulated to the agencies for discussion. Heated discussions ensued, and in the end Solicitor General McCree, Assistant Attorney General Days, and several of their assistants (I was one of them) spent several days and nights together in a conference room rewriting the brief, which was filed in September 1977. It is alleged that officials in the White House attempted to influence the content of the brief. If that was so, those of us in the career staff who participated in that exercise were well insulated from the White House pressure.[38]

When the United States' participation in a case in which it has no statutory interest responds to a request from a court, arguably the government acts as a true amicus. However, when it participates *sua sponte*, it is more analogous to an intervenor because it is participating to advance either a statutory interest or a priority of the administration. Such a use of the amicus role arguably conflicts with Congress's decision not to adopt Part 3 legislation. One response to this criticism is that the power to serve as an amicus is less subject to abuse than the power to initiate litigation since an amicus may only participate in already existing litigation. Another is that the United States may have an articulable interest even in cases that do not affect particular statutes. For example, it was legitimate for the Truman administration to file as amicus in *Shelley v. Kraemer*[39] because as a section of its brief argued, "Enforcement of racial restrictive covenants is contrary to the public policy of the United States."[40]

ESTABLISHING LITIGATION POSITIONS

The principal litigation objective of the Civil Rights Division, broadly speaking, is to secure the civil rights created by the Constitution and laws of the United States. This objective arguably warrants liberal construction of the law to maximize those rights. There is a tension between two objectives of the Reconstruction amendments and the civil rights laws: to forbid certain types of classifications and to protect certain classes. The primary and immediate motivation for enacting the Reconstruction amendments and the civil rights laws was to solve the problem of discrimination against members of groups such as African Americans, Hispanics, women, and the disabled. However, with the exception of the laws protecting the disabled, the nondiscrimination laws do more than forbid discrimination against those protected groups. For example, they ban discrimination based on race, which encompasses discrimination against African Americans but also against members of other racial groups. These more broadly applicable protections enshrine as a second objective the nondiscrimination principle as to the enumerated classes. Moreover, Congress entrusted enforcement to the attorney general in part because of a perception that she would exercise that authority responsibly, with due regard for competing values such as fairness to affected groups, comity, and workability.

Infrequently, litigation positions in enforcement actions are dictated from above by the president or the attorney general. More typically, the Department of Justice has shaped litigation positions through the use of two principal techniques. First, its decisions are often forged with quasi common law tools,[41] that is, litigation positions are determined by fact-intensive analysis and reliance on precedent and tend to evolve incrementally. As Oliver Wendell Holmes noted, the common law technique relies heavily on experience.[42] It is case-specific rather than general in scope and often favors narrow arguments as the department attempts to convince a court to adopt a specific position.

The advantages of the common law technique include its facial syllogistic style, its ability to recognize and accommodate competing values, and its grounding in reality. Weaknesses include the illusoriness of its syllogisms and the survival of precedents "long after the use they once served is at an end and the reason for them has been forgotten."[43] Both sides of the coin are reflected in civil rights law. For example, as one of the case histories later in this chapter demonstrates, the standards for southern school desegregation evolved in a careful, rational, but very slow manner, with each decision building on earlier cases and on experience. However, the "all deliberate speed" doctrine of *Brown II* in 1955 held irrational sway until 1969, long past the time when the articulated reasons for it might have justified delay.

The second technique the department has employed is reliance on regulations and guidelines of other federal agencies with responsibilities under the civil rights acts—administrative law. As the principal attorney for the United States, the department has an obligation to defend the tenable positions of other agencies when they are at issue in litigation. Moreover, most administrations have sought cooperation among agencies in civil rights enforcement. Regulations and guidelines differ greatly from the common law. Although agencies may attempt to base them on facts and precedents, regulations and guidelines are generally written at a higher level of abstraction than judicial opinions and are meant not so much to respond to the facts of a particular case as to govern conduct generally. They stem from the exercise of specialized agency expertise rather than from the generalists who sit on the bench.

Change by regulations is more likely to be sweeping in contrast to incremental common law change. The courts normally exercise deference to agency rule making, so that the government is held to a lesser burden in attempting to sustain a regulation than when it tries to convince the court to adopt a "common law" type of rule.[44] Agency regulations and guidelines with respect to civil rights normally will coincide with the department's views, because the Office of Legal Counsel and the Civil Rights Division usually will have reviewed the regulations and guidelines before the agency finally adopted them.[45]

These two disparate techniques, reliance on common law and reliance on administrative law, play complementary roles in the Justice Department's adoption of litigation positions. Other determinants also claim a role in position setting: the underlying values of the civil rights laws and the evolving political pressures from the president, Congress, and interest groups. A final complication is the relationship between positions in the trial court and in the appellate courts, especially the Supreme Court. The litigating divisions normally decide trial court positions, though the attorney general may play a role in very high-visibility or policy-sensitive cases. However, not only may the solicitor general veto the taking of a government appeal, but that official also dictates the government's position in Supreme Court cases. Often a sort of minilitigation occurs in which various government agencies and private litigants try to influence the solicitor general to deviate from or follow the position taken by the litigating division in the lower courts.

Even when, as is normally the case, the solicitor general follows the litigating division's position taken in the lower courts, he may articulate the position in a different manner. For example, the Civil Rights Division had opposed dissolving a desegregation decree in Pasadena, California; Solicitor General Bork's argument in the Supreme Court supporting the division's position surprisingly opined that "if, as petitioners have represented, they have complied with the District Court's order during the intervening two years, they will probably be entitled to a lifting of the District Court's order in its entirety."[46] This opinion represented a new twist in the case and one at odds with the views of the division.

The following two case studies illustrate how the department develops litigation positions: the effects test under Title VII and southern school desegregation. The first case study demonstrates the impact of these techniques and forces on the department's position as to how to prove a violation of the civil rights laws; the second studies their impact on the department's position on matters of relief.

Case Study: Griggs

The interplay of common law technique and reliance on regulations and guidelines is well illustrated by the development of the department's position in *Griggs v. Duke Power Co.*[47] and subsequent cases. In *Griggs* black employees challenged the employer's rule that applicants for transfer to formerly all-white jobs be high school graduates or pass certain general intelligence tests. The lower courts had upheld the rule, finding that the employer had lacked discriminatory motive in adopting it. The department, together with the EEOC, participated in the case as amicus curiae, both in the court of appeals and, at the invitation of the Court, in the Supreme Court.[48] According to the counsel for the plaintiffs, Department of Justice lawyers had thought *Griggs* was a weak case on the testing issue and advised against appealing it.[49] Once the plaintiffs presented the issue to the Supreme Court, however, the United States filed a brief urging the Court to hear the case "to review the issue of the use of aptitude tests and general education requirements as conditions for employment and transfer which disqualify a disproportionate number of blacks and which are not shown to be predictive of job performance."[50]

The department had, in a series of voting rights cases, developed the important doctrine that facially neutral policies that perpetuate the effects of past discrimination are themselves unlawfully discriminatory; for example, *United States v. Louisiana* held that black applicants for voter registration could not be subjected to more onerous requirements than had in the past been applied to white applicants.[51] This ruling became known as "freezing relief" because it froze in place the prior white standard. In a case where the right to vote was "a simple corollary of citizenship . . . exclusively enjoyed by the white people of" Panola County, Mississippi, the court of appeals froze "in effect, at least temporarily, those requirements for qualification to vote, which were in effect, to the benefit of others, at the time the Negroes were being discriminated against."[52] A related rule evolved in school desegregation cases, which required school districts to adopt desegregation plans designed to eradicate the racially separate patterns of enrollment established by past policies.[53] The voting rule simply applied to one race the standards that already applied to the other, while the school desegregation rule required restructuring of the school system. The two rules are linked by their dependence on the notion of overcoming the effects of past discrimination.

In the first Title VII cases to reach the appellate courts, the United States successfully transferred this doctrine to the Title VII context. Its argument was in harmony with a recommendation of the Kerner Commission in 1968 that "artificial barriers to employment and promotion must be removed."[54] Two years after issuance of the Kerner Commission report, the court in *Local 53, International Association of Heat and Frost Insulators v. Vogler,* relying in part on *United States v. Louisiana,* upheld affirmative action relief and held that a nepotism practice discriminated.[55] Judge John Minor Wisdom subsequently relied on *Vogler, United States v. Louisiana,* and earlier voting and school desegregation cases in holding that where an employee selection device perpetuates the effects of past discrimination the controlling issue is "business necessity."[56] He cited *Vogler* for the proposition that "when an employer or union has discriminated in the past and when its present policies renew or exaggerate discriminatory effects, those policies must yield, unless there is an overriding legitimate, non-racial business purpose."[57] Judge Wisdom compared the case to *United States v. Louisiana,* where, he said, the court found "a change in system that is apparently fair on its face but in fact freezes into the system advantages to whites and disadvantages to Negroes."[58] After citing seven prior voting and school desegregation cases, he concluded by citing the Supreme Court's decision in a Voting Rights Act case, *Gaston County v. United States,*[59] which he said held that where a test continued the effects of past discrimination "neither the fair administration of the test, nor its legitimate public purpose could save it."[60]

When *Griggs* reached the Supreme Court, there was thus a preexisting body of law, developed largely in Department of Justice litigation, regarding facially neutral employee selection devices such as those used by the Duke Power Company. That body of law focused heavily on the relationship of those devices to past discrimination, but the court of appeals in *Griggs* had already granted relief with respect to "Negroes employed in the Labor Department at a time when there was no high school or test requirement for . . . whites hired contemporaneously."[61] The department's brief treated the lower court precedents as standing for a broader proposition: "An employment practice that appears neutral but has

the effect of discrimination on the basis of race without business necessity is prohibited."[62] That argument in the government's brief relied on common law reasoning, using analogous Supreme Court cases as well as the lower court cases.
For example, the concept of business necessity came from the *Local 189* case.
The brief also carefully developed the factual record which showed that the two
high school and test requirements resulted in virtually all the higher paying jobs
going to white employees, while African-American employees who were as
qualified as incumbent whites were confined to the lowest paying department,
"labor." Yet the evidence failed to show any correlation between these requirements and performance of the jobs. In fact, many satisfactorily performing white
employees did not meet these job requirements, which had been adopted after
they were hired.

The defendants not only argued that discriminatory purpose must be shown
but also argued that Section 703(h) of the act, which provided that "it shall not
be an unlawful employment practice for an employer . . . to give and to act upon
the results of any professionally developed ability test provided that such test, its
administration or action upon the results is not designed, intended, or used to
discriminate because of race, color, religion, sex or national origin," authorized
their use of the tests. The government's brief did not rely on any cases interpreting that section of the act but instead began by arguing that the language of Section 703(h), its legislative history, and EEOC guidelines all precluded "tests
which do not predict success in the jobs for which they are given."[63] The EEOC
had issued a guideline in 1966 that interpreted the words "professionally developed ability test" in Section 703(h) to "mean a test which fairly measures the
knowledge or skills required by the particular job or class of jobs."[64] That guideline did not articulate the "disparate impact" rule but simply "advocated" that
employers use "a total personnel assessment system that is non-discriminatory
within the spirit of the law and places special emphasis on" test validation.[65]
After the Supreme Court granted certiorari, the EEOC elaborated further in
"Guidelines on Employee Selection Procedures,"[66] which the government's brief
also cited for authority. Section 1607.3 of those guidelines adopted the position
stated in the government's brief at the petition stage and provided:

> The use of any test which adversely affects . . . any . . . employment . . . op-
> portunity of classes protected by title VII constitutes discrimination unless:
> (a) the test has been validated and evidences a high degree of utility as
> hereinafter described, and (b) the person giving or acting upon the results
> of the particular test can demonstrate that alternative suitable hiring, trans-
> fer or promotion procedures are unavailable for his use.

The unanimous decision of the Supreme Court followed the government's approach and held that facially neutral selection devices "cannot be maintained if
they operate to 'freeze' the status quo of prior discriminatory employment practices."[67] The Court adopted the business necessity test and held that if such a

selection "cannot be shown to be related to job performance, the practice is prohibited."[68] It accorded "great deference" to the EEOC guidelines.[69] David Rose,
who served as chief of the Civil Rights Division's Employment Litigation Section from 1969 to 1987, has noted that with the Court's decision in *Griggs* "the
initial work of securing interpretation of the substantive provisions of Title VII
was complete."[70]

Some commentators have criticized *Griggs* as inconsistent with Congress's intent,[71] while others have praised it.[72] Congress arguably ratified it in 1972, with
the Senate Report explaining that the extension of Title VII to federal government employment should prompt "a thorough re-examination of [the federal]
testing and qualification program to ensure that the standards enunciated in the
Griggs case are fully met."[73] Congress explicitly adopted the *Griggs* rule in 1991,
in Section 105 of the Civil Rights Act of 1991, which specifically recognizes that
practices with a racially disparate impact are unlawful if the employer "fails to
demonstrate that the challenged practice is job related for the position in question and consistent with business necessity."

Griggs involved a close question of statutory interpretation and continues to
pose important policy issues that were perhaps only dimly perceived in 1970
when the government filed its brief. The two primary issues *Griggs* raises are
whether it "may cause firms to abandon testing and move to more subjective . . .
methods of screening applicants—or, on the other hand, to proportional hiring
on a racial basis in order to avoid charges of discrimination."[74] Note, however,
that subjective selection devices have since been held subject to the *Griggs* rule.[75]

Several factors converged to lead the government to its position in *Griggs,*
which built on prior positions developed by the United States as a litigant both
in employment discrimination cases and in other civil rights cases. Although
Griggs did not follow inescapably from those prior cases, they provided respect-
able support for the government's position. Experience had shown that tests
were subject to abuse and manipulation and tended to perpetuate past discrimination. The disparate impact test of *Griggs* furthered the policies of the fair employment law because absent business necessity, "the two attributes of race that
make it an inappropriate basis for allocating jobs—unrelatedness to productivity
and absence of individual control—also [are] attributes of the criterion in question."[76] The Kerner Commission had proposed a similar rule based on its belief
that it would advance national unity and the EEOC had adopted the rule in its
guidelines, so the department's position supported its normal role as lawyer for
other agencies.[77] The department had begun formulating its position regarding
disparate impact during the Kennedy and Johnson administrations, and the initial EEOC position on testing had been drafted under President Johnson. The
subsequent, more specific EEOC guideline and the department's brief were
drafted by officials of the Nixon administration. The focus on disparate impact was consistent with President Nixon's support for affirmative action requirements in the Philadelphia Plan. In short, the position stemmed from an

amalgam of litigating precedent, core values, views of the Labor Department and EEOC, and presidential policy.

Much Title VII law, as well as law under other civil rights acts, has built on the foundation *Griggs* laid.[78] One critic commented that "the courts and the Equal Employment Opportunity Commission (EEOC) acted as if *Griggs* were a line of scrimmage from which to march the football steadily downfield" and have served "the revisionists' civil rights agenda [which] requires the abandonment of objective standards in order to produce proportional results."[79] The department relied on *Griggs* both in subsequent cases[80] and in joining with other agencies to draft "Uniform Guidelines on Employee Selection Procedures."[81] In one remarkable episode, Solicitor General Bork and Assistant Attorney General Rex Lee of the Civil Division argued in *Washington v. Davis*[82] that *Griggs* governed a claim that the use of a test which disproportionately excluded African-American applicants for police trainee positions in the District of Columbia police department was unconstitutional. The brief was drafted in close consultation with the Civil Rights Division. The solicitor general represented the Civil Service Commission, which had formulated the test being used to determine eligibility for employment as a police cadet and admission to the Police Academy. Although the complaint alleged a violation of the Constitution and had been filed before Title VII applied to the District of Columbia, the brief of the United States, along with the briefs of all other parties, assumed that the *Griggs* standard applied.

At oral argument Justice Lewis Powell raised for the first time the question whether the constitutional standard was identical to the standard that *Griggs* had formulated for statutory cases. Assistant to the Solicitor General Mark Evans replied, "I think that in essence the standards are the same under Title VII as they are under the equal protection concept."[83] There can be no doubt that the prior strong position of the department in support of plaintiffs in *Griggs* and *Albemarle Paper* influenced the solicitor general to make this response despite its adverse implications for the client agency. However, once the Supreme Court ruled in *Washington v. Davis* that the *Griggs* standard did not apply in cases brought under the equal protection clause, the department's approach in cases under the Constitution changed. The year after *Washington v. Davis* the department simply declined to file an amicus brief in a case involving a claim that municipal land-use decisions had an adverse disparate impact on African Americans in the Chicago region, thereby foregoing the opportunity to influence the development of the legal standard.[84]

In *Personnel Administrator v. Feeney*,[85] a challenge to the Massachusetts veterans' preference for state employment as depriving women of equal protection of the laws, the government filed two briefs, one by the solicitor general and one by general counsels of four affected agencies. The veterans' preference had a strong adverse impact on women, but Title VII did not apply because it specifically exempted veterans' preference statutes from its application. The solicitor general argued that the " 'intent' requirement plays an important role in constitutional adjudication," and that "awareness of probable disparate effect is not the same as purposeful discrimination."[86] The emphasis of the general counsels' brief was different. They argued that "in some circumstances, the method chosen by the legislature may be so arbitrary and extreme in effect as to warrant a finding of discriminatory intent."[87] However, all conceded that the *Griggs* standard did not apply.

In sum, the Court took its initial direction in *Griggs* from the department's position, which in turn reinforced the power of the disparate impact standard in determining future departmental positions. Yet, once the Court on its own motion ruled that the standard did not apply to equal protection cases, the department quickly backed off. Because the department defends federal agencies sued for alleged employment discrimination while at the same time acting as plaintiff in other fair employment suits, strong countervailing forces contend in setting the department's position. The Civil Rights Division's preference for the *Griggs* standard initially prevailed, but once *Washington v. Davis* was decided, the solicitor general concluded that federal agencies were entitled to defend against suits under the Fourteenth Amendment by insisting on proof of intentional discrimination.

Minna J. Kotkin has pointed out that the structure of *Griggs* analysis, in which the claim is based on disparate impact, "has created certain enduring principles that fit within the model of public law litigation." She refers, for example, to the class nature of the claim and the typical result of successful disparate impact claims—"the negotiation of detailed changes in the employer's policies and the imposition of affirmative action requirements as a remedy."[88] She contrasts *Griggs*-type cases with disparate treatment cases, which tend to involve "private" forms of discrimination and therefore arguably fall on the other side of the public/private dichotomy.[89] If the Department of Justice's civil rights enforcement function should concentrate on systemic discrimination, *Griggs* would provide the department's most powerful litigative tool.

The centrality of *Griggs* to public law statutory litigation led the Reagan administration to reconsider it in the 1980s. President Reagan's campaign had criticized quotas and other race-based decisions, and his new attorney general, William French Smith, perhaps influenced by White House adviser Ed Meese, appointed an assistant attorney general firmly committed to changing the department's positions on a range of issues. An unsigned report, issued several years later by the department's Office of Legal Policy (rather than the Civil Rights Division), explained the administration's hostility to the effects test by arguing that *Griggs* had led to "the moral evils of race-based decision-making" and would lead to an "economic toll in reduced productivity."[90] As the top career attorney in the Civil Rights Division during the Reagan administration (as well as before and after) has noted, "This crowd singlemindedly insisted that the exceptions were the rule; that the perceived abuses were the policies; and that there had to be changes to civil rights fundamentals, not just mid-course corrections."[91]

In implementing this policy change, the department argued unsuccessfully against applying *Griggs* to subjective selection devices[92] and subsequently pressed more successfully "for a more thorough re-examination of what the lower courts had been doing in *Griggs*-type cases." In 1986 the United States petitioned for certiorari in *Tisch v. Shidaker,* seeking review of a Seventh Circuit decision allowing a Title VII plaintiff to state a cause of action based on an alleged disparate impact arising from a subjective decision-making process. The government argued that while objective selection devices "arguably can be validated" empirically, subjective selection devices "are not susceptible to such rigorous validation and, practically speaking, may not be susceptible to validation at all." The government concluded that employers using subjective selection devices would be driven to use quotas to avoid disparate impact, and that this would be contrary to the policies of Title VII.[93]

Two weeks after the Court disposed of *Tisch v. Shidaker* without reaching this issue, the Court invited the solicitor general to file a brief expressing the views of the United States on a question presented by the petition in *Watson v. Fort Worth Bank and Trust,*[94] "Is the racially adverse impact of an employer's practice of simply committing employment decisions to the unchecked discretion of a white supervisory corps subject to the test of *Griggs vs. Duke Power Co.,* 401 U.S. 424?"[95] The government's brief on the merits refined and expanded its position in *Tisch v. Shidaker,* arguing again that it was virtually impossible to validate subjective selection devices and that

> Ruling that the disparate impact theory is applicable to decisions resulting from subjective selection processes would, therefore, create an irresistible incentive for employers to abandon subjective selection processes in favor of objective ones or, where such replacement is too difficult or expensive, to eliminate the statistical disparity by superimposing quotas upon them. Neither result would be consistent with the intent of the 1964 Congress.[96]

These cases culminated in *Wards Cove Packing Company v. Atonio,* where the Court substantially watered down the business necessity defense by holding that if the employer claims that the "challenged practice serves, in a significant way, the legitimate employment goals of the employer," the burden shifts to the plaintiffs to negate the claim.[97] During this period the department tended to ignore EEOC guidelines and prior government positions,[98] a pattern that began with the government's switch of position in the *Bob Jones University* case.[99] The brief of the United States in *Wards Cove* does not once mention the EEOC guidelines standards for showing that an employer practice is justified, nor does it mention the government's position in cases such as *Albemarle.* The brief gives lip service to *Griggs* but proposes to merge the employer's burden in disparate impact cases with the less demanding standard of the disparate treatment cases.[100]

It has been argued that the Reagan administration "severely damaged" the credibility of the department.[101] It is, however, worth noting that the continuity of position from cases such as *United States v. Louisiana* to the present day has been far more powerful than the episodic departures from those positions. A more measured approach by the Reagan administration arguably would have cured perceived abuses without any lapse in credibility. By insisting on challenging long-settled doctrines whose adoption the department had previously urged and by ignoring the advice of career lawyers who could have helped devise a credible position, the Reagan administration laid the foundation for what happened next: Congress reacted to *Wards Cove* by enacting a law intended "to codify the concepts of 'business necessity' and 'job related' enunciated by the Supreme Court in Griggs . . . , and in the other Supreme Court decisions prior to Wards Cove."[102] In short, while prevailing in the Supreme Court, the administration's failure to reckon with the strength of the commitment of other players to preexisting doctrine led to the statutory entrenchment of *Griggs*.

Continuity, however, has arguably been interrupted in one important respect: *Griggs* was limited to Title VII cases. The issue has remained whether the principles of *Griggs* should be extended to other areas, such as fair housing. *Griggs* had built on the foundation of the voting cases, and a natural common law progression might have been expected to lead to the expansion of the effects test to other areas of discrimination law.

Prior to 1981 the department had taken the position that the effects test applied to fair housing[103] and Title VI.[104] However, in hearings on his nomination to become President Reagan's assistant attorney general for civil rights, William Bradford Reynolds responded to a question regarding application of the effects test to fair housing cases in a manner suggesting that he would abandon the prior position:

> My personal view is that the constitutional standard of "wrongful purpose or intent" should apply except in those instances where Congress has required the use of an "effects" or "disproportionate impact" test. In this regard, it is not, in my opinion, a proper role for the Department of Justice to use its litigating responsibility as a vehicle for seeking to rewrite Federal statutes in a manner that Congress never intended.[105]

Subsequently the department filed a Supreme Court brief as amicus curiae, arguing that the Fair Housing Act did not adopt the *Griggs* standard, even though, as the brief conceded, the language of Title VII and Title VIII was similar.[106] The Supreme Court avoided the issue,[107] and testimony of Clinton administration nominee Deval Patrick at the hearing on his nomination as assistant attorney general for civil rights suggests that the department will again argue in favor of the applicability of the effects test to Title VIII. As he argued,

I think that the position that the Department of Justice takes through the Civil Rights Division, if I am confirmed, has to be firmly grounded in case law and good sense. And my understanding is that all of the courts of appeals who have addressed the subject have found a disparate impact theory appropriate under the Fair Housing Act. That doesn't mean, necessarily, that every case is appropriate for a disparate impact approach. I think that has to be taken on a case by case basis.[108]

The history of *Griggs* thus includes continuity of position through the Kennedy, Johnson, Nixon, Ford, and Carter administrations, departures during the Reagan era, ambivalence under President Bush, and a resumption of the long-standing position under President Clinton. The application of the standard in the fair housing arena shows that when, as is often the case, precedents are not directly on point the department enjoys greater leeway in establishing its position.

Case Study: Southern School Desegregation[109]

The story of *Brown* and its progeny has been told numerous times,[110] but it is important to recount it from the Department of Justice perspective. The development of litigation policy with respect to school desegregation also illustrates the interplay of presidential and congressional policy, common law techniques, and agency policies.

President Truman's Committee on Civil Rights had concluded that in education "it is the South's segregated school system which most directly discriminates against the Negro." Apparently it based this conclusion on its determination that "the 'separate but equal' rule has not been obeyed in practice."[111] The committee also found that the doctrine "brands the Negro with the mark of inferiority and asserts that he is not fit to associate with white people."[112] Without explicitly calling for the overruling of *Plessy v. Ferguson,* the committee stated that the doctrine "creates inequality by imposing a caste status on the minority group."[113] Although the Committee therefore recommended that Congress end segregation in the schools of the District of Columbia and urged the elimination of segregation from American life, its action plan as to states simply recommended that state legislatures prohibit racial discrimination in education.[114]

Although lacking statutory authority to attack segregation, the Department of Justice followed up on the committee's report by participating as amicus curiae in several Supreme Court cases challenging various forms of race discrimination. In the October 1949 term, the solicitor general filed a brief in two higher education cases, arguing that the separate but equal doctrine should be overruled.[115] The department built on that brief when it filed its amicus brief in *Brown v. Board of Education* in December 1952, when President Truman was a lame-duck president.[116]

The Department of Justice's first brief in *Brown* noted that the federal government has a "special responsibility for assuring vindication of the fundamental civil rights guaranteed by the Constitution."[117] The brief focused on official race discrimination, observing that it "inevitably tend[s] to undermine the foundations of a society dedicated to freedom, justice, and equality."[118] Finally, the brief expressed concern that "the existence of discrimination against minority groups in the United States has an adverse effect upon our relations with other countries."[119] Thus, the main concern of the federal government was not with private rights but with national unity, enforcing constitutional norms, and the public interest.

The Court had expressly declined to reach the contention of the plaintiffs and the United States in *Sweatt* and *McLaurin* that the separate but equal doctrine should be overruled. The United States in *Brown* therefore argued that the plaintiffs could win without overruling *Plessy v. Ferguson,* but that if the Court reached the issue, *Plessy* should be overruled. Children do not enjoy equality when they "know that because of their color the law sets them apart from others, and requires them to attend separate schools specially established for members of their race."[120] The government concluded that "the Fourteenth Amendment forbids the classification of students on the basis of race or color so as to deny one group educational advantages and opportunities afforded to another."[121]

As to relief, the brief recommended that the Court remand to the lower courts "with directions to devise and execute such program for relief as appears most likely to achieve orderly and expeditious transition to a non-segregated system."[122] Relief need not occur "forthwith." As justification for this gradual approach, the brief argued that a "reasonable period of time will obviously be required to permit formulation of new provisions of law governing the administration of schools in areas affected by the Court's decision."[123]

After hearing initial arguments during its October 1952 term, the Supreme Court set the case down for reargument in order to seek the views of the parties as to questions propounded by the Court. By this time the Eisenhower administration had taken office, and the Court asked it to file an amicus brief. Thus, the litigation policy of the prior administration placed the new administration into a posture of having to endorse, repudiate, or stand mute on the government's prior position. The brief of the United States on rehearing addressed the questions the Court had asked and took no position on the outcome, but at oral argument Assistant Attorney General J. Lee Rankin said, "It is the position of the Department of Justice that segregation in public schools cannot be maintained under the Fourteenth Amendment, and we adhere to the views expressed in the original brief of the Department in that regard."[124] Unlike the briefs of the parties, which gave partisan versions of history to justify their positions, the brief of the United States impartially surveyed the historical record and concluded that it neither explicitly supported nor repudiated school segregation, but "that the general aims of the Fourteenth Amendment permitted the Supreme Court now to 'abolish all legal distinctions based on race or color.' "[125]

Turning to relief, the United States noted the success of New Jersey in desegregating its schools and noted various issues of school administration that the state would have to address. It assumed that neighborhood schools would be permissible even if they were substantially of one race[126] and argued that relief should be entered "as expeditiously as the particular circumstances permit."[127]

The story of the government's participation in *Brown I* foreshadows later federal actions. The Truman administration had actively supported nondiscrimination, partly out of conviction and partly to woo the African-American vote.[128] The support by one administration for desegregation placed the next administration on a path that was difficult to reverse. President Eisenhower, who had opposed desegregation of the armed forces in 1948 and had broken the long-standing southern boycott of Republican candidates by carrying four southern states in 1952, was indecisive as to whether to support school desegregation; the momentum of the outgoing administration's briefs seemingly tipped the balance.[129] The federal arguments, unlike those of the parties, treated the cases as involving values of both nondiscrimination and order and made a case for accommodating both values. The briefs were limited to the issues before the Court and did not attempt to resolve all the implementation issues that inevitably followed *Brown I.* Finally, when both the plaintiffs and the federal government prevailed in arguing for an end to the separate but equal doctrine, a ratchet effect began in which, however slowly, increasingly stringent rules were imposed on segregated school systems for the next twenty years.[130]

After the Court in *Brown I* ruled for the plaintiffs, the government filed a brief in *Brown II.* In arguing that "the vindication of the constitutional rights involved should be as prompt as feasible," the department pointed out that "the 'personal and present' right . . . of a colored child not to be segregated while attending public school is one which, if not enforced while the child is of school age, loses its value."[131] The federal government argued that the "right of children not to be segregated because of race or color . . . is a fundamental human right, supported by considerations of morality as well as law," and that "racial segregation affects the hearts and minds of those who segregate as well as those who are segregated, and it is also detrimental to the community and the nation."[132] Several sentences of the brief, drafted by President Eisenhower,[133] also noted countervailing values that might affect relief.[134]

The initial federal foray into school desegregation law was inspired by President Truman and his Committee on Civil Rights. The filing in *Brown* was a natural extension of the *McLaurin* and *Sweatt* filings. The legacy of the Truman administration made it difficult for the Eisenhower administration to remain mute and apparently led Attorney General Brownell to take up the issue with the president.[135] The participation in *Brown I* made participation in *Brown II* virtually inevitable, and the government's litigating position there built on ideas from the prior briefs. However, the position as to relief was subtly altered to reflect President Eisenhower's concern about "insensitive" implementation. That shift in the government's emphasis may have influenced the Court to adopt the "all deliberate speed" formula.

The 1957 act bestowed no school desegregation enforcement authority on the attorney general; one of the primary reasons for Congress's rejection of Part 3 in 1957 was opposition to *Brown*.[136] Theoretically, the attorney general might have brought criminal prosecutions against school officials who willfully violated *Brown*.[137] However, the ambiguities of *Brown* could have made it difficult to prove the requisite specific intent to deny a constitutional right.[138] Attorney General Brownell opined that "the discretion vested in the district courts" by *Brown* was a barrier to a Section 242 prosecution of school officials.[139] Although the Civil Rights Section had urged consideration of criminal prosecution of the conspirators who had interfered with school desegregation in the *Hoxie* case,[140] then–Deputy Attorney General William Rogers disapproved the proposal.[141] Moreover, it was believed that the right to jury trial would have led to jury nullification even if adequate proof had been presented. Finally, the government had primarily used Section 242 to prosecute crimes of violence and fraud; the section was available but exceedingly awkward.[142]

Although initially taking a hands-off attitude toward post-*Brown* school desegregation, the executive branch later took action in 1957 to enforce the order to desegregate the Little Rock, Arkansas, schools in the face of defiance by Governor Faubus.[143] There were at least twelve incidents of violent interference with school desegregation between 1954 and 1960; the Department of Justice intervened in five of those cases but "only after local officials begged for help." In the other seven cases, "federal executive authorities refused to intervene."[144] Responding to acts of private violence against school desegregation, Congress did make obstruction of federal court orders a crime in 1960.[145] The Department of Justice participated as a "litigating amicus" in other school desegregation cases[146] and attempted to initiate cases to desegregate schools attended by large numbers of children of federal employees.[147]

Finally, ten years after *Brown,* Congress authorized a strong federal enforcement role, but the authorization was hedged. It empowered the attorney general to bring school desegregation suits, but only after receiving a meritorious complaint from a parent who is unable to maintain appropriate proceedings for relief and only if the attorney general finds that "the institution of an action will materially further the orderly achievement of desegregation in public education."[148] Moreover, the 1964 Civil Rights Act specified that it did not empower any court or official to "issue any order seeking to achieve a racial balance in any school by requiring the transportation of pupils or students from one school to another or one school district to another in order to achieve such racial balance."[149] It also authorized the federal government to provide technical assistance for desegregation and banned discrimination in federally assisted programs. The 1964 act thus signaled Congress's desire to bring de jure segregation to an end but to keep the federal government out of de facto segregation cases.

The department identified two primary needs that governed the school litigation program under the new act. First, it sought "to secure recognition of *Brown v. Board of Education* as the law in school systems throughout the South."[150] Second, it used "federal court litigation to support the school desegregation program of the Department of Health, Education, and Welfare under Title VI of the 1964 Act."[151] In the years that followed, the litigation policy of the Department of Justice contributed to these objectives and to the development of the legal standards governing school desegregation. The Department of Justice participated as a party or amicus in every Supreme Court school desegregation case and many lower court cases.

The ambiguity of *Brown* spawned litigation to define the extent of school authorities' obligation to desegregate. In a series of cases, the courts considered succeeding responses to *Brown* by school authorities: massive resistance, under which the states refused to follow *Brown* on the grounds that the Court had acted improperly in deciding it; pupil placement laws and pupil transfer laws, which placed a series of hurdles in the path of African Americans who wished to attend white schools; and freedom of choice plans, which made all students choose whether they wished to attend a white school or a black school.[152] The Office of Civil Rights of the Department of Health, Education, and Welfare developed guidelines for measuring compliance by formerly dual school systems with the requirements of Title VI of the 1964 act. The initial guidelines required that at least four grades be desegregated for the 1965–1966 school year and established criteria for judging geographical and free choice systems of student assignment.[153] These guidelines represented HEW's evaluation of the state of the law and of feasibility in light of the "all deliberate speed doctrine." The federal courts began applying the HEW guidelines to school desegregation cases.[154]

The following year HEW issued revised guidelines which made explicit that the test of a valid desegregation plan is whether it will "eliminate the dual school system . . . as expeditiously as possible."[155] School systems in the South had begun to adopt plans under which students were to "choose" whether to enroll in a white school or a black school. Those plans generally resulted in most schools remaining segregated. The revised guidelines treated free choice not as the objective of the plan but as an instrument "for a gradual move away from a dual structure."[156] Among the factors for determining whether the plan promised to eliminate the dual system expeditiously were steps taken "to eliminate the identifiability of schools on the basis of race" and the "progress actually made in eliminating past discrimination and segregation."[157] A Department of Justice brief described the theory underlying the revised guidelines: "The substantive requirements of the proposed decree derive from the Fourteenth Amendment and the decisions of the courts. The administrative details are largely drawn from the HEW Guidelines."[158] The secretary of HEW stated that the revised guidelines were based on court decisions.[159]

The leading case in which these positions were first presented to the courts was *United States v. Jefferson County Board of Education.*[160] The brief of the United States in that case relied on two voting rights cases in urging the court to adopt a model decree for school systems in the Fifth Circuit and to base it on the revised guidelines.[161] The brief relied not only on prior case law requiring abolition of the dual school system[162] but also on a voting case requiring that the remedy "eradicate the effects of former discrimination."[163] Appendices to the government's brief contained the history of every school desegregation case in the Fifth Circuit, reflecting both the lack of compliance with *Brown* and the lack of uniform treatment by the lower court judges. These appendices supported the need for a model decree.

Judge Wisdom's opinion in *United States v. Jefferson County Board of Education,* noting that the revised guidelines represent "for the most part standards the Supreme Court and this Court established *before the Guidelines were promulgated,*"[164] did fashion such a model decree. His opinion stresses the systemic nature of school segregation and allows free choice plans only "in a bona fide unitary system where schools are not white schools or Negro schools—just schools."[165] The opinion requires as well that the plan achieve substantial integration; if it fails to do so, the school officials must try an alternative.[166] The result was to transfer from the students to the school authorities the burden of complying with *Brown.* The Department of Justice and the Department of Health, Education, and Welfare agreed that the time was right to work toward a rule of law under which "free choice would not be permitted unless it achieved 'complete desegregation.' "[167]

The department's opportunity to press for complete desegregation came three months later when the Supreme Court agreed to review the remedial issue in *Green v. County School Board.*[168] *Jefferson County* laid the foundation for the department's amicus curiae brief in *Green.* The solicitor general's office prepared a draft brief in *Green* which argued in part that freedom of choice plans were per se unconstitutional. Assistant Attorney General Stephen J. Pollak objected, based on "the experience acquired under the Division's school litigation program."[169] He argued that if the Supreme Court adopted the argument, it would be placed "out on a limb . . . that neither the Fifth Circuit nor the Federal Executive . . . had previously been prepared to climb out to."[170] He stressed as well that arguing for per se invalidity of free choice was "inconsistent with the Department's established enforcement program" and expressed doubt that "this Division (with only 25 lawyers assigned to the Fifth Circuit) or HEW could abruptly abandon that program and meaningfully implement the principle" of per se invalidity.[171] Finally, Pollak argued that the draft "may underestimate the Negro" and expressed the view that in a nondiscriminatory climate "Negroes have the gumption to choose what they truly want."[172]

The brief as filed in *Green* did not argue that free choice was per se invalid but instead built on the *Jefferson County* reasoning. The United States argued that "so-called 'freedom of choice' plans satisfy the State's obligation only if they are part of a comprehensive program which actually achieves desegregation."[173] The government identified the continued existence of "all-Negro schools, attended by an overwhelming majority of the Negro children," as the mark of an ineffective desegregation plan. Quoting *Jefferson County,* the United States argued, "Against the background of educational segregation long maintained by law, the duty of school authorities is to accomplish 'the conversion of a de jure segregated dual system to a unitary, nonracial (nondiscriminatory) system—lock, stock, and barrel."[174] Further, "the Fourteenth Amendment bars State action which unnecessarily creates opportunities for the play of private prejudice."[175]

The Supreme Court in *Green* unanimously adopted the approach of *Jefferson County,* holding that "the transition to a unitary, nonracial system of public education was and is the ultimate end to be brought about."[176] The Court found "an affirmative duty to take whatever steps might be necessary to convert to a unitary system" and required adoption of "a plan that promises realistically to work, and promises realistically to work *now.*"[177] Echoing Judge Wisdom, the Court said the plan must "promise realistically to convert promptly to a system without a 'white' school and a 'Negro' school, but just schools."[178] *Green* resolved ambiguity of prior case law by imposing a stringent test for desegregation, thus tightening the ratchet well beyond the limited progress that most southern school systems had achieved.

Following *Green* the issue in most cases was not what *Brown* required or even whether individual school systems had achieved compliance; most had not. Private plaintiffs and the government set about enforcing the Supreme Court's new standard, which effectively required most school systems to abandon free choice plans, which had failed to produce unitariness, and adopt various other forms of student reassignment, often through "busing." The department filed motions in its pending cases to require conformity with *Green* and intervened in other cases.[179] HEW pursued administrative enforcement under Title VI.[180] The two agencies followed "the policy assumption . . . that in school desegregation matters, the Department of Justice should be in the law development business, and HEW should be concerned with volume."[181]

These actions to enforce the holding in *Green* were initiated by the outgoing administration of President Lyndon Johnson and placed constraints on the options available to the incoming administration of President Richard Nixon.[182] For example, less than six weeks after President Nixon was inaugurated the Supreme Court agreed to hear an appeal initiated by the Johnson administration from an appellate ruling that disapproved Judge Frank Johnson's order requiring the Montgomery, Alabama, school board to "move toward a goal" of racially balanced faculties. The new administration, required to brief that case on the merits, supported the order, arguing it was "designed as a *remedy for* past [discrimination]."[183] The Court agreed. Nathan Lewin, a high-ranking official during the Johnson administration who stayed on during the early Nixon administration, observed:

The Southerners expected it all to be different, but it's clear now that it won't be. I haven't seen even minor, let alone major, shifts in civil-rights policies here. A new Administration couldn't turn things around here even if it wanted to. In a place like this, the self-perpetuating mechanism of the law makes any basic change unlikely.[184]

Although Lewin's optimism proved wrong in a short-term sense, his faith in the self-perpetuating mechanism of the law proved correct insofar as it predicted administration enforcement of *Green*.

Despite its early support for the principles of *Green* in the Montgomery case, the Nixon administration initially wavered in its support for the *Green* motions that it had inherited; when the secretary of Health, Education, and Welfare concluded that prompt compliance with *Green* would cause "chaos, confusion and a catastrophic educational setback" to students in twenty-three Mississippi school districts,[185] the department filed a motion asking for a delay of the very desegregation it had been seeking. When the case reached the Supreme Court, the government agreed that the doctrine of all deliberate speed should be abandoned but argued that a delay of one semester in the desegregation of the defendant school districts was permissible. However, when the Supreme Court held in *Alexander* that there were to be no further delays in school desegregation,[186] the Nixon administration eventually complied. The department then filed a series of *Alexander* motions and statewide desegregation cases and HEW took enforcement action under Title VI in order to bring about immediate school desegregation in the remaining dual systems.[187]

The issue then arose whether the Court's approach in *Green* to desegregation of a rural county would apply as well to a densely populated urban school system in which residential segregation prevailed. Some lower courts had begun requiring busing to desegregate such systems. President Nixon released a policy statement on school desegregation in which he took issue with those decisions and said, "Unless affirmed by the Supreme Court, I will not consider them as precedents to guide administration policy elsewhere."[188]

In *Swann v. Charlotte-Mecklenburg Board of Education*,[189] the brief of the United States accordingly struck a cautious note. The brief did embrace *Green*, saying

We think the right of school children articulated in *Brown* is to attend school in a system where the school board exercises its decision-making powers so as to operate a non-racial unitary school system free from discrimination, and that where this has not been done there is a violation of the rights of such children requiring remedial adjustments which give proper weight to that which is feasible and that which is just. If choices exist which may have a racial impact, they cannot be exercised in a racially neutral manner where to do so is to perpetuate segregation.[190]

Thus, the courts should "require that the governmental decisions affecting racial segregation be so made and implemented, when feasible alternatives are available, as to disestablish the dual system and eliminate its vestiges."[191] However, echoing Congress's ambivalence on the matter and the president's opposition to busing, the United States also concluded that "the Fourteenth Amendment does not require . . . racial balance in all public schools or integration of every all-white or all-Negro school."[192] Contrary to the prior norm, the government's position in a school desegregation case diverged substantially but not wholly from that of the black plaintiffs.

In deciding *Swann* the Court departed from the government's position and applied *Green,* holding that Congress had not intended to interfere with remedies for de jure segregation and creating a presumption of invalidity of one-race schools in a former dual system. The department once again filed a series of motions, this time to bring about compliance with *Swann.*[193] One such motion was filed in the Austin, Texas, school desegregation case. When the district court approved the defendant school board's proposed desegregation plan rather than the busing plan devised by HEW, the Department of Justice appealed. In a possibly unprecedented statement, President Nixon explained that the attorney general had decided that appeal was required but the president disavowed the HEW plan. The government filed a brief arguing that both the school board's plan and the HEW plan should be rejected and that a plan should be fashioned which would remedy only the racial imbalance at those schools infected with de jure segregation. The brief was the subject of intense high-level consideration; one page was deleted after a phone call from the attorney general placed from the White House.[194] The court of appeals agreed that the lower court should be reversed but ordered implementation of a comprehensive busing plan rather than the more limited measures sought by the government, observing that the government "has never asserted this position before."[195]

The Nixon administration, although it had campaigned against busing, found itself in a dilemma after *Green* and *Swann.* If it failed to enforce those decisions it would appear to be joining forces with those who had defied the mandate of *Brown.* Moreover, the Nixon administration had also campaigned for law and order, and *Green* and *Swann* had transformed busing into a law enforcement issue. On the other hand, enforcement of those decisions could endanger the so-called southern strategy of catering to southern white voters. In this political context, the Nixon administration opted to enforce the decisions but to seek to make those lawyerly arguments that were still available to limit their reach. An interesting by-product of this strategy was a strange sort of credibility, with many courts and school boards believing that if the Nixon administration said they must bus it must be so, while if it said they should not be required to bus the argument was deemed suspicious. I well remember one desegregation case in particular. The Johnson administration had filed an intradistrict desegregation suit, and private plaintiffs had later intervened seeking interdistrict desegregation. After I explained the department's position to the U.S. district judge—a position which had not actually changed when the Nixon administration took office—the judge said, "Tell Attorney General Mitchell that [the state in question] will vote to re-elect President Nixon, no matter what position the government takes in this case."

In the years that followed *Swann,* the government has continued its homage to *Brown* while sometimes urging the Court to limit *Brown*'s applicability. On the one hand the government took the position that metropolitan-wide remedies could be ordered only where a metropolitan violation has been found.[196] On the other hand the government argued that system-wide busing was appropriate in Columbus, Ohio, because the record reflected a system-wide violation. The government argued that a unitary school system is entitled to be released from a desegregation decree while agreeing that eliminating the vestiges of discrimination is a prerequisite to a unitariness finding.[197]

Congress, while rejecting proposed constitutional amendments to overrule *Swann,* has signaled its disapproval of busing by denying desegregation funding for it, by denying the Department of Education authority to require it, and by prohibiting any "court, department, or agency of the United States [from ordering] transportation" to distant schools, language that has been construed not to apply to desegregation orders in de jure segregation cases.[198] Nonetheless, the division has taken its cue from the Court's decisions rather than Congress's apparent dislike of busing and, although at times seeking to minimize busing, has enforced the *Swann* rule. Congress has placed more rigid restrictions on the Department of Education's ability to require busing under Title VI than on the Department of Justice's ability to seek busing in the course of its litigation under Titles IV and IX of the 1964 act, presumably because the Justice Department litigates constitutional rights in the courts while the Education Department administratively enforces statutory rights.

To some extent the fluctuations in the government's position have been due to political changes from one administration to the next. For example, Assistant Attorney General for Civil Rights William Bradford Reynolds stressed cessation of busing and dissolution of desegregation decrees as central themes of the government's program for enforcing *Brown.*[199] This stance represents a change from the position of the Carter administration, and one may expect the Clinton administration to reject these themes as well.

There is much more detail to this story, but the essential point is that the department primarily built its school desegregation positions on its congressional mandate to promote "the orderly achievement of desegregation" and on its own enforcement experience, case law, and the administrative positions of HEW. The administrative positions and case law built on one another, with a ratchet effect of increasingly stringent criteria for desegregation. Where external, probably political, considerations intruded on decision making, as with the Mississippi desegregation delay in 1969 and the Austin case in 1971, the credibility of the department suffered. The department's earlier positions had a moderating influence on its later ones, and the actions taken by one administration placed constraints on the options available to its successors. The department, as well as the plaintiffs and the Court, started down a path in its amicus brief in *Brown* without full understanding of where that path might lead but with a clear comprehension of the underlying values it sought to advance. As has been said of private interest group litigation,[200] much of the government's subsequent school desegregation litigation may have been "responsive and reflexive," but much of it qualifies as "planned litigation" that achieved the objective of bringing the South into compliance with *Brown*.

The department began with the normative value expressed by President Truman's Committee on Civil Rights. President Eisenhower had no enthusiasm for the department's position in *Brown* but did nothing to countermand it. Rather, he insisted in *Brown II* that the department recognize the competing value of public order. The Kennedy administration began to initiate a few cases involving segregation of military dependents, but it was not until passage of the 1964 act that the department, now reporting to President Johnson, took a proactive role in seeking school desegregation. That act did not, however, arm the department with a strong mandate but instead placed limits on the department's right to sue and insisted on a de jure–de facto distinction that undermined efforts to achieve nationwide desegregation. The department found unsettled law and widespread noncompliance. It participated in efforts to clarify the law, such as the *Green* case, while at the same time teaming with HEW to seek to require southern school systems to comply with the evolving standards.

The Nixon administration came into office opposed to busing to achieve desegregation, a posture that it continued to espouse even as under the pressure of *Green* and then *Swann* it enforced the Supreme Court's busing mandates. The Johnson-Nixon years were the formative period for enforcement policy, just as the Truman-Eisenhower years had been the formative period for the normative rule of *Brown*. The political changes during these periods did influence litigation policy but only within relatively narrow limits that the case law dictated. No administration wished to be painted as lawless, and a powerful subtext of the department's enforcement of *Brown* was always the importance of public order and uniform compliance with the Supreme Court's later rulings. Where those rulings were ambiguous, the political preferences of the administrations were more strongly felt. The Johnson administration made a calculated judgment to seek the pragmatic test that the Court adopted in *Green*. The Nixon administration made a calculated judgment to seek to limit the scope of busing plans, which the Court adopted in *Milliken*. But where the rulings were clear, as in *Alexander* and *Swann,* the Nixon administration enforced them. In short, the department's actions stemmed from substantive policy choices of succeeding administrations, the Supreme Court, Congress, the Department of Health, Education, and Welfare, and the department's own personnel. They took place in the context of the activity of private litigants and civil rights groups, public opinion, and state re-calcitrance. No precise calculus defines the litigation policy-making process, but the ingredients are clear enough: the Constitution, statutes, case law, application of common law litigation methods, presidential policy, and continuity.

CHANGING LITIGATION POSITIONS

Three types of circumstance may lead department officials to wish to change litigation position: a change in administration policy, a change in the law, or the discovery that the initial position was ill-advised. The change in position may take the form of switching sides in a pending case or in a completed case. Change could also occur in a completely new case about an issue that the department has addressed in an earlier case.

In most of the above situations, considerations of repose, staying power, and credibility dictate caution in changing positions. Repose relates to the expectations of those outside the department. Courts, litigants, and the public are normally entitled to act on the suppositions that the litigation position of the United States is based on careful consideration of the law and the facts and will not shift with every new wind, and that the Supreme Court often gives greater weight to the government's original position than to revised positions that result from changes in administration.[201] Staying power imparts increased effectiveness to an enforcement program.[202] Credibility relates to the department's future ability to carry out its mission, and the Supreme Court's words about its own credibility apply to the department as well:

> Only the most convincing justification under accepted standards of [precedent] could suffice to demonstrate that a later decision overruling the precedent was anything but a surrender to political pressure and an unjustified repudiation of the principle on which the Court staked its authority in the first instance.[203]

Repose, staying power, and credibility are closely related. If the department declines to follow its own position, continuity of enforcement is undermined and the disappointed expectations of others lead them to doubt the integrity of future departmental positions. Thus, as one observer has noted, "In some sense, high Executive officials were educated by and locked into the positions that the Department attorneys—the professionals—took for the United States in civil rights litigation. Those positions could on occasion be abandoned or repudiated, but only with a good explanation."[204]

This need for continuity has often been stressed in congressional debates over the placement of enforcement power in the department.[205] The political leadership of the Department of Justice has also understood the importance of continuity. Drew Days, for example, noted that when he became assistant attorney general for civil rights, "it became clear to me . . . that I had stepped into a tradition, that I had to adhere to some positions taken by prior administrations even though I disagreed with them. Of course, I was committed to making changes that I thought would advance the course of civil rights, but I understood that progress would be slow and painful."[206]

On the other hand, it would be unrealistic to expect that the department should never change litigation position. Its initial position may have been poorly conceived, may have been taken without adequate review, or may reflect a policy judgment that a new administration finds impossible to swallow. Facts may emerge in the course of litigation that dictate change, or the legal landscape may be legislatively or judicially altered in such a way as to make the initial position untenable. As Justice Frankfurter's famous aphorism holds, "Wisdom too often never comes, and so one ought not to reject it merely because it comes late."[207]

The very fact that the United States is the litigant entitles the public to assume that when the government discovers its position is wrong, it will correct the error.[208] Indeed, the Supreme Court has commented that "in addition to those institutional concerns traditionally considered by the Solicitor General, the panoply of important public issues raised in governmental litigation may quite properly lead successive administrations of the Executive Branch to take differing positions with respect to the resolution of a particular issue."[209] These considerations favoring changing positions act as a restraint on the initial staking out of position. Knowledge that ill-conceived positions may be changed by future administrations leads to greater care in their formulation.

For the above reasons, no absolute rule should govern changes in government position, and the practical value of continuity will normally outweigh the need for such change. However, where the law and facts permit, policy considerations may sometimes trump continuity. When the department does change position, it can expect heightened and highly visible criticism of its action; that criticism will be cloaked in concern for the neutral principle of continuity. When the Reagan administration changed the government's position from support to opposition to affirmative action under the Birmingham, Alabama, fair employment case consent decree that the government had previously signed, attorneys for the city accused the assistant attorney general of misconduct, duplicitousness, and betrayal of the public trust.[210] One attorney concluded that "the Department interprets the Decree as its convenience, as opposed to its conscience, dictates."[211] Similarly, when the Clinton administration decided to change the government's position in another case from opposition to support of an affirmative action plan, the attorney for the white complainant was the one who cried foul. He claimed the change was bad faith,[212] and another observer charged that the reversal of position was "apparently unprecedented" and raised "serious ethical concerns."[213] Such criticisms are designed to persuade even those who agree with the merits of the new position that it was improper for the department to switch sides. These criticisms also create doubt about the merits of the department's new position as being based on politics rather than on the law and facts. Whether or not such criticisms are valid, they should lead the department to apply to itself a presumption against changing position.

Note that because the above changes took place during the course of litigation, the courts, not the attorney general, had the final word as to the outcome of the case. Civil rights litigation often involves more than two parties, so a change of position by one party alone is not enough to moot the case. For example, the Carter administration had objected under Section 5 of the Voting Rights Act to a change in the city of Lockhart's voting practices and had prevailed in the city's district court suit seeking a declaratory judgment approving the change. On the city's appeal the Reagan administration changed the government's position, but because a private party had intervened in the case in the district court there was still a live case; the private party defended the district court's decision in the Supreme Court.[214] Even where no third party is present, a change of government position will not always moot the case. For example, in the *Bob Jones* case, although the government changed its position it did not rescind the administrative action that Bob Jones University challenged. Therefore the Supreme Court heard the case and appointed an amicus curiae to defend the challenged administrative action.

The election of a new president normally leads to reconsideration of policies. Campaign speeches and party platforms often address issues pertaining to law enforcement, and a new administration may be expected to review litigation priorities and positions in light of promises made during the political campaign. As Solicitor General Drew Days observed, "If there weren't changes in position from one administration to another, it would be very unusual, and it would cause the average voter to wonder why she went to the polls in the first place."[215] For example, President Nixon opposed busing and spoke out against it during his campaign, allegedly as part of a "southern strategy" to woo the South to the Republican party. Subsequent positions of the department argued for limiting court-ordered busing to the extent that the state of the law permitted. The United States argued that busing in Charlotte, North Carolina, need not be as extensive as the trial court had ordered, and that interdistrict busing was not an appropriate remedy in the Richmond, Virginia, and Detroit, Michigan, school desegregation cases. Note, however, that the argument against busing in big cities represented a change in direction but not a change in position, since the Johnson administration had never directly confronted the question of how far to push the *Green* decision in the urban-suburban setting. The Nixon administration never asked the Court to overturn prior decisions favoring African-American claims to nondiscrimination.

One legacy from the Johnson administration that should be noted was a set of urban school desegregation cases brought by the department. The Nixon administration did not abandon those cases, and the ultimate remedies in such places as Tulsa, Oklahoma, Indianapolis, Indiana, and Pasadena, California, included extensive busing. The department's legal position was based on its reading of the *Green* and *Swann* cases and held that the extent of the remedy should be determined by the nature of the violation. Where only a limited violation was proved, only limited busing would be appropriate, but system-wide discrimination might require more extensive busing. The Ford administration continued the call to limit busing while also acknowledging that the case law often required some busing.

When the Carter administration took office, the department immediately faced the question of what position to take in the Dayton, Ohio, school desegregation case, where the Supreme Court had agreed to consider whether "the imposition of a district wide racial balance remedy exceed[ed] the remedial and equitable powers" of the lower courts. Under President Carter's attorney general, Griffin Bell, the department's public stance was that it was not changing its position on busing. However, since the position all along had been to comply with Supreme Court rulings, the department, led by new Assistant Attorney General Drew Days, was able to file a brief in the *Dayton* case which found that under existing law the busing plan was constitutionally proper: "The remedial order in this case was proper in light of the far-reaching constitutional violations shown."[216] The brief argued that to determine the proper remedy the Court must "seek to determine the consequences of the acts constituting the illegal discrimination and to eliminate their continuing effects," and it noted that the United States had "taken a similar position in other recent school cases" including cases argued in the Ford administration.[217] Thus, the brief supported busing while stressing the continuity of government position.

This approach was true to the common law orientation of the department but also true to the orientation of the new administration. Not only did the Carter administration not change position in cases in which the prior administration had played a role, but it eschewed dramatic breaks with the earlier positions of the division even in *Dayton,* a case in which the former administration had played no role. In essence, the change of administrations brought a new perspective of the facts and a more expansive view of how the legal standard should apply. The new politically appointed staff at the head of the department and the division had subtly changed direction.

From the founding of the Civil Rights Section in 1939 to the end of the Carter administration, the department's civil rights policies followed "a long-standing, bipartisan tradition of incrementally progressive civil rights enforcement."[218] In the few cases in which the department changed its position, it did so because the department lawyers in the lower court had woodenly defended racially discriminatory positions of federal agencies without regard to the developing understanding and case law that was undermining the separate but equal doctrine. For example, in the *Henderson* case the Antitrust Division had defended an Interstate Commerce Commission (ICC) ruling upholding a railway's segregation of dining car passengers. On appeal the solicitor general told the ICC, "We're not only not going to support them, we're going to oppose," and the government argued that *Plessy* should be overruled.[219] The department had taken a similar position, resting solely on statutory grounds,[220] nine years earlier, and the ICC-Antitrust Division position in *Henderson* simply ignored administration policy. Although the Supreme Court did not reach the constitutional issue in *Henderson,* it ruled without dissent that the dining car segregation violated the Interstate Commerce Act.[221]

The department's role in the Seattle busing case provides an interesting contrast to *Henderson.* The Reagan administration took office determined to reverse the department's prior positions on school desegregation, and in the Seattle busing case it quickly found a vehicle to do so in the Supreme Court. The Carter administration had intervened in the case to support the Seattle school district's defense of its voluntarily adopted desegregation plan. The plan had led to the adoption of a state initiative that banned busing as a desegregation technique, and Seattle sued for a declaration that the initiative was unconstitutional. The school district and the department succeeded in the lower courts, and the state of Washington sought review. The department, acknowledging that it was repudiating its prior position, urged the Court to hear the case and subsequently argued in favor of the constitutionality of the antibusing initiative. The department gave no explanation for its switch in position except to say that it had concluded that the prior position was wrong. The Court, noting the switch without commenting on its appropriateness, ruled against the state and the department and affirmed the lower courts, albeit by a 5 to 4 margin.

The switch of position in the *Seattle* case, along with a contemporaneous switch in the *Bob Jones University* case, brought to the fore the question of the propriety of repudiating a position taken in the same case. In *Bob Jones University,* the department was the only respondent. It had initially filed a memorandum with the Court supporting the lower court's ruling that the Internal Revenue Service had correctly denied tax-exempt status to a racially discriminatory university. When the department reversed position, the Court had to resort to the extraordinary device of appointing an "amicus curiae in support of the judgments below" to defend the government's prior position. *Seattle,* unlike *Bob Jones University,* was a case in which there were other parties, including the original plaintiff, supporting the position the department had taken below. It was argued at the time that the department should be deprived of its status as a party[222] and that it could not ethically switch sides in light of the government's prior relations with its coparties.[223]

The Supreme Court did not bar the government from asserting its newly formed positions in these cases. It also did not address the issue of party status. Section 902 of the 1964 act governs that issue and provides that the United States "shall be entitled to the same relief as if it had instituted the action." In a sense, the party status issue was trivial, since the government was free to participate as amicus curiae even if it could not participate as a party. The ethical charge is tenuous, for the attorney general at no point purported to represent any party other than the United States. The attorney general sues to vindicate the public interest and does not represent the private interests of other parties.[224] No rule imposes a duty on a party to support coparties. Perhaps confidences were exchanged, though in a case such as Seattle, which concerned matters of public record, it is doubtful that there were confidences of any consequence. In any event, the rules impose no obligation to respect confidences of coparties, and it seems more realistic to say that parties act at their own risk in such confidences.

The changes in position thus were not legally improper, but they nonetheless should not have occurred. The change in *Bob Jones* denied the Treasury Department a defense of its regulation, which was arguably valid and the Supreme Court ultimately upheld it. Moreover, the regulation also advanced the very nondiscrimination values that the department has been assigned to uphold. The change in *Seattle* suggested that the department's antipathy toward busing extended not only to court-ordered busing but also to local efforts to fashion workable desegregation plans. The department did not need to use the *Seattle* case as a pulpit for its opposition to court-ordered busing, for it filed a brief that same year in the Los Angeles busing case where that was an issue. The two briefs were unprecedented in the boldness and gratuitousness of their attacks on governmental efforts to advance school desegregation.

Is there a principled distinction between the change in position in *Henderson* and those in *Bob Jones* and *Seattle*? If the role of the United States is to advance the constitutional and statutory values of nondiscrimination, the government did so in its Supreme Court filing in *Henderson* but not in *Bob Jones* or *Seattle*. True, the *Henderson* filing contradicted a federal agency, but prior cases had rendered the agency's position tenuous. By contrast, the positions of the United States in the lower courts in *Bob Jones* and *Seattle* were well supported by the case law. The Reagan administration's filings not only turned their back on the department's lower court positions but also gave forced and grudging readings to the Supreme Court case law that supported the lower court rulings. In short, *Bob Jones* and *Seattle* represented serious lapses of legal judgment in which the policy agenda of the Reagan administration was allowed to displace careful consideration of the many factors counseling against changing position in those cases. One further distinction between *Henderson* and these two Reagan administration filings is, of course, the end result: an unqualified legal success in *Henderson* and embarassing defeats in *Bob Jones* and *Seattle,* although some justices did agree with the Reagan administration position. Taken alone, losing a case does not mean the position in the case was misguided, but when objective analysis concludes that the odds of losing are as great as they were in *Bob Jones* and *Seattle,* the normal values of sticking to the government's prior position are further enhanced.

An interesting variant on the change in position occurs when a federal agency charged with responsibility for executing a statute disagrees with the Department of Justice enforcement position. In *Georgia Ass'n of Retarded Citizens v. McDaniel,*[225] the Department of Justice in 1980 took one position on behalf of the Department of Education during the Carter administration. The Reagan Department of Justice then reversed position in 1983. However, apparently the administration was not unified on the issue, because the Department of Education issued a memorandum reiterating the 1980 position. The memorandum reached the court of appeals, which chose to follow the Department of Education (and the original Department of Justice) position, saying: "The United States, invited to file a brief as amicus curiae has blown hot, cold and hot as to the coverage under Section 504. . . . [The] last word from the Department [of Education], of course, supports the views we have expressed above." This case shows that although the Department of Justice may make the final determination about position to be taken, it should not lightly ignore the positions of client agencies, especially when deciding whether to change position in a case.[226]

As the *Lockhart* case described above reflects, individuals who stand to be affected by government litigation can protect against possible changes in government position by timely intervention in the case. So long as the government's position in the case coincides with the private person's position, intervention is not necessary and under the applicable rules the court may deny intervention. At such time as the government's position fails to vindicate the private interest, the individual may intervene on the ground that the government no longer adequately represents his or her interest.[227]

One peculiar aspect of the general tendency not to make drastic changes in litigation positions is the great suspicion with which an incoming administration views the lame-duck activities of its predecessor. For example, the Reagan administration conducted a review of several cases that the Carter administration had filed after President Carter was defeated for reelection. The purpose of the review was to ensure that these filings were justified and were not departures from proper procedures and policies. To its credit, the Reagan administration ultimately decided to move forward with all the postelection cases.

Another such episode ended differently. At the end of the Bush administration, less than two weeks before President Clinton's inauguration, Solicitor General Starr filed amicus curiae briefs in two Voting Rights Act cases that the losing parties were asking the Supreme Court to hear. Professor C. Lani Guinier, who later was President Clinton's first nominee as assistant attorney general for civil rights (a nomination that the president subsequently withdrew), reacted vehemently to the filings: "The Justice Department is acting gratuitously in its rush to file these briefs. The deadline they were apparently trying to meet is Inauguration Day." According to the *New York Times,* Starr responded that "he was just trying to 'clear the decks' so his successor would not be overburdened."[228] Four months later, after the Court agreed to hear one of the cases, the Clinton administration filed a brief explicitly rejecting one of Starr's arguments and urging that the Court rule in favor of the African-American plaintiffs.[229] Although the *New York Times* had predicted that "in practice it will be awkward for" the Clinton administration to change position, the fact that President Bush's assistant attorney general for civil rights, John Dunne, had favored backing the plaintiffs ameliorated any appearance of improper haste by the Clinton administration in adopting its position.

SETTING LITIGATION POSITIONS TODAY

The Civil Rights Division was created to secure the rights of disenfranchised African Americans. Its mission has expanded considerably since 1957, but the core duty to employ law enforcement tools to eradicate the racial caste system remains. Litigation policy should reflect that central duty. The ambiguity of the duty leads, however, to considerable leeway in fashioning appropriate litigation positions. The chemistry that leads to a particular position is complex, involving a mixture of constitutional and statutory common law techniques along with fact development and administration policy which itself is shaped by the politics of a democratic country.

Once the division has taken a position, the courts respond by either accepting or rejecting it, and that response in turn influences the division's future development of positions. The division normally does not lightly adopt abrupt changes in position, but litigation policies evolve. Abrupt departures from past policies may undermine the division's credibility but may in rare instances be justified by a strong showing that the prior position was wrong or was not carefully formed.

Litigation policy is closely related to priority setting, the topic of Chapter 6, and a pattern of progressive phases of enforcement emerges. First comes the definition of some core principle, such as the nondiscrimination principle that the department helped develop during the period from *Shelley* through *Brown* or the ban on employment discrimination that Congress established in Title VII, again with assistance from the department. Next there is a period of seeking compliance with the core principle and either subsequent or concurrent litigation refining that principle. The compliance efforts inevitably lead to litigation over relief, and the department first helps define standards of relief and then seeks to apply these new standards. Finally, the department may seek adjustments in principles and standards, based on experience.

All these steps require fidelity to the ultimate objective of eliminating racial discrimination, but they also call upon the department to recognize other values, such as state autonomy, workability, and the rights of third parties. The competing values inevitably cross over into the political arena; administration policies formed in response to broader currents in American life influence the department's position as to some issues but normally have been constrained by the statutes, case law, and prior positions of the department. Thus, litigation policy and priorities stem from an intricate interplay of the Constitution, the courts, the Congress, the president, the agencies, and the people.

9

The Role of Civil Servants
and Political Appointees

Although the Constitution and laws of the United States are clear in forbidding various forms of discrimination, numerous issues of legal interpretation have been left in the first instance to the courts. This situation has thrust the Civil Rights Division into the policy arena, not only with regard to setting priorities but also in selecting legal positions on a variety of unsettled issues profoundly important to the country. Those issues have ranged from the development of remedies for violation of voting rights to busing and affirmative action in employment. My discussion of the forces that influence the department's priorities and litigation policy would be incomplete without illustrating how individuals within the department shape the division's activities. Those persons fall into two groups: political appointees (the officials nominated by the president and confirmed by the Senate) and civil servants.

The relations between these two groups are initially a function of basic judgments of the framers of the Constitution and of later legislation leading to the creation of a tripartite executive branch: an elected president, political appointees primarily loyal to the president but beholden to the Senate, and apolitical civil servants whose primary loyalty flows to the department that employs them. The Department of Justice is an executive agency, reporting to the president. It is not a lawmaking body but depends on Congress for its mandate and on the courts for definitive judgment and interpretation. As Locke pointed out, "It is necessary there should be a power always in being, which should see to the execution of the laws that are made and remain in force; and thus the legislative and executive power come often to be separated."[1]

The department thus must be responsive to its immediate superior, the president; to the creator of its authority (and budget), the Congress; and to the ultimate authority to which it must appeal, the courts. Congress has also created the two tiers of executive personnel. Under Article 2, Section 2, of the Constitution the attorney general and assistant attorney general are officers of the United States, and the system of presidential appointment and senatorial confirmation ensures that they will be political appointees. Most personnel, however, are "inferior Officers" whose appointment Congress may vest in the heads of departments and whom Congress has classified as civil servants, forbidden by the Hatch Act to engage in political activities. The Supreme Court noted in 1882 that the Hatch Act was intended to promote "efficiency and integrity in the discharge of official duties, and to maintain proper discipline in the public service."[2] The resulting system contains two types of separation of powers, one horizontal and one vertical. Theoretically the three branches of government coexist on a horizontal plane, with specialized duties of law creation (Congress), law execution (president), and issuance of legal judgments (courts). Although oversimplified, this well-known picture is essentially accurate. Within the executive branch, a vertical separation exists in which the president provides overall policy guidance, the political appointees are charged with executing that policy guidance, and the civil servants are charged with executing the laws and court rulings that are products of horizontal separation of powers while simultaneously responding to the policy guidance from above. In effect, Congress has created a system of internal checks within the executive branch very roughly analogous to the internal checks that the bicameralism requirement of Article 1, Section 7, imposes on the Congress. Just as the two chambers of Congress, with different bases of representation, are thought to bring differing perspectives to the consideration of legislation, the differing perspectives of the two sets of executive branch personnel ideally will result in wiser administration.

My theses are simple. Although the job of the Department of Justice is to enforce binding legal norms, three factors set up the potential for conflict between political appointees, who represent the policies of the administration then in power, and civil servants, whose tenure is not tied to an administration and whose loyalties are to the department where they work and the laws they enforce: the horizontal and vertical separation of powers; the indeterminacy of some legal norms; and the lack of a concrete client. The vertical separation of powers was designed to enable both civil service attorneys and political appointees to influence policy. This design, as well as wise policy, requires cooperation between the two groups to achieve the proper balance between carrying out administration policy and carrying out core law enforcement duties. Where one group shuts itself out from influence by the other, the department's effectiveness suffers.

Basic descriptive information about the two groups will set the foundation for understanding their relative roles. Two obvious distinguishing features are method of selection and tenure. The attorney general, solicitor general, and assistant attorney general for civil rights are appointed by the president with the advice and consent of the Senate. The Senate's power is not toothless; twice in recent years the Senate's opposition has led to the withdrawal of nominations for assistant attorney general for civil rights, and one assistant attorney general was denied promotion because of Senate unhappiness with the manner in which he had discharged his duties.[3] The presidential appointees may select a small number of noncareer assistants.

In contrast, the members of the civil service are selected through a facially nonpolitical process. Although attorneys do not take a civil service examination, the law requires that they be hired based solely on merit with no regard for political affiliation.[4] Since 1954 the primary source of lawyers in the department has been the attorney general's honors program, which Attorney General Brownell instituted in order to end perceived personnel practices "marked by allegations of cronyism, favoritism and graft."[5]

Political appointees have come from a variety of places. Some came from the world of politics. For example, two assistant attorneys general for civil rights came from positions as state senators (Jerris Leonard, from Wisconsin,[6] and John Dunne, from New York). Some were lawyers in private practice who had supported the electoral winner (Harold Tyler, Burke Marshall, and J. Stanley Pottinger). Some were promoted from positions as deputy assistant attorney general (John Doar, Stephen Pollak, and David L. Norman). In the division's early years, the Eisenhower, Kennedy, and Johnson administrations thought the division should "maintain a neutral, disinterested, almost quasi-judicial image." During that period, "none of the men chosen to head the Civil Rights Division—White, Ryan, Tyler, Doar, and Marshall—were in any way identified with civil rights aims before taking office."[7] Indeed, Attorney General Kennedy's director of public information, Ed Guthman, believes that Attorney General Kennedy decided "that someone who had been in the forefront of any rights or racial cause might be handicapped by ideology or past associations in civil rights enforcement." That led to the choice of Burke Marshall, an "enlightened, conservative, brilliant Yale lawyer," as Kennedy's assistant attorney general for civil rights.[8] However, some later appointees, such as Drew S. Days III and Deval Patrick, had been active in civil rights organizations prior to their appointments. Days apparently was selected at least in part because President Carter's attorney general, Griffin Bell, had been impressed with Days's performance in cases that Bell had heard when serving as a judge of the U.S. Court of Appeals for the Fifth Circuit.[9]

The political appointee must ensure that the civil service lawyers enforce the law and that to the extent possible they do so in a manner consistent with administration policies.[10] This understanding was pithily explained by Assistant Attorney General Reynolds: "I subscribe to the policies of the administration and I have certainly followed those policies, and in doing so, I have made every effort that I possibly could, to do so within the letter and the spirit of the laws that are on the books, and that I am charged with enforcing."[11] Thus, the political appointee is subject to countervailing pressures of law and politics, with the latter sometimes at odds with the former. "More than in any other office, lawyers in the attorney general's office must make a schizophrenic choice between the office's role as a neutral expositor of the law and its role as a political advocate for the administration."[12]

Early in the Reagan administration, I recall a meeting in the office of President Reagan's new solicitor general, Rex Lee. We were discussing the position to be taken in the government's brief in a case pending in the Supreme Court. The political appointees of another department were arguing that our brief should reverse the position taken in the lower courts by the Carter administration. Lee listened patiently but seemed unpersuaded. Finally, the proponents for a changed position pulled out their trump card: "But Mr. Solicitor General, you must remember that we won the election." Fortunately, the law and the facts trumped politics, and the government's brief in that case did not reverse our prior position.

The tenure of most political appointees will be no longer than that of the president who appointed them, and typically it is shorter. Since the creation of the Civil Rights Division of the Justice Department in 1957, nine persons have served as president of the United States. A larger number have served as attorney general (sixteen)[13] and assistant attorney general for civil rights (twelve).[14] (William Bradford Reynolds is the only assistant attorney general for civil rights to serve through two presidential terms.) In contrast with this high turnover of political appointees, the civil service lawyer serves as a source of stability. True, hundreds of civil service lawyers have passed through the division during the past forty years. During the period 1971–1984, a total of 403 attorneys left the division, or an average of 29 per year. Total authorized attorney strength during that time ranged from 157 in 1971 and 1972 to 201 in 1979. Departures during this thirteen-year period ranged from 11 percent to 22 percent of the authorized attorney strength in a given year.[15] However, careers of twenty or thirty years are not uncommon among this cadre.

Discussion of the division's personnel tends to focus on its political leadership and to pay scant attention to the civil service lawyer except for the occasional cause célèbre, such as the delay of desegregation in Mississippi in 1969[16] or the volte-face in the *Bob Jones University* case in 1981.[17] And it is not uncommon for political appointees to aim generalized barbs or praise at civil servants, as when Charles Fried, in his account of his tenure as solicitor general, states that the career lawyers in the Civil Rights Division "sabotaged [Assistant Attorney General William Bradford Reynolds's] rightful claim to leadership in every way they could."[18]

No focused and thorough examination of the role and influence of civil servants in the Civil Rights Division exists. A study of Civil Division attorneys shows that on average their age is young; their tenure is shorter, on average, than other government lawyers; and for the most part they come from large eastern law schools. It also shows that they have a different outlook, which stems from their being generalists and litigators, in contrast with agency lawyers, who tend to be specialists and counselors. Civil Rights Division lawyers, by contrast with both of these groups, tend to be specialists and litigators,[19] having more in common with Antitrust Division attorneys of whom "a significant number . . . have joined or remain because they want to bring antitrust cases and win them. Their goals and opinions are overwhelmingly those that one associates with legal advocates and prosecutors, and their opinions on various questions that are important in shaping antitrust enforcement are largely determined by the imperatives of prosecution."[20]

The typical lawyer in the division was a high achiever in law school.[21] Most were hired under the attorney general's honors program initiated in 1955 by Attorney General Herbert Brownell to substitute for the prior practice of hiring young lawyers "off the street."[22] Most were attracted to the division both because of their commitment to the laws that it enforces and because of the division's general reputation as a good place to gain experience in complex litigation.[23] Many leave after a few years, generally moving on to attractive jobs as litigators with law firms or with U.S. attorneys. One can count among the alumni of the Civil Rights Division several federal judges, numerous law professors, and many leaders of the bar. But another large group makes the Civil Rights Division a career. They do so not because they lack mobility, but because a variety of factors make their jobs desirable. Chief among those factors is the understanding that their work promotes justice. One of my former colleagues, the late Walter W. Barnett, has been described as having "entered government not to enrich his contacts and then spin through the revolving door into lucrative private practice, but to work for a cause in which he believed and for people whom he felt had been deprived."[24]

The type of work—litigation in federal court—also tends to mold those who do it. Early in the history of the division, it became apparent that success in civil rights litigation in the Deep South required extraordinary lawyering. Because many trial court judges were unsympathetic, every case had to be tried so as to provide to a more balanced appellate court compelling grounds for reversal of adverse findings of fact as clearly erroneous.[25] Further, Assistant Attorney General John Doar stressed that division attorneys must be the epitome of rectangular rectitude. Turning around the famous Holmes phrase, "Men must turn square corners when they deal with the Government,"[26] he required that government attorneys always turn square corners. This rule recognizes that government attorneys "are in an odd situation because [they] almost always litigate against the people of the United States, who are the very people that [they] ultimately serve."[27]

From these circumstances grew a tradition of thoroughness and care that disfavors knee-jerk responses to issues and persists to the present day.[28] John Doar insisted that each lawyer use "the technique that the Division believes is best suited to producing maximum results."[29] A lawyer who disagreed with this pragmatic approach would not last long in the division. As Doar said, "If you play for Green Bay, you only block one way; if you litigate in this Division, you only prepare one way."[30] The early modus operandi of Burke Marshall and John Doar continues to exert influence on the career attorneys. In the Civil Rights Division, as in the Antitrust Division, "younger lawyers' attitudes toward and practice of enforcement are ... heavily formed through emulation of their senior colleagues."[31] For example, a generation of Civil Rights Division lawyers was taught the "Owen option," named after Deputy Assistant Attorney General D. Robert Owen: always take the option that places the most demands on you.

A memorandum that John Doar sent to all section chiefs in 1967 exemplifies the standards he applied. The memorandum quoted suggestions of a senior career lawyer, David L. Norman, who had been reviewing the work of the sections while Doar was prosecuting the conspirators who had killed three civil rights workers in Mississippi in 1964. Norman suggested that the remedy for substandard work "lies not so much in preaching but in rejecting matters on the ground that they need more careful work." For example, he criticized an investigative request for the lack of analysis of prior investigative results and for vagueness and incompleteness. He found fault with a recommendation under Section 5 of the Voting Rights Act that "reflects a philosophy that we would be representing the defeated Negro candidate, and that therefore a major consideration is whether she would like for us to sue or not," and which failed to cite any of the major applicable case law. He noted that pleadings in two proposed desegregation suits were "mass-production jobs—an approach which I believe must be abandoned in the school litigation area," and he recommended rejecting a proposed public accommodations suit against a small restaurant whose owner had expressed a willingness to comply with Title II of the Civil Rights Act.[32] This memorandum reflects that although not all the work being produced in the division was of top quality, the leadership was committed to insisting on top quality even during a period when the division was under enormous pressure to produce.

Arthur Schlesinger, Jr., once described the difference between lawyers in the Civil Rights Commission and those in the Civil Rights Division: "One was an agency of recommendation and the other of action."[33] Lawyers at the two agencies began with similar backgrounds but subsequently diverged in their attitudes depending on whether their role was gadfly (the commission)[34] or litigator (the division). In short, the division has attracted employees looking for more than just another job, people committed to equality under the law and to litigation as the instrument for securing that right.

This configuration of the division's enforcement staff hardly presents the problem of a runaway bureaucracy out of touch with reality. Nonetheless, some problems are inherent. First, the job of the law enforcer is to find violations of the law and to correct them. Zeal to uncover wrongdoing may lead to a lack of rigor in critically evaluating cases and positions[35] or a failure to consider competing values. Assistant Attorney General Reynolds felt he had been a victim of a failure to consider competing values when early in his tenure the appellate section failed to consider filing an amicus brief supporting the defendant in a voting rights case pending in the Supreme Court; the division had previously followed a practice of presumptively either supporting the civil rights plaintiff or not participating in the case. In a memorandum to the solicitor general, Reynolds complained:

> Regrettably, because I received the appellate section's analysis and recommendation in this case after petitioner's brief on the merits had been filed, the preferred course of action—which would be to participate as amicus in support of petitioners—is foreclosed. Accordingly, my recommendation—albeit with considerable disappointment—is that the United States not participate.[36]

Second, the civil service staff is hired by and serves under political appointees, each of whom may seek to mold that staff into the image most compatible with the policy views of the president. This situation may lead to a real or perceived lack of responsiveness to new leadership when administrations change. Unfortunately, new administrations often view the career leadership with great suspicion, which is fed by disgruntled groups who objected to decisions made under the prior administration, which the career lawyers faithfully carried out. Ironically, it is this loyalty to one administration that engenders distrust by the next administration.

Reassignments of career staff early in the new administration are common. For example, the Clinton administration removed three section chiefs from their positions and when the sole remaining career deputy assistant attorney general retired, passed over all the section chiefs in replacing him. Perhaps the most dramatic example of distrust of career holdovers is the story of Lawrence Wallace, a deputy solicitor general who began his career in the solicitor general's office in 1968 during the Johnson administration and was one of the authors of the government's brief in *Green v. County School Board*. During the Carter administration he was characterized by Secretary of Health, Education, and Welfare Joseph Califano as a "Nixon holdover" in the course of Califano's effort to influence the content of the government's brief in the *Bakke* case.[37] Yet, "when Wallace became a target for the anger of Reagan conservatives after the Bob Jones debacle, they tried to link the source of his obstinacy to his political views,"[38] and he was removed from any further participation on civil rights cases. In short, this Johnson administration hire was considered a Nixon holdover under President Carter and a Carter holdover under President Reagan.

Third, some of the civil service staff may develop a degree of expertise and a commitment to particular law enforcement policies that can overwhelm a new leader, who is inundated with paper. Justice Powell's observation regarding submissions under Section 5 of the Voting Rights Act has some application to the assistant attorney general's other duties:

No senior officer in the Justice Department—much less the Attorney General—could make a thoughtful, personal judgment on an average of 25 pre-clearance petitions per day. Thus, important decisions made on a democratic basis in covered subdivisions and States are finally judged by unidentifiable employees of the federal bureaucracy, usually without anything resembling an evidentiary hearing.[39]

Fourth, civil service staff may form alliances with outside groups concerned with the laws the staff enforces. Former Deputy Attorney General Tyler believed that

> Some offices and divisions within the Department of Justice have informally affiliated with public pressure groups in our society. They feel that it is incumbent upon them in their official capacity to be in cheek-to-jowl with these groups, even to the extent of bringing them in to put on a "dog and pony show"—as it is called in Washington—on the fifth or fourth floor of the Department of Justice and sometimes even in the White House. This has happened within the civil rights sphere, the antitrust sphere, and in other offices.[40]

Tyler seems to have drawn this conclusion from the pattern of advocacy groups seeking an opportunity to convince him or the attorney general or solicitor general of the correctness of their position. Because that position sometimes corresponded to the position of a litigating division, he seems to assume that the advocacy group and the division must be acting in concert. On the other hand, when Tyler met with other advocacy groups whose positions conflicted with those of a litigation division, he presumably saw no such cabal. Tyler's position seems at odds with those of his former boss, Attorney General Edward H. Levi, who believed strongly in "government by discussion."

Fifth, "there are significant pressures to place decisions beyond the control—even beyond the consideration—of policymaking officials by identifying policy questions as questions of law and therefore as peculiarly within the province of the courts."[41] Finally, we know that over time bureaucracies tend to ossify, to lose their sense of purpose, to look more to the past than to the future, to reject new ideas because they differ from what they have always done.

The Civil Rights Division is a party or amicus in over a thousand ongoing suits; it brings between one hundred and two hundred new suits each year[42] and files numerous briefs, motions, and pleadings. That work is done primarily by the roughly two hundred civil service lawyers. They are not fungible, and absent some controls, litigation decisions could turn on which lawyer is assigned to the matter. The basic control is, or at least should be, the law itself. For example, Congress did not grant division lawyers carte blanche to initiate civil rights litigation. It withheld from them until recently the right to bring a civil suit seeking injunctive relief against patterns of brutality by a police department.[43] It defeated a proposal to allow them to bring civil actions to remedy racial discrimination in jury selection.[44] Even where such suits are authorized, Congress has attached limiting conditions.[45] Finally, the civil service lawyer must follow the substantive provisions of the law as construed by the courts. Even with all these restraints, however, the division retains tremendous flexibility both in setting its priorities and in addressing unsettled areas of the law.[46]

Nongovernment lawyers typically labor under the most basic restraint of all: the wishes of the client. But who is the client of the government lawyer? As a District of Columbia Bar committee has pointed out, some argue that the government lawyer's responsibility is to the "public interest" and his or her client is "the people as a whole," while others argue that his or her client is "the entire government."[47] Calling "We the People" the clients of the Department of Justice[48] would not provide sufficient guidance to department lawyers as to the wishes of the client. The committee, in an attempt to provide greater specificity, concluded that "the employing agency should in normal circumstances be considered the client of the government lawyer." If the employing agency is the client, then ordinarily the lawyer will learn the client's wishes from the political appointee (the attorney general and assistant attorney general for civil rights). This shift of discretion from the civil service lawyer to the political appointee allows democratic processes, rather than mandarins, to determine what litigation decisions promote the public interest. At the same time, the participation of civil servants in the process helps insulate the political appointee from the appearance of undue partisanship in decision making. As President Theodore Roosevelt wrote in 1904:

> Of all the officers of the Government, those of the Department of Justice should be kept most free from any suspicion of improper action on partisan or factional grounds, so that there shall be gradually a growth, even though a slow growth, in the knowledge that the Federal courts and the representatives of the Federal Department of Justice insist on meting out evenhanded justice to all.[49]

Both the civil service employee and the political appointee bring disadvantages to the problem that a former general counsel of the Office of Management and Budget calls "clientless lawyering."[50] Where lawyering is clientless, the reins that tether most lawyers are absent and the lawyer is both the maker of policy and its advocate. The civil servant has no claim to represent the wishes of "We the People"; the political appointee may take a narrow, partisan view of those wishes. The former may be tied to the positions of the past; the latter may be unaware of the lessons of the past. One answer to this dilemma is joint decision making, building on the strengths of each and on the responsibility that falls on each to faithfully execute the laws of the United States.[51] Other answers—raw exercise of political power or the creation of a completely apolitical Department of Justice—would magnify one or the other prong of the dilemma.

Although political appointees and civil service attorneys differ in many respects, they share several characteristics. First, their training in the law tends to lead both groups to approach law enforcement issues through the use of legal analysis, relying on close reading of statutes, fidelity to binding precedent, and careful development of facts. Second, most members of both groups chose to work in the Civil Rights Division because of their commitment to the nondiscrimination principle, to the federal role in law enforcement, and to quality work. Third, both groups work in the executive branch and, with varying intensity, recognize the attorney general and the president as their superiors in the chain of command. In most instances these shared characteristics prove more important than the differences discussed above.

The importance of the shared characteristics is heightened by the interdependence of the two groups. The political appointees need the legal expertise, institutional memory, and sheer numbers of the civil service lawyers. Moreover, the existence of a quasi-independent civil service may enhance the credibility of the department with the courts and some members of the public. Conversely, the civil service lawyers need the political expertise and connections of the political appointees, who provide a crucial link to the president and Congress as well as to the electorate. Given the importance of the issues that the division addresses and the potential for interference from the political branches, the division needs leaders who can speak with authority and receive respect from those branches. For example, it took the Clinton administration over a year to put an assistant attorney general into place. During that year the division lacked the political credibility to gain departmental approval for a defined set of enforcement policies. It reported to Associate Attorney General Webster Hubbell, who was unable to devote substantial time to the division's affairs. Many litigation decisions were simply placed on hold.[52]

The political appointees also bring fresh perspectives and a healthy distance that may facilitate rethinking of substantive positions and organizational structure. The question, then, is how best to configure the relationship between the two groups. Joint decision making has been the norm in the Civil Rights Division. Of course, the attorney general, solicitor general, and assistant attorney general for civil rights must have the final word, but normally they have done so only after consulting with civil service attorneys. By and large, the two components of the division have recognized that both public interest and self-interest dictate cooperation and communication: the political appointee's impact on policy will be minimal unless he or she can enlist the aid of the career staff.

As Justice Powell has noted, "Implementation of policy often depends upon the cooperation of public employees who do not hold policymaking posts."[53] Sheer volume of work, the need for expertise, and the maintenance of credibility with the courts and Congress all lead in the direction of joint decision making. Moreover, even if there are disagreements as to specific policies, both components share a common commitment to enforcement of the civil rights laws. In

general, "the Department's lawyers are professionals who realize that each administration is entitled to make its mark on federal law."[54] The civil servant has
other incentives to cooperate. Not only does the political appointee hold the up-
per hand on matters such as promotions and assignments, but the civil service
attorney needs approval from the political appointee to file the cases or briefs
he thinks should be filed.

Other forces, however, lead to tension between the political leader and the
civil service follower. A study of the relationship between political and civil service attorneys might fruitfully be advanced by examining various models of law
enforcement management. Since no administration has adhered to one model
exclusively, the differences have been in emphasis. What follows is an examination of two polar models: government by discussion (toward which I am biased)
and government by fiat. These models are fleshed out with a few case histories
that span several administrations and different phases in the development of civil
rights enforcement and are drawn primarily from published accounts of the
means used by each component to respond to the tension between them.

Attorney General Edward H. Levi, who served under President Ford, es-
poused what he called a "government by discussion."[55] The development of the
department's decision not to file a Supreme Court brief in the Boston school
desegregation case is a good illustration of this model. In 1975 Solicitor General
Robert Bork wished to file a brief in the Supreme Court urging the grant of
certiorari in the Boston school desegregation case,[56] because in his view the busing order in that case went too far. The case was a cause célèbre, and proponents
and opponents of the lower court decision vigorously lobbied the department.
Bork sought the views of Assistant Attorney General Pottinger, who headed the
Civil Rights Division. Pottinger opposed the filing. Attorney General Levi discussed the case with the president, presumably because the proposal related to
the president's general policy opposing school busing. When the president left
the decision to the department,[57] a period of intense deliberation ensued there.
This was not a case of civil servant versus political appointee; indeed the attorney general simply sought the advice of the solicitor general, assistant attorney
general for civil rights, and civil service attorneys such as Deputy Solicitor General Lawrence Wallace and me (in my role as head of the Civil Rights Division's
Appellate Section). In keeping with his practice, he also consulted with others,
such as his special assistants.

Despite the political controversy swirling around us and our divergent views,
we each spoke our minds freely and the discussions focused on the merits of the
issue whether to file. In the end the attorney general decided not to file. The discussions did, however, ultimately lead to further meetings to discuss a legislative
approach. Levi "led in the development of proposed legislation, under the direction of the President, designed to guide use of the busing remedy in school desegregation cases in order to achieve the purposes articulated in the courts' decisions while interfering as little as possible with other values."[58] The end result

reflected proper consideration of legal standards, law enforcement concerns, and administration policy.

Attorney General Levi was not, of course, the only attorney general to favor government by discussion. For example, Attorney General Robert F. Kennedy employed an open style of leadership that called on a variety of career and political appointee attorneys for their views.[59] Similarly, in 1969, early in the tenure of Attorney General John Mitchell, a free-flowing debate ensued as to the desired shape of federal school desegregation policy. Career attorneys Bob Owen and Dave Norman joined Assistant Attorney General Jerris Leonard and officials of the Department of Health, Education, and Welfare in these discussions that resulted in "a document that supported strong enforcement of the law."[60] President Carter's assistant attorney general for the Civil Rights Division Drew S. Days III referred to this style of decision making as "internal due process" and argued that it is the traditional mode in the Department of Justice.[61]

Government by discussion requires trust between the civil service lawyers and political appointees. Trust cannot exist without some common denominator about basic objectives, but it does not require agreement about subsidiary issues. Mutual trust will rarely exist at the beginning of a new administration and must be built; it is difficult in Washington, D.C., where the "leak" is a way of life and the significance of the leak tends to be magnified out of all proportion to its actual importance. The building of trust requires civil service attorneys to honor confidences and political appointees to resist pointing the finger when leaks occur. Civil service attorneys must have confidence that they will not be punished for expressing their views to the political appointee, or the well-known dangers of Washington sycophancy will insulate the political appointee from the range of information and views needed to make wise choices.

No doubt it was easier to maintain an atmosphere of trust in the 1960s, when the division was small enough for the assistant attorney general to spend time in the trenches with his troops and when the common objectives of the career and political staff were clearer than today. One answer to the problems occasioned by growth of staff and diffusion of responsibilities and attitudes is effective use of a pyramidal organization. The assistant attorney general and the civil service leadership (deputy assistant attorneys general and section chiefs and their deputies) can create or destroy an atmosphere of trust. If the political and civil service leadership engage in cooperative law enforcement, the line lawyers who work in the various litigation sections are likely to follow that example.

One cannot claim that discussion will always lead to the right decision, but involvement of civil service lawyers in the decision-making discussions tends to lend legitimacy to those decisions and motivate the civil service lawyers to zealously represent the position of the department. A former political appointee has observed that if the civil service attorneys are fully involved in the decision-making process but the political appointees ultimately decide not to follow their advice, the career lawyers "would do their best to support the position adopted," provided that "plausible legal arguments exist in support of [that] position."[62] Indeed, discussion may cause the career lawyers to rethink their entrenched positions. I engaged in many heated discussions with Assistant Attorney General Reynolds. Although often unconvinced by his reasoning, I noted that Reynolds had, "through his keen and questioning intellect, challenged the complacency and settled views of many of us, forcing us to analyze anew basic issues. I believe this process has substantially deepened our understanding of civil rights law and policy."[63]

Moreover, government by discussion will often prevent error.[64] One of the many mistakes that led to the *Bob Jones* debacle during the Reagan administration was the failure to listen to civil service attorneys from the Tax Division, Civil Rights Division, solicitor general's office, and Department of Treasury.[65] Government by discussion is enhanced by procedural regularity—a regularity that was bypassed in *Bob Jones*—which in litigation matters comes from the J-memo approach (see Chapter 7). As to review of submissions under Section 5 of the Voting Rights Act, Assistant Attorney General Reynolds noted that "the internal process of review has been the same for a number of years." Using that process,

> There has been a considerable amount of disagreement on a number of these, but . . . while there are decisions that I have made, which the staff has disagreed with, after I've received the staff's recommendations, we've had meetings on numerous occasions, and sometimes I've persuaded them that my view of the matter differs from what they stated in their memorandum, and sometimes they've persuaded me that their view is better than the one that I thought after I read their memorandum.[66]

Government by discussion in the Boston school desegregation case during the Ford administration may have been, in part, a reaction against the government by fiat[67] that marked the Nixon administration's approach to busing. Busing is not a politically popular remedy, and the Nixon administration was firmly opposed to it. Nevertheless, the Supreme Court had required the use of busing where necessary to overcome the effects of past racial discrimination by school systems.[68] Following that decision, many school systems in large southern cities were placed under busing plans and challenged those plans in the higher courts. At that time the president "ordered the Justice Department to actively oppose busing plans. Instead of using the department to argue the conservative position on the unsettled issues of constitutional law, he attempted to use the Civil Rights Division as a weapon against enforcement of the settled law."[69]

There ensued a series of hasty, ill-informed misadventures by the division. For example, twenty-four hours before the Nashville school desegregation case was to be argued before the U.S. Court of Appeals for the Sixth Circuit, the division moved for leave to file an amicus curiae brief that argued against busing. The court granted the motion and invited the division to present oral argument. According to the court's opinion, Deputy Assistant Attorney General K. William

O'Connor, who drew the unenviable assignment, "had not had the opportunity to read the District Court record in this case and was not aware in advance of hearing that the claimed practical problems had never been presented to or adjudicated by the District Judge."[70] In another case, involving Prince George's County, Maryland, Solicitor General Erwin Griswold, ordered to support a stay of a busing order, could find no legal argument for it, so Attorney General Richard Kleindienst alone signed the government's amicus brief urging a stay.[71] These shenanigans did not substantially harm the law but did undermine judicial confidence in the Department of Justice. They also were very demoralizing to civil service attorneys in the Department of Justice, who reacted by refusing to sign some briefs and by sending letters to newspapers, signing a statement of opposition, and resigning.[72]

Another technique of government by fiat is the end run, in which normal procedures are breached in order to avoid discussion of proposed courses of action. Early in the Reagan administration Assistant Attorney General Reynolds stated his opposition to employment quotas, goals, and timetables.[73] Apparently dissatisfied with the civil service staff's responsiveness to his announcement, he hired non–civil service attorneys and authorized them to act independently of the normal structure. Thus, for example, the department took the unusual but not unheard-of step of intervening in a fair employment suit in the court of appeals in order to seek rehearing en banc of the court's initial decision, which had reversed a district court order refusing to enter an affirmative action consent decree. The department's filing was a secret operation handled by two non–civil service attorneys who did not consult with the division personnel normally responsible for employment cases and appeals until the eve of filing.[74] Unlike the department's brief in the Nashville school desegregation case, the department filed lawyerlike papers in this case and it partially prevailed in the court of appeals.[75]

The costs of maintaining a shadow Civil Rights Division, referred to by civil service lawyers as commissars, include inefficiency, lack of balanced consideration of positions, and poor morale among the civil service attorneys. Such an expression of distrust breeds distrust in return.[76] Advantages of such a system include its effectiveness in developing expertise among non–civil service attorneys, its responsiveness to an administration's agenda,[77] and its implicit warning to civil service lawyers to conform or leave. Aside from the issue of whether the advantages are outweighed by the disadvantages, one might also ask whether government by fiat is necessary in light of the availability of other governing techniques. Former Attorney General Nicholas Katzenbach is said to have observed:

> The big job a President has is to make the bureaucracy work for him. Most Presidents resist this. They don't have confidence in it. They create other mechanisms to short-cut it, to go around it. The one thing Robert Kennedy

did was he *made* the Department of Justice work for him and President Kennedy, and if you can translate that into government you can make the whole government work.[78]

Although government by unilateral command is available only to the political appointee, government by end run may at times be available to the civil service lawyer as well. The political appointee is physically incapable of monitoring every court appearance, and it is difficult to monitor every court filing. Where the goals of the political appointee and the civil service lawyers differ radically, the latter may be tempted to become a loose cannon. A well-known example is the oral argument of a civil service lawyer in the court of appeals shortly after the Mississippi school desegregation debacle, where the lawyer publicly chastised the attorney general.[79] There may be occasional examples of civil service lawyers soliciting invitations from federal judges for the government to participate in litigation, where the political appointees might have resisted *sua sponte* participation by the government.

Nonresponsiveness to policy direction is an indirect way of advancing the civil servant's personal agenda. For example, the Nixon and Ford administrations had avoided bringing cases attacking discriminatory zoning and had concentrated on cases of private discrimination.[80] On taking office, Assistant Attorney General Days ordered a reversal of priorities,[81] but the attorneys in the section continued to produce primarily individual cases. After the assistant attorney general disapproved the filing of a complaint because the apartment complex in question was too small,[82] he later disapproved a meritorious appeal of a similar case to enforce his policy. As Joel Selig reports,

> The reappraisal which Mr. Days desired met with some resistance on the part of career attorneys who had led or been associated with the Division's fair housing litigation in the past. Attorneys who had investigated and proposed small, low impact cases for litigation were not enthusiastic when some of their cases were disapproved or referred to a local United States Attorney's office for handling.[83]

Eventually the career and political leadership compromised, and it was agreed that 25 percent of the section's resources would be devoted to high-impact land-use cases.[84]

It has long been recognized that "of all manifestations of power, restraint impresses men most."[85] The Madisonian vision of government imposed restraint through structural devices such as the separation of powers. Congress has bestowed considerable power upon both the political appointee and the civil service attorney in the Department of Justice. Each labors under the awesome responsibility of enforcing the laws of the nation, a responsibility that exists within the framework of horizontal separation of powers. Although both are constrained by each of the three branches of government, the political appointee owes primary allegiance to the president, while the civil service lawyer's allegiance is perhaps more diffuse because it is more long-term. Government by discussion draws on the strengths of each to produce proper restraint in setting law enforcement policy. Government by fiat tends to abandon restraint, because each element of the department ignores the legitimate concerns of the other.

10

The Future of the Civil Rights Division

On my first trip as a lawyer in the Civil Rights Division in January 1964, I interviewed an African American who had tried to register to vote in Eutaw, Alabama, county seat of Greene County, an 80 percent black county with virtually no African-American voters. The unpainted home of the frustrated voter was located on a dirt street, and one had to cross the open storm sewer to reach it. The chill of the bitter winter (two days later it would snow) was only slightly softened by embers in the only heat source, a fireplace. The elderly interviewee received us in his bedroom, where he lay under piles of blankets. However, he invited us to move to the living room, carefully unscrewing the naked lightbulb hanging from the bedroom ceiling and installing it in the living room.

The tools given to the Civil Rights Division to address this man's plight were limited and indirect. The right to vote might lead to African-American representation in government; certainly the streets in the black neighborhood would then be paved and proper sewers installed. Economic progress, however, would come more slowly. Today, the black majority is represented in government in Greene County, as are African Americans in Selma and throughout the South. The division's powers, too, have been supplemented in order to address discrimination in education, employment, and housing. Yet it is far from clear that antidiscrimination laws alone will suffice to erase the racial chasm in Greene County or elsewhere.

In the 1950s and 1960s race discrimination was so palpable that it could be photographed. Pictures of state officials barring the schoolhouse door, of soldiers escorting children to school, of burnt-out interstate freedom ride buses, of well-dressed students being dragged from lunch counters, of police dogs attacking orderly marchers, of baton-swinging sheriff's deputies on horseback at the Edmund Pettus Bridge in Selma, and of the funeral of three African-American girls killed in a church bombing in Birmingham, Alabama, dramatically exposed the evils of the official racial caste system. Thankfully, while such pictures occa-

171

sionally still intrude, they have become relatively rare. A large proportion of white Americans no longer believes that racial discrimination against African Americans is a pressing problem. What is the role of the Civil Rights Division in this new era?

Much has changed since 1957, and much has remained the same. The political landscape, always in transition, continues to affect the responsibilities of the division. The division's policies have emphasized a more activist role in bringing cases and in shaping the law, but the core policy remains the enforcement of laws against racial discrimination. The country's understanding of federalism has evolved from Burke Marshall's "Federalism and Civil Rights" book, to the Voting Rights Act and the imposition on the states of Title VII and the Americans with Disabilities Act, to the current unsettled condition in which Congress increasingly attempts to legislate in areas traditionally reserved to the states and the Supreme Court increasingly imposes restrictions on such legislation.

The influence of the president on the division has evolved. Under President Eisenhower the division was reactive and cautious, with little direct contact with the president. President Kennedy's style was different, his brother was attorney general, and the times required an active approach to enforcement. John Doar "would say that the chain of command at the Division was short and straight: Doar to Marshall to Robert Kennedy to the President of the United States."[1] Over time the national sense of urgency of the task abated, the personal relationships between the division's leadership and the president attenuated, and other issues such as Vietnam, Watergate, deregulation, and the economy came to the fore. It is startling to visit President Carter's library and museum and to see that the displays featuring the primary issues of his presidency include the Iran hostage crisis, the energy crisis, the Camp David accords, the protection of the environment, and international human rights, but there is no display concerning race discrimination in the United States. The so-called imperial presidency was severely challenged in the wake of Watergate, but today's presidents are more likely to be insulated from the Civil Rights Division by multiple layers of aides in the White House and in the Department of Justice. In 1961, Attorney General Kennedy "was impressed by the fact that [John Doar] seemed to have gotten an awful lot done in the five months between July 1960 [when Doar joined the Republican administration as number two person in the division] and January 1961" and "decided that the Republican from Wisconsin could stick around."[2] Today, by contrast, retention of a holdover political deputy would be inconceivable. Instead, great emphasis is placed on filling the second tier of jobs in the Civil Rights Division with politically vetted individuals, and even career attorneys are viewed with suspicion if they are high-ranking holdovers.

Most important, officially imposed racial segregation in the South is no longer tolerated, but racial divisions remain a powerful force. The most desegregated school systems in the country are the formerly de jure segregated schools of the

Deep South. The state with the largest number of elected African-American public officials is now Mississippi, which had none in 1957. African Americans hold high positions in law enforcement in the southern states. Where "white" and "colored" signs once directed individuals to separate rest rooms, water fountains, theater entrances, and restaurant areas, the races freely mingle largely without incident. Housing and financing have more gradually opened up to African-American buyers. Yet the African-American underclass has grown, and virtually every city has its low-income black ghetto with concomitant high crime rates and failures of the education system. An undercurrent of racial mistrust still runs through American life.

The need for a Civil Rights Division to enforce laws against race discrimination has, unhappily, not ended. In 1964 a prescient observer noted, "Desegregation may be the problem of the last decade and integration of this one, but the problem of the casualties of the long period before and the decade after the *Brown* decision promises to be with us for a long time to come."[3] Although a national consensus against race discrimination has emerged and massive overt resistance to racial equality has ended, intentional discrimination still flourishes, there is much to learn about less obvious forms of discrimination, and as of yet a consensus has not been reached about remedies. Although the broad need to combat racial discrimination remains, the battle against the official, formal racial caste system for which the division was initially created has largely ended with victory. The role of the division must evolve to meet current and future problems, unless it is, like the Interstate Commerce Commission,[4] to lose its relevance and then its existence.

The formal, moral, and pragmatic reasons that supported the adoption of the civil rights acts continue. The Supreme Court has often and emphatically reaffirmed the nondiscrimination principle of the Reconstruction amendments and the enforcement power of the Congress. As a national consensus has developed that race discrimination in particular is morally wrong, deviations from that moral norm become arguably even more intolerable. The racial caste system mocks that consensus and continues to undermine national unity. "While the legislatures and federal courts were pursuing their individualist, rights-oriented course, social scientists discovered the permanent underclass, a subculture of poverty, suspiciously congruent with concentrations of black Americans in the urban ghettos, and impervious to changes in the economic structure."[5]

Racial discrimination saps our economic strength by shrinking markets, depriving American business of an educated workforce, and creating large economic wastelands in urban centers. Threats to public order from official discrimination have abated but have not disappeared, as the state violence to Rodney King attests. The growth of white supremacist groups has led to an increase in hate crimes. And the threat of riots in inner cities is never far from the surface. For all these reasons, and despite the growth of its responsibilities regarding matters in addition to race discrimination, the division should continue to have responsibility for combating race discrimination and should accord high priority to race cases.

Prior to 1957, civil rights enforcement in the United States was relegated primarily to civil suits by private individuals and to very limited authority of the attorney general to prosecute those who criminally deprived individuals of civil rights. The creation of the Civil Rights Division in 1957 was accompanied by a narrow expansion of authority to seek civil judicial relief for violations of the Fifteenth Amendment right to vote. No federal enforcement structure existed outside the Department of Justice. Today the picture is much different.

First, the Congress has created new rights to be free from private discrimination. Second, a large federal enforcement structure has been erected. Every federal agency has responsibility to ensure that federal funds are not expended in programs or activities that discriminate based on race, national origin, or disability. Many agencies have similar responsibilities as to gender discrimination. Federal banking agencies share with the Department of Justice responsibility to enforce the Equal Credit Opportunity Act. The Department of Labor and other agencies enforce Executive Order 11246 banning discrimination by federal contractors. The Department of Justice shares with HUD enforcement of the Fair Housing Act and with the EEOC enforcement of the fair employment law, Title VII. This list is by no means an exhaustive one. Congress has authorized employment of over 5,800 federal employees to enforce the civil rights laws, of whom only 569 are in the Department of Justice.

The federal enforcement structure has developed without a master plan, and the resulting edifice could benefit from renovation. Restructuring requires careful thought about the proper role of the various players—the Department of Justice, other federal departments and agencies, and private individuals. Broadly speaking, the Department of Justice should pursue structural reform and the punishment of egregious violations, while private individuals should pursue vindication of their private interests. The other federal departments and agencies should bring to bear their pinpointed expertise on such matters as employment, housing, lending, and education and should facilitate both the department's structural reform litigation and private individuals' vindication of private interests. The Department of Justice should function primarily as a litigator but should retain other roles that are ancillary to litigation.

The creation of the Civil Rights Division began a shift of emphasis from criminal to equitable sanctions such as injunctions. More recent cases and legislation arguably have shifted emphasis from equitable to legal sanctions (damages). Yet as we have seen there seems to be a stronger justification for the Department of Justice to litigate equitable than legal issues, because equitable relief requires the defendant to conform to the civil rights acts' vision of the public interest, while damages for private individuals seem much more to vindicate "private" than "public" interests, although they may incidentally promote public ends. Moreover, the department should not be considered a representative of the individuals harmed by the defendant's conduct, and therefore it lacks a principled basis for negotiating damage settlements.[6]

Greater emphasis on criminal enforcement against open and notorious acts of discrimination should be considered. In 1957 discrimination was so widespread that criminal sanctions for voting discrimination would potentially have subjected a large proportion of the leadership of the southern states to prosecution. Alexander Bickel's observation that under the school desegregation cases "the task of the law . . . was not to punish law breakers but to diminish their numbers"[7] may have been correct in 1962, but conditions have changed since then. Discrimination is no longer an accepted norm, and the reasons that may have precluded criminalizing it have largely vanished. Current law, which is a clumsy vehicle for bringing criminal prosecutions for racial discrimination, needs to be changed. Racial discrimination under color of state law does violate the general prohibition of 18 U.S.C.A. §242.[8] However, a much more specific criminal prohibition would be more effective.[9] Such a vehicle does exist for violations of the Voting Rights Act.[10] Even where violence occurs, the federal law against race violence contains loopholes, applying only if the violence occurred "because" the individual was engaging in an activity enumerated in the statute.[11]

One possible objection to criminalizing nondiscrimination law is the fear of chilling affirmative action. Indeed, some opponents of affirmative action have proposed making it a crime.[12] However, it should not be difficult to draft a statute that punishes only invidious discrimination and allows affirmative race-based efforts to overcome a pattern of racial exclusion.

It may also be argued that too many crimes have been federalized in recent years, and that we should not further enlarge the federal criminal sphere.[13] However, my proposal is not to federalize a crime but to criminalize some existing federal civil offenses. Even critics of the modern tendency to federalize a wide range of crimes acknowledge that some nonviolent activities, such as counterfeiting, federal tax evasion, and espionage, should be made federal crimes.[14] For example, Judge Stanley Marcus of the federal District Court for the Southern District of Florida has listed five areas of appropriate federal criminal concern. He argues that "enforcing and protecting the rights of insular minorities is a fourth area where the federal government has had a powerful and historical interest."[15]

The current federal enforcement structure is in some respects incompatible with the above division of labor. Most notably, current laws increasingly stress Department of Justice suits for money damages rather than structural reform; they place barriers in the way of structural reform litigation; they mandate some types of Justice Department suits on behalf of individuals, regardless of the impact of such litigation; they leave major gaps in the department's enforcement authority; and they fail to provide for punishment of many wrongdoers.

The current hierarchy of civil rights laws renders it easier for the Justice Department to protect some rights than others. Whether wittingly or not, Congress has created a spectrum that ranges from requiring the department to bring some cases, for example, so-called election cases under the Fair Housing Act, to giving it discretionary authority under other acts to sue whenever it finds discrimination. The spectrum also includes more limited authority under other acts to sue to remedy a pattern or practice of discrimination and statutory limits on suits by the attorney general to instances where she has received a written complaint, where there is an existing suit to intervene in, or where she has completed various presuit prerequisites. The acts variously authorize the attorney general to sue for injunctive relief, for equitable restitutionary-type relief, for damages, for punitive damages, for penalties, or for criminal sanctions.

Many of the differences in enforcement structure of the various federal civil rights laws are difficult to explain except as accidents of history. It makes no sense to allow an attorney general to bring suit for damages and civil penalties against a privately owned public accommodation that discriminates against the disabled but not against one that discriminates based on race. Nor can one readily explain why the United States may sue to remedy private housing discrimination but not private discrimination against minority contractors. Why should one who physically blocks an abortion clinic be guilty of a crime, while one who willfully engages in unlawful racial discrimination is not? Similarly, why should the attorney general be authorized to bring suit to remedy a pattern or practice of discrimination by laundromats or grocery stores or private schools based upon disability but not authorized to bring suit where the discrimination is based on race?

The rejection of Part 3 authority has left further gaps and anomalies. In many instances, it is easier for the attorney general to remedy private discrimination than to enforce the Fourteenth Amendment's prohibition of racial discrimination by the states. If the proprietor of an apartment house will not rent to African Americans, the department may bring suit. If a state university engages in racial discrimination, the department may sue only if it receives a written complaint from the victim. If a jury commission discriminates based on race, the department may not initiate a civil suit but is relegated to waiting for the filing of a private suit in which the attorney general may intervene. This anomaly has only been heightened by adoption in 1994 of partial Part 3–type authority. Now, if a police department engages in a pattern or practice of race discrimination, the division may seek judicial relief under 42 U.S.C.A. §14141, but if government officials other than law enforcement officials do so, §14141 does not authorize suit.

Anomalies exist as well in the division of authority between the attorney general and other federal departments and agencies. Why is private-sector pattern-or-practice employment discrimination litigation placed with the EEOC rather than the Justice Department, while private-sector housing and credit discrimination litigation is placed with the department rather than HUD or the banking regulatory agencies? Why is HUD given administrative enforcement powers while the EEOC is not, and why not leave Section 706 cases against state and local governments in the hands of the EEOC? Perhaps these questions only open the "can of worms" of increased interagency rivalries, but in this era of reinventing government they must be asked.

Many of the changes to correct the above problems would require legislation. Although such legislation might take a variety of forms, I believe that the principles outlined above provide a sound starting point. The Department of Justice should be given general authority to sue for injunctive relief and civil penalties against a pattern or practice of racial discrimination that violates the Constitution or laws of the United States. It should not be required to await a written complaint, a referral, or the filing of a private lawsuit before commencing pattern-or-practice litigation. In addition, Congress should explicitly make it a crime to engage in intentional racial discrimination in violation of the Constitution or laws of the United States. Authority to bring employment or housing suits on behalf of individuals should reside primarily with the individuals themselves and with the EEOC and the Department of Housing and Urban Development. Fair Housing Act election cases, whether housed in the Justice Department or HUD, should not be mandatory; instead, the agency should have discretion as to whether to bring the action. These changes would simplify and rationalize the federal enforcement role. Coordination problems would remain, but sufficient techniques already exist to deal with them. They can be modeled on solicitor general control of Supreme Court litigation, which ensures relative consistency of government position. The Department of Justice, the EEOC, and HUD each have been given coordination functions by statute and executive order.

Whether or not legislation is enacted, the division will continue to encounter change. How should it approach the future? Past practices offer much of value. John Doar summarized his vision of the Civil Rights Division in 1967:

1. This is a litigating Division with the assignment of using the coercive power of the federal court to bring about the desired objective, i.e., elimination of the caste system.
2. The people in the Civil Rights Division are litigators whose assignment is to persuade, or, if necessary, to compel white officials or other white persons to comply with the law. Persuasion is a fundamental part of our operation. For example, we rarely file a civil suit without first attempting to resolve the matter informally.
3. We have used an empirical approach to civil rights problems and to arrive at legal and effective solutions for them. This means we learn from a case-by-case approach, and it means we establish and document every fact as carefully as we can.
4. In solving civil rights problems, whether by persuasion or litigation, we

strive not only for the elimination of present discrimination and to insure against future discrimination, but, where reasonable, to correct the
effects of past discrimination.
5. We place maximum emphasis on the big important cases. This means
putting our best men[16] on them regardless of where they are assigned in
the organizational structure.[17]

This vision weds pragmatism with idealism. Keeping these two approaches in
balance has been the key to success; losing that balance has been the door to failure. The distinctiveness of the Civil Rights Division grew out of its unique mission, its litigation focus, its abandonment of the desk lawyer model, its leadership's close control of litigation, its intermixing of career and political leadership,
and its relative independence from case-specific political pressure. The division's
decision making is based on a variable mixture of law, pragmatism, idealism, high
policy, and partisan politics. Ideally the first four elements predominate. No matter what the mixture, the division cannot satisfy all constituents.

It is hard to evaluate the extent to which the Civil Rights Division of the 1960s
and 1970s was responsible for the impressive changes during that period. Many
forces played a role in bringing about change, so one might argue that the division was simply facilitating the inevitable. However, while change may have been
inevitable, the shape and pace of the change was substantively influenced by the
presence in the federal government of the Civil Rights Division as a defining
and mediating force in the struggle for equal rights. The department was a credible and effective voice for going beyond paying ineffective lip service to nondiscrimination. In its stead, the department helped convince the courts that nothing short of structural reform would vindicate the rights proclaimed by the
Reconstruction amendments to the Constitution.

The methods that led to the Civil Rights Division's success are at risk. The
transformation of the Civil Rights Division from a small band of litigators to a
large bureaucratic organization has disabled the division's top leadership from
the hands-on role that Burke Marshall, John Doar, and Steve Pollak played in
the 1960s. John Doar *tried* cases, spending months in Alabama and Mississippi;
even when he was not trying a case, he closely supervised case preparation.

One incident illustrates the degree of Assistant Attorney General Doar's su-
pervision. On May 4, 1966, election officials in Selma, Alabama, attempted to
throw out ballots of voters from six predominantly African-American precincts
who had overwhelmingly voted against Jim Clark as sheriff. The United States
promptly brought suit under the Voting Rights Act, and eight days later the case
came to trial. With such a compressed time schedule, most cases—and most lawyers—would be in a state of pandemonium. Nonetheless, on the eve of the trial
that led to the counting of the disputed ballots and the unseating of Jim Clark
as sheriff, Doar delivered a lecture on trial techniques to the trial attorney and

his staff. My cursory notes of the May 16, 1966, lecture, somewhat edited, include the following:

> For most trials of big cases—
> One attorney deals with judge and handles witnesses—Develop strategy and tactics; choose witnesses; make motions.
> One attorney at counsel table handling exhibits and taking trial notes—Get substance of testimony; use witness's words to extent possible; tell lead attorney other questions to ask; handle witness folders in court-room.
> One attorney coordinating witnesses—Have them ready to testify and let attorney in courtroom know they are ready, and give him feel for witness; keep ahead of inside attorneys; pass in witness folders to #2 inside attorney.
> Other outside attorneys work on particular witnesses and particular areas of proof.
> Act as your own court reporter or get official reporter to commit himself to quick transcription—Be prepared to move fast in court of appeals with unofficial transcript and copies of record.
> Don't oversell case or try to give impression everything is pure as snow.

The lecture is extraordinary, not for its content but for the commitment it displays to quality, mentoring, and leadership. This sort of leadership from the top seems inconceivable today.[18]

Although the general level of advocacy remains high, size and changes in leadership style have led to a relaxed review system and some resultant sloppiness.[19] Similarly, the growth of the division has led to the creation of relatively inflexible organizational lines and resistance from the career leadership to breaches in those lines. The assistant attorney general should take steps to restore the system of choosing the lawyers who are best suited to address high-priority matters, without artificial bureaucratic restraints.

During the 1950s and early 1960s, the division was forced to try its cases before a largely hostile district court bench under legal standards that placed a heavy burden of persuasion on the government. Knowing that the district courts were likely to rule against the government, the division concentrated on presenting such strong proof that adverse district court fact-findings would be held clearly erroneous on appeal. This approach meant that even a relatively straightforward case required a large trial staff and months of preparation.

The division faced the double barriers of being required to prove discriminatory intent and appearing before hostile district court judges who even denied basic discovery rights of access to voting records. It surmounted those barriers, as the U.S. Court of Appeals for the Fifth Circuit graphically summarized in an early case: "Notwithstanding the well-nigh impossible task of showing the true facts, the witnesses produced by the government proved without question that certain serious discriminations had taken place during the term of office of the defendant Lynd."[20] Every case was tried with a view to satisfying the extremely demanding standard of appellate review of district court findings of fact: that the lower court's findings may not be overturned unless clearly erroneous. The effects test is a valuable and justifiable tool, adopted by Congress in part to avoid "the inordinate amount of time and energy required to overcome the obstructionist tactics invariably encountered in" discrimination suits.[21] The effects test also addresses the unfairness of applying selection devices that screen out people of color but do not accurately measure merit. But in making litigation decisions, the department must balance the legitimacy of the effects test with the desirability of presenting a convincing record of discrimination.

Return to the painfully slow progress that prevailed during the earlier era would obviously be undesirable. It was that slowness that led Congress and the federal courts to respond with relaxed legal standards. The Voting Rights Act, *Griggs,* and *Green* each shifted substantial burdens to defendants whose practices had a discriminatory effect. The pace of progress quickened under the new regime as the need diminished for the division to present an ironclad case of intentional discrimination. However, something may have been lost in the process. The ability of the division to educate the courts and the American people regarding the continued existence and nature of race discrimination has fallen victim to the successes of the effects test's shift of burden to the defendant.[22]

As America seemingly enters a period of retrenchment in race relations, paradoxically a new opportunity arises for the division to reinvigorate its litigative approaches, although it will not be easy to do so. Leadership must come from the ranks of experienced litigators. Demands must be placed on career attorneys. Priorities and litigation policies must give adequate attention to the need to expose the nature of race discrimination and to develop fair and workable remedies. Although the effects test is a valuable tool that the division should not abandon, it should wherever possible present evidence of intentional discrimination as well, despite the burden that might place on division resources. Excessive reliance on effects alone would cause the division attorneys to lose sight of the harms that the division should combat and would contribute to the false sense among white Americans that racial discrimination against African Americans is no longer a national problem.

The division should use its criminal authority to prosecute not only violent crimes but also those few acts of discrimination that violate existing criminal law, such as the provisions of the Voting Rights Act that criminalize deprivations of the rights which it guarantees.[23] It should recognize that racial discrimination is simply a more sophisticated form of violence than beatings and bombings.

The division must take pains to avoid confusion of roles. Its job is evenhanded and effective enforcement of the laws against race discrimination, not representation of private interests. It will be pressed by civil rights advocates and opponents to embrace their positions. In response, the division must ask whether the urged position will further responsible enforcement of the civil rights laws. The division must show a balance that is not required of private interests. It must recognize competing interests and must take the long view.

The division's primary method has stressed steady, incremental progress in eliminating racial discrimination. Even the few great leaps forward, such as the rapid transformation in voter registration wrought by enforcement of the Voting Rights Act and the rapid transformation of southern schools in the wake of *Green* and *Swann,* sprang from the foundation laid in prior case-by-case litigation of voting and school desegregation cases. Affirmative action, too, was a natural outgrowth of these litigative efforts, as was the careful tailoring of affirmative action required under cases such as *Bakke.* The most striking departure from the pattern of careful, incremental efforts came under President Reagan with the department's dramatic shift in position on race-conscious remedial measures. Affirmative action remains high on the nation's policy agenda, but unlike other issues, since 1981 the department has not provided the kind of balanced leadership that would promise constructive resolution of the issue. Burke Marshall noted in the 1980s the consensus that "colorblindness is an ideal for an ideal society" but "that ours is not an ideal society."[24] The great need now is not a cataclysmic abandonment of affirmative action but the development of standards for using it or phasing it out. The sensitive balancing of public and private need that has long guided the Supreme Court and the department in addressing race issues must be revived in the department's analysis of affirmative action.

The United States has made several false starts toward the ideals of the Declaration of Independence, which holds it self-evident that all human beings are created equal. The Constitution countenanced African-American slavery, the *Dred Scott* decision overturned the Missouri Compromise, and the dismantling of Reconstruction betrayed the promise of the post–Civil War amendments to the Constitution. Each false start has led to a national nightmare: slavery, the Civil War, and the modern racial caste system symbolized by the separate-but-equal doctrine. No foolproof defense exists against the possibility that the modern civil rights acts might be just another in a series of false starts. The division is not wholly insulated from national politics. But for forty years it has provided effective law enforcement and leadership toward the goal of an equal opportunity society.

We cannot expect the Civil Rights Division to provide the cure for all our racial ills. We can and should expect the division to give its highest priority to eradicating the continuing manifestations of America's racial caste system and to bring to the task quality, principled analysis of law and facts, and a commitment to basic fairness. Here lies the way to avoid another false start. Here lies the way toward racial harmony and fairness.

Notes

CHAPTER 1. INTRODUCTION

1. Deut. 16:20, Torah.

2. *Missouri v. Holland,* 252 U.S. 416, 433 (1920).

3. For example, in 1983 appropriations for the Civil Rights Division, U.S. Department of Justice, amounted to $18.7 million out of a total of $589.8 million appropriated to all federal civil rights programs. Executive Office of the President, Office of Management and Budget, "Special Analysis J: Civil Rights Activities," in *Special Analysis: Budget of the United States Government, Fiscal Year 1984* (Washington, D.C.: Government Printing Office, 1984), J-3.

4. Sanford Levinson, *Identifying the Compelling State Interest: On "Due Process of Lawmaking" and the Professional Responsibility of the Public Lawyer,* 45 Hastings L. J. 1035, 1036 (1994).

5. Id., citing Karl N. Llewellyn, *A Realistic Jurisprudence—The Next Step,* 30 Colum. L. Rev. 431 (1930).

6. Statement of William Bradford Reynolds, assistant attorney general, Civil Rights Division, before the Subcommittee on Civil and Constitutional Rights, Committee on the Judiciary, and Subcommittee on Employment Opportunities, Committee on Education and Labor, House of Representatives, concerning affirmative action, September 1981, 5.

7. Statement of Deval L. Patrick, assistant attorney general, Civil Rights Division, before the Subcommittee on the Constitution, Committee on the Judiciary, U.S. House of Representatives, regarding H.R. 2128; the Equal Opportunity Act of 1995, December 7, 1995, p. 10.

8. William N. Eskridge, Jr., and Philip P. Frickey, *Foreword: Law as Equilibrium,* 108 Harv. L. Rev. 26, 35 (1994).

9. Stephen J. Pollak, "Remarks to the Lawyers' Committee for Civil Rights Under Law on Receipt of Whitney North Seymour Award," New York, October 1994, 1–2. Pollak noted: "The Lawyers' Committee was born in an era of nonviolent direct action to break the racial caste system. Its birth was accompanied by a spirit of optimism—an optimism that was bolstered through the next decade and a half as the barriers to equality were toppled one after another in the courts and legislatures."

10. See Owen M. Fiss, *The Civil Rights Injunction* (Bloomington: Indiana University Press, 1978).

184 NOTES TO PAGES 6–7

CHAPTER 2. THE EVOLUTION OF ATTORNEY GENERAL AUTHORITY

1. Record on Appeal at 614–15, *United States v. McLeod,* 385 F.2d 734 (5th Cir. 1967) (no. 21475) (testimony of Jim Clark) (filed April 24, 1964).

2. In 1960 the voting age population of Dallas County, Alabama, was 14,400 whites and 15,115 blacks. House Committee on the Judiciary, Subcommittee no. 5, *Voting Rights: Hearings on H.R. 6400,* 89th Cong., 1st sess., March–April 1965, 137.

3. See *United States v. McLeod,* 385 F.2d 734 (5th Cir. 1967); *United States v. Dallas County,* 385 F.2d 734 (5th Cir. 1967).

4. The Fifteenth Amendment provides: "Section 1. The right of citizens of the United States to vote shall not be denied or abridged by the United States or by any State on account of race, color, or previous condition of servitude. Section 2. The Congress shall have power to enforce this article by appropriate legislation."

5. "The United States is not entitled to relief unless the defendant's acts were for the purpose of interfering with the Negroes' right to vote." *United States v. McLeod,* 385 F.2d at 741.

6. The Fourteenth Amendment reads, in part: "Section 1. . . . No State shall make or enforce any law which shall abridge the privileges or immunities of citizens of the United States; nor shall any State deprive any person of life, liberty, or property, without due process of law; nor deny to any person within its jurisdiction the equal protection of the laws. . . . Section 5. The Congress shall have power to enforce, by appropriate legislation, the provisions of this article."

7. Indeed, later efforts to indict law enforcement officials for violent deprivations of rights in Selma failed. See Associated Press wire, September 21, 1965, reporting that a federal grand jury had decided not to issue indictments for violence by state troopers and sheriff's deputies during the attempted civil rights march from Selma to Montgomery in March 1965.

8. John T. Elliff, *The United States Department of Justice and Individual Rights, 1937–1962* (New York: Garland Publishing, 1987), 650.

9. For example, in 1870 the Selma *Southern Argus* had editorialized in favor of "a solution of the labor question [and] . . . the proper subordination of the inferior race among us." Eric Foner, *Reconstruction: America's Unfinished Revolution, 1863–1877* (New York: Harper and Row, 1988), 420.

10. 347 U.S. 483 (1954).

11. *United States v. Clark,* 249 F. Supp. 720, 723–27 (S.D. Ala. 1965).

12. *Williams v. Wallace,* 240 F. Supp. 100, 104 (M.D. Ala. 1965) (Judge Frank M. Johnson, Jr.).

13. *United States v. Clark,* 249 F. Supp. at 724. That same day Sheriff Clark closed a movie theater when African-American patrons attempted to desegregate it.

14. See Michal R. Belknap, *Federal Law and Southern Order: Racial Violence and Constitutional Conflict in the Post-Brown South* (Athens: University of Georgia Press, 1987), 184; Jack Bass, *Taming the Storm: The Life and Times of Judge Frank M. Johnson, Jr., and the South's Fight over Civil Rights* (New York: Doubleday, 1993), chap. 17. As described by Judge Frank M. Johnson, Jr., the peaceable and orderly marchers were met at the east side of the Edmund Pettus Bridge by state troopers, deputy sheriffs, and members of Sheriff Clark's "posse." The state troopers rolled "approximately 20 canisters of tear gas, nausea gas and canisters of smoke . . . into the Negroes. . . . The Negroes were then prodded, struck, beaten and knocked down by members of the Alabama State Troopers. The mounted 'possemen,' supposedly acting as an auxiliary law enforcement unit of the Dallas County sheriff's office, then, on their horses, moved in and chased and beat the fleeing

Negroes. Approximately 75 to 80 of the Negroes were injured, with a large number being hospitalized." *Williams v. Wallace,* 240 F. Supp. at 105.

15. Leonard Larsen, "Selma: Marking Where They Marched," *Sacramento Bee,* May 28, 1996, sec. B, p. 7 (describing the bulletin board in Sheriff Clark's office).

16. See *United States v. Atkins,* 323 F.2d 733 (5th Cir. 1963) (pattern or practice of racial discrimination in voter registration practices); *United States v. McLeod, 385 F.2d 734 (5th Cir. 1967)* (voter intimidation by district attorney, circuit judge, and sheriff); *United States v. Clark,* 249 F. Supp. 720 (S.D. Ala. 1965) (three-judge court) (more voter intimidation by district attorney, circuit judge, and sheriff).

17. By the spring of 1965 the department was a party to "six separate suits in Dallas County," Alabama, "pertaining to voter discrimination and intimidation." Letter from John Doar to Charles Dinson, March 15, 1965.

18. *Federal Register* 30, no. 152 (August 7, 1965): 9897, microfiche.

19. *Voting Rights Act of 1965, U.S. Statutes at Large* 79 (1966): 437, 439 (42 U.S.C. §1973d).

20. *United States v. Atkins,* 323 F.2d at 736.

21. *United States v. Executive Comm. of the Democratic Party of Dallas County, Ala.,* 254 F. Supp. 537 (S.D. Ala. 1966).

22. See, e.g., the suits challenging racially discriminatory districting of school board and county commission seats, whose history is recounted in *United States v. Dallas County Comm'n,* 850 F.2d 1430 (5th Cir. 1988), 850 F.2d 1433 (5th Cir. 1988).

23. The early history of the attorney general's enforcement is described in Robert J. Kaczorowski, *The Politics of Judicial Interpretation: The Federal Courts, Department of Justice and Civil Rights, 1866–1876* (New York: Oceana Publications, 1985).

24. Eugene Gressman, *The Unhappy History of Civil Rights Legislation,* 50 Mich. L. Rev. 1323, 1343 (1952). See also Will Maslow and Joseph B. Robison, *Civil Rights Legislation and the Fight for Equality, 1862–1952,* 20 U. Chi. L. Rev. 363 (1953); Homer Cummings and Carl McFarland, *Federal Justice: Chapters in the History of Justice and the Federal Executive* (1937; reprint, New York: Da Capo Press, 1970), chap. 12; Kaczorowski, *Politics of Judicial Interpretation.*

25. See Robert K. Carr, *Federal Protection of Civil Rights: Quest for a Sword* (Ithaca, N.Y.: Cornell University Press, 1947), 24. The section was initially called the Civil Liberties Unit but was renamed the Civil Rights Section in 1941.

26. *United States v. Carolene Products Co.,* 304 U.S. 144 (1938). The famous footnote 4 referred to "legislation which restricts those political processes which can ordinarily be expected to bring about repeal of undesirable legislation," "statutes directed at particular religious, or national, or racial minorities," and the question whether "prejudice against discrete and insular minorities may be a special condition, which tends seriously to curtail the operation of those political processes ordinarily to be relied upon to protect minorities." Id. at 152, citations omitted. See David M. Bixby, *The Roosevelt Court, Democratic Ideology, and Minority Rights: Another Look at* United States v. Classic, 90 Yale L. J. 741, 781 (1981), as to the parallel reasoning of the Court and the Department of Justice during the 1930s and 1940s.

27. Attorney General, Order no. 3204, February 3, 1939.

28. For example, in 1941 President Roosevelt issued an executive order forbidding racial discrimination in war industries and apprenticeship programs. President, "Executive Order No. 8802," *Federal Register* 6, no. 125 (June 27, 1941): 3109, microfiche.

29. President's Committee on Civil Rights, *To Secure These Rights* (Washington, D.C.: Government Printing Office, 1947), 152.

30. Id. at 160.

31. Carr, *Quest for a Sword,* 205–8.

32. Harry S. Truman, "Special Message to Congress on Civil Rights," in *Public Papers of the Presidents of the United States: Harry S. Truman, 1948* (Washington, D.C.: Government Printing Office, 1964), 121.

33. House Committee on the Judiciary, Subcommittee no. 3, *Hearings on Antilynching and Protection of Civil Rights,* 81st Cong., 1st and 2d sess., 1950, 70. The first bill to propose establishment of a Civil Rights Division in the Department of Justice of which I am aware was S. 1725 and its House counterpart. See Thomas I. Emerson and David Haber, *Political and Civil Rights in the United States: A Collection of Legal and Related Materials* (Buffalo, N.Y.: Dennis and Company, 1952), 94–100. The bill would have clarified the criminal statutes enforced by the Department of Justice but would not have created civil enforcement authority.

34. Letter from Attorney General Brownell to Vice President Nixon, April 9, 1956.

35. Bernard Schwartz, ed., *Statutory History of the United States: Civil Rights* (New York: Chelsea House Publishers, 1970), pt. 2, 914. The legislative history of the 1957 act is recounted in Robert Fredrick Burk, *The Eisenhower Administration and Black Civil Rights* (Knoxville: University of Tennessee Press, 1984), chap. 10. John Weir Anderson, *Eisenhower, Brownell, and the Congress* (Tuscaloosa: Published for the Inter-University Case Program by the University of Alabama Press, 1964) describes the unsuccessful effort to pass a civil rights act in 1956, but that effort did pave the way for the 1957 act.

36. Schwartz, *Statutory History,* 914. See also the statement of Senator J. W. Fulbright (D-Ark.) in the debates on the Civil Rights Act of 1960: Reconstruction was "one of the darkest and most unhappy eras since the founding of this Nation." Id. at 998.

37. *Civil Rights Act of 1957,* Public Law 85-315, 85th Cong., 1st sess. (September 9, 1957), §101.

38. The formal order establishing the Civil Rights Division was issued by Attorney General William P. Rogers on December 9, 1957. Attorney General, Order no. 155-57, December 9, 1957.

39. See *United States v. City of Philadelphia,* 644 F.2d 187 (3d Cir. 1980).

40. The House Report on the bill notes that "the provision permitting the Attorney General to bring suit to recover damages for an aggrieved party because of a deprivation of civil rights or the right to vote was eliminated, thus limiting the Attorney General in such cases to civil actions for injunctive relief." House Committee on the Judiciary, *Civil Rights Act of 1957,* 85th Cong., 1st sess., 1957, H. Rept. 291, reprinted in 1957 U.S.C.C.A.N. (U.S. Code Congressional and Administrative News) 1966, 1968.

41. Sec. 121 of H.R. 6127 would have added the following to 42 U.S.C. 1985: "Fourth. Whenever any persons have engaged or there are reasonable grounds to believe that any persons are about to engage in any acts or practices which would give rise to a cause of action pursuant to paragraphs First, Second, or Third, the Attorney General may institute for the United States, or in the name of the United States, a civil action or other proper proceeding for preventive relief, including an application for a permanent or temporary injunction, restraining order, or other order." The first three paragraphs of Sec. 1985 authorized private civil suits against conspiracies to prevent officers from performing their duties, to obstruct justice, or to deprive persons of their rights to the equal protection of the laws and equal privileges under the laws. In Fact Paper no. 217, April 12, 1956, the Executive Branch Liaison Office, the White House, explained the need for Part 3 thus: "In attempting to achieve the constitutional goal of the observance of the civil rights, the Administration feels that it has been a mistake for the Congress to have relied so heavily upon the criminal law and to have made so little use of the more flexible and often more effective processes of the civil courts.... Criminal prosecution can never begin until after the harm is done and it can never be invoked to forestall a violation of civil rights no

matter how obvious the threat of violation may be. Moreover, criminal prosecution for civil rights violations, when they involve state or local officials as they often do, stir up ill feeling in the community and tend to cause bad relations between state and local officials on the one hand and the federal officials responsible for the investigation and prosecution on the other. Much of this could be avoided if Congress would authorize the Attorney General to seek preventive relief from the civil courts in civil rights cases."

42. A limited Part 3–type proposal appeared as late as H.R. 7191, a 1965 voting rights bill. The bill that became the Voting Rights Act of 1965 contained no such provision. Attorney General Nicholas Katzenbach opposed adding a Part 3 provision because such a provision might endanger passage of the bill. He also said that the proposal would require the government to hire a national police force. House Committee on the Judiciary, Subcommittee no. 5, *Voting Rights: Hearings on H.R. 6400,* 108–9 (testimony of Attorney General Katzenbach). A Part 3–type proposal passed the House on August 9, 1966, but the Senate did not act on it. See House Committee on the Judiciary, *Civil Rights Act of 1966,* 89th Cong., 2d sess., 1966, H. Rept. 1678 (to accompany H.R. 14765). The Violent Crime Control Act, enacted in 1994, does authorize the attorney general to sue law enforcement officers who engage in a pattern or practice of deprivation of rights secured by the Constitution or laws of the United States. 42 U.S.C.A. §14141.

43. Schwartz, *Statutory History,* 930 (Sen. Richard Russell [D-Ga.]). Sen. Russell added that Part 3 would have vested "vast, yea, limitless power . . . in a political Federal appointee, [who] could have moved simultaneously against every school board of trustees in every Southern State. At the same time, he could have brought thousands of lawsuits at the expense of the American taxpayer and supported by the full power of the Federal Government to break down every scintilla of separation of the races in every walk of life in every public place." Id. at 932.

44. Burk, *Eisenhower Administration,* 223. The president added, "If in every locality every person . . . is permitted to vote . . . he has got a means of getting what he wants in democratic government, and that is the one [right] on which I place the greatest emphasis."

45. 18 U.S.C. §§241, 242.

46. Indeed, one author concludes that in 1957 the southern senators did not filibuster "a watered-down version of a House-approved bill . . . because the amended bill seemed harmless enough." They wanted to preserve the filibuster for "any measures which smacked of Reconstruction. In fact, they viewed [Part] III . . . in exactly that way. It would have authorized the Attorney General to seek injunctive relief in the federal courts whenever an individual's rights were violated." Carl M. Brauer, *John F. Kennedy and the Second Reconstruction* (New York: Columbia University Press, 1977), 10. They did filibuster the stronger measure proposed in 1959, and Senator Paul H. Douglas observed, "The United States Congress, after eight weeks of Senate debate and weeks of House debate, passed what can only by courtesy be called a civil rights . . . bill." Id. at 11.

47. See Burk, *Eisenhower Administration,* chap. 11. The act also provided for court appointment of federal voting referees in jurisdictions where the Department of Justice proved a pattern or practice of voting discrimination. The referees would be empowered to review applications of individuals to be declared qualified to vote. 42 U.S.C. 1971(e). The referee provisions responded to concerns that the 1957 act had been ineffective. See Daniel M. Berman, *A Bill Becomes a Law: Congress Enacts Civil Rights Legislation,* 2d ed. (New York: Macmillan, 1966), 2, 54–55 (comparing the legislative histories of the 1960 and 1964 acts). Thurgood Marshall is said to have stated, "The Civil Rights Act of 1960 isn't worth the paper it's written on." Id. at 135.

48. H.R. 3147 would have authorized the attorney general to seek injunctive relief

against denials of equal protection of the laws based on race, color, religion, or national origin. This authority was limited to instances where the attorney general received a signed complaint from an individual who was financially unable to afford litigation or was in fear of reprisals. Similar provisions were proposed in bills introduced by Sen. Jacob Javits (R-N.Y.; S. 456) and Sen. Paul Douglas (D-Ill.; S. 810).

49. Senate Committee on the Judiciary, Subcommittee on Constitutional Rights, *Civil Rights—1959: Hearings on S. 435, S. 456, S. 499, S. 810, S. 957, S. 958, S. 959, S. 960, S. 1084, S. 1199, S. 1277, S. 1848, S. 1998, S. 2001, S. 2002, S. 2003, and S. 2041,* 86th Cong., 1st sess., March-April-May 1959, 199 (testimony of Attorney General William Rogers). See also id. at 223; House Committee on the Judiciary, Subcommittee no. 5, *Civil Rights: Hearings on H.R. 300, 352, 353, 353, 400, 430, 461, 617, 618, 619, 759, 913, 914, 1902, 2346, 2479, 2538, 2786, 3090, 3147, 3148, 3212, 3559, 4169, 4261, 4338, 4339, 4342, 4348, 4457, 5008, 5170, 5189, 5217, 5218, 5276, 5323, 6934, 6935,* 86th Cong., 1st sess., March 1959, 223, 225.

50. The legislative history of the 1964 act is recounted in Charles Whalen and Barbara Whalen, *The Longest Debate: A Legislative History of the 1964 Civil Rights Act* (Cabin John, Md.: Seven Locks Press, 1985).

51. Burke Marshall, *Federalism and Civil Rights* (New York: Columbia University Press, 1964), 57. Attorney General Kennedy testified, "We thought that by the provisions of the public accommodations bill and the school bill, a good portion of [Part III] was covered. This was a better way in which to do it." House Committee on the Judiciary, Subcommittee no. 5, *Civil Rights: Hearings on Miscellaneous Proposals Regarding the Civil Rights of Persons Within the Jurisdiction of the United States,* 88th Cong., 1st sess., June 1963, 1428. He later testified against a proposed authorization for the attorney general to bring suits under 42 U.S.C. 1983, which he thought "injects Federal executive authority into some areas which are not its legitimate concern and vests the Attorney General with broad discretion in matters of great political and social concern." House Committee on the Judiciary, *Civil Rights: Hearings on 7152, as Amended by Subcommittee No. 5,* 88th Cong., 1st Sess., October 1963, 2658. See also id. at 2701, 2728, 2753–55; Brauer, *Second Reconstruction,* 248.

52. Marshall, *Federalism and Civil Rights,* 78. See also Taylor Branch, *Parting the Waters: America in the King Years, 1954–1963* (New York: Simon and Schuster, 1988), 808 (describing the discussions within the Kennedy administration regarding Part 3).

53. Robert G. Dixon, Jr., "The Attorney General and Civil Rights, 1870–1964," in *Roles of the Attorney General of the United States* (Washington, D.C.: American Enterprise Institute, 1968), 105, 148.

54. Owen M. Fiss, *The Fate of an Idea Whose Time Has Come: Antidiscrimination Law in the Second Decade After Brown v. Board of Education,* 41 U. Chi. L. Rev. 742, 746 (1974).

55. *Civil Rights Act of 1964, U.S. Statutes at Large* 78 (1965): 241, 246 (42 U.S.C.A. §§2000b[a]), 248 (2000c-6[a]).

56. Id. at 241, 245 (42 U.S.C.A. §2000a-5[a]), 261 (42 U.S.C.A. §2000e-6[a]). The pattern or practice notion came from the 1960 act's provision for voting referees where the court has found that race-based deprivations of the right to vote were "pursuant to a pattern or practice." *Civil Rights Act of 1960, U.S. Statutes at Large* 74 (1961): 86, 90 (42 U.S.C. §1971[e]).

57. *Civil Rights Act of 1964, U.S. Statutes at Large* 78 (1965): 241, 266 (42 U.S.C.A. §2000h-2).

58. Id. at 241, 252 (42 U.S.C.A. §2000d et seq.).

59. Id. at 241, 258 (42 U.S.C. §2000e-4).

60. Id. at 241, 244 (42 U.S.C. §2000a-4).

61. Id. at 241, 247 (42 U.S.C. §2000c-2).

62. Other organizations responsible for civil rights enforcement are the Office for Civil Rights of the Department of Education, which currently has 824 employees and a $58,325,000 budget; the Office for Civil Rights of the Department of Health and Human Services, which currently employs 274 people and has a budget of $21,330,000; the Equal Employment Opportunity Commission, which currently has approximately 3,219 employees and a $268,000,000 budget; the Office of Fair Housing and Equal Opportunity of the Department of Housing and Urban Development, which has a staff of 725 and a budget of $57,337,000; and the Office of Federal Contract Compliance Programs of the Department of Labor, which employs 808 and has a budget of $63,831,000. Together these organizations employ 5,850 people with a combined budget of $468,823,000 compared with the Department of Justice, Civil Rights Division, which has 569 employees and a budget of $65,304,000. Staff estimates for 1996 are from Commission on Civil Rights, *Funding Federal Civil Rights Enforcement: A Report of the United States Commission on Civil Rights, June 1995,* prepared by Conner Ball (Washington, D.C., n.d.).

63. Hugh Davis Graham, *Civil Rights and the Presidency: Race and Gender in American Politics, 1960–1972* (New York: Oxford University Press, 1992), 129.

64. *Fair Housing Act of 1968, U.S. Statutes at Large* 82 (1969): 73, 88 (42 U.S.C. §3613[a]). "By 1968 the role of the Department in civil rights litigation was so well established that it seemed perfectly natural to give it a similar role in the enforcement of the newly enacted fair housing law." Fiss, *Fate of an Idea,* 754.

65. *U.S. Statutes at Large* 82 (1969): 73 (18 U.S.C. §245[b]). Belknap, *Federal Law and Southern Order,* chap. 9, provides a legislative history of the criminal provisions of the 1968 act.

66. Senate Committee on the Judiciary, Subcommittee on Constitutional Rights, *Hearings on the Nomination of John Doar, of New Richmond, Wis., To Be Assistant Attorney General, Civil Rights Division, U.S. Department of Justice,* 89th Cong., 1st sess., February 1965, 6.

67. The legislative histories of the Voting Rights Act of 1965 and the 1982 amendments to the act are explored in Abner J. Mikva and Eric Lane, *Legislative Process* (Boston: Little, Brown and Company, 1995).

68. These powers are similar to the powers that the Force Act of 1871, 16 Stat. 433, conferred on federal supervisors of election appointed by federal judges. The Force Act was repealed in 1894, 28 Stat. 36.

69. Federal examiners were sent to Selma five days after the Voting Rights Act became law. Sheriff Clark proclaimed, "The whole thing's so ridiculous I haven't gotten over laughing at it yet," and added that the new black registrants would be able to vote only "if they can find their way into town." Eric F. Goldman, *The Tragedy of Lyndon Johnson* (New York: Knopf, 1969), 332.

70. *Georgia v. United States,* 411 U.S. 526, 536 (1973) (upholding authority of the attorney general to promulgate regulations, 28 CFR Part 51, although "§5 itself does not authorize the Attorney General to promulgate any regulations"; authority is granted by the Administrative Procedure Act, 5 U.S.C. §301). The regulations were issued after the department was excoriated by a federal court for its "Pilate-like response" to a section five submission of Mississippi's open primary law. *Evers v. State Bd. of Election Comm'rs,* 327 F. Supp. 640, 642 (S. D. Miss. 1971), appeal dismissed, 405 U.S. 1001 (1972).

71. *Civil Rights of Institutionalized Persons Act, U.S. Statutes at Large* 94 (1981): 349, 352 (42 U.S.C. §1997e).

72. *Civil Liberties Act of 1988, U.S. Statutes at Large* 102 (1990): 903, 905 (50 U.S.C.A. App. §1989b-4).

73. 42 U.S.C. §12188.

74. 42 U.S.C. §12134.

75. See, e.g., *Craig v. Boren,* 429 U.S. 190 (1976) (gender); *City of Cleburne v. Cleburne Living Ctr.,* 473 U.S. 432 (1985) (disability).

76. *Americans with Disabilities Act of 1990, U.S. Statutes at Large* 104 (1991): 327, 328 (42 U.S.C.A. §§12101 et seq.).

77. 42 U.S.C.A. §§3601 et seq.

78. *Freedom of Access to Clinic Entrances Act of 1994,* Public Law 103-259, 103d Cong., 2d sess. (26 May 1994). The act adds §248 to Title 18 of the U.S. Code. It forbids various forms of interference with the right to obtain or provide reproductive health services and provides the attorney general with both criminal and civil remedies as well as creating a private right of action for injured persons and for state attorneys general on behalf of such persons. The 1995 Civil Rights Division's "Activities and Programs" brochure states (p. 7 of version found on Civil Rights Division website) that "the Criminal Section, along with other Department of Justice components, . . . began enforcing the" act.

79. See Clarice E. Gaylord and Geraldine W. Twitty, *Protecting Endangered Communities,* 21 Fordham Urb. L. J. 771, 780 (1994) (describing several pending legislative proposals on environmental justice).

80. See James A. Kushner, *The Fair Housing Amendments Act of 1988: The Second Generation of Fair Housing,* 42 Vand. L. Rev. 1049 (1989); Leland B. Ware, *New Weapons for an Old Battle: The Enforcement Provisions of the 1988 Amendments to the Fair Housing Act,* 7 Admin. L. J. Am. U. 59 (1993).

81. See remarks of Rep. Hamilton Fish, Jr. (R-N.Y.), June 23, 1988: "My amendment addresses constitutional concerns over the bill's enforcement provisions, which allow an administrative law judge to award damages but do not guarantee the right to a trial by jury." *Congressional Record,* 100th Cong., 2d sess., 1988, 134, pt. 11:15848.

82. 42 U.S.C.A. 3612(o)(1).

83. See generally Stephen L. Wasby, "The Political Environment of Civil Rights Litigation," in *Race Relations Litigation in an Age of Complexity* (Charlottesville: University Press of Virginia, 1995), 1–25.

84. See 42 U.S.C. 14141, authorizing the attorney general to sue to eliminate a pattern or practice of deprivations of constitutional or statutory rights by law enforcement officers. See also Mark Curriden, *When Good Cops Go Bad,* 82 A.B.A. J. 62 (1996).

85. John Doar and Dorothy Landsberg, "The Performance of the FBI in Investigating Violations of Federal Laws Protecting the Right to Vote, 1960–1967" (1971), 56. This unpublished paper prepared for a conference on the FBI can be found in Senate, *Intelligence Activities, Senate Resolution 21: Hearings Before the Select Committee to Study Governmental Operations with Respect to Intelligence Activities,* 94th Cong., 1st sess., November–December 1975, vol. 6, 888.

86. 42 U.S.C. §2000d. Agencies that enter into large contracts must ensure that federal contractors do not discriminate in employment.

87. Agencies with other enforcement responsibilities include the EEOC, Department of Education, Department of Labor, Department of Housing and Urban Development, Federal Reserve Board, Federal Home Loan Bank Board, Comptroller of the Currency, and Department of the Treasury.

CHAPTER 3. REASONS FOR FEDERAL ROLE

1. Charles Whalen and Barbara Whalen, *The Longest Debate: A Legislative History of the 1964 Civil Rights Act* (Cabin John, Md.: Seven Locks Press, 1985), 185.

2. For accounts of the political maneuvering and interests at stake during considera-

tion of the 1957, 1960, and 1964 acts, see John Weir Anderson, *Eisenhower, Brownell, and the Congress* (University: Published for the Inter-University Case Program by the University of Alabama Press, 1964) (a history of the unsuccessful effort to pass an act in 1956, which discusses the Powell amendment at 72–81); Daniel M. Berman, *A Bill Becomes a Law: Congress Enacts Civil Rights Legislation*, 2d ed. (New York: Macmillan, 1966) (a history of the 1960 act); Whalen and Whalen, *The Longest Debate.* See also Michael J. Klarman, Brown, *Racial Change, and the Civil Rights Movement,* 80 Va. L. Rev. 7, 129ff (1994) (attempting to establish a chain of causation for the civil rights legislation of the mid-1960s); Carl M. Brauer, *John F. Kennedy and the Second Reconstruction* (New York: Columbia University Press, 1977), 266. Eric F. Goldman, *The Tragedy of Lyndon Johnson* (New York: Knopf, 1969), describes President Johnson's political strategy for enacting the Voting Rights Act of 1965.

3. U.S. Constitution, Article 1, Sec. 8.

4. *H. P. Hood & Sons, Inc. v. Du Mond,* 336 U.S. 525, 537 (1949).

5. See *Heart of Atlanta Motel, Inc. v. United States,* 379 U.S. 241 (1964); *Katzenbach v. McClung,* 379 U.S. 294 (1964).

6. See *Fitzpatrick v. Bitzer,* 427 U.S. 445 (1976).

7. Compare *Garcia v. San Antonio Metro. Transit Auth.,* 469 U.S. 528 (1985); *New York v. United States,* 505 U.S. 144 (1992).

8. *United States v. Raines,* 362 U.S. 17, 27 (1960).

9. The Thirteenth Amendment provides: "Section 1. Neither slavery nor involuntary servitude, except as a punishment for crime whereof the party shall have been duly convicted, shall exist within the United States, or any place subject to their jurisdiction. Section 2. Congress shall have power to enforce this article by appropriate legislation."

10. The Thirteenth Amendment authorized Congress to forbid private persons from holding slaves and from imposing badges and incidents of slavery. *Jones v. Alfred H. Mayer Co.,* 392 U.S. 409 (1968).

11. See *United States v. Carolene Products Co.,* 304 U.S. 144, 152 n.4 (1938), described in Chapter 2 n.26.

12. Brief for the United States as amicus curiae at 6, *Brown v. Board of Education,* 347 U.S. 483 (1954) (no. 8). Philip B. Kurland and Gerhard Casper, eds., *Landmark Briefs and Arguments of the Supreme Court of the United States: Constitutional Law,* vol. 49 (Arlington, Va.: University Publications of America, 1975), 121.

13. John F. Kennedy, "Annual Message to the Congress on the State of the Union," in *Public Papers of the Presidents of the United States: John F. Kennedy, 1961* (Washington, D.C.: Government Printing Office, 1962), 22.

14. Klarman, Brown, *Racial Change, and the Civil Rights Movement* 27 (footnote omitted) (referring to nine sources taking that position).

15. President's Committee on Civil Rights, *To Secure These Rights* (Washington, D.C.: Government Printing Office, 1947), 139.

16. See A. Leon Higginbotham, Jr., *In the Matter of Color: Race and the American Legal Process, The Colonial Period* (New York: Oxford University Press, 1978).

17. Martin Luther King, Jr., "Letter from Birmingham Jail," in *Why We Can't Wait* (New York: New American Library, Signet Books, 1964), 83.

18. John F. Kennedy, "Radio and Television Report to the American People on Civil Rights," in *Public Papers of the Presidents of the United States: John F. Kennedy, 1963* (Washington, D.C.: Government Printing Office, 1964), 469.

19. Deval Patrick, "Reclaiming America's Conscience," *Legal Times,* April 23, 1994, 16.

20. *Congressional Record,* 90th Cong., 2d sess., 1968, 114, pt. 3–4. Senator Ervin was a leader of the opposition to several of the civil rights acts.

21. Richard A. Epstein, *Forbidden Grounds: The Case Against Employment Discrimination Laws* (Cambridge, Mass.: Harvard University Press, 1992), 497.

22. Sanford Levinson, *Processes of Constitutional Decisionmaking: Cases and Materials,* 3d ed. (Boston: Little, Brown and Company, 1992), 297 (quoting *Essays of William Graham Sumner,* 2 vols., ed. Albert G. Keller and Maurice R. Davie (New York: Gorden Press, 1934), 2:56.

23. Alexis de Tocqueville, *Democracy in America,* vol. 2 (New York: Knopf, Vintage Books, 1954), 100.

24. Declaration of Independence.

25. See Robert J. Reinstein, *Completing the Constitution: The Declaration of Independence, Bill of Rights, and Fourteenth Amendment,* 66 Temp. L. Rev. 361 (1993).

26. "For when any number of men have, by the consent of every individual, made a community, they have thereby made that community one body, with a power to act as one body, which is only by the will and determination of the majority." John Locke, *The Second Treatise of Civil Government and a Letter Concerning Toleration* (Oxford: Basil Blackwell, 1948), 48.

27. Num. 5:6, New English Bible.

28. John F. Kennedy, "Radio and Television Report," 470.

29. Bureau of the Census, *1968 Statistical Abstract of the United States* (Washington, D.C.: Government Printing Office, 1968), 23 (showing the population by race from 1790 to 1967 in table 21; 10.5 percent of the population was black in 1960).

30. See Mark V. Tushnet, *Making Civil Rights Law: Thurgood Marshall and the Supreme Court, 1936–1961* (New York: Oxford University Press, 1994), 247–56 (discussing massive resistance to desegregation and *Brown v. Board of Education* in particular); Commission on Civil Rights, "Education," bk. 2 of *1961 United States Commission on Civil Rights Report* (Washington, D.C.: Government Printing Office, 1961), 65–77 (discussing the massive, statewide resistance in the South to desegregation and various state legislative attempts to circumvent the Constitution and federal law).

31. See, e.g., King, "Letter from Birmingham Jail," 93.

32. Id. at 85.

33. *Report of the National Advisory Commission on Civil Disorders,* New York Times edition (New York: E. P. Dutton and Company, 1968), 410. Among the commission's "objectives for national action" were "opening up opportunities to those who are restricted by racial segregation and discrimination, and eliminating all barriers to their choice of jobs, education and housing." Id. at 413.

34. See Brauer, *Second Reconstruction.* As Burke Marshall argued, "The federal system must be made to work quickly if the racial conflict is to stay within the boundaries of law." Burke Marshall, *Federalism and Civil Rights* (New York: Columbia University Press, 1964), 34.

35. Hanes Walton, Jr., *When the Marching Stopped: The Politics of Civil Rights Regulatory Agencies* (New York: State University of New York Press, 1988), 11.

36. As to public accommodations, see Senate Report on 1964 act, Bernard Schwartz, ed., *Statutory History of the United States: Civil Rights* (New York: Chelsea House Publishers, 1970), 1085–87; as to employment, see John F. Kennedy, "Special Message to the Congress on Civil Rights and Job Opportunities," in *Public Papers of the Presidents of the United States* (Washington, D.C.: Government Printing Office, 1964), 483; as to schools, see remarks of Rep. Celler in Schwartz, *Statutory History,* 1100; as to housing, see remarks of Sen. Robert F. Kennedy, id. at 1679–81. See generally *Report of the National Advisory Commission on Civil Disorders.*

37. Harry S. Truman, "Special Message to Congress on Civil Rights," in *Public Papers*

of the Presidents of the United States: Harry S. Truman, 1948 (Washington, D.C.: Government Printing Office, 1964), 121–22.

38. 325 U.S. 91, 140 (1945). Frankfurter's version of history is reminiscent of the views found in a treatise on reconstruction history that was influential at the time and which summarized the postwar history of the South thusly: "the Civil War; the great work of Lincoln; the abolition of slavery; the defeat of the South; Reconstruction based upon universal Negro suffrage; the oppression of the South by the North; the final triumph of Southern intelligence and character over the ignorance that so long had thriven under Northern misconceptions." James Ford Rhodes, *History of the United States, 1850–1877,* vol. 7 (New York: Macmillan Company, 1906), 290.

39. 109 U.S. 3 (1883).

40. Eric Foner, *Reconstruction: America's Unfinished Revolution, 1863–1877* (New York: Harper and Row, 1988). Foner points out that the view of Reconstruction as a time of "savage tyranny" was "accorded scholarly legitimacy—to its everlasting shame—by the nation's fraternity of professional historians" (p. 609) and that "few interpretations of history have had such far-reaching consequences as this image of Reconstruction" (p. 610). See also Randall Kennedy, *Reconstruction and the Politics of Scholarship,* 98 Yale L. J. 521 (1989) (reviewing Foner, *Reconstruction*).

41. For example, Justice Robert Jackson, speaking for the Supreme Court, referred to reconstruction legislation based on the "conquered province" theory. *Collins v. Hardyman,* 341 U.S. 651, 656 (1951) (internal quotation marks omitted). Relying on the discredited book, Claude Gernade Bowers, *The Tragic Era* (New York: Halcyon, 1929), he characterized the legislation that included 42 U.S.C. §1985 as having been "passed by a partisan vote in a highly inflamed atmosphere." Id. at 657 n.8. Even Attorney General Homer Cummings regarded Reconstruction as an unfortunate episode in the history of the Department of Justice, referring to enforcement of the civil rights acts during that period as "the most difficult, the most dramatic, and the most sordid task to be performed by the new Department of Justice." Homer Cummings and Carl McFarland, *Federal Justice: Chapters in the History of Justice and the Federal Executive* (1937; reprint, New York: Da Capo Press, 1970), 230. He spoke thankfully of the time when "the sword of force began to rust in its scabbard and the attempt to impose a new order upon the South by legislative fiat and executive decree ended." Id. at 249.

42. Brauer, *Second Reconstruction,* 153.

43. James Madison, "Federalist Paper No. 39," in *The Federalist Papers* (New York: New American Library, Mentor Books, 1961), 244.

44. Motion of Mr. Bedford, July 17, 1787, reproduced in Daniel A. Farber and Suzanna Sherry, *A History of the American Constitution* (St. Paul, Minn.: West Publishing Company, 1990), 136–37 (internal quotation marks omitted).

45. See, e.g., *U.S. Term Limits, Inc. v. Thornton,* 115 S.Ct. 1842, 1875 (1995) (Thomas, J., dissenting): "The ultimate source of the Constitution's authority is the consent of the people of each individual State, not the consent of the undifferentiated people of the Nation as a whole."

46. 17 U.S. (4 Wheat.) 316, 403, 405 (1819).

47. *Screws v. United States,* 325 U.S. 91, 139 (1945).

48. Id. at 142.

49. Id. at 144.

50. Id. at 158.

51. Id. at 160.

52. Id. at 160–61. See also *Monroe v. Pape,* 365 U.S. 167 (1961) and *South Carolina v. Katzenbach,* 383 U.S. 301 (1966).

53. 460 U.S. 226 (1983) (Burger, C. J., dissenting, joined by Powell, Rehnquist, and O'Connor, JJ.); id. at 265 (Powell, J., joined by O'Connor, J.).

54. *Fitzpatrick v. Bitzer,* 427 U.S. 445 (1976). Of the four dissenters in *EEOC v. Wyoming,* three were on the Court that unanimously upheld the extension of Title VII to the states.

55. 383 U.S. 301, 360 (1966).

56. *United States v. Louisiana,* 225 F. Supp. 353, 356–57 (E.D. La. 1963), *aff'd,* 380 U.S. 145 (1965).

57. House Committee on the Judiciary, Subcommittee no. 5, *Voting Rights: Hearings on H.R. 6400,* 89th Cong., 1st sess., March–April 1965, 66–67.

58. Letter from Attorney General Nicholas Katzenbach to registrars in seven southern states, August 7, 1965.

59. Commission on Civil Rights, *The Voting Rights Act: Ten Years After* (Washington, D.C., January 1975), 33.

60. See Walter Hartwell Bennett, *American Theories of Federalism* (Kingsport, Tenn.: University of Alabama Press, 1964), 205–11 (explaining this theory and recounting the story of the failed effort of interposition).

61. See, e.g., *Martin v. Hunter's Lessee,* 14 U.S. (1 Wheat.) 304 (1816); *Cooper v. Aaron,* 358 U.S. 1 (1958).

62. See Taylor Branch, *Parting the Waters: America in the King Years, 1954–1963* (New York: Simon and Schuster, 1988), 222–24, 647–49.

63. *H. P. Hood & Sons, Inc. v. Du Mond,* 336 U.S. 525, 537 (1949) (Jackson, J.).

64. Klarman, *Brown, Racial Change, and the Civil Rights Movement,* 37.

65. Treaty of Rome, Article 119. Eric Stein, Peter Hay, and Michael Waelbroeck, *Documents for European Community Law and Institutions in Perspective* (Charlottesville, Va.: Michie Company, 1976), 65. See also Directive 75/117 (equal pay directive); Directive 76/207 (equal treatment directive).

66. Schwartz, *Statutory History,* 1292. For more recent economic arguments that competitive markets with free entry provide better protection against invidious discrimination than do antidiscrimination laws, see Epstein, *Forbidden Grounds,* 2, 4, 9 (also arguing that antidiscrimination laws focus on irremediable historical injustices while imposing present and future costs). In Epstein's view antidiscrimination laws are covertly redistributive and operate in a capricious, expensive, and wasteful manner. Id. at 494. Judge Posner, while acknowledging the moral repugnance of some causes of sex discrimination, concludes that "there is no strong theoretical reason to believe that sex discrimination, even if not prohibited by law, would be a substantial source of inefficiency in American labor markets today." Richard A. Posner, *An Economic Analysis of Sex Discrimination Laws,* 56 U. Chi. L. Rev. 1311, 1321 (1989). But see John J. Donohue III, *Prohibiting Sex Discrimination in the Workplace: An Economic Perspective,* 56 U. Chi. L. Rev. 1337, 1355 (1989) (the law against sex discrimination "has generated annual benefits of roughly $6.66 billion").

67. John F. Kennedy, "Excerpts from Annual Message to the Congress: The Economic Report of the President," in *Public Papers of the Presidents of the United States: John F. Kennedy, 1963* (Washington, D.C.: Government Printing Office, 1964), 71.

68. *Equal Credit Opportunity Act of 1974, U.S. Statutes at Large* 88 (1976): 1500, 1521. Assistant Attorney General J. Stanley Pottinger, testifying on behalf of the Department of Justice, supported passage of the act: "To deny credit to an individual because of an immutable characteristic denies that person the ability to function fully within the national stream of commerce. Such an inability may be accompanied by a sense of personal humiliation and frustration, the implications of which may extend beyond the economic sphere. Further, I would assume that the national production of goods and services is constricted whenever commercial financing, a cornerstone of the economy, is either denied or offered under unreasonable conditions to a segment of our population or business com-

munity." House Committee on Banking and Currency, Subcommittee on Consumer Affairs, *Credit Discrimination: Hearings on H.R. 14856 and H.R. 14908,* 93d Cong., 2d sess., June 1974, 35.

69. President's Committee on Civil Rights, *To Secure These Rights,* 142–43.

70. "Antitrust, at its origin and in its development, is about public policy and ideology. It is about a market economy and limited government. At its core, antitrust attempts to harmonize and synthesize a body of law designed to correct market imperfections. It invites government intervention when market failures or externalities occur, but it does so only through ad hoc interdiction and without the remedy of a personal industrial policy or a systemic regulatory scheme." E. Thomas Sullivan, ed., *The Political Economy of the Sherman Act: The First One Hundred Years* (Athens: Ohio University Press, 1991), 4. See also Robert Cooter, *Market Affirmative Action,* 31 San Diego L. Rev. 133, 153 (1994) (pointing out several parallels between antitrust law and antidiscrimination law that flow from the fact that "discriminatory social groups are much like cartels, and a discriminatory norm is analogous to a price- fixing agreement").

71. *Northern Securities Co. v. United States,* 193 U.S. 197, 351 (1904).

72. "The approach to constitutional adjudication recommended here is akin to what might be called an 'antitrust' as opposed to a 'regulatory' orientation to economic affairs—rather than dictate substantive results it intervenes only when the 'market,' in our case the political market, is systemically malfunctioning." John Hart Ely, *Democracy and Distrust: A Theory of Judicial Review* (Cambridge, Mass.: Harvard University Press, 1980), 102-3 (footnote omitted). Using Ely's taxonomy the civil rights laws take both the "antitrust" and the "regulatory" approach, both dictating substantive results and addressing market malfunctions. Nondiscrimination is treated as a substantive value, and discrimination is thought to reflect a market malfunction. However, the underlying purpose of the civil rights laws is structural: to deal with the caste system in American life.

73. Compare Robert Bork's "wealth maximization" rationale for the Sherman Act with Richard Hofstadter's political and cultural interpretation and Robert Lande's emphasis on distributive objectives. Sullivan, *Political Economy of the Sherman Act,* 6-11.

74. Id. at 19. For another, similar comparison of these two organic and somewhat vague statutes, with a different perspective, see Owen M. Fiss, *Troubled Beginnings of the Modern State, 1888-1910,* vol. 8 of *History of the Supreme Court of the United States* (New York: Macmillan Company, 1993), 142.

75. See Gerald Gunther, *Constitutional Law,* 12th ed. (Westbury, N.Y.: Foundation Press, 1991), 147-51.

76. Willard Hurst, "The Law in United States History," in *American Law and the Constitutional Order: Historical Perspectives,* ed. Lawrence M. Friedman and Harry N. Scheiber (Cambridge, Mass.: Harvard University Press, 1978), 4. Cf. Frank H. Easterbrook, *The State of Madison's Vision of the State: A Public Choice Perspective,* 107 Harv. L. Rev. 1328 (1994).

77. See *In re Debs,* 158 U.S. 564 (1895). See also Owen M. Fiss, "Debs and the Maintenance of Public Order," in *Troubled Beginnings of the Modern State,* 65: "The intellectual challenge posed by the *Debs* case arose because it was the national rather than the state government that restored order and because the national government had used the injunction as part of its overall strategy for doing so. To justify this course of action, [Justice] Brewer drew from three different political and legal sources: the Commerce Clause, the Civil War, and public nuisance doctrine."

78. See Arthur Bestor, "The American Civil War as a Constitutional Crisis," in *American Law and the Constitutional Order: Historical Perspectives,* ed. Lawrence M. Friedman and Harry N. Scheiber (Cambridge, Mass.: Harvard University Press, 1978), 223-34.

79. E.g., U.S. Constitution, Article 4, Section 2: "No Person held to Service or Labour in one State, under the Laws thereof, escaping into another, shall, in Consequence of any

Law or Regulation therein, be discharged from such Service or Labour, but shall be delivered up on Claim of the Party to whom such Service or Labour may be due."

80. See *Screws v. United States,* 325 U.S. 91 (1945).

81. See Jack Bass, *Unlikely Heroes: The Dramatic Story of the Southern Judges of the Fifth Circuit Who Translated the Supreme Court's* Brown *Decision into a Revolution for Equality* (New York: Simon and Schuster, 1981), 118.

82. See Klarman, Brown, *Racial Change, and the Civil Rights Movement,* 97ff.

83. See, e.g., *United States v. Wood,* 295 F.2d 772 (5th Cir. 1961) (person attempting to help black citizens register to vote battered by voter registrar and arrested by sheriff).

84. See Branch, *Parting the Waters,* 432–91.

85. John F. Kennedy, "Special Message to the Congress on Civil Rights and Job Opportunities," 484.

86. Memorandum from the attorney general to the president, June 1964, quoted in John Doar and Dorothy Landsberg, "The Performance of the FBI in Investigating Violations of Federal Laws Protecting the Right to Vote, 1960–1967" (1971), 97 n.35 (reproduced in Senate, *Intelligence Activities, Senate Resolution 21: Hearings Before the Select Committee To Study Governmental Operations with Respect to Intelligence Activities,* 94th Cong., 1st sess., November–December 1975, vol. 6, 888, 984 n.35).

87. See, e.g., *United States v. Barnett,* 376 U.S. 681 (1964); see also 330 F.2d 369, 391 (5th Cir. 1963) ("the sovereign's presence was needed by this Court to effectuate its decrees and to maintain and uphold the rule of law"); *Faubus v. United States,* 254 F.2d 797 (8th Cir. 1958), and President's Power to Use Federal Troops to Suppress Resistance to Enforcement of Federal Court Orders—Little Rock, Arkansas, 41 Op. Att'y Gen. 313 (1957).

88. *Faubus,* 254 F.2d at 805.

89. *Marbury v. Madison,* 5 U.S. (1 Cranch) 137, 176 (1803).

90. Senate Committee on the Judiciary, *Nomination of W. Wilson White: Hearings Before the Committee on the Judiciary on Nomination of W. Wilson White, of Pennsylvania, To Be an Assistant Attorney General, To Head the Civil Rights Division of the Department of Justice,* 85th Cong., 2d sess., February 1958, 9–14.

91. J. W. Peltason, *Fifty-Eight Lonely Men: Southern Federal Judges and School Desegregation* (New York: Harcourt, Brace and World, 1961), 165–68.

92. Michal R. Belknap, *Federal Law and Southern Order: Racial Violence and Constitutional Conflict in the Post-*Brown *South* (Athens: University of Georgia Press, 1987), 46.

93. Id. at 37.

94. The women declined; one eventually married me. Sheriff Clark was later convicted of marijuana trafficking. "Ex-Sheriff Is Sentenced to 2 Years," *New York Times,* December 2, 1978, p. 12.

95. See, e.g., *Brewer v. Hoxie School Dist. No. 46,* 238 F.2d 91 (8th Cir. 1956).

96. See, e.g., *Kasper v. Brittain,* 245 F.2d 92 (6th Cir. 1957).

97. Robert Fredrick Burk, *The Eisenhower Administration and Black Civil Rights* (Knoxville: University of Tennessee Press, 1984), 240.

98. *Civil Rights Act of 1960, U.S. Statutes at Large* 74 (1961): 86 (18 U.S.C. §1509).

99. Id. at 87 (18 U.S.C. §837; repealed in 1970 and replaced by the more comprehensive Organized Crime Control Act of 1970, U.S. Statutes at Large 84 [1971]: 922, 952 [18 U.S.C. §§841–48]). This responded to bombings of desegregating schools. See Schwartz, *Statutory History,* 947. Private violence was also often directed at individuals.

100. John F. Kennedy, "Special Message to the Congress on Civil Rights and Job Opportunities," 484.

101. Klarman, Brown, *Racial Change, and the Civil Rights Movement,* 141.

102. Id. at 44 (footnote omitted).

103. Derrick A. Bell, Jr., Brown v. Board of Education *and the Interest-Convergence Dilemma,* 93 Harv. L. Rev. 518, 525 (1980).

104. Senate Committee on Commerce, *Civil Rights—Public Accommodations: Hearings on S. 1732,* 88th Cong., 1st sess., July 1963, serial 26, pt. 1, 873 (testimony of Ivan Allen, Jr.).

105. Id. at 866. His reference to "rights that the Court" has conferred is unclear, since the Court had conferred no right to nondiscrimination by public accommodations.

106. Belknap, *Federal Law and Southern Order,* 239.

107. Walton, *When the Marching Stopped,* 181.

108. *Report of the National Advisory Commission on Civil Disorders,* 32.

109. See Hugh Davis Graham, *The Civil Rights Era: Origins and Development of National Policy, 1960–1972* (New York: Oxford University Press, 1990), 270–73. But see Neal Devins, *The Civil Rights Hydra,* 89 Mich. L. Rev. 1723, 1728 (1991) ("While the King murder accelerated House action, Congress' action appears not to have been driven by expediency")(reviewing Graham, *The Civil Rights Era.*)

110. *U.S. Statutes at Large* 82 (1969): 73, 75–76 (18 U.S.C. 2101, 2102).

111. See Kimberlè Williams Crenshaw, *Race, Reform, and Retrenchment: Transformation and Legitimation in Antidiscrimination Law,* 101 Harv. L. Rev. 1331, 1332 n.3 (1988). Professor Crenshaw describes a danger that the reforms which the civil rights laws have wrought could legitimate the continuation of subordination of African Americans. Id. at 1349, 1368, 1382.

112. Henry J. Friendly, *Federal Jurisdiction: A General View* (New York: Columbia University Press, 1973), 90.

113. See, e.g., *Hernandez v. Texas,* 347 U.S. 475 (1954) (national origin).

114. See Chapter 2 n.75.

115. Schwartz, *Statutory History,* 857 (Rep. Emanuel Celler, [D-N.Y.].

116. Epstein, *Forbidden Grounds.* But see Drew S. Days III, *Reality,* 31 San Diego L. Rev. 169, 170 (1994) (Epstein fails "to take the history of racial discrimination seriously and to portray accurately the workings of Title VII law").

117. Albert O. Hirschman, *The Rhetoric of Reaction: Perversity, Futility, Jeopardy* (Cambridge, Mass.: Harvard University Press, 1991), 7–8.

118. Id. at 168.

119. Id. at 78.

120. See id. at 28.

121. Id. at 153.

122. Id. at 43; "the more it changes, the more it is the same thing."

123. Derrick A. Bell, Jr., *Race, Racism and American Law,* 3d ed. (Boston: Little, Brown and Company, 1992), 46.

124. Days, *Reality,* 178.

125. Crenshaw, *Race, Reform, and Retrenchment,* 1347 n.62.

126. Derrick Bell, *The Racism Is Permanent Thesis: Courageous Revelations or Unconscious Denial of Racial Genocide,* 22 Cap. U. L. Rev. 571 (1993).

127. "A 1994 survey of Americans found that [s]ixty-eight percent . . . favored full integration; 17 percent favored integration in some areas; while 7 percent favored separation of the races." Anne Stein, "Race Relations in America: What We Really Think of Each Other," *Human Rights* 21, no. 3 (summer 1994): 38. Compare the authorities mentioned in Days, *Reality,* 179 n.57.

128. Bell, *Race, Racism and American Law,* 46.

129. See Richard A. Posner, *The Economics of Justice* (Cambridge, Mass.: Harvard University Press, 1981), 352. Indeed, Richard Epstein argues that Title VII "has brought in its

wake more discrimination (and for less good purpose) than would exist in an unregulated system." Epstein, *Forbidden Grounds,* 497. This theory discounts the force of racism, which is rooted both in noneconomic factors and in the arguable countervailing interest in maintaining an underclass that can be economically exploited. Epstein concedes that "it would be a mistake to insist that all forms of discrimination would disappear in a competitive market." Id. at 496.

130. Bell, *Race, Racism and American Law,* 49.

131. Id. at 7.

132. E.g., Bell notes the limits placed on school desegregation, id. at 565–607, the constraints of the disparate treatment doctrine, id. at 854ff, and the weakening of the disparate impact doctrine, id. at 841ff.

CHAPTER 4. ENFORCEMENT ROLES OF INDIVIDUALS, STATES, AND FEDERAL GOVERNMENT

1. Stephen Wasby reports that individual plaintiffs' attorney's fees and costs in the Detroit case totaled just under $4 million and in Dayton, $1.8 million. Stephen L. Wasby, *The Multi-Faceted Elephant: Litigator Perspectives on Planned Litigation for Social Change,* 15 Cap. U. L. Rev. 143, 180 (1986).

2. See Deborah L. Rhode and David Luban, *Legal Ethics* (Westbury, N.Y.: Foundation Press, 1992), 810–13.

3. See *Alyeska Pipeline Service Co. v. Wilderness Society,* 421 U.S. 240 (1975).

4. See Council for Public Interest Law, *Balancing the Scales of Justice: Financing Public Interest Law in America* (n.p.: Council for Public Interest Law, 1976) for a thorough review of methods of financing private interest law.

5. As to the NAACP and its Legal Defense and Education Fund (LDF), see Jack Greenberg, *Crusaders in the Courts: How a Dedicated Band of Lawyers Fought for the Civil Rights Revolution* (New York: HarperCollins, Basic Books, 1994), 14–21. As to the ACLU, see Samuel Walker, *In Defense of American Liberties: The History of the ACLU* (New York: Oxford University Press, 1990), 4–6.

6. See Wasby, *Multi-Faceted Elephant,* 147 (the NAACP Legal Defense Fund has twenty-two lawyers; NAACP has sixteen, including many performing house counsel duties and therefore unavailable for public interest litigation). Greenberg, *Crusaders in the Courts* (describing the work and resources of the NAACP Legal Defense Fund).

7. In addition, the client's wishes may not coincide precisely with the public values that the organization seeks to pursue. See Derrick A. Bell, Jr., *Serving Two Masters: Integration Ideals and Client Interests in School Desegregation Litigation,* 85 Yale L. J. 470 (1976).

8. 42 U.S.C. 1988. See also the attorney's fee award provisions of the 1964 act, 42 U.S.C. 2000a-3(b), 2000e-5(k); the Voting Rights Act, 42 U.S.C. 1973l(e); the Fair Housing Act, 42 U.S.C. 3613(c)(2); and the Freedom of Access to Clinic Entrances Act of 1994, 18 U.S.C. 248(c)(1)(B). Although the court ordinarily must award attorney's fees to prevailing plaintiffs under these acts (see, e.g., *Newman v. Piggie Park Enterprises,* 390 U.S. 400 [1968], it may award attorney's fees to prevailing defendants only where the "action was frivolous, unreasonable or without foundation." *Christiansburg Garment Co. v. EEOC,* 434 U.S. 412, 421 (1978).

9. *Civil Rights Act of 1991, U.S. Statutes at Large* 105 (1992): 1071, 1079 (Sec. 113, Civil Rights Act of 1991, 42 U.S.C.A).

10. The NAACP Legal Defense Fund receives in the neighborhood of $1 million in fees under these statutes each year. Stephen L. Wasby, *Race Relations Litigation in an Age of Complexity* (Charlottesville: University Press of Virginia, 1995), 96.

11. Wasby, *Multi-Faceted Elephant,* 181. See also Vicki Quade, "Treating Civil Rights Law as a Business: Interview with Guy Saperstein," *Human Rights* 21, no. 2 (spring 1994).

12. 26 U.S.C. 162.

13. 26 U.S.C. 501(c).

14. See Wasby, *Race Relations Litigation,* 93.

15. *Legal Services Corporation Act of 1974, U.S. Statutes at Large* 88 (1976): 378–90 (42 U.S.C. §2996 et seq.). The corporation is an outgrowth of the Legal Services Program of the Office of Economic Opportunity, part of President Johnson's War on Poverty. See Historical and Statutory Notes to 42 U.S.C.A. §2996b.

16. Rhode and Luban, *Legal Ethics,* 824.

17. Law reform suits generally challenge a government law or practice as invalid and seek to substitute a new law or practice deemed more favorable to the plaintiff class. See Bryant Garth, *Neighborhood Law Firms for the Poor: A Comparative Study of Recent Developments in Legal Aid and in the Legal Profession* (Rockville, Md.: Sijthoff and Noordhoff, 1980), 172–78.

18. See, e.g., 42 U.S.C.A. §2996f(b).

19. Rhode and Luban, *Legal Ethics,* 821.

20. For a general review of government assistance to public interest litigation, see Wasby, *Race Relations Litigation,* chap. 4. He notes that for a short period the EEOC provided some direct assistance for fair employment cases, but "what is given can be taken away," and it was. Id. at 92.

21. For a survey of state laws by the mid-1960s, see Joseph P. Witherspoon, *Civil Rights Policy in the Federal System: Proposals for a Better Use of Administrative Process,* 74 Yale L. J. 1171 (1965). Witherspoon also advocates delegating enforcement to local human relations commissions. However, we cannot rely on a general commitment to local enforcement of nondiscrimination laws. Indeed, it has been argued that "localism may be more of an obstacle to achieving social justice and the development of public life than a prescription for their attainment." Richard Briffault, *Our Localism: Part I—The Structure of Local Government Law,* 90 Colum. L. Rev. 1, 2 (1990). In Selma, Alabama, localism was part of the problem, not the solution.

22. Michal R. Belknap, *Federal Law and Southern Order: Racial Violence and Constitutional Conflict in the Post-Brown South* (Athens: University of Georgia Press, 1987), 236–37.

23. See 9 United States Attorneys Manual §2.142 (no dual prosecution "unless there is a compelling federal interest supporting" it). The policy is described and approved in *Rinaldi v. United States,* 434 U.S. 22 (1977); see also *Petite v. United States,* 361 U.S. 529 (1960).

24. House Committee on Banking and Currency, Subcommittee on Consumer Affairs, *Credit Discrimination: Hearings on H.R. 14856 and H.R. 14908,* 93d Cong., 2d sess., June 1974, 70.

25. Mauro Cappelletti, *Governmental and Private Advocates for the Public Interest in Civil Litigation: A Comparative Study,* 73 Mich. L. Rev. 793, 883 (1975).

26. "In our received tradition, the lawsuit is a vehicle for settling disputes between private parties about private rights." Abram Chayes, *The Role of the Judge in Public Law Litigation,* 89 Harv. L. Rev. 1281, 1282 (1976).

27. Lon L. Fuller, *The Forms and Limits of Adjudication,* 92 Harv. L. Rev. 353, 387 (1978).

28. "Vindicating the *public* interest (including the public interest in Government observance of the Constitution and laws) is the function of Congress and the Chief Executive." *Lujan v. Defenders of Wildlife,* 504 U.S. 555, 576 (1992) (denying private right of action to enforce extraterritorial enforcement of Endangered Species Act).

29. The distinction between private and public rights differs from that drawn by

Crowell v. Benson, 285 U.S. 22, 50 (1932): "The distinction . . . between cases of private right and those which arise between the government and persons subject to its authority in connection with the performance of the constitutional functions of the executive or legislative departments." "Public rights" refer to the rights of the public at large under the Constitution and under laws that vindicate constitutional rights. They are rights that private citizens enjoy against infringement by either the government or by private actors.

30. Chayes, *The Role of the Judge in Public Law Litigation,* 1283.

31. See *Hawaii v. Standard Oil Co.,* 405 U.S. 251 (1972). "Traditionally, the term was used to refer to the King's power as guardian of persons under legal disabilities to act for themselves." Id. at 257.

32. See Harold J. Krent, *Executive Control over Criminal Law Enforcement: Some Lessons from History,* 38 Am. U. L. Rev. 275, 297 (1989) ("Through the qui tam actions, private citizens helped enforce the criminal laws").

33. *Linda R.S. v. Richard D.,* 410 U.S. 614, 617 n.3 (1973).

34. Thus, the Supreme Court has noted that references to the attorney general in §12 of the Voting Rights Act "were included to give the Attorney General power to bring suit to enforce what might otherwise be viewed as 'private' rights." *Allen v. State Bd. of Elections,* 393 U.S. 544, 555 n.18 (1969).

35. *Newman v. Piggie Park Enterprises,* 390 U.S. 400, 401 (1968).

36. Id.

37. Id. at 402. See also *Cornelius v. NAACP Legal Defense & Educ. Fund, Inc.,* 473 U.S. 788, 827 (1985) (Blackmun, J., dissenting) ("respondents work to enforce the rights of minorities, women, and others through litigation, a task that various Governmental agencies otherwise might be called upon to undertake").

38. U.S. Constitution, Article 2, Section 1.

39. For example, Justice John Paul Stevens's opinion in *Regents of the Univ. of Cal. v. Bakke,* 438 U.S. 265, 421 n.28 (1978), first characterizes the rights under the Voting Rights Act and Title VI of the 1964 act as "personal rights" and then says that the private right of action will "supplement" federal enforcement.

40. *General Telephone Company v. EEOC,* 446 U.S. 318, 326 (1980).

41. House, *Civil Rights of Institutionalized Persons Act: Conference Report to Accompany H.R. 10,* 96th Cong., 2d sess., 1980, H. Rept. 897, 13.

42. Alexander M. Bickel, *The Decade of School Desegregation: Progress and Prospects,* 64 Colum. L. Rev. 193, 221 (1964).

43. In addition to the elimination of Part 3 in 1957, the elimination of similar broad authority from the bill that became the 1964 act, and the elimination of federal authority to bring civil suits attacking state jury discrimination practices from the bill that became the 1968 act, see the Indian Civil Rights Act, 28 U.S.C. §1301, et seq., enacted in 1968 ("Congress considered and rejected proposals for federal review of alleged violations of the Act arising in a civil context. As initially introduced, the Act would have required the Attorney General to 'receive and investigate' complaints relating to deprivations of an Indian's statutory or constitutional rights, and to bring 'such criminal or other action as he deems appropriate to vindicate and secure such right to such Indian.' Notwithstanding the screening effect this proposal would have had on frivolous or vexatious lawsuits, it was bitterly opposed by several tribes. . . . In response, this provision . . . was completely eliminated from the ICRA." *Santa Clara Pueblo v. Martinez,* 436 U.S. 49, 67–68 (1978) (footnotes omitted). Note, however, that some believe the provision was deleted because "the proposals gave the Attorney General no more authority than he already possessed." Id. at 78 (White, J., dissenting)).

44. See, e.g., *Yates v. Unites States,* 354 U.S. 298 (1957); *Scales v. United States,* 367 U.S. 203 (1961); *Noto v. United States,* 367 U.S. 290 (1961).

45. Senate Amendment no. 817 to H.R. 14765, 89th Cong., 2d sess., September 6, 1966. The Civil Rights Act of 1875 had made it a crime to discriminate based on race in jury selection. See Earl M. Maltz, *The Civil Rights Act and the Civil Rights Cases: Congress, Court, and Constitution,* 44 Fla. L. Rev. 605, 623–26 (1992); *Ex parte Virginia,* 100 U.S. 339 (1879). The modern version is 18 U.S.C. 243.

46. *U.S. Statutes at Large* 62 (1949): 683, 696 (18 U.S.C. 243).

47. *Castaneda v. Partida,* 430 U.S. 482 (1977); *White v. Crook,* 251 F. Supp. 401 (M.D. Ala. 1966).

48. See, e.g., *Colegrove v. Green,* 328 U.S. 549, 552 (1946) (plurality opinion of Frankfurter, J.), in which the Court refused to allow a private suit in federal court challenging congressional malapportionment because, "The basis for the suit is not a private wrong, but a wrong suffered by Illinois as a polity."

49. 42 U.S.C.A. 2000c-6(a).

50. Senate Committee on the Judiciary, Subcommittee on Constitutional Rights, *Civil Rights—1957: Hearings on S. 83, an amendment to S. 83, S. 427, S. 428, S. 429, S. 468, S. 500, S. 501, S. 502, S. 504, S. 505, S. 508, S. 509, S. 510,* S. Con. Res. 5, 85th Cong., 1st sess., February–March 1957, 60. House Committee on the Judiciary, Subcommittee no. 5, *Civil Rights: Hearings on H.R. 140, 142, 143, 159, 359, 360, 363, 374, 395, 424, 438, 439, 440, 441, 542, 548, 549, 550, 551, 552, 555, 887, 956, 957, 958, 959, 1097, 1099, 1100, 1101, 1102, 1134, 1151, 1254, 2145, 2153, 2375, 2835, 3088, 3481, 3613, 3616, 3617, 3618, 3793, 3945, 3946, 3951, 3955, 3956, 3957, 3959, 4121, 4126, 4269, 4420, 4496, 4782,* 85th Cong., 1st sess., February 1957, 599.

51. House Committee on the Judiciary, Subcommittee no. 5, *Civil Rights: Hearings on H.R. 140, . . . 4782,* 602.

52. *Civil Rights Act of 1964, U.S. Statutes at Large* 78 (1965): 241, 252 (42 U.S.C. §2000d). President, Executive Order, "Equal Employment Opportunity, Executive Order 11246," *Federal Register* 30, no. 187 (September 28, 1965): 12319, microfiche.

53. *Allen v. State Bd. of Elections,* 393 U.S. 544, 556 (1969).

54. *Trafficante v. Metropolitan Life Ins. Co.,* 409 U.S. 205, 211 (1972) ("since the enormity of the task of assuring fair housing makes the role of the Attorney General in the matter minimal, the main generating force must be private suits").

55. Id. at 209.

56. *Occidental Life Ins. Co. v. EEOC,* 432 U.S. 355 (1977).

57. Id. at 368. The Court did suggest that equitable principles might limit available relief if the EEOC's delay in filing suit was "inordinate" and the defendant was prejudiced by the delay. Id. at 373. Note, however, that to deny a victim of discrimination relief because of the failure of an administrative agency to comply with time periods would raise due process concerns. See *Logan v. Zimmerman Brush Co.,* 455 U.S. 422 (1982).

58. *General Telephone Company v. EEOC,* 446 U.S. 318, 331 (1980).

59. See generally Maimon Schwarzschild, *Public Law by Private Bargain: Title VII Consent Decrees and the Fairness of Negotiated Institutional Reform,* 1984 Duke L. J. 887.

60. *United States v. Reserve Mining Co.,* 56 F.R.D. 408, 419 (D. Minn. 1972).

61. Schwarzschild, *Public Law by Private Bargain,* 914.

62. Id. at 919.

63. 490 U.S. 755 (1989).

64. 42 U.S.C.A. §703(n).

65. As to school desegregation, see Randolph D. Moss, Note, *Participation and Department of Justice School Desegregation Consent Decrees,* 95 Yale L. J. 1811 (1986) (arguing that a Rule 23-type procedure should be required when the department seeks judicial approval of a school desegregation consent decree).

66. 295 F.2d 772 (5th Cir. 1961).

67. Id. at 781.

68. Id. at 783.
69. Id.
70. *Newman v. Piggie Park Enterprises,* 390 U.S. 400, 401 (1968). In a footnote to the above language the Court noted that the attorney general could sue "only where a 'pattern or practice' of discrimination is reasonably believed to exist." Id. at 401 n.2.
71. Id. at 402. The Court concluded that Title II's authorization for an award of attorney's fees to the prevailing party should ordinarily lead to an award to a prevailing plaintiff "unless special circumstances would render such an award unjust."
72. *Northcross v. Board of Educ.,* 412 U.S. 427 (1973).
73. See *Albemarle Paper Co. v. Moody,* 422 U.S. 405, 415 (1975).
74. See *Newman,* 390 U.S. at 401.
75. See 42 U.S.C. §1988.
76. *Hensley v. Eckerhart,* 461 U.S. 424, 445–46 (1983) (alteration in original) (footnote omitted) (Brennan, J., concurring in part and dissenting in part).
77. Philip Selznick, *The Moral Commonwealth: Social Theory and the Promise of Community* (Berkeley and Los Angeles: University of California Press, 1992), 174.
78. House Committee on the Judiciary, Subcommittee on Courts, Civil Liberties, and the Administration of Justice, *Civil Rights of Institutionalized Persons: Hearings on H.R. 10,* 96th Cong., 1st sess., February 1979, 2 (statement of Subcommittee Chairman Robert W. Kastenmeier).
79. *Giles v. Harris,* 189 U.S. 475, 488 (1903).
80. Burke Marshall, *Federalism and Civil Rights* (New York: Columbia University Press, 1964), 7.
81. Bickel, *Decade of School Desegregation,* 219.
82. Id.
83. Id.
84. Id. at 222.
85. See Chapter 8 of this volume.
86. Bernard Schwartz, ed., *Statutory History of the United States: Civil Rights* (New York: Chelsea House Publishers, 1970), pt. 1, 148. This language suggests that the government is the lawyer for the victim, but the context—support for federal criminal prosecution—negates that suggestion.
87. See Taylor Branch, *Parting the Waters: America in the King Years, 1954–1963* (New York: Simon and Schuster, 1988), 333–35; *United States v. Wood,* 295 F.2d 772 (5th Cir. 1961); Jack Bass, *Unlikely Heroes: The Dramatic Story of the Southern Judges of the Fifth Circuit Who Translated the Supreme Court's Brown Decision into a Revolution for Equality* (New York: Simon and Schuster, 1981), 216.
88. See, e.g., 18 U.S.C. 245, 42 U.S.C. 3617, 42 U.S.C. 1973(i)(b), 42 U.S.C. 2000e-3.
89. See, e.g., 42 U.S.C. 2000a-5, 42 U.S.C. 2000c-6.
90. *Sobol v. Perez,* 289 F.Supp. 392 (E.D. La. 1968)(arrest); Branch, *Parting the Waters,* 868, 871, 888 (bombing).
91. Victor S. Navasky, *Kennedy Justice* (New York: Atheneum, 1971), 20.
92. Thus, in concurring with the Court's refusal to allow a federal private right of action under 42 U.S.C. 1985(3) for conspiracy to deprive women of the right to interstate travel to seek an abortion, Justice Anthony Kennedy noted that if state law enforcement officials deemed it necessary, federal help was available from the attorney general under 42 U.S.C. 10501. Justice Kennedy noted, "I have little doubt that such extraordinary intervention into local controversies would be ordered only after a careful assessment of the circumstances, including the need to preserve our essential liberties and traditions." *Bray v. Alexandria Women's Health Clinic,* 113 S.Ct. 753, 769 (1993) (Kennedy, J., concurring).

93. Jack Bass, *Taming the Storm: The Life and Times of Judge Frank M. Johnson, Jr., and the South's Fight over Civil Rights* (New York: Doubleday, 1993), 223 (quoting an interview with Owen M. Fiss).

94. One experienced practitioner notes the sharp decline in class actions to enforce Title VII (from 1,174 in 1976 to 48 in 1980) and concludes that "it has become increasingly difficult for those harmed by discriminatory employment practices to find counsel who can and will represent their interests effectively." David L. Rose, *Twenty-Five Years Later: Where Do We Stand on Equal Employment Opportunity Law Enforcement?* 42 Vand. L. Rev. 1121, 1160-61 (1989). But see Michael Selmi, *The Value of the EEOC: Reexamining the Agency's Role in Employment Discrimination Law,* 57 Ohio St. L. J. 1, 42 (1996), arguing that 1991 amendments to Title VII, providing for jury trial and punitive and compensatory damages, should "render employment discrimination cases significantly more attractive to attorneys than they previously were."

95. See Minna J. Kotkin, *Public Remedies for Private Wrongs: Rethinking the Title VII Back Pay Remedy,* 41 Hastings L. J. 1301, 1363 (1990).

96. Id. at 1368.

97. The Court and the Congress have established some protections against federal discrimination. See, e.g., *Davis v. Passman,* 442 U.S. 228 (1979); 42 U.S.C. §794 (handicap discrimination in federally conducted programs); 42 U.S.C. §2000e-16 (employment discrimination by federal government).

98. The paradigm is the NAACP's litigation strategy for ending school segregation.

99. Joseph L. Sax, *Defending the Environment: A Strategy for Citizen Action* (New York: Knopf, 1971), 56.

100. Senate Committee on the Judiciary, Subcommittee on Constitutional Rights, *Civil Rights—1957,* 29.

101. The department has successfully prosecuted election officials under the predecessor of §241 for conspiring to discriminate against African Americans in the voting process. E.g., *Guinn v. United States,* 238 U.S. 347 (1915) (application of grandfather clause); see also *United States v. Mosley,* 238 U.S. 383 (1915) (reversing dismissal of indictment for conspiracy to deny right to vote for Congress). Justice Holmes, in *Mosley,* noted that the statute "naturally did not confine itself to conspiracies contemplating violence." Id. at 387-88.

102. 18 U.S.C. §245; 42 U.S.C. §§1973j(c), 3617.

103. See, e.g., the Fugitive Slave Acts of 1793 and 1850; Sherman Antitrust Act of 1890.

104. Henry M. Hart, Jr., *The Aims of the Criminal Law,* 23 Law and Contemp. Probs. 401, 405 (1958).

105. Although the Fair Housing Act does not explicitly limit civil penalties to cases of intentional discrimination, it seems unlikely that courts which recognize disparate impact claims under the act would grant civil penalties in the absence of a showing of intent. One court, in awarding a civil penalty of $10,000 instead of the $50,000 authorized by §814 of the act (42 U.S.C.A. 3614), said a penalty was warranted because "officials acted with an intent to discriminate on the basis of a handicap." However, a larger award was not warranted because the case was "an aberration." *United States v. Borough of Audubon,* 797 F. Supp. 353, 363 (D.N.J. 1991), *aff'd mem.,* 968 F.2d 14 (3rd Cir. 1992).

106. John T. Elliff, *The United States Department of Justice and Individual Rights, 1937–1962* (New York: Garland Publishing, 1987) 170-71, 222-24.

107. Letter from Joseph M. F. Ryan, Jr., acting assistant attorney general, Civil Rights Division, to Dr. John A. Hannah, chairman, Commission on Civil Rights, June 19, 1959, described in Commission on Civil Rights, *Reports of the United States Commission on Civil Rights, 1959* (Washington, D.C.: Government Printing Office, 1959), 131.

108. Id. at 130.

109. Attorney General, *Annual Report of the Attorney General of the United States for Fiscal Year ended June 30, 1960,* 185–89. The one conviction was for arresting a Native American, beating him unconscious and bleeding, and dumping him outside the Blackfoot, Idaho, city limits. Id. at 186.

110. Senate Committee on the Judiciary, *Civil Rights—The President's Program, 1963: Hearings on S. 1731 and S. 1750,* 88th Cong., 1st sess., July-August-September 1963, 111, 113.

111. Id. at 113.

112. Senate Committee on the Judiciary, Subcommittee on Constitutional Rights, *Civil Rights—1957,* 6. A study of French employment discrimination law suggests that criminalization of employment discrimination is an ineffective device even in a country without jury trial; in any event, only two or three employers are convicted of race discrimination under the French law in a year. Donna M. Gitter, Comment, *French Criminalization of Racial Employment Discrimination Compared to the Imposition of Civil Penalties in the United States,* 15 Comp. Lab. L. J. 488, 525 (1994).

113. House Committee on the Judiciary, *Civil Rights: Hearing on Legislation Regarding the Civil Rights of Persons Within the Jurisdiction of the United States,* 84th Cong., 2d sess., April 1956, 571. This preference for preventive rather than retrospective relief echoes the decision in *In re Debs,* 158 U.S. 564 (1895), where "the vastness and importance of the interests threatened . . . made it inappropriate for the government to rely exclusively on such after-the-fact legal remedies as criminal prosecution, which must await the harm or a good measure of it before the actual proceeding is begun." Owen M. Fiss, *Troubled Beginnings of the Modern State, 1888–1910,* vol. 8 of *History of the Supreme Court of the United States* (New York: Macmillan Company, 1993).

114. Senate Committee on the Judiciary, Subcommittee on Constitutional Rights, *Civil Rights—1957,* 81.

115. House Committee on the Judiciary, Subcommittee no. 5, *Civil Rights: Hearings on H.R. 140, . . . 4782,* 591.

116. The attorney general is authorized to seek a civil penalty of up to $50,000 for a first offense under the Fair Housing Act or under the Americans with Disabilities Act's public accommodations provisions and up to $100,000 for any subsequent offense. 42 U.S.C.A. §§3614(d)(1)(C) and 12188(b)(2)(C). She may seek a civil penalty of up to $10,000 for the first nonviolent physical obstruction of an abortion clinic and $15,000 for other first violations of the Freedom of Access to Clinic Entrances Act of 1994 and up to $15,000 for subsequent nonviolent physical obstruction and $25,000 for other subsequent violations. 18 U.S.C.A. §248(c)(2)(B). Punitive damages are now available to private plaintiffs in cases under some civil rights acts. See, e.g., 42 U.S.C. §1981a (punitive damages in fair employment cases, up to $300,000 per complaining party), 42 U.S.C. §3613(c) (punitive damages in fair housing cases).

117. *Tull v. United States,* 481 U.S. 412, 422 n.7 (1987). The Court added that "the remedy of civil penalties is similar to the remedy of punitive damages."

118. James Madison, "Federalist Paper No. 10," in *The Federalist Papers* (New York: New American Library, 1961), 77– 84. Madison defined faction as citizens "united and actuated by some common impulse of passion, or of interest, adverse to the rights of other citizens, or to the permanent and aggregate interests of the community" (p. 78).

119. Robert F. Kennedy, foreword to Marshall, *Federalism and Civil Rights,* ix.

120. See Carl M. Brauer, *John F. Kennedy and the Second Reconstruction* (New York: Columbia University Press, 1977), 152–53. Earlier, Justice Jackson had sounded a similar concern: "I cannot say that our country could have no central police without becoming totalitarian, but I can say with great conviction that it cannot become totalitarian without a centralized national police. . . . All that is necessary is to have a national police competent to investigate all manner of offenses, and then, in the parlance of the street, it will

have enough on enough people, even if it does not elect to prosecute them, so that it will find no opposition to its policies." Robert H. Jackson, *The Supreme Court in the American System of Government* (Cambridge, Mass.: Harvard University Press, 1955), 70–71.

121. Marshall, *Federalism and Civil Rights,* 6–7. A review of Assistant Attorney General Marshall's book minimizes the federalism concern: "*Federalism and Civil Rights* is an important book because it so largely reflects the contemporary as well as prior governmental ideology concerning the appropriate reach and kind of federal involvement in the enforcement of federal law. This ideology holds that the Government's role in the legal enforcement and protection of civil rights should be a restricted one. It consists, further, of the commitment to secure voluntary compliance from state and local officials. And it insists, finally, that the federal system itself is not at fault—only the persons functioning within the system are to blame." The review concludes that "the hard question that Mr. Marshall's book does not answer satisfactorily is how, in the light of the dismal record of enforcement to date and the injuries all too long endured and still suffered daily, the continued imposition of these constraints on federal action can still seem defensible." Richard A. Wasserstrom, book review, 33 U. Chi. L. Rev. 406, 409, 413 (1966) (footnote omitted). A more balanced critique argues: "There are ways of approaching the problem which embrace neither a large-scale take-over of what are properly state functions nor a policy of refraining from action in the interest of federalism. . . . What is needed . . . is not a Federal occupation, but what is called in the civil rights movement a greater 'Federal presence.' " Haywood Burns, "The Federal Government and Civil Rights," in *Southern Justice,* ed. Leon Friedman (Westport, Conn.: Greenwood Press, 1965), 241–42. Historian Michal Belknap, after examining the results of Kennedy administration policies, concluded that "by 1965 Southern policemen and jurors were proving Burke Marshall had been correct when he insisted that the South and its institutions could be counted on eventually to assume responsibility for protecting blacks and civil rights workers." Michal R. Belknap, *The Vindication of Burke Marshall: The Southern Legal System and the Anti–Civil-Rights Violence of the 1960s,* 33 Emory L. J. 93, 131 (1984). Increasing black political power combined with white concern about law and order led to what he characterizes as "the Southern crackdown on racist violence." Id. at 115–16.

122. Bickel, *Decade of School Desegregation,* 220.

123. Id. at 221.

124. Id. at 220.

125. Id.

126. Id. at 220–21.

127. House Committee on the Judiciary, Subcommittee no. 5, *Civil Rights: Hearings on H.R. 300, 351, 352, 353, 400, 430, 461, 617, 618, 619, 759, 913, 914, 1902, 2346, 2479, 2538, 2786, 3090, 3147, 3148, 3212, 3559, 4169, 4261, 4338, 4339, 4342, 4348, 4457, 5008, 5170, 5189, 5217, 5218, 5276, 5323, 6934, 6935,* 86th Cong., 1st sess., March-April-May 1959, 225.

128. Id. at 228.

129. *Civil Rights Act of 1964, U.S. Statutes at Large* 78 (1965): 241, 244 (42 U.S.C. §2000a[3][c]), 259 (42 U.S.C. §2000e[5][b]).

CHAPTER 5. ENFORCEMENT ROLES WITHIN THE EXECUTIVE BRANCH

1. Section 35 of the Judiciary Act of 1789 created the Office of Attorney General of the United States "to prosecute and conduct all suits in the Supreme Court in which the United States shall be concerned, and to give his advice and opinion upon questions of

law when required by the heads of any of the departments, touching any matters that may concern their departments." *Judiciary Act of 1789, U.S. Statutes at Large* 1 (1845): 73, 92.

2. *Department of Justice Act of 1870, U.S. Statutes at Large* 16 (1871): 348. For a history of the department, see Homer Cummings and Carl McFarland, *Federal Justice: Chapters in the History of Justice and the Federal Executive* (1937; reprint, New York: Da Capo Press, 1970); see also Nancy V. Baker, *Conflicting Loyalties: Law and Politics in the Attorney General's Office, 1789-1990* (Lawrence: University Press of Kansas, 1992).

3. Robert L. Rabin, *Federal Regulation in Historical Perspective,* 38 Stan. L. Rev. 1189, 1216 (1986).

4. *In re Debs,* 158 U.S. 564 (1895).

5. See generally Rabin, *Federal Regulation in Historical Perspective.*

6. See 28 U.S.C. §516 ("Except as otherwise authorized by law, the conduct of litigation in which the United States . . . is a party . . . is reserved to officers of the Department of Justice, under the direction of the Attorney General").

7. Bernard Schwartz, ed., *Statutory History of the United States: Civil Rights* (New York: Chelsea House Publishers, 1970), 1562.

8. Calif. Govt. Code §12901; Race Relations Act, 1965, §2 (Eng.); Race Relations Act, 1968, §14 (Eng.); Race Relations Act, 1976, §43 (Eng.) (replacing Race Relations Board with Commission for Racial Equality); Sex Discrimination Act 1975, §53 (Eng.) (Equal Opportunities Commission).

9. For use of "institutional equilibrium," see William N. Eskridge, Jr., and Philip P. Frickey, *Foreword: Law as Equilibrium,* 108 Harv. L. Rev. 26, 35 (1994).

10. Hugh Davis Graham, *Civil Rights and the Presidency: Race and Gender in American Politics, 1960-1972* (New York: Oxford University Press, 1992), 227.

11. Robert G. Dixon, Jr., "The Attorney General and Civil Rights, 1870-1964," in *Roles of the Attorney General of the United States* (Washington, D.C.: American Enterprise Institute, 1968), 115.

12. Graham, *Civil Rights and the Presidency,* 81.

13. John M. Rosenberg, *Personal Reflections of a Life in Public Interest Law: From the Civil Rights Division of the United States Department of Justice to Appalred,* 96 W. Va. L. Rev. 317, 319 (1993-1994).

14. Id. at 319-20.

15. For the history of the Title VII enforcement provisions, see Minna J. Kotkin, *Public Remedies for Private Wrongs: Rethinking the Title VII Back Pay Remedy,* 41 Hastings L. J. 1301 (1990).

16. Senate Committee on Labor and Public Welfare, Subcommittee on Labor, *Legislative History of the Equal Employment Opportunity Act of 1972,* 92d Cong., 2d sess., November 1972, 1576.

17. *Fair Housing Amendments Act of 1988,* 100th Cong., 2d sess., H.R. 1158, *Congressional Record* 134, pt. 14:19718. See also Sen. Karnes remarks, id. at 19723 ("superior nationwide resources and expertise of the Justice Department, including local U.S. attorneys"); memorandum submitted by Sens. Kennedy and Spector, id. at 19712 ("The authority to litigate fair housing cases is consolidated in the Justice Department, while it is made clear that the Department is required to bring cases authorized by the Secretary under the bill's provisions regarding prompt judicial action and regarding federal court enforcement of cases in which a party to an administrative proceeding elects to have the charge heard in federal court").

18. *Fair Housing Amendments Act of 1988,* 100th Cong., 2d sess., H.R. 1158, *Congressional Record* 134, pt. 2:16492 (referring to prompt judicial action cases).

19. Susan M. Olson, "Challenges to the Gatekeeper: The Debate over Federal Litigating Authority," *Judicature* 68, no. 1 (June-July 1984), 72.

20. The arguments for and against centralizing litigation authority in the Department of Justice are well summarized in Olson, "Challenges to the Gatekeeper," 78-83. See also Neal Devins, *Unitariness and Independence: Solicitor General Control over Independent Agency Litigation,* 82 Cal. L. Rev. 255, 321-27 (1994).

21. Federal resources include 6,419 staff members from the Office of Fair Housing and Equal Opportunity, Department of Housing and Urban Development; Office for Civil Rights, Department of Education; Office for Civil Rights, Department of Health and Human Services; Equal Employment Opportunity Commission (1994 actual staff), Department of Labor; and Office of Federal Contract Compliance Programs, Department of Justice, Civil Rights Division. Staff estimates for 1996 from Commission on Civil Rights, *Funding Federal Civil Rights Enforcement: A Report of the United States Commission on Civil Rights, June 1995,* prepared by Conner Ball (Washington, D.C., n.d.). There are 422 litigation lawyers at the Department of Justice's Civil Rights Division and the Equal Employment Opportunity Commission. Agency staff, telephone interviews, June 7, 10, and 17, 1996.

22. Schwartz, *Statutory History,* 926.

23. Id. at 1312.

24. Id. at 1331. Sen. Clark endorsed, however, Section 707 pattern and practice authority as "a real net gain," though he feared "that the office of the Attorney General . . . through the entire history of the Republic has tended to be a political one, and that the extent to which any particular laws or set of laws are enforced depends largely if not entirely on the political philosophy of the particular individual . . . who holds the office of Attorney General. . . . The fact remains that the power has been taken away from the Federal Commission which would be created by the bill—a commission expert in dealing with the employment aspects of the civil rights problem—and has been given to a political officer, who has a host of other duties and other heavy responsibilities to perform, requiring him to find in each instance a pattern of discrimination before he can invoke Federal power."

25. Senate Committee on Labor and Public Welfare, Subcommittee on Labor, *Legislative History of the Equal Employment Opportunity Act of 1972,* 193.

26. See Brian K. Landsberg, Book Review, 6 Const. Commentary 165, 179 (1989) (reviewing Lincoln Caplan, *The Tenth Justice: The Solicitor General and the Rule of Law* [New York: Knopf, 1987]).

27. See Devins, *Unitariness and Independence,* 299. See also David L. Rose, *Twenty-Five Years Later: Where Do We Stand on Equal Employment Opportunity Law Enforcement?* 42 Vand. L. Rev. 1121, 1173 n.264 (1989) (the commission's "functions are those of a law enforcement agency, which is the essence of the executive branch").

28. Frank H. Easterbrook, *The State of Madison's Vision of the State: A Public Choice Perspective,* 107 Harv. L. Rev. 1328, 1342 (1994).

29. Id. at 1341. Suzanne Weaver has pointed out that the independent regulatory commissions "are accused of having been co-opted by the industries under their jurisdiction and diverted from their proper allegiance to the interest of the public as a whole; they are accused of making bad decisions because of the intrusion of partisan politics; and they are accused of simple inattention to their primary goals." Suzanne Weaver, *Decision to Prosecute: Organization and Public Policy in the Antitrust Division* (Cambridge, Mass.: MIT Press, 1977), 174.

30. See, e.g., *General Electric Co. v. Gilbert,* 429 U.S. 125, 142 (1976) (rejecting Nixon administration EEOC guideline because it "flatly contradicts the position which the agency had enunciated at an earlier date" during the Johnson administration); *Bob Jones University v. United States,* 461 U.S. 574 (1983) (upholding long-standing position of Internal Revenue Service that Reagan Justice Department had attempted to abandon).

31. See Neal Devins, *The Civil Rights Hydra,* 89 Mich. L. Rev. 1761 (1991); William N. Eskridge, Jr., *Reneging on History? Playing the Court/Congress/President Civil Rights Game,* 79 Cal. L. Rev. 613 (1991).

32. See Devins, *Unitariness and Independence,* 295–300, discussing the briefs in *Metro Broadcasting, Inc. v. FCC,* 497 U.S. 547 (1990); *Williams v. City of New Orleans,* 729 F.2d 1554 (5th Cir. 1984); *Local 28, Sheet Metal Workers' Int'l Ass'n v. EEOC,* 478 U.S. 421 (1986). The plurality in *Local 28* pointed out that the "Government urged a different interpretation of *Stotts* earlier in this lawsuit," referring to the submission of the EEOC in the Court of Appeals. Id. at 474 n.46.

33. See Stephen L. Wasby, *Race Relations Litigation in an Age of Complexity* (Charlottesville: University Press of Virginia, 1995), 247–51.

34. Eric Foner, *Reconstruction: America's Unfinished Revolution, 1863–1877* (New York: Harper and Row, 1988), 69.

35. Id. at 142.

36. President, Executive Order, "Leadership and Coordination of Nondiscrimination Laws, Executive Order 12250," *Federal Register* 45, no. 215 (November 2, 1980): 72995, microfiche (transferring coordination of §504 from the Department of Health and Human Services to the Department of Justice). "The rationale for this move of coordinating responsibility was to place authority for implementing section 504 in the agency responsible for other civil rights laws. Disability interest groups generally applauded this action, which they felt emphasized the rights nature of section 504 and its relation to other civil rights laws." Stephen L. Percy, *Disability, Civil Rights, and Public Policy: The Politics of Implementation* (Tuscaloosa: University of Alabama Press, 1989), 86.

37. 163 U.S. 537, 540 (1896) (upholding state law requiring "separate railway carriages for the white and colored races").

38. 189 U.S. 475 (1903) (denial of injunctive relief to register African-American plaintiff who was denied registration pursuant to racially discriminatory voting law).

39. See Richard Kluger, *Simple Justice: The History of* Brown v. Board of Education *and Black America's Struggle for Equality* (New York: Random House, 1975).

40. Conciliation, however, proved ineffectual as long as the commission lacked power to enforce Title VII. For example, the commission's conciliation failed in 507 of 890 efforts in 1967 and 731 of 1,244 efforts in 1968. See note, *The Scope of the Attorney General's Power Under Title VII: Appraisal and Reform,* 2 Rut.-Cam. L. J. 185, 186 n.6 (1970).

41. See 42 U.S.C. 2000d-2, which provides for judicial review of agency decisions to terminate federal financial assistance under Title VI.

42. President, Executive Order, "Equal Employment Opportunity, Executive Order 11246," *Federal Register* 30, no. 187 (September 28, 1965): 12319, microfiche.

43. Under Executive Order 11246, the Office of Federal Contract Compliance of the Department of Labor may debar from future federal contracts any contractor found to discriminate or to fail to comply with affirmative action requirements in its employment practices. See Hugh Davis Graham, *The Civil Rights Era: Origins and Development of National Policy, 1960–1972* (New York: Oxford University Press, 1990), 186, 282–97, 322–45.

44. See Chapter 2 of this volume. A recent review of Fair Housing Act enforcement found that "in the majority of cases, the parties elected to proceed in district court rather than before an ALJ." Leland B. Ware, *New Weapons for an Old Battle: The Enforcement Provisions of the 1988 Amendments to the Fair Housing Act,* 7 Admin. L. J. Am. U. 59, 111 (1993).

45. 29 U.S.C. 160.

46. See, e.g., House Committee on Education and Labor, *Equal Employment Opportunities Enforcement Act of 1971,* 92d Cong., 1st sess., June 1971, H. Rept. 238 (reproduced in Senate Committee on Labor and Public Welfare, Subcommittee on Labor, *Legislative*

History of the Equal Employment Opportunity Act of 1972, 62–71). Professor Blumrosen argues that the proponents were misguided, ignoring how well civil rights supporters had done in the courts and how poor the enforcement record of state fair employment practice agencies had been. Alfred W. Blumrosen, *Modern Law: The Law Transmission System and Equal Employment Opportunity* (Madison: University of Wisconsin Press, 1993), 48–49.

47. "It had become the heart of the Johnson administration's Senate bill in 1967 and 1968." Graham, *The Civil Rights Era,* 420. See also Rose, *Twenty-Five Years Later,* 1134; Clarence Mitchell, *Moods and Changes: The Civil Rights Record of the Nixon Administration,* 49 Notre Dame Law. 63, 71 (1973).

48. Mitchell, *Moods and Changes,* 119–22.

49. See *Occidental Life Ins. Co. v. EEOC,* 432 U.S. 355 (1977) for a history of Congress's consideration of the cease and desist issue.

50. Senate Committee on Labor and Public Welfare, Subcommittee on Labor, *Legislative History of the Equal Employment Opportunity Act of 1972,* 156. Professor Blumrosen notes that the language of the transfer of power could have been read to transfer all pattern and practice authority to the EEOC, but that congressional intent was to assign pattern and practice cases against state and local governments to the Department of Justice. Blumrosen, *Modern Law,* 390 n.10.

51. 8 U.S.C.A. §1324b.

52. The House Report on the act argued, "Administrative tribunals are better equipped to handle the complicated issues involved in employment discrimination cases." House Committee on Education and Labor, *Equal Employment Opportunities Enforcement Act of 1971,* 10 (reproduced in Senate Committee on Labor and Public Welfare, Subcommittee on Labor, *Legislative History of the Equal Employment Opportunity Act of 1972,* 70).

53. Administrative tribunals are better because "efficiency and predictability will be enhanced if the necessarily detailed case by case findings of fact and fashioning of remedy is performed by experts in the subject matter." Id. at 11 (reproduced in Senate Committee on Labor and Public Welfare, Subcommittee on Labor, *Legislative History of the Equal Employment Opportunity Act of 1972,* 71).

54. Id. at 10 (reproduced in Senate Committee on Labor and Public Welfare, Subcommittee on Labor, *Legislative History of the Equal Employment Opportunity Act of 1972,* 70). "Further, congested Court calendars necessitate inordinate delays in bringing cases to trial." Id. at 11 (reproduced in *Legislative History,* 71). Senate Committee on Labor and Public Welfare Report no. 92-415 (October 28, 1971) recounts the arguments as to whether the EEOC should have cease and desist powers or court enforcement powers. Civil rights groups supported the former while the administration and employer groups supported the latter. Senate Committee on Labor and Public Welfare, *Equal Employment Opportunities Enforcement Act of 1971,* 92d Cong., 1st sess., October 1971, S. Rept. 415, 2–3 (reproduced in *Legislative History,* 411–12). The report supports the cease and desist approach.

55. House Committee on Education and Labor, *Equal Employment Opportunities Enforcement Act of 1971,* 92d Cong., 1st sess., June 1971, H. Rept. 238, 58 (minority views on H.R. 1746) (reproduced in Senate Committee on Labor and Public Welfare, Subcommittee on Labor, *Legislative History of the Equal Employment Opportunity Act of 1972,* 118). "The EEOC has attained an image as an advocate of civil rights, and properly so. For this very reason, we submit that it cannot be an impartial arbiter of the law." Id. at 59 (*Legislative History,* 119). Direct resort to the courts was said to be preferable because of "Timeliness of Relief and Remedy," id.; "Greater Prestige of Federal Judges," id. at 62 (*Legislative History,* 122); and "Evidentiary Matters" (referring to discovery), id. As to the NLRB, see *Congressional Record* 92d Cong., 1st sess., 117, pt. 24:31959, (Rep. Martin, R-Nebr.), microfiche. Finally, the federal courts handle cases more expeditiously than the commis-

sion, which has a tremendous backlog. Id. See also Sen. Dominick's individual views. Senate Committee on Labor and Public Welfare, *Equal Employment Opportunities Enforcement Act of 1971*, 88 (reproduced in *Legislative History*, 410–97). Graham, *Civil Rights Era*, 424–25, describing then–Assistant Attorney General William H. Rehnquist's opposition to cease and desist authority.

56. House Committee on Education and Labor, *Equal Employment Opportunities Enforcement Act of 1971*, 64 (reproduced in Senate Committee on Labor and Public Welfare, Subcommittee on Labor, *Legislative History of the Equal Employment Opportunity Act of 1972*, 124).

57. Federal Courts Study Committee, "Tentative Recommendations for Public Comment," December 22, 1989, 50.

58. Federal Courts Study Committee, *Report of the Federal Courts Study Committee* (n.p.: April 2, 1960), 60.

59. Id. at 61–62.

60. Senate Committee on Labor and Public Welfare, *Equal Employment Opportunities Enforcement Act of 1971*, 25 (reproduced in *Legislative History of the Equal Employment Opportunity Act of 1972*, 424).

61. *Age Discrimination in Employment Act of 1967, U.S. Statutes at Large* 81 (1968): 602, 607 (29 U.S.C. §633).

62. See, e.g., *Mitchell v. United States*, 313 U.S. 80 (1941); *Henderson v. United States*, 339 U.S. 816 (1950). In both cases the solicitor general filed a brief for the United States supporting black plaintiffs and opposing the position of the Interstate Commerce Commission.

63. Commission on Civil Rights, *Report of the United States Commission on Civil Rights, 1959* (Washington, D.C.: Government Printing Office, 1959), 141.

64. J. W. Peltason, *Fifty-eight Lonely Men: Southern Federal Judges and School Desegregation* (New York: Harcourt, Brace and World, 1961), 252.

65. Id. at 253.

66. See Chapter 2 n.53.

67. Even the 1965 act had its statutory precedents in the Force Act of 1871, which had authorized federal judges to appoint federal "supervisors of election" who could supercede state registrars and election officials. *Force Act of 1871, U.S. Statutes at Large* 16 (1871): 433. See the comments of Sen. Philip Hart (D.-Mich.) during debate on the Voting Rights Act. Schwartz, *Statutory History*, 1520. As Sen. Hart points out, the Supreme Court upheld that system in *Ex parte Siebold*, 100 U.S. 371 (1879).

68. *U.S. Statutes at Large* 82 (1969): 73, 88 (42 U.S.C. 3612[c]) allowed an award of "actual damages and not more than $1,000 punitive damages," as well as injunctive relief and costs. There is no longer a cap on damages in private fair housing cases. See 42 U.S.C. 3613(c).

69. *United States v. Long*, 537 F.2d 1151 (4th Cir. 1975), *cert. denied*, 429 U.S. 871 (1976).

70. *Fair Housing Amendments Act of 1988, U.S. Statutes at Large* 102 (1990): 1619, 1634 (42 U.S.C. 3614[d]).

71. *Civil Rights Act of 1991, U.S. Statutes at Large* 105 (1992): 1071, 1072 (42 U.S.C.A. 1981a). Also in 1991 Congress authorized the attorney general to recover actual and punitive damages for violations of the Equal Credit Opportunities Act. *Federal Deposit Insurance Corporation Act of 1991, U.S. Statutes at Large* 105 (1992): 2236, 2306 (15 U.S.C.A. §1691e[h]).

72. House Committee on Banking and Currency, Subcommittee on Consumer Affairs, *Credit Discrimination: Hearings on H.R. 14856 and H.R. 14908*, 93d Cong., 2d Sess., June 1974, 35.

73. House Committee on Banking and Currency, Subcommittee on Consumer Affairs,

To Amend the Equal Credit Opportunity Act of 1974: Hearings on H.R. 3386, 94th Cong., 1st sess., April 1975, 15.

74. Senate Committee on Banking, Housing, and Urban Affairs, Subcommittee on Consumer Affairs, *Equal Credit Opportunity Act Amendments and Consumer Leasing Act—1975, Hearings on S. 483, S. 1900, S. 1927, S. 1961, and H.R. 5616,* 94th Cong., 1st sess., July 1975, 327.

75. Id.

76. Id. at 321–22.

77. *United States v. Beneficial Corp.,* 492 F. Supp. 682 (D.N.J. 1980), *aff'd mem.,* 673 F.2d 1302 (3d Cir. 1981).

78. 15 U.S.C.A. §1691e(h).

79. 15 U.S.C.A. §1691e(g).

80. 15 U.S.C.A. §1691e(k).

81. Senate Committee on Banking, Housing, and Urban Affairs, *Comprehensive Deposit Insurance Reform and Taxpayer Protection Act of 1991,* 102d Cong., 1st sess., 1991. S. Rept. 167, 92.

CHAPTER 6. SETTING PRIORITIES

1. "The Attorney General has a limited staff and often might be unable to uncover quickly new regulations and enactments passed at the varying levels of state government." *Allen v. State Bd. of Elections,* 393 U.S. 544, 556 (1969). See also *Newman v. Piggie Park Enterprises,* 390 U.S. 400, 401 (1968); *Trafficante v. Metropolitan Life Ins. Co.,* 409 U.S. 205, 211 (1972); House Committee on Banking and Currency, Subcommittee on Consumer Affairs, *Credit Discrimination: Hearings on H.R. 14856 and H.R. 14908,* 93d Cong., 2d sess., June 1974, 70 (testimony of Assistant Attorney General Pottinger). Most federal law enforcement is given limited resources, perhaps because Congress sees underenforcement as less repugnant than overenforcement. William M. Landes and Richard A. Posner, *The Private Enforcement of Law,* 4 J. Legal Stud. 1, 36–40 (1975).

2. Civil Rights Division Full-Time Permanent Staff Summary, December 29, 1993.

3. Senate Committee on the Judiciary, Subcommittee on Constitutional Rights, *Hearings on the Nomination of John Doar, of New Richmond, Wis., To Be Assistant Attorney General, Civil Rights Division, U.S. Department of Justice,* 89th Cong., 1st sess., February 1965, 8.

4. As to the limited resources of the Antitrust Division and its consequent need to set priorities, see Suzanne Weaver, *Decision to Prosecute: Organization and Public Policy in the Antitrust Division* (Cambridge, Mass.: MIT Press, 1977), 5.

5. Senate Committee on the Judiciary, *Department of Justice Confirmations: Hearings on the Nominations of Rex E. Lee To Be Solicitor General of the United States, and William Bradford Reynolds To Be Assistant Attorney General, Civil Rights Division, Department of Justice,* 97th Cong., 1st sess., June–July 1981, serial no. J-97-7, pt. 2, 96.

6. *Moses v. Kennedy,* 219 F. Supp. 762, 764 (D.D.C. 1963).

7. Id. at 765. See also *United States v. Cox,* 342 F.2d 167 (5th Cir. 1965), *cert. denied,* 381 U.S. 935 (1965) (district court may not require U.S. attorney to prepare and sign indictment).

8. *Adams v. Richardson,* 480 F.2d 1159, 1162 (D.C. Cir. 1973) (en banc).

9. John T. Elliff, *The United States Department of Justice and Individual Rights, 1937–1962* (New York: Garland Publishing, 1987), 553.

10. The General Litigation Section was composed of three units, responsible for due process, equal protection, and federal custody issues. See Commission on Civil Rights, *Re-*

port of the United States Commission on Civil Rights, 1959 (Washington, D.C.: Government Printing Office, 1959), 129. As John Doar later explained, "Because there was a concern among the people in the Justice Department at that time that the Division would not have enough to do, responsibility for the enforcement of a number of miscellaneous statutes was given to the Civil Rights Division." Memorandum from John Doar to deputy attorney general, September 11, 1967, quoted in David L. Norman, "The Civil Rights Division of the U.S. Department of Justice, 1954–1973" (unpublished manuscript, 1992), 117. The federal custody unit, which was responsible for issues regarding federal prisoners, did not rightly belong in the division at all, and its functions were shifted to the Criminal Division in 1966. Attorney General, *Annual Report of the Attorney General of the United States for Fiscal Year Ended June 30, 1966,* 226.

11. Not only was the Voting and Elections Section responsible for enforcing the remedial provisions of the Civil Rights Act of 1957, but it also was assigned the Hatch Act, the Corrupt Practices Act, and federal criminal statutes forbidding election fraud. Commission on Civil Rights, *Report of the United States Commission on Civil Rights, 1959,* 129–30. The latter three responsibilities were transferred to the Criminal Division in 1964 (except where race discrimination or intimidation is involved). Attorney General, *Annual Report of the Attorney General of the United States for Fiscal Year Ended June 30, 1964,* 179 n.1 (citing Department Order no. 318–64, as amended July 30, 1964).

12. This allocation is reflected in a circular and two memoranda from the assistant attorney general, contained in Michal R. Belknap, ed., *Justice Department Civil Rights Policies Prior to 1960: Crucial Documents from the Files of Arthur Brann Caldwell,* vol. 16 of *Civil Rights, the White House, and the Justice Department, 1945–1968* (New York: Garland Publishing, 1991), 246, 255–65. According to the attorney general's annual report for FY 1960, the Equal Protection Unit was abolished in 1959 and the Trial Staff Section created. Attorney General, *Annual Report of the Attorney General of the United States for Fiscal Year Ended June 30, 1960,* 184. Over the years numerous such minor adjustments of organizational structure have occurred.

13. "Legends in the Law: A Conversation with Harold Greene," *Bar Report* 24, no. 5 (April/May 1996): 10.

14. Commission on Civil Rights, *Report of the United States Commission on Civil Rights, 1959,* 131 ("Nearly two years after passage of the Act, the Department of Justice had brought only three actions under its new powers to seek preventive civil relief").

15. The attorney general's annual report for 1959, the first full fiscal year after the creation of the Civil Rights Division, emphasizes in its summary of Civil Rights Division activities three cases under the Civil Rights Act of 1957. Attorney General, *Annual Report of the Attorney General of the United States for Fiscal Year Ended June 30, 1959,* 180–81. However, the detailed description of activities reveals that of the five Supreme Court merits briefs prepared by the division four "involved unique questions of court-martial jurisdiction," id. at 182; that none of the equal protection unit's prosecutions involved race discrimination, id. at 189–90; that the federal custody unit was involved in at least six cases, id. at 190–91; and that the majority of the voting and elections section's cases involved violations of laws governing federal elections rather than race discrimination, id. at 192–97. The report lists one peonage and eight police brutality cases presented to grand juries, of which three are identified as involving race. Id. at 187–89. Grand juries failed to indict in two of the race cases, and the petit jury returned a not guilty verdict in the third.

16. The Civil Rights Division currently is responsible for enforcing civil rights laws protecting against discrimination in voting, public accommodations, public facilities, public schools, state and local government employment, housing, and credit. It also enforces the Civil Rights of Institutionalized Persons Act, the Motor Voter Act, the Overseas Voting Rights Act, the criminal civil rights laws, and the Americans with Disabilities Act.

17. For example, when John Dunne's nomination as assistant attorney general was before the Senate, he responded to a question as to his priorities: "Following the 1990 census, the examination of reapportionment will be an important priority for the Civil Rights Division under the Voting Rights Act. The rise in hate crimes, exemplified by the recent bombings of a judge and lawyer in the South, will also require top priority of the Civil Rights Division under my leadership, if I am confirmed. The new amendments to the Fair Housing Act and the Japanese redress provisions will also be vigorously and effectively enforced by the division, as will all of our civil rights laws if I am confirmed." Senate Committee on the Judiciary, *Confirmation Hearings on Federal Appointments: Hearings on Confirmation Hearings on Appointments to the Federal Judiciary,* 101st Cong., 2d sess., serial no. J-101-6, pt. 5, 186 (1990).

18. 42 U.S.C. 1973gg, et seq. The act provides for voter registration to occur concurrent with obtaining a driver's license. The attorney general is given authority to sue "for such declaratory or injunctive relief as is necessary to carry out this Act." 42 U.S.C. 1973gg-9(a).

19. Morroe Berger, *Equality by Statute,* rev. ed. (Garden City, N.Y.: Doubleday, 1967), 13.

20. The staff grew from forty attorneys in 1963 to fifty-two in 1964 to eighty-six in 1965 to ninety-five in 1966. See Attorney General, *Annual Report for Fiscal Year 1966,* 182; Attorney General, *Annual Report of the Attorney General of the United States for Fiscal Year Ended June 30, 1965,* 168; House Committee on Appropriations, Subcommittee on Departments of State, Justice, Commerce, the Judiciary, and Related Agencies Appropriations, *Departments of State, Justice, and Commerce, the Judiciary, and Related Agencies Appropriations for 1965, Hearings: Department of Justice,* 88th Cong., 2d sess., 1965, 145. House Committee on Appropriations, Subcommittee on Departments of State, Justice, Commerce, the Judiciary, and Related Agencies Appropriations, *Departments of State, Justice, and Commerce, the Judiciary, and Related Agencies Appropriations for 1964, Hearings: Department of Justice,* 88th Cong., 1st sess., 1964, 11.

21. The Commission on Civil Rights noted that by 1968 the department had brought only one suit to enforce Section 5. Commission on Civil Rights, *Political Participation: A Report of the United States Commission on Civil Rights—1968* (Washington, D.C.: Government Printing Office, 1968), 164–65 (referring to *United States v. Crook,* 253 F. Supp. 915 [M.D. Ala. 1966]).

22. Nadine Cohodas, "Remembering the Voting Rights Revolution," *Legal Times* 18, no. 12 (August 7, 1995): 12.

23. *Federal Register* 36, no. 176 (September 10, 1971): 18186. The current version is at 28 C.F.R. Part 51. See generally authorities cited by David Garrow, *Protest at Selma: Martin Luther King, Jr. and the Voting Rights Act of 1965* (New Haven: Yale University Press, 1982), 308 nn.60–61.

24. Stephen L. Wasby, "Civil Rights Litigation by Organizations: Constraints and Choices," *Judicature* 68, no. 9–10 (April–May 1985): 352.

25. U.S. Department of Justice, *The Department of Justice Manual,* vol. 6 (Clifton, N.J.: Prentice-Hall, 1988), §§8-2.215, 8-2.223.

26. See Burke Marshall, *Federalism and Civil Rights* (New York: Columbia University Press, 1964). When Marshall resigned as assistant attorney general in early 1964, a southern newspaper editorialized: "At the first hint of difficulties between the races here and elsewhere, [Marshall] did not rush in loudly with a sermon and a summons. Instead, he made himself available for discussion of the difficulty. Then, he gave the community all the necessary time to handle its problem at the local level, quietly and voluntarily. He believed deeply that local solutions were the most meaningful." Editorial, "The South Loses a Friend," *The Anniston Star,* reprinted in *Montgomery Advertiser,* January 7, 1965, p. 4.

27. Memorandum from John Doar to attorneys assigned to work on Alabama elections, March 2, 1966, 6.

28. Robert G. Dixon, Jr., "The Attorney General and Civil Rights, 1870–1964," in *Roles of the Attorney General of the United States* (Washington, D.C.: American Enterprise Institute, 1968), 105, 119. Dixon also explains that "voting rights suits were delayed for three years while the constitutionality of the act was being tested."

29. See "U.S. Countersues Virginia over Motor Voter Law," *New York Times,* July 9, 1995, p. 18, reporting that Virginia had become the sixth state to be sued by the Justice Department for failing to comply with the motor voter law.

30. *United States v. Biloxi Mun. School Dist.,* 219 F. Supp. 691 (S.D. Miss. 1963), *aff'd sub nom. United States v. Madison County Bd. of Educ.,* 326 F.2d 237 (5th Cir. 1964), *cert. denied,* 379 U.S. 929 (1964) (segregation of federal military and civilian dependents in public schools), and *United States v. County School Bd. of Prince George County,* 221 F. Supp. 93 (E.D. Va. 1963); *United States v. Brittain,* 319 F. Supp. 1058 (N.D. Ala. 1970) (ban on interracial marriage applied to U.S. military personnel). See generally Richard Seldin, *Eradicating Racial Discrimination at Public Accommodations Not Covered by Title II,* 28 Rutgers L. Rev. 1, 19ff (1974).

31. See, e.g., *United States v. U.S. Klans, Knights of Ku Klux Klan, Inc.,* 194 F. Supp. 897 (M.D. Ala. 1961) (segregated bus terminal); *United States v. City of Shreveport,* 210 F. Supp. 36 (W.D. La. 1962), *aff'd mem.,* 316 F.2d 928 (5th Cir. 1963) (segregated municipal airport).

32. See *United States v. Brand Jewelers, Inc.,* 318 F. Supp. 1293 (S.D.N.Y. 1970) (sewer service of summons). The government also relied on a commerce clause theory in this case.

33. See, e.g., *United States v. City of Philadelphia,* 644 F.2d 187, 197 (3d Cir. 1980).

34. See Chapter 2 n.56.

35. See, e.g., 42 U.S.C. 2000h-2 (intervention in equal protection case), 3614(a) (fair housing).

36. 42 U.S.C. 2000b(a) (discrimination in public facilities); 2000c-6(a) (discrimination in public education).

37. 42 U.S.C. 1973h(b).

38. After passage of the Voting Rights Act, the Civil Rights Division concentrated its voting enforcement on the examiner and observer provisions, cases to enforce the act, and filing "suits . . . to eliminate the payment of poll tax as a prerequisite to voting in the states of Alabama, Mississippi, Virginia, and Texas." Attorney General, *Annual Report for Fiscal Year 1966,* 186. See *Harper v. Virginia Bd. of Elections,* 383 U.S. 663 (1966) (United States as amicus curiae); *Texas v. United States,* 384 U.S. 155 (1966) (per curiam), *aff'g* 252 F. Supp. 234 (W.D. Texas 1966).

39. E.g., 42 U.S.C. 1971(c), 1973j (reasonable grounds to believe a person is practicing voting discrimination); 42 U.S.C. 2000e-5(f) (employment discrimination).

40. See, e.g., *Allen v. State Bd. of Elections,* 393 U.S. 544, 556 (1969): "The achievement of the Act's laudable goal could be severely hampered, however, if each citizen were required to depend solely on litigation instituted at the discretion of the Attorney General."

41. *McKennon v. Nashville Banner Publishing Co.,* 115 S.Ct. 879, 884 (1995).

42. *Alexander v. Gardner-Denver Co.,* 415 U.S. 36, 45 (1974).

43. For example, several courts of appeals concluded that the 1968 Fair Housing Act confined the attorney general to equitable relief, which did not include damages for victims of discrimination. *United States v. Rent-A-Homes Sys. of Ill., Inc.,* 602 F.2d 795 (7th Cir. 1979), *United States v. Mitchell,* 580 F.2d 789 (5th Cir. 1978), *United States v. Long,* 537 F.2d 1151 (4th Cir. 1975), *cert. denied,* 429 U.S. 871 (1976). The 1988 amendments to the act, however, authorize the attorney general to obtain damages for individuals. 42 U.S.C. §3614(d)(1)(B).

44. Elliff, *The United States Department of Justice,* 143–44.

45. Senate Committee on the Judiciary, Subcommittee on Constitutional Rights, *Civil Rights—1957: Hearings on S. 83, an Amendment to S. 83, S. 427, S. 428, S. 429, S. 468, S. 500, S. 501, S. 502, S. 504, S. 505, S. 508, S. 509, S. 510, S. Con. Res. 5,* 85th Cong., 1st sess., February–March 1957, 49. See also id. at 78 ("if we had a complaint filed with us . . . we would have a preliminary inquiry made").

46. Id. at 182.

47. See Elliff, *The United States Department of Justice,* 558, quoting a memorandum from Joseph Ryan to Due Process Unit of the General Litigation Section, August 5, 1958. Elliff reports that "the subsequent course of this new policy is not clear." See also memorandum of August 5, 1958, from Joseph Ryan, Jr., stating that investigations must be predicated on complaints or reports from public officials or citizens, not on the basis of newspaper articles alone. Belknap, *Justice Department Civil Rights Policies,* 234.

48. House Committee on the Judiciary, Subcommittee no. 5, *Civil Rights: Hearings on H.R. 300, 351, 352, 353, 400, 430, 461, 617, 618, 619, 759, 913, 914, 1902, 2346, 2479, 2538, 2786, 3090, 3147, 3148, 3212, 3559, 4169, 4261, 4338, 4339, 4342, 4348, 4457, 5008, 5170, 5189, 5217, 5218, 5276, 5323, 6934, 6935,* 85th Cong., 1st sess., March-April-May 1959, 214.

49. Id. at 216.

50. Robert Fredrick Burk, *The Eisenhower Administration and Black Civil Rights* (Knoxville: University of Tennessee Press, 1984), 247.

51. Senate Committee on the Judiciary, *Nomination of Burke Marshall: Hearings on the Nomination of Burke Marshall To Be an Assistant Attorney General,* 87th Cong., 1st sess., March 1961, 4.

52. See David L. Norman, *The Strange Career of the Civil Rights Division's Commitment to Brown,* 93 Yale L. J. 983, 987 (1984). The first of these suits, *Lee v. Macon County, Ala.* is described in Jack Bass, *Taming the Storm: The Life and Times of Judge Frank M. Johnson, Jr., and the South's Fight over Civil Rights* (New York: Doubleday, 1993), chap. 16.

53. House Committee on the Judiciary, Subcommittee no. 5, *Voting Rights: Hearings on H.R. 6400,* 89th Cong., 1st sess., March–April 1965, 71.

54. Id. at 72.

55. J. Stanley Pottinger, assistant attorney general, *Civil Rights Division Program Objective Submission: Fiscal Year 1976, Program Objective no. 17* (July 1974).

56. Letter from Deputy Attorney General Rogers to Sen. Eastland, *Congressional Record,* 85th Cong., 1st sess., 1957, 103, pt. 9:11839, quoted in an unattributed document, "Legislative Histories of Civil Rights Statutes," in Belknap, *Justice Department Civil Rights Policies,* 333.

57. Attorney General Bonaparte filed a brief and argued orally as amicus curiae in *Bailey v. Alabama,* 211 U.S. 452 (1908) and Attorney General Wickersham filed two more amicus briefs in *Bailey v. Alabama,* 219 U.S. 219 (1911). These amicus briefs were part of a series of "strenuous efforts on the part of the Department of Justice to stamp out peonage." Homer Cummings and Carl McFarland, *Federal Justice: Chapters in the History of Justice and the Federal Executive* (1937; reprint, New York: Da Capo Press, 1970), 444.

58. 18 U.S.C. §1581.

59. 334 U.S. 1 (1948).

60. 339 U.S. 629 (1950).

61. Stephen Gillers, "Letter to the Editor," *New York Times,* August 5, 1985, sec. A, p. 14. Professor Gillers's letter contains serious inaccuracies. He states that "before Brown the Government had never tried to overturn Plessy." Yet the briefs of the United States in *Sweatt v. Painter,* 339 U.S. 629 (1950), and *Henderson v. United States,* 339 U.S. 816 (1950), had argued that separate was inherently unequal. For example, its brief in *Henderson* said at page 10 that "the legal and factual assumptions upon which *Plessy v. Ferguson* was decided have been demonstrated to be erroneous, and that the doctrine of that case should

now be re-examined and overruled." Gillers implies that the government did not try to overturn *Plessy* in its brief in *Brown,* but the brief of the United States argued at page 17 that "if the Court should reach the question, the 'separate but equal' doctrine should be reexamined and overruled."

62. Elliff, *The United States Department of Justice,* 578.

63. Brief of the United States as amicus curiae at 35, *Henderson v. United States,* 339 U.S. 816 (1950) (no. 25). Michal R. Belknap, ed., *Justice Department Briefs in Crucial Civil Rights Cases: 1948–1968,* vol. 18, pt. 1, of *Civil Rights, the White House, and the Justice Department, 1945–1968* (New York: Garland Publishing, 1991), 125.

64. *Louisiana v. United States,* 380 U.S. 145 (1965).

65. *United States v. Guest,* 383 U.S. 745, 757 (1966).

66. See Elliff, *The United States Department of Justice,* 548.

67. *Breedlove v. Suttles,* 302 U.S. 277 (1937).

68. 42 U.S.C.A. §1973h.

69. *United States v. Texas,* 252 F. Supp. 234 (W.D. Texas 1966); *United States v. Alabama,* 252 F. Supp. 95 (M.D. Ala. 1966).

70. *Harper v. Virginia Bd. of Elections,* 383 U.S. 663 (1966).

71. See Marc Galanter, *Why the "Haves" Come Out Ahead: Speculations on the Limits of Legal Change,* 9 Law and Soc'y 98 (1974).

72. Id.

73. *Perkins v. Matthews,* 400 U.S. 379, 391 (1971).

74. *United States v. Board of Comm'rs of Sheffield, Ala.,* 435 U.S. 110, 131 (1978).

75. *Georgia v. United States,* 411 U.S. 526 (1973).

76. *Perkins,* 400 U.S. 379 (1971). See also *Regents of the Univ. of Cal. v. Bakke,* 438 U.S. 265, 345 n.19 (1978) (opinion of Brennan, White, Marshall, and Blackmun, JJ., concurring in the judgment in part and dissenting in part) (because the president delegated to the attorney general responsibility for coordinating federal enforcement of Title VI of the Civil Rights Act of 1964, "the views of the Solicitor General, as well as those of HEW, that the use of racial preferences for remedial purposes is consistent with Title VI are entitled to considerable respect").

77. *Dougherty Co., Georgia, Bd. of Educ. v. White,* 439 U.S. 32, 39 (1978) (attorney general's determination that a school board rule was a voting change within the meaning of §5 of the Voting Rights Act "is entitled to particular deference"). See also *United Jewish Org. v. Carey,* 430 U.S. 144, 175 (1977) (Brennan, J., concurring): "The participation of the Attorney General, for example, largely relieves the judiciary of the need to grapple with the difficulties of distinguishing benign from malign discrimination. Under §5 of the Act, the Attorney General in effect is constituted champion of the interests of minority voters, and accompanying implementing regulations ensure the availability of materials and submissions necessary to discern the true effect of a proposed reapportionment plan."

78. See, e.g., John Doar, "The Voting Rights Act: 25 Years Later," *Civil Rights Division Journal,* December 9, 1992, 13; H. Rept. no. 439, 89th Cong., 1st sess., 6–13 (1965); *South Carolina v. Katzenbach,* 383 U.S. 301, 312–15, 328, 330, 333–34, 336 (1966).

79. Symposium, *The Department of Justice and the Civil Rights Act of 1964,* 26 Pac. L. J. 765, 770 (1995) (remarks of Janet Reno).

80. The reports include "Original Meaning Jurisprudence: A Sourcebook, March 12, 1987"; "Redefining Discrimination: Disparate Impact and the Institutionalization of Affirmative Action, November 4, 1987"; and "Justice Without Law: A Reconsideration of the 'Broad Equitable Powers' of the Federal Courts, August 31, 1988." They are written in the form of legal scholarship, complete with colon-laden titles. However, they are essentially briefs for the Meese agendas of "strict construction," color blindness, and limiting the structural injunction. A Westlaw search of Allfeds, Allstates, and law reviews and jour-

nals revealed that "Original Meaning Jurisprudence" was cited once, in Robert N. Clinton, *Original Understanding, Legal Realism, and the Interpretation of "This Constitution,"* 72 Iowa L. Rev. 1177, 1182 n.5 (1987), and the others not at all.

81. Attorney General, *Annual Report of the Attorney General of the United States for Fiscal Year Ended June 30, 1974,* 79. The figure of 150 in 1971 is a typographical error; it should read 250. See Attorney General, *Annual Report of the Attorney General of the United States for Fiscal Year Ended June 30, 1972,* 87.

82. J. Stanley Pottinger, assistant attorney general, *Civil Rights Division Program Objective Submission: Fiscal Year 1976, Program Objective no.4* (July 1, 1974).

83. *Board of Educ. v. Dowell,* 498 U.S. 237 (1991); *Freeman v. Pitts,* 503 U.S. 467 (1992).

84. *Warth v. Seldin,* 422 U.S. 490 (1975). Private plaintiffs may, however, challenge as racially discriminatory the refusal to grant zoning to a builder who proposes a specific low-income project. *Village of Arlington Heights v. Metropolitan Housing Dev. Corp.,* 429 U.S. 252 (1977).

85. *Rizzo v. Goode,* 423 U.S. 362 (1976).

86. *O'Shea v. Littleton,* 414 U.S. 488 (1974).

87. Joel L. Selig, *The Justice Department and Racially Exclusionary Municipal Practices: Creative Ventures in Fair Housing Act Enforcement,* 17 U.C. Davis L. Rev. 445, 457 (1984).

88. *Rizzo v. Goode,* 423 U.S. 362 (1976).

89. *United States v. City of Philadelphia,* 644 F.2d 187, 197 (3d Cir. 1980).

90. *Violent Crime Control and Law Enforcement Act of 1994,* Public Law 322, 103d Cong., 2d sess. (September 13, 1994).

91. See *United States v. Board of Educ. of the Township of Piscataway,* 832 F. Supp. 836 (D.N.J. 1993), *aff'd en banc,* 91 F.3d 1547 (3d Cir. 1996).

92. *Wygant v. Jackson Bd. of Educ.,* 476 U.S. 267 (1986).

93. Senate Committee on the Judiciary, *Department of Justice Confirmations: Hearings on the Nominations of Rex E. Lee and William Bradford Reynolds* (testimony of William Bradford Reynolds). Reynolds testified that class relief for individual wrongs was inappropriate.

94. Fair Housing Amendments Act of 1988, 100th Cong., 2d sess., H.R. 1158, *Congressional Record,* 100th Cong., 2d Sess., 1988, 134, pt. 2:15848–50 (Rep. Edwards).

95. See Jeffrey D. Robinson, "Fair Housing Act Amendments of 1988," in Citizens' Commission on Civil Rights, *One Nation, Indivisible: The Civil Rights Challenge for the 1990s* (Washington, D.C., 1989), 304, 309.

96. Robert G. Schwemm, *The Future of Fair Housing Litigation,* 26 J. Marshall L. Rev. 745, 769 (1993).

97. See, e.g., 42 U.S.C. §706 (E.E.O.C.) and 42 U.S.C. §3610 (H.U.D.). The wholesale-retail dichotomy is described in Symposium, *The Department of Justice and the Civil Rights Act of 1964* (remarks of William N. Eskridge, Jr.). See also Michael Selmi, *The Value of the EEOC: Reexamining the Agency's Role in Employment Discrimination Law,* 57 Ohio St. L. J. 1 (1996) (suggesting that we rethink the role of the EEOC and rely more heavily on private attorneys).

98. Senate Committee on Banking, Housing, and Urban Affairs, Subcommittee on Consumer Affairs, *Equal Credit Opportunity Act Amendments and Consumer Leasing Act—1975, Hearings on S. 483, S. 1900, S. 1927, S. 1961, and H.R. 5616,* 94th Cong., 1st sess., July 1975, 323.

99. Attorney General, *Annual Report of the Attorney General of the United States for Fiscal Year Ended June 30, 1984,* 149.

100. Schwemm, *The Future of Fair Housing Litigation,* 749.

101. The precise nature of the government attorney's ethical responsibilities is unclear. As one scholar has noted, "The [government] lawyer's duties of zeal, loyalty, and confiden-

tiality are less clearly defined because of the multiplicity of constituencies to which the lawyer is said to have responsibilities. . . . [N]either the *Model Code* nor the *Model Rules* reflects much detailed consideration of the government lawyer's role in the advocacy system. To the extent that they address government lawyers at all, the ethical codes suggest that government lawyers are subject to different ethical considerations than other lawyers, but the nature of these considerations remains ambiguous." Catherine J. Lanctot, *The Duty of Zealous Advocacy and the Ethics of the Federal Government Lawyer: The Three Hardest Questions,* 64 S. Cal. L. Rev. 951, 967 (1991) (footnote omitted).

102. "As a representative of all citizens, the government lawyer actually owes a duty to the opposing party, who is a citizen and a taxpayer and who seeks protection under a law that the government lawyer is committed to uphold." Id. at 981. The tension between organizational goals and client desires noted above also exists in litigation brought by civil rights organizations. See Stephen L. Wasby, *Race Relations Litigation in an Age of Complexity* (Charlottesville: University Press of Virginia, 1995), 287. However, those organizations do not hold the same responsibilities to opposing parties.

103. The Federal Bar Association has promulgated its own "Model Rules of Professional Conduct for Federal Lawyers," which do not have the force of law but represent the most complete effort to define the ethical obligations of federal lawyers. These rules do not resolve the issues discussed above but may be read as consistent with the suggestion in the text. Rule 1.13(e) provides, "A Government lawyer shall not form a client-lawyer relationship or represent a client other than the Federal Agency unless specifically assigned or authorized by competent authority." Under Rule 1.13(g), "A Government lawyer who has been duly assigned or authorized to . . . provide civil legal assistance to an individual has, for those purposes, a lawyer-client relationship with that individual." Arguably the government lawyer who brings a suit denominated "United States v. Defendant" has not been "duly assigned or authorized" to represent or provide legal assistance to the individual on whose behalf the government is suing. If I am correct in this assumption, then the representation is governed by Rule 1.13(a), which reads in relevant part, "Except when representing another client pursuant to paragraphs (e), . . . and (g), a Government lawyer represents the Federal Agency that employs the Government lawyer."

104. Memorandum from Janet Reno, attorney general, to all U.S. attorneys, November 10, 1993, re fair housing litigation. See discussion of the role of U.S. attorneys in Chapter 7 under "Organizing Around the Priorities."

105. Robinson, "Fair Housing Act Amendments of 1988," 309.

106. Reorg. Plan no. 2 of 1973; Reorg. Plan no. 1 of 1978, reprinted in 5 U.S.C.S. §903 (Law. Co-op. 1994); President, Executive Order, "Leadership and Coordination of Nondisrimination Laws, Executive Order 12250," *Federal Register* 45, no. 215 (November 2, 1980): 72995, microfiche.

107. House Committee on the Judiciary, *Civil Rights: Hearing on Legislation Regarding the Civil Rights of Persons Within the Jurisdiction of the United States,* 84th Cong., 2d sess., April 1956, 570.

108. Attorney General, *Annual Report for Fiscal Year 1966,* 184–85.

109. House Committee on Appropriations, Subcommittee on Departments of State, Justice, Commerce, the Judiciary, and Related Agencies Appropriations, *Departments of State, Justice, and Commerce, the Judiciary, and Related Agencies Appropriations for 1968: Hearings Before a Subcommittee of the House Committee on Appropriations,* 90th Cong., 1st sess., 1967, 368. Richard P. Nathan, "Jobs and Civil Rights," prepared for Commission on Civil Rights by the Brookings Institute, Washington, D.C., 1969, 81.

110. Attorney General, *Report of the Attorney General of the United States for Fiscal Year Ended June 30, 1968,* 60.

111. See Hugh Davis Graham, *The Civil Rights Era: Origins and Development of Na-*

tional Policy, 1960–1972 (New York: Oxford University Press, 1990), 236–37. According to Graham, the Civil Rights Division had only eighty-seven lawyers in 1967, and voting rights, school desegregation, and criminal cases involving violence, local defiance, and intimidation had a higher priority than employment discrimination. David L. Rose tells a slightly different story, stating that after passage of the 1964 act the division decided "to give priority first to public accommodations, then to voting, and then to school desegregation. As a result only two employment law suits were brought in 1965 and 1966 by the Division." David L. Rose, *Twenty-Five Years Later: Where Do We Stand on Equal Employment Opportunity Law Enforcement?* 42 Vand. L. Rev. 1121, 1137 (1989). Rose points out, however, that the 1967 decision to place a high priority on employment discrimination suits led to the filing of six in 1967 and twenty-six in 1968. Id. at 1138.

112. The report added erroneously, "Indeed, for several years it has accorded the lowest priority to employment discrimination cases." The committee did give some positive recognition to the division, saying that "those selected suits which the Division has been able to bring, however, have contributed significantly to the Federal effort to combat employment discrimination." House, *Equal Employment Opportunities Enforcement Act of 1971,* H. Rept. 238, 92d Cong., 1st sess., 1971, 13 (reprinted in *Legislative History of the Equal Employment Opportunity Act of 1972,* 92d Cong., 2d sess., November 1972, 73).

113. Alfred W. Blumrosen, *Modern Law: The Law Transmission System and Equal Employment Opportunity* (Madison: University of Wisconsin Press, 1993), 367–68 n.32.

114. See J. Stanley Pottinger, *Civil Rights Division Program Objective Submission: Fiscal Year 1976, Objective no. 3* (1974), reflecting that the Education Section had brought seven Title VII cases against school districts under Title VII by FY 1974.

115. *Hazelwood School Dist. v. United States,* 433 U.S. 299, 309 (1977).

116. House Committee on the Judiciary, *Civil Rights: Hearing on Legislation Regarding the Civil Rights of Persons Within the Jurisdiction of the United States,* 569. Brownell gave as an example the department's participation "as a friend of the court in a civil suit to prevent by injunction, unlawful interference with the efforts of the school board at Hoxie, Ark., to eliminate racial discrimination in the school in conformity with the Supreme Court's decision."

117. Jack Greenberg, *Crusaders in the Courts: How a Dedicated Band of Lawyers Fought for the Civil Rights Revolution* (New York: Harper Collins, Basic Books, 1994), 238.

118. Id. at 287.

119. *Heart of Atlanta Motel, Inc. v. United States,* 379 U.S. 241 (1964); *Katzenbach v. McClung,* 379 U.S. 294 (1964).

120. See Attorney General, *Annual Report for Fiscal Year 1964,* 182. See also Harrell R. Rodgers, Jr., and Charles S. Bullock III, *Law and Social Change: Civil Rights Laws and Their Consequences* (New York: McGraw-Hill, 1972), 62–66.

121. Rodgers and Bullock, *Law and Social Change,* 63–64.

122. Attorney General, *Annual Report for Fiscal Year 1968,* 67.

123. See *South Carolina v. Katzenbach,* 383 U.S. 301 (1966).

124. See, e.g., *United States v. Executive Comm. of the Democratic Party of Dallas County, Ala.,* 254 F. Supp. 537 (S.D. Ala. 1966) (failing to count ballots from black polling places).

125. See 28 C.F.R. Part 51; *Georgia v. United States,* 411 U.S. 526 (1973).

126. *Civil Rights Act of 1957, U.S. Statutes at Large* 71 (1958): 634, 637 (42 U.S.C. 1971[a][1]).

127. Senate Committee on the Judiciary, Subcommittee on Constitutional Rights, *Civil Rights—1957: Hearings on S. 83, . . . S. Con. Res. 5,* 14.

128. Although Congress does treat some forms of sex discrimination in separate laws, for example the Equal Pay Act, it has generally opted for unified enforcement mechanisms

for various forms of discrimination, in contrast with Great Britain, which established separate mechanisms for combating race discrimination and sex discrimination. See Race Relations Act 1965, §2 (Eng.) (Race Relations Board), and Race Relations Act 1968, §14 (Eng.) (same); Sex Discrimination Act 1975, §53 (Eng.) (Equal Opportunities Commission).

129. See Graham, *Civil Rights Era*, 403.

130. Attorney General, *Annual Report of the Attorney General of the United States for Fiscal Year Ended June 30, 1970*, 82, citing *United States v. Libbey-Owens Ford Co.*, no. C-70-212 (N.D. Ohio, filed July 20, 1970).

131. In 1973, the division began to "give greater emphasis to the protection of Spanish-speaking Americans and American Indians" as well as "increased attention . . . to the problem of sex discrimination, with particular reference to employment rights." Attorney General, *Annual Report of the Attorney General of the United States for Fiscal Year Ended June 30, 1973*, 65.

132. James A. Kushner, *The Fair Housing Amendments Act of 1988: The Second Generation of Fair Housing*, 42 Vand. L. Rev. 1049, 1097 (1989).

133. See Suzanna Sherry, *Selective Judicial Activism in the Equal Protection Context: Democracy, Distrust, and Deconstruction*, 73 Geo. L. J. 89, 105 (1984) (distinguishing between "the *classification* itself—the general characteristic by which the statutory line is drawn. . . . [and] a disfavored *class:* those persons who, because they possess one particular aspect of the identifying characteristic, are disadvantaged by the statute").

134. See, e.g., Kimberlè Williams Crenshaw, *Race, Reform, and Retrenchment: Transformation and Legitimation in Antidiscrimination Law*, 101 Harv. L. Rev. 1331 (1988); Senate Committee on the Judiciary, *Department of Justice Confirmations: Hearings Before the Committee on the Judiciary*, 97th Cong., 1st sess., 1989, 75, 113. Norman C. Amaker, *Civil Rights and the Reagan Administration* (Arlington, Va.: University Press of America, 1988).

135. Hanes Walton, Jr., *When the Marching Stopped: The Politics of Civil Rights Regulatory Agencies* (New York: State University of New York Press, 1988), 188.

136. Senate Committee on the Judiciary, *Department of Justice Confirmations: Hearings on the Nominations of Rex E. Lee and William Bradford Reynolds*, 112.

137. Elliff, *The United States Department of Justice*, 649.

138. Rodgers and Bullock, *Law and Social Change*, 154.

CHAPTER 7. FOLLOWING PRIORITIES

1. William French Smith, "Address of Attorney General William French Smith Before the American Law Institute," Philadelphia, Pennsylvania, May 22, 1981.

2. "Affirmative Action," memorandum from William Bradford Reynolds to William French Smith, June 10, 1981.

3. William French Smith, *Urging Judicial Restraint*, 68 A.B.A. J. 59 (1982).

4. Senate Committee on the Judiciary, *Nomination of William Bradford Reynolds To Be Associate Attorney General of the United States: Hearings on the Confirmation of William Bradford Reynolds To Be Associate Attorney General of the United States*, 99th Cong., 1st sess., June 1985, serial no. J-99-29, 1012–13.

5. See, e.g., 28 U.S.C.A. §§ 503, 516, 519 (1993). See also Executive Order no. 6166, reprinted in 5 U.S.C.A. S901 (1977); The Attorney General's Role as Chief Litigator for the United States, 6 Op. Att'y. Gen. 47 (1982).

6. See *Smith v. United States*, 375 F.2d 243 (5th Cir. 1967), *cert. denied*, 389 U.S. 841 (1967); *Powell v. Katzenbach*, 359 F. 2d 234 (D. C. Cir. 1965), *cert. denied*, 384 U.S. 906 (1965).

7. The organization chart for the Department of Justice as of May 1993, reproduced

as Figure 7.1, is found in U.S. Department of Justice, *United States Department of Justice: Legal Activities, 1993–1994* (Washington, D.C.: Office of Attorney Personnel Management, n.d.), v.

8. For an excellent analysis of the work of U.S. attorneys and their relationship with the divisions in Washington, see James Eisenstein, *Counsel for the United States: U.S. Attorneys in the Political and Legal Systems* (Baltimore: John Hopkins University Press, 1978).

9. See Sanford J. Ungar, *FBI* (Boston: Little, Brown and Company, 1976).

10. See Eisenstein, *Counsel for the United States*, 94.

11. Management Programs and Budget Staff, U.S. Department of Justice Office of Management and Finance, Justice Litigation Management: Executive Summary, 2 (April 1975).

12. Memorandum from Drew S. Days III, assistant attorney general for civil rights, to Michael J. Egan, associate attorney general, November 23, 1977, re Justice Department reorganization—Circuit solicitor proposal.

13. Memorandum from John Doar to deputy attorney general, September 11, 1967, quoted in David L. Norman, "The Civil Rights Division of the U.S. Department of Justice, 1954–1973" (unpublished manuscript, 1992), 118.

14. Norman, "The Civil Rights Division," 5.

15. The information about the events during the 1950s is taken from a notebook compiled by the late David L. Norman, primarily containing retyped versions of the relevant documents. Norman joined the Civil Rights Section in 1956 and later rose to become assistant attorney general for civil rights in 1971. His distinguished career in the Civil Rights Division is described by Monica Gallagher in Symposium, *The Department of Justice and the Civil Rights Act of 1964*, 26 Pac. L. J. 765, 807–8 (1995).

16. E.g., "You may . . . be assured that Mr. Cox will perform his duties in keeping with the solemn oath of office which he has taken, as a public official of the State of Mississippi." Letter from Lester Clark, attorney, to Robert E. Hauberg, U.S. attorney, February 15, 1955.

17. Senate Committee on the Judiciary, *Voting Rights: Hearings on S. 1564*, 89th Cong., 1st sess., March–April 1965, pt. 2, 1205.

18. Id.

19. Commission on Civil Rights, *Political Participation: A Report of the United States Commission on Civil Rights—1968* (Washington, D.C.: Government Printing Office, 1968), 244–45.

20. John Doar and Dorothy Landsberg, "The Performance of the FBI in Investigating Violations of Federal Laws Protecting the Right to Vote, 1960–1967" (1971), 12. The Doar and Landsberg manuscript, which has been reprinted in Senate, *Intelligence Activities, Senate Resolution 21: Hearings Before the Select Committee To Study Governmental Operations with Respect to Intelligence Activities*, 94th Cong., 1st sess., November–December 1975, vol. 6, 888, not only provides an excellent account of the relations between the division and the FBI but also explains in detail the fact analysis techniques employed by the division.

21. Id. at 17a. See also Ungar, *FBI*, 409–21.

22. Memorandum from David L. Norman, director, Office of Planning and Coordination, to Assistant Attorney General Jerris Leonard, February 9, 1969, p. 7.

23. U.S. Department of Justice, *United States Department of Justice Legal Activities, 1993–94* (Washington, D.C.: Office of Attorney Personnel Management, n.d.), 3.

24. Memorandum from Brian K. Landsberg to David L. Norman, October 14, 1968.

25. In 1995 Attorney General Reno amended the U.S. attorneys' manual to provide for the Civil Rights Division and U.S. attorneys to "work as partners." Except on matters of "national importance," U.S. attorneys are granted considerable autonomy in criminal ci-

vils rights matters (memorandum from Janet Reno to Holders of United States Attorneys' Manual Title 8, May 10, 1995).

26. See memorandum from John Doar to deputy attorney general, September 11, 1967, p. 4.

27. Frank E. Schwelb, "Promotion of Civil Liberties by the Department of Justice," 3 (undated manuscript apparently sent to Assistant Attorney General Drew S. Days III on November 30, 1977); see memorandum from Larry Hammond, deputy assistant attorney general, Office of Legal Counsel, to Frederick D. Baron, special assistant to the attorney general, re Department of Justice civil liberties policy, dated June 8, 1979.

28. Memorandum from Attorney General Benjamin Civiletti to all heads of offices, boards, and divisions and all U.S. attorneys, re civil liberties policy, January 28, 1980.

29. Barbara Allen Babcock, *Defending the Government: Justice and the Civil Division*, 23 J. Marshall L. Rev. 181, 183 (1990).

30. Michal R. Belknap, ed., *Administrative History of the Civil Rights Division of the Department of Justice During the Johnson Administration*, vol. 17, *Civil Rights, the White House, and the Justice Department, 1945–1968* (New York: Garland Publishing, 1991), pt. 1, 6.

31. Hugh Davis Graham, *The Civil Rights Era: Origins and Development of National Policy, 1960–1972* (New York: Oxford University Press, 1990), 362.

32. See Belknap, *Administrative History*, 6–8.

33. Id. at 9.

34. Id. at 13.

35. Id.

36. Miriam R. Eisenstein, "The Civil Rights Division at Thirty-Five: A Retrospective," *Civil Rights Division Journal* (December 9, 1992): 4, 6.

37. Attorney General, *Annual Report of the Attorney General of the United States for Fiscal Year Ended June 30, 1973*, 67.

38. David L. Rose, *Twenty-Five Years Later: Where Do We Stand on Equal Employment Opportunity Law Enforcement?* 42 Vand. L. Rev. 1121, 1143 (1989).

39. Chandler Burr, "The Better Part of Valor," *California Lawyer* 15, no. 7 (July 1995): 44, 48.

40. Id.

41. Attorney General, *Annual Report of the Attorney General of the United States for Fiscal Year Ended June 30, 1979*, 113; see also, Joel L. Selig, *The Justice Department and Racially Exclusionary Municipal Practices: Creative Ventures in Fair Housing Act Enforcement*, 17 U.C. Davis L. Rev. 445, 450 n.19 (1984) (merger of the Housing and Credit Section with the Education Section).

42. See Selig, *The Justice Department and Racially Exclusionary Municipal Practices*, 489, and Burr, "The Better Part of Valor," 48, describing *United States v. Yonkers Board of Educ.*, 837 F.2d 1181 (2d Cir. 1987).

43. Attorney General, *Annual Report of the Attorney General of the United States for Fiscal Year Ended June 30, 1984*, 145.

44. Eisenstein, "Civil Rights Division at Thirty-Five," 6; Attorney General, *Annual Report of the Attorney General of the United States for Fiscal Year Ended June 30, 1974*, 77.

45. Eisenstein, "Civil Rights Division at Thirty-Five," 6. See also President, Executive Order, "The Task Force on Legal Equality for Women, Executive Order 12336," *Federal Register* 46, no. 246 (December 23, 1981): 62239, ordering the attorney general to review U.S. laws and to report to the president as to any language or provision that "unjustifiably differentiates, or which effectively discriminates, on the basis of sex."

46. Eisenstein, "Civil Rights Division at Thirty-Five," 8.

47. See Race Relations Act, 1976, §43 (Eng.) and Sex Discrimination Act, 1975, §53 (Eng.).

48. The duties of the section are outlined in a memorandum from John Doar to the deputy attorney general, September 11, 1967, p. 6. An early analogue was the Economics Section of the Antitrust Division, which Assistant Attorney General Thurmond Arnold established in the late 1930s in an effort to overcome Antitrust Division "lawyers' particularism and their failure to think of antitrust enforcement in objective, systematic, economic terms." Suzanne Weaver, *Decision to Prosecute: Organization and Public Policy in the Antitrust Division* (Cambridge, Mass.: MIT Press, 1977), 30. Arnold also created a Complaints Section to "enable the division to be more efficient in its decisions about which complaints were to be accepted for field investigation." Id. Weaver notes that neither of these techniques was fully successful. Id. at 31–32. The Antitrust Division now looks to a Legal Policy Section for analysis of complex antitrust matters and an Office of Operations to supervise the litigating sections' investigative and litigative activities. U.S. Department of Justice, *United States Department of Justice Legal Activities, 1993–94*, 31.

49. Memorandum from John Doar to the deputy attorney general, September 11, 1967, p. 6.

50. Reorganization memorandum of January 18, 1969 (Directive no. 10), quoted in memorandum from David L. Norman, director, Office of Planning and Coordination, to Assistant Attorney General Jerris Leonard, February 9, 1969.

51. Memorandum from John Doar to all section chiefs, October 26, 1967. Memorandum from Brian Landsberg to Assistant Attorney General Pollak, September 9, 1968.

52. Attorney General, *Annual Report of the Attorney General of the United States for Fiscal Year Ended June 30, 1968*, 63; Attorney General, *Annual Report of the Attorney General of the United States for Fiscal Year Ended June 30, 1969*, 44.

53. The elements are "to develop litigation (20%), conduct litigation (20%), respond to correspondence (8%), public information (1%), legislative activity (1%), and respond to agency referrals (50%)." J. Stanley Pottinger, *Civil Rights Division Program Objective Submission: Fiscal Year 1976, Objective no. 1* (Internal budget submission, 1974), 3.

54. Id.

55. For example, the milestones for objective 2 are: "1. *September, 1975.* To develop a program for enforcement of Title IX of the Education Amendments. 2. *December, 1975.* Through district court action, develop bilingual standards to implement the Supreme Court decision in *Lau* v. *Nichols.* 3. *June, 1976.* Initiate two suits to enforce Title IX, two suits to enforce Title I, and two new urban student assignment suits. 4. *June, 1976.* Complete district court action in two urban student assignment suits and one Title I suit. 5. *June, 1976.* Complete appellate action in Omaha, Kansas City, Conway County, Kinloch and Indianapolis." Id. at 3.

56. Weaver, *Decision to Prosecute*, 95.

57. See Chapter 8 n.180.

58. Civil Rights Division memorandum no. 68-2, March 14, 1968, re: coordination of HEW and Department of Justice school desegregation programs.

59. Robert Pear, "Justice Dept. Challenges Its Civil Rights Division," *New York Times,* January 20, 1993, sec. A, p. 14, national edition. Although supporting Bleckley County's argument on the merits, Solicitor General Starr recommended denial of the Georgia county's petition for Supreme Court review. Brief for the United States as amicus curiae at 19, *Holder v. Hall*, 114 S.Ct. 2581 (1994) (no. 91-2012). However, the Court heard the case on the merits and ruled for Bleckley County, rejecting the Clinton administration's argument that the African-American plaintiffs should prevail. *Holder v. Hall*, 114 S.Ct. 2581 (1994). In accordance with Solicitor General Starr's recommendation, the Court

summarily affirmed the judgment in favor of the state in the other case, involving Alabama congressional districting. *Figures v. Hunt,* 113 S.Ct. 1233 (1993).

60. Brief for the United States as amicus curiae, *Morales v. Turman,* 535 F.2d 864 (5th Cir. 1976), *reh'g denied,* 539 F.2d 710, *rev'd* 430 U.S. 322 (1977) (no. 74-3436).

61. See, e.g., organizational charts in Attorney General, *Annual Report of the Attorney General of the United States for Fiscal Year Ended June 30, 1980,* 126; Attorney General, *Annual Report of the Attorney General of the United States for Fiscal Year Ended June 30, 1982,* 154.

62. See Attorney General, *Annual Report for Fiscal Year 1984,* 144.

63. As to the coordination function, see Hanes Walton, Jr., *When the Marching Stopped: The Politics of Civil Rights Regulatory Agencies* (New York: State University of New York Press, 1988).

64. See Victor S. Navasky, *Kennedy Justice* (New York: Atheneum, 1971), 181.

65. President Johnson's news conference of March 13, 1965, 1 Pub. Papers 274 (March 13, 1965).

66. Memorandum from John Doar to attorneys assigned to work on Alabama elections, March 2, 1966.

67. Weekends were considered prime time for interviewing witnesses rather than for leisure.

68. 254 F. Supp. 537 (S.D. Ala. 1966). The case is described in Chapter 2.

CHAPTER 8. LITIGATION POLICY

1. Alexander Hamilton, "Federalist Paper No. 78," in *The Federalist Papers* (New York: New American Library, Mentor Books, 1961), 464–72. See Alexander M. Bickel, *The Least Dangerous Branch: The Supreme Court at the Bar of Politics,* 2d ed. (New Haven: Yale University Press, 1986).

2. *Brown v. Board of Education,* 345 U.S. 972 (1953) (reargument), 347 U.S. 483 (1954) (requesting brief on remedial issues).

3. *Allen v. State Bd. of Elections,* 393 U.S. 544 (1969).

4. For the Antitrust Division's standard for filing suit, see Suzanne Weaver, *Decision to Prosecute: Organization and Public Policy in the Antitrust Division* (Cambridge, Mass.: MIT Press, 1977), 167–68.

5. "U.S. Seeks to Balk Alabama Inquiry: Use of Government Car by Dr. King Queried by State," *New York Times,* November 13, 1963, p. 31, col. 1; "Court Restrains Alabama Inquiry: Calling Justice Department Officials Is Forbidden," *New York Times,* November 14, 1963, p. 14, col. 1. It also led to an Alabama state grand jury investigation, which diverted the United States into litigation peripheral to the primary objective of enforcing the civil rights laws. *United States v. McLeod,* 385 F.2d 734, 750–52 (1967) (United States entitled to an injunction against the grand jury's investigation).

6. See *Alexander v. Holmes County Bd. of Educ.,* 396 U.S. 19 (1969) (per curiam).

7. See text in Chapter 8 at note reference 32.

8. Symposium, *The Department of Justice and the Civil Rights Act of 1964,* 26 Pac. L. J. 765, 788 (1995).

9. Burke Marshall, "The Control of the Public Lawyer," in *Law and the American Future,* ed. Murray L. Schwartz (Englewood Cliffs, N.J.: Prentice-Hall, Spectrum, 1976), 177.

10. *General Building Contractors Ass'n, Inc. v. Pennsylvania,* 458 U.S. 375 (1982).

11. *Guardians Ass'n v. Civil Service Comm'n,* 463 U.S. 582 (1983).

12. 100 U.S. 303, 307 (1879).

13. *United Steelworkers of America v. Weber,* 443 U.S. 193, 194 (1979).

14. Statement of William Bradford Reynolds, assistant attorney general, Civil Rights Division, before the Subcommittee on Civil and Constitutional Rights, Committee on the Judiciary, and Subcommittee on Employment Opportunities, Committee on Education and Labor, House of Representatives, concerning affirmative action, July 11, 1985, p. 9.

15. *Local 28 of the Sheet Metal Workers' Int'l Ass'n v. EEOC,* 478 U.S. 421 (1986).

16. *Joint Anti-Fascist Refugee Comm. v. McGrath,* 341 U.S. 123, 172 (1951) (Frankfurter, J., concurring).

17. *Johnson v. Miller,* 864 F. Supp. 1354, 1362 (S.D. Ga. 1994).

18. Michael Kelley, "Segregation Anxiety," *New Yorker,* November 20, 1995, 55. See also Charles Fried, *Foreword: Revolutions?* 109 Harv. L. Rev. 13, 66 n.355 (1995).

19. *Miller v. Johnson,* 115 S.Ct. 2475, 2485 (1995).

20. Brief for the United States at 35, *Miller v. Johnson,* 115 S.Ct. 2475 (1995) (no. 94-631). As to undue coziness with the ACLU, the United States pointed out that "the governing DOJ regulations provide that any information received from any individual or group 'shall be considered along with the materials submitted [by the jurisdiction] and materials resulting from any investigation,' " id. at 34, and that "such consideration was accorded in this case."

21. Nonetheless, in *Shaw v. Hunt,* no. 94-923, 1996 WL 315870, at *8 (U.S. 1996) the Court still was not convinced. ("It appears that the Justice Department was pursuing in North Carolina the same policy of maximizing the number of majority-black districts that it pursued in Georgia").

22. See *Allen v. State Bd. of Elections,* 393 U.S. 544 (1969); *United States v. Cox,* 342 F.2d 167 (5th Cir. 1965), *cert. denied,* 381 U.S. 935 (1965); *Moses v. Kennedy,* 219 F. Supp. 762 (D.D.C. 1963).

23. See Robert Fredrick Burk, *The Eisenhower Administration and Black Civil Rights* (Knoxville: University of Tennessee Press, 1984), 247.

24. Michal R. Belknap, *Federal Law and Southern Order: Racial Violence and Constitutional Conflict in the Post-Brown South* (Athens: University of Georgia Press, 1987), 72.

25. For example, the "Criminal Section reviews approximately 8,000-10,000 complaints annually for prosecutorial merit and seeks indictment in 50-60 cases per year." U.S. Department of Justice, *United States Department of Justice Legal Activities, 1993-94* (Washington, D.C.: Office of Attorney Personnel Management, n.d.), 42.

26. For instance, the Department of Justice recently announced a $16 million settlement against an insurance company for allegedly refusing to insure African-American homes. The press release describing the settlement noted that the "Justice Department first started to investigate the company in 1988 after receiving numerous complaints about American Family's discriminatory behavior." U.S. Department of Justice press release, March 30, 1995.

27. Joel Brenner and Lisa Spayd, "Justice Dept. Probes Area Banks for Loan Bias," *Washington Post,* June 17, 1993, sec. B, p. 11.

28. 42 U.S.C. 2000e-8(c)(1).

29. See, e.g., 42 U.S.C.A. §3608(a) (information regarding fair housing); 42 U.S.C.A. §§1974-1974d (information regarding voter registration); 15 U.S.C.A. §1691(e), (g), (h), and (k) (information regarding equal credit). See also Senate Committee on Banking, Housing, and Urban Affairs, *Comprehensive Deposit Insurance Reform and Taxpayer Protection Act of 1991,* 102d Cong., 1st sess., 1991, S. Rept. 167, 84-94 (need for additional information regarding equal credit).

30. Cf. Suzanne Weaver, *Decision to Prosecute,* 58.

31. 24 C.F.R. §103.410(e) provides for consultation between HUD and DOJ where new facts or law suggest reconsideration of a matter referred to Justice under the act. Subtitle

B, ch. 1, subc. A, app. 1 of 24 C.F.R., explains that this provision is designed to ensure compliance with rule 11, Federal Rules of Civil Procedure. New facts include those that DOJ uncovers during its own investigation of the election case.

32. 461 U.S. 574 (1983).

33. Neal Devins, *Unitariness and Independence: Solicitor General Control over Independent Agency Litigation,* 82 Cal. L. Rev. 255, 276 (1994). For a description of the debacle, see Brian K. Landsberg, book review, 6 Const. Commentary 165, 177–79 (1989) (reviewing Lincoln Caplan, *The Tenth Justice: The Solicitor General and the Rule of Law* [New York: Knopf, 1987]). See also Philip B. Heymann and Lance Liebman, *The Social Responsibilities of Lawyers* (Westbury, N.Y.: Foundation Press, 1988), 136–82 (containing some of the primary source material regarding the department's handling of this case).

34. Memorandum no. 70-1 from Assistant Attorney General Jerris Leonard to all attorneys, re: procedure for handling division cases on appeal and as amicus curiae, January 29, 1970, p. 3. The memorandum states that "the Solicitor General and I have established the following guidelines governing our amicus participation in private civil rights cases. Except in rare cases, our participation will be limited to the following types of cases: (a) Cases in which the Court requests our participation; (b) Cases which involve the validity or interpretation of statutory provisions which the Department of Justice (or another federal agency) is empowered to enforce; (c) Cases which raise issues the resolution of which will likely affect the scope of our enforcement jurisdiction (e.g. cases involving the concept of State action under the Fourteenth Amendment); (d) Cases where a special federal interest is clear and is not likely to be well served by the private litigants."

35. Memorandum from Assistant Attorney General J. Stanley Pottinger to all personnel, September 3, 1974, regarding the Appellate Section, p. 5. The policies now appear in U.S. Department of Justice, *The Department of Justice Manual,* vol. 6 (Clifton, N.J.: Prentice-Hall, 1988), §8-2.170.

36. The solicitor general represents the United States in the Supreme Court, but the litigating divisions normally participate in the process. See generally Rebecca Mae Salokar, *The Solicitor General: The Politics of Law* (Philadelphia: Temple University Press, 1992). For a description of the interaction in an important civil rights case, see Timothy J. O'Neill, *Bakke and the Politics of Equality: Friends and Foes in the Classroom of Litigation* (Middletown, Conn.: Wesleyan University Press, 1985), 179–91.

37. See, e.g., *Lee v. Macon County Bd. of Educ.,* 221 F. Supp. 297 (M.D. Ala. 1963); *Carr v. Montgomery County Bd. of Educ.,* 232 F. Supp. 705 (M.D. Ala. 1964). See John T. Elliff, *The United States Department of Justice and Individual Rights, 1937–1962* (New York: Garland Publishing, 1987), 437, citing J. W. Peltason, *Fifty-Eight Lonely Men: Southern Federal Judges and School Desegregation* (New York: Harcourt, Brace and World, 1961), 151–52. Its activity as a litigating amicus in cases challenging conditions of confinement in institutions for the mentally ill, retarded, juvenile delinquents, and criminals served as a basis for passage of the Civil Rights of Institutionalized Persons Act. See generally Michael K. Lowman, comment, *The Litigating Amicus Curiae: When Does the Party Begin After the Friends Leave?* 41 Am. U. L. Rev. 1243 (1992).

38. The story of the *Bakke* brief has been told from many vantage points but not from the vantage point of the solicitor general's office or the Civil Rights Division. See, e.g., Griffin B. Bell with Ronald J. Ostrow, *Taking Care of the Law* (New York: William Morrow and Company, 1982), 28–32. Caplan, *The Tenth Justice,* 39–48.

39. 334 U.S. 1 (1948).

40. Philip B. Kurland and Gerhard Casper, eds., *Landmark Briefs and Arguments of the Supreme Court of the United States: Constitutional Law,* vol. 46 (Arlington, Va.: University Publications of America, 1975), 324; quotation is in all caps in the original.

41. The common law is traditionally understood to refer to nonstatutory decisions. See

R. Randall Kelso and Charles D. Kelso, *Studying Law: An Introduction* (St. Paul, Minn.: West Publishing Company, 1984), 43.

42. "The life of the law has not been logic: it has been experience." Oliver Wendell Holmes, *The Common Law* (Boston: Little, Brown and Company, 1881), 1.

43. Id. at 35.

44. See *Chevron U.S.A. Inc. v. Natural Resources Defense Council, Inc.*, 467 U.S. 837 (1984). Although agency guidelines may lack the force of law, courts have often given them deference as well, depending on the statutory scheme and how the agency adopted them. See, e.g., *Griggs v. Duke Power Co.*, 401 U.S. 424, 433–34 (1971) (EEOC guidelines "entitled to great deference"). But see *General Electric Co. v. Gilbert*, 429 U.S. 125, 141 (1976) ("Congress . . . did not confer upon the EEOC authority to promulgate rules or regulations. . . . [C]ourts properly may accord less weight to such guidelines than to administrative regulations which Congress has declared shall have the force of law").

45. President, Executive Order, "Leadership and Coordination of Nondiscrimination Laws, Executive Order no. 12250," *Federal Register* 45, no. 215 (November 2, 1980): 72995, microfiche.

46. *Pasadena City Bd. of Educ. v. Spangler*, 427 U.S. 424, 441 (1976).

47. 401 U.S. 424 (1971).

48. 399 U.S. 926 (1970).

49. Robert Belton, *A Comparative Review of Public and Private Enforcement of Title VII of the Civil Rights Act of 1964*, 31 Vand. L. Rev. 905, 943 (1978); Jack Greenberg, *Crusaders in the Courts: How a Dedicated Band of Lawyers Fought for the Civil Rights Revolution* (New York: Harper Collins, Basic Books, 1994), 419.

50. Attorney General, *Annual Report of the Attorney General of the United States for Fiscal Year Ended June 30, 1970*, 83.

51. See *United States v. Louisiana*, 225 F. Supp. 353, 392–96 (E.D. La. 1963) (Wisdom, J.), *aff'd per curiam*, 380 U.S. 145 (1965), and cases there cited. See also *United States v. Duke*, 332 F.2d 759 (5th Cir. 1964).

52. *United States v. Duke*, 332 F.2d at 762, 769.

53. *United States v. Jefferson Co. Bd. of Educ.*, 372 F.2d 836 (5th Cir. 1966) (Wisdom, J.), *modified*, 380 F.2d 385 (5th Cir.1967) (en banc), *cert. denied*, 389 U.S. 840 (1967); *Green v. County School Bd.*, 391 U.S. 430 (1968).

54. *Report of the National Advisory Commission on Civil Disorders*, New York Times edition (New York: E. P. Dutton and Company, 1968), 416. The commission argued, "Racial discrimination and unrealistic and unnecessarily high minimum qualifications for employment or promotion often have the same prejudicial effect."

55. *Local 53 of the Int'l Ass'n of Heat and Frost Insulators v. Vogler*, 407 F.2d 1047, 1052, 1054 (5th Cir. 1969).

56. *Local 189, United Papermakers v. United States*, 416 F.2d 980 (5th Cir. 1969), *cert. denied*, 397 U.S. 919 (1970). See also *United States v. Sheet Metal Workers Int'l Ass'n, Local Union No. 36*, 416 F.2d 123, 131 (8th Cir. 1969) (employment referral systems "carry forward the effects of former discriminatory practices"); *United States v. Hayes Int'l Corp.*, 415 F.2d 1038, 1044 ("present application of lay-off rights gained by whites but denied to blacks in the past could . . . result in a Title VII violation").

57. *Local 189*, 416 F.2d at 989.

58. Id. at 990.

59. 395 U.S. 285 (1969).

60. *Local 189*, 416 F.2d at 991.

61. *Griggs v. Duke Power Co.*, 401 U.S. 424, 429 n.4 (1971).

62. Brief for the United States as amicus curiae on writ of certiorari at 12, *Griggs v. Duke Power Co.*, 401 U.S. 424 (1971) (no. 124).

63. Id.

64. *Griggs,* 401 U.S. at 433 n.9 (internal quotation marks omitted).

65. Equal Employment Opportunity Commission, "Guidelines on Employment Testing Procedures," *U.S. Law Week* 35 (August 24, 1966): 2137.

66. *Federal Register* 35, no. 149 (August 1, 1970): 12333.

67. *Griggs,* 401 U.S. at 430.

68. Id. at 431.

69. Id. at 433–34.

70. David L. Rose, *Twenty-Five Years Later: Where Do We Stand on Equal Employment Opportunity Law Enforcement?* 42 Vand. L. Rev. 1121, 1144 (1989).

71. See, e.g., Donald L. Horowitz, *The Courts and Social Policy* (Washington, D.C.: Brookings Institution, 1977), 15 ("the Court's handling of the legislative history is halting and embarrassed"); Hugh Davis Graham, *The Civil Rights Era: Origins and Development of National Policy, 1960–1972* (New York: Oxford University Press, 1990), 387 ("Burger's interpretation in 1971 of the legislative intent of Congress in the Civil Rights Act would have been greeted with disbelief in 1964").

72. See, e.g., Alfred W. Blumrosen, *Strangers in Paradise:* Griggs v. Duke Power Co. *and the Concept of Employment Discrimination,* 71 Mich. L. Rev. 59 (1972).

73. Senate Committee on Labor and Public Welfare, *Equal Employment Opportunities Enforcement Act of 1971,* 92d Cong., 1st sess., October 1971, S. Rept. 415, 14–15 (reproduced in *Legislative History of the Equal Employment Opportunity Act of 1972,* 92d Cong., 2d sess., November 1972, 423–24). See also *Connecticut v. Teal,* 457 U.S. 440, 447 n.8 ("legislative history of the 1972 amendments to Title VII . . . demonstrates that Congress recognized and endorsed the disparate-impact analysis employed by the Court in *Griggs*"). But see U.S. Department of Justice, Office of Legal Policy, Report to the Attorney General, *Redefining Discrimination: Disparate Impact and the Institutionalization of Affirmative Action,* November 4, 1987, 75–76.

74. Horowitz, *The Courts and Social Policy,* 15.

75. *Watson v. Fort Worth Bank & Trust,* 487 U.S. 977 (1988).

76. Owen M. Fiss, *A Theory of Fair Employment Laws,* 38 U. Chi. L. Rev. 235, 299 (1971).

77. The history is slightly more complex than that. As stated above in note 65, the 1966 EEOC guideline did interpret 703(h) as exempting only those tests that were sufficiently job-related, but it did not contain the adverse impact test. The government's brief at the petition stage, filed in June 1970, articulated the disparate impact test, and the August 1, 1970, guidelines adopted that articulation. The government's brief on the merits reiterates the prior articulation of the disparate impact test but relies on the 1966 and 1970 guidelines only for its argument that 703(h) did not foreclose application of the disparate impact test to unvalidated tests.

78. See Rose, *Twenty-Five Years Later,* 1144ff.

79. Clint Bolick, *Unfinished Business: A Civil Rights Strategy for America's Third Century* (San Francisco: Pacific Research Institute, 1990), 116, 118.

80. E.g., *Albemarle Paper Co. v. Moody,* 422 U.S. 405 (1975).

81. *Federal Register* 43, no. 166 (August 25, 1978): 38290, microfiche.

82. 426 U.S. 229 (1976).

83. Philip B. Kurland and Gerhard Casper, eds., *Landmark Briefs and Arguments of the Supreme Court of the United States: Constitutional Law,* vol. 88 (Arlington, Va.: University Publications of America, 1977), 369.

84. *Village of Arlington Heights v. Metropolitan Housing Dev. Corp.,* 429 U.S. 252 (1977) (race-based equal protection challenge to village's land-use decisions).

85. 442 U.S. 256 (1979).

86. Brief for the United States as amicus curiae at 22, 25, *Personnel Adm'r. v. Feeney,*

442 U.S. 256 (1979) (no. 78-233). Philip B. Kurland and Gerhard Casper, eds., *Landmark Briefs and Arguments of the Supreme Court of the United States: Constitutional Law,* vol. 110 (Arlington, Va.: University Publications of America, 1980), 526.

87. Brief for the Office of Personnel Management, U.S. Department of Defense, U.S. Department of Labor, and the Equal Employment Opportunity Commission as amici curiae at 5, *Personnel Adm'r. v. Feeney,* 442 U.S. 256 (1979) (no. 78-233). Kurland and Casper, *Landmark Briefs,* 110:526.

88. Minna J. Kotkin, *Public Remedies for Private Wrongs: Rethinking the Title VII Back Pay Remedy,* 41 Hastings L. J. 1301, 1331 (1990) (footnote omitted).

89. Id. at 1332–33. Kotkin exempts from this observation cases involving "systemic disparate treatment." Id. at 1335 (internal quotation marks omitted).

90. U.S. Department of Justice, *Redefining Discrimination,* 84. The department was not alone in that view. For example, a leading scholar refers to *Griggs's* "implicit model of proportional representation in the workplace." Graham, *Civil Rights Era,* 390.

91. James P. Turner, unpublished manuscript (1996), 11.

92. U.S. petition for certiorari in *Tisch v. Shidaker,* 782 F.2d 746 (7th Cir. 1986), *cert. granted, cert. vacated & remanded,* 481 U.S. 1001 (1987) (no. 86-468); brief for the United States as amicus curiae supporting respondent, *Watson v. Fort Worth Bank & Trust,* 487 U.S. 977 (1988) (no. 86-6139). See Brian K. Landsberg, *Race and the Rehnquist Court,* 66 Tul. L. Rev. 1267, 1290 n.115 (1992).

93. U.S. petition for certiorari at 17, *Tisch v. Shidaker,* 782 F.2d 746 (7th Cir. 1986), *cert. granted, cert. vacated & remanded,* 481 U.S. 1001 (1987) (no. 86-468). The Court granted the petition and remanded the case for further consideration in light of *Johnson v. Transportation Agency,* 480 U.S. 616 (1987), which had been decided two weeks earlier. Apparently the remand concerned the other issue presented by the government, concerning the proper statistical base for comparison in a disparate impact case.

94. The order appears at 481 U.S. 1012 (1987).

95. *Watson v. Fort Worth Bank & Trust,* 487 U.S. 977, 1011 (1988) (Stevens, J., concurring in the judgment) (internal quotation marks omitted).

96. Brief for the United States as amicus curiae supporting respondent at 23, *Watson v. Fort Worth Bank and Trust,* 487 U.S. 977 (1988) (no. 86-6139) (footnote omitted).

97. 490 U.S. 642 (1989). Charles Fried, the solicitor general who briefed both cases for the United States, says that "*Watson* had been crucial in preparing the Court for what we would ask it to do now [in *Wards Cove*]. . . . [Justice O'Connor's opinion] . . . gave us our signal to press for a more thorough re-examination of what the lower courts had been doing in *Griggs*-type cases." Charles Fried, *Order and Law: Arguing the Reagan Revolution—A Firsthand Account* (New York: Simon and Schuster, 1991), 226 n.64.

98. See Rose, *Twenty-Five Years Later,* 1156–57.

99. See Landsberg, book review, 6 Const. Commentary 165, 177–79. See also Devins, *Unitariness and Independence,* 301 (noting the "decline of EEOC authority relative to the Solicitor General" and the greater influence of the Civil Division and Civil Rights Division of the department, which "both have power to interpret employment discrimination legislation in statutorily designated spheres of authority").

100. The brief sums up: "Nothing about disparate impact cases justifies a departure from the model for litigating disparate treatment cases." Brief for the United States as amicus curiae at 27, *Wards Cove,* 490 U.S. 642 (1989) (no. 87-1387).

101. Rose, *Twenty-Five Years Later,* 1170.

102. *Civil Rights Act of 1991, U.S. Statutes at Large* 105 (1992): 1071.

103. See Joel L. Selig, *The Justice Department and Racially Exclusionary Municipal Practices: Creative Ventures in Fair Housing Act Enforcement,* 17 U.C. Davis L. Rev. 445, 460 (1984).

104. Brief for the United States as amicus curiae at 10–11, *Lau v. Nichols*, 414 U.S. 563 (1974) (no. 72-6520).

105. Senate Committee on the Judiciary, *Department of Justice Confirmations: Hearings on the Nominations of Rex E. Lee To Be Solicitor General of the United States, and William Bradford Reynolds To Be Assistant Attorney General, Civil Rights Division, Department of Justice,* 97th Cong., 1st sess., June–July 1981, serial no. J-97-7, pt. 2, 100.

106. Brief for United States as amicus curiae at 14–16, *Town of Huntington v. Huntington Branch, NAACP,* 488 U.S. 15 (1988) (no. 87-1961). The government argued that Title VIII's use of the words "because of" "strongly suggests a requirement of discriminatory motivation." However, footnote 18 of the government's brief acknowledges that in *Griggs* "the Court construed the 'because of' language in 42 U.S.C. 2000e-2(a)(2) as prohibiting employment practices that had discriminatory effects and rejected the contention that the language barred only intentional discriminatory practices." Id. at 15 n.18.

107. *Town of Huntington v. Huntington Branch, NAACP,* 488 U.S. 15 (1988).

108. U.S. Senate Committee on the Judiciary, *Senate Judiciary Committee Confirmation Hearing of Deval Patrick To Be Assistant Attorney General for Civil Rights,* March 10, 1994, available in LEXIS, Legis Library, Fednew file.

109. Statutes required the schools of the South to be racially segregated. The department's school desegregation responsibilities extend as well to other forms of de jure segregation, but this case study concentrates on the eradication of traditional state-mandated dual school systems.

110. See, e.g., Richard Kluger, *Simple Justice: The History of* Brown v. Board of Education *and Black America's Struggle for Equality* (New York: Random House, 1975); J. Harvie Wilkinson III, *From* Brown *to* Bakke (New York: Oxford University Press, 1979); Derrick A. Bell, Jr., *Race, Racism, and American Law,* 3d ed. (Boston: Little, Brown and Company, 1992).

111. President's Committee on Civil Rights, *To Secure These Rights* (Washington, D.C., Government Printing Office, 1947), 63.

112. Id. at 79.

113. Id. at 82.

114. Id. at 166–71.

115. "The United States . . . urges the Court to repudiate the 'separate but equal' doctrine as an unwarranted deviation from the principle of equality under law." Memorandum for the United States as amicus curiae at 9–10, *Sweatt v. Painter,* 339 U.S. 629 (1950) (no. 44), and *McLaurin v. Oklahoma State Regents for Higher Educ.,* 339 U.S. 637 (1950) (no. 34). The brief relies in part on the recommendations of the President's Committee on Civil Rights. Id. at 10 n.1.

116. See Kluger, *Simple Justice,* 558–60; Philip Elman, interviewed by Norman Silber, *The Solicitor General's Office, Justice Frankfurter, and Civil Rights Litigation, 1946–1960: An Oral History,* 100 Harv. L. Rev. 817 (1987).

117. Brief of United States as amicus curiae at 2, *Brown v. Board of Education,* 347 U.S. 483 (1954) (no. 1); Philip B. Kurland and Gerhard Casper, eds., *Landmark Briefs and Arguments of the Supreme Court of the United States: Constitutional Law,* vol. 49 (Arlington, Va.: University Publications of America, 1975), 117.

118. Id. at 3 (Kurland and Casper, *Landmark Briefs,* 49:118).

119. Id. at 6 (Kurland and Casper, *Landmark Briefs,* 49:121).

120. Id. at 18 (Kurland and Casper, *Landmark Briefs,* 49:133).

121. Id.

122. Id. at 27 (Kurland and Casper, *Landmark Briefs,* 49:142).

123. Id. at 29 (Kurland and Casper, *Landmark Briefs,* 49:144).

124. Kluger, *Simple Justice,* 675 (internal quotation marks omitted). President Eisen-

hower insisted that this was the position of the attorney general as a lawyer and not as an administration spokesperson. See Burk, *The Eisenhower Administration,* 138, 166.

125. Elliff, *The United States Department of Justice,* 395. See also Herbert Brownell, *Civil Rights in the 1950s,* 69 Tul. L. Rev. 781 (1995).

126. Supplemental brief for the United States on reargument at 184, *Brown v. Board of Education,* 347 U.S. 483 (1954) (no. 1); Kurland and Casper, *Landmark Briefs,* 49:1050.

127. Id. at 188 (Kurland and Casper, *Landmark Briefs,* 49:1054).

128. See, e.g., Elman, *The Solicitor General's Office,* 818, suggesting that the amicus brief in *Shelley v. Kraemer* was motivated by both moral and political considerations.

129. See, e.g., Kluger, *Simple Justice,* 322–23, 650–51.

130. The Supreme Court's decision in *Milliken v. Bradley,* 418 U.S. 717 (1974) (school systems not involved in the violation may not be required to participate in the remedy) arguably marked the end of that ratchet.

131. Brief for the United States on the further argument of the questions of relief at 4–5, *Brown v. Board of Education,* 347 U.S. 483 (1954); Philip B. Kurland and Gerhard Casper, eds., *Landmark Briefs and Arguments of the Supreme Court of the United States: Constitutional Law,* vol. 49A (Arlington, Va.: University Publications of America, 1975), 745–46.

132. Id. at 6 (Kurland and Casper, *Landmark Briefs,* 49A:747).

133. See Caplan, *Tenth Justice,* 31.

134. The brief noted that school segregation had previously enjoyed Supreme Court approval and public support on moral and legal grounds and that just as *Brown I* rested in part on psychological factors, so also "psychological and emotional factors are involved—and must be met with understanding and good will—in the alterations that must now take place in order to bring about compliance with the Court's decision." Brief for the United States on the further reargument of the questions of relief at 8 (Kurland and Casper, *Landmark Briefs,* 49A:749). See Elliff, *The United States Department of Justice,* 397.

135. Caplan, *Tenth Justice,* 28.

136. See Chapter 2 n.43. See also John Weir Anderson, *Eisenhower, Brownell, and the Congress* (University: Published for the Inter-University Case Program by the University of Alabama Press, 1964), 86–87.

137. See 18 U.S.C. 242.

138. See *Screws v. United States,* 325 U.S. 91 (1945).

139. Senate Committee on the Judiciary, Subcommittee on Constitutional Rights, *Civil Rights—1957: Hearings on S. 83, an amendment to S. 83, S. 427, S. 428, S. 429, S. 468, S. 500, S. 501, S. 502, S. 504, S. 505, S. 508, S. 509, S. 510, S. Con. Res. 5,* 85th Cong., 1st sess., February–March 1957, 7.

140. *Brewer v. Hoxie School Dist. No. 46,* 238 F.2d 91 (8th Cir. 1956).

141. Elliff, *The United States Department of Justice,* 417.

142. See David L. Norman, *The Strange Career of the Civil Rights Division's Commitment to Brown,* 93 Yale L. J. 983, 984 (1984). Judge Norman notes that there is "only one reported case in which a public school official was prosecuted under [§242]. See *United States v. Buntin,* 10 F. 730 (C.C.S.D. Ohio 1882)." Id. at 984 n.4. Although the case preceded *Plessy v. Ferguson,* 163 U.S. 537 (1896), in *Buntin* the issue presented to the jury was whether the black school in an adjoining district was equal to the white school from which the defendant had excluded a black child.

143. *Cooper v. Aaron,* 358 U.S. 1 (1958). See Kluger, *Simple Justice,* 754 (1977); Elliff, *The United States Department of Justice,* 462–87; Attorney General, *Annual Report of the Attorney General of the United States for the Fiscal Year Ended June 30, 1958,* 178.

144. Peltason, *Fifty-Eight Lonely Men,* 51. "Spokesmen for the Administration excused their inaction . . . on the ground that they lacked legal authority." Id. at 54. However, a

study of the Eisenhower administration concludes that the department's "passive role in investigating acts of obstruction" stemmed from President Eisenhower's "dictating a bland position on desegregation." Burk, *Eisenhower Administration,* 166.

145. *Civil Rights Act of 1960, U.S. Statutes at Large* 74 (1961): 86 (18 U.S.C. §1509).

146. J. W. Peltason notes that under the Kennedy administration the Department of Justice "started to take a more active role in desegregation suits." Peltason, *Fifty-Eight Lonely Men,* 253. See, e.g., Attorney General, *Annual Report of the Attorney General of the United States for the Fiscal Year Ended June 30, 1962,* 169 (amicus curiae participation in school desegregation cases in Orleans, St. Helena, and East Baton Rouge parishes, Louisiana, and New Rochelle, New York).

147. See Attorney General, *Annual Report for Fiscal Year 1962,* 170 ("A 'pilot' case was filed on September 17, 1962 [*United States v. County School Board of Prince George County, et al.*], and others will follow where local authorities refuse to desegregate their schools"). See also *United States v. Madison Co. Bd. of Educ.,* 326 F.2d 237 (5th Cir. 1964), *cert. denied,* 379 U.S. 929 (1964).

148. *Civil Rights Act of 1964, U.S. Statutes at Large* 78 (1965): 241, 248 (§407[a]).

149. Id.

150. Attorney General, *Annual Report of the Attorney General of the United States for the Fiscal Year Ended on June 30, 1967,* 173.

151. Id. at 174.

152. See Bell, *Race, Racism and American Law,* 548–51.

153. The initial guidelines are reproduced in the appendix to *Price v. Denison Indep. School Dist. Bd. of Educ.,* 348 F.2d 1010, 1015 (5th Cir. 1965).

154. See, e.g., *Price,* 348 F.2d 1010 (5th Cir. 1965); *Singleton v. Jackson Municipal Separate School Dist.,* 348 F.2d 729 (5th Cir. 1965). In *Singleton* Judge Wisdom noted that H.E.W. was the "more appropriate federal body to weigh administrative difficulties inherent in school desegregation plans." *Singleton,* 348 F.2d at 731.

155. Statement of policies for school desegregation plans under Title VI of the Civil Rights Act of 1964, *Federal Register* 31, no. 69 (April 9, 1966): 5623, 5625 (§181.11). Justice Department officials John Doar and David Filvaroff were involved in the drafting of the 1966 guidelines. Summary of deposition of Harold Howe II, U.S. commissioner of education, in *Alabama NAACP State Conference of Branches and United States of America v. George C. Wallace and John W. Gardner (impleaded defendants),* C.A. no. 2457-N, M.D. Ala. (November 2, 1966), 1.

156. Howe deposition summary, in *Alabama NAACP State Conference,* 9–10.

157. Revised statement, *Federal Register* 31, no. 69 (April 9, 1966): 5623, 5628 (§181.54). This section adds, "The single most substantial indication as to whether a free choice plan is actually working to eliminate the dual school structure is the extent to which Negro . . . students have in fact transferred from segregated schools." The section also contains rough numerical guidelines for measuring success.

158. Brief for the United States at 32, *United States v. Jefferson County Bd. of Educ.,* 372 F.2d 836 (5th Cir. 1966) (no. 23345). Judge Wisdom adopted the substance of that language. *United States v. Jefferson County Bd. of Educ.,* 272 F.2d 836, 894 (5th Cir. 1966), *aff'd en banc,* 380 F.2d 385 (1967), *cert. denied,* 389 U.S. 840 (5th Cir. 1967).

159. Letter from Secretary of Health, Education, and Welfare John Gardner to congressmen and governors, April 9, 1966, reproduced in House Committee on Rules, *Hearings on H.R. 826,* 89th Cong., 2d sess., 1966, 31–32.

160. 372 F.2d 836 (5th Cir. 1966), *aff'd en banc,* 380 F.2d 385 (5th Cir. 1967), *cert. denied,* 389 U.S. 840 (1967).

161. Brief for the United States at 29–30, *Jefferson County,* 372 F.2d 836 (5th Cir. 1966) (no. 23345), citing two voting discrimination cases in which the United States had con-

vinced the Fifth Circuit to fashion a detailed decree to be entered on remand by the district court. *United States v. Ward,* 349 F.2d 795 (5th Cir. 1965); *United States v. Palmer,* 356 F.2d 951 (5th Cir. 1966). The brief also cited "decided cases in which the courts, in their decrees, have used provisions the same as, or similar to, the provisions of the decree here proposed." Appendix to briefs of the United States, *Johnson v. Jackson Parish School Bd.,* 423 F.2d 105 (5th Cir. 1970) (no. 23173), and six other cases including *Jefferson County* (vol. 4 of Appendix).

162. Brief for the United States at 9, *Jefferson County,* 372 F.2d 836 (5th Cir. 1966) (no. 23345), citing *Brown v. Board of Education,* 347 U.S. 483 (1954); *Lockett v. Board of Educ.,* 342 F.2d 225, 228 (5th Cir. 1965).

163. Brief for the United States at 20, *Jefferson County,* 372 F.2d at 836 (5th Cir. 1966) (no. 23345), citing *United States v. Duke,* 332 F.2d 759, 768–69 (5th Cir. 1964).

164. *Jefferson County,* 372 F.2d at 851; emphasis in original.

165. Id. at 890.

166. Id. at 895–96.

167. See memorandum from Assistant Attorney General John Doar to Owen Fiss, September 9, 1967, summarizing a meeting with Peter Libassi of HEW.

168. 389 U.S. 1003 (1967) (granting certiorari).

169. Memorandum from Assistant Attorney General Stephen J. Pollak to the solicitor general, February 23, 1968, in Michal R. Belknap, ed., *Administrative History of the Civil Rights Division of the Department of Justice During the Johnson Administration,* vol. 17, *Civil Rights, the White House, and the Justice Department, 1945–1968* (New York: Garland Publishing, 1991), pt. 1, 10.

170. Id.

171. Id. at 11.

172. Id. at 12.

173. Memorandum for the the United States as amicus curiae at 3, *Green v. County School Board,* 391 U.S. 430, 436 (1968) (no. 695).

174. Id. at 4.

175. Id. at 15.

176. *Green v. County School Board,* 391 U.S. 430, 436 (1968).

177. Id. at 437–39.

178. Id. at 442.

179. See Attorney General, *Annual Report of the Attorney General of the United States for Fiscal Year Ended June 30, 1968,* 63.

180. The enforcement program is described in a memorandum for the attorney general from Assistant Attorney General Stephen J. Pollak, dated June 28, 1968, in Belknap, *Administrative History,* pt. 2, 16–20. See also Civil Rights Division memorandum no. 68-2, March 14, 1968, re: coordination of HEW and Department of Justice school desegregation programs, which directed division lawyers that "we should use the administrative remedies available to HEW where its processes can achieve a result comparable to that which we could achieve in court; and we should save the litigative remedy for situations where the administrative remedy is no longer available (*e.g.,* the terminated systems) or not particularly effective (*e.g.,* intimidation or harassment), or when the litigative remedy can perform a special function for the desegregation process (*e.g.,* establish important legal principles)."

181. Memorandum from David L. Norman to Assistant Attorney General Jerris Leonard, June 2, 1969, quoted in David L. Norman, "The Civil Rights Division of the U.S. Department of Justice, 1954–1973" (unpublished manuscript, 1992), 120, 121.

182. A former head of the Department of Health, Education, and Welfare's Office for Civil Rights during the Nixon administration provides a vivid description of the clash be-

tween the desire of some administration officials to embrace free choice and the need to comply with the legal standards imposed by *Green.* See Leon E. Panetta and Peter Gall, *Bring Us Together: The Nixon Team and the Civil Rights Retreat* (Philadelphia: J. B. Lippincott Company, 1971), 110ff.

183. *United States v. Montgomery County Bd. of Educ.,* 395 U.S. 225, 236 (1969); emphasis in original.

184. Richard Harris, *Justice: The Crisis of Law, Order, and Freedom in America* (New York, E. P. Dutton and Company, 1970), 193.

185. Panetta and Gall, *Bring Us Together,* 255. The Nixon administration had initially pressed for compliance. The Department of Justice had requested the federal court to order the school systems to implement desegregation plans drafted by the Department of Health, Education, and Welfare. Id. at 252–53.

186. *Alexander v. Holmes County Bd. of Educ.,* 396 U.S. 19 (1969) (per curiam); *Carter v. West Feliciana Parish School Bd.,* 396 U.S. 290 (1970); see Graham, *Civil Rights Era,* 382; Harrel R. Rodgers, Jr. and Charles S. Bullock III, *Law and Social Change: Civil Rights Laws and Their Consequences,* (New York: McGraw-Hill, 1972), 93.

187. Attorney General, *Annual Report for Fiscal Year 1970,* 83–84. The report noted that "prior to the 1969–70 school year, 5.2 percent of the black public school children in 11 southern States attended school in desegregated systems; that as of June 4, 1970, systems enrolling 58.9 percent of those children were committed to desegregate by September 1970; and that the figure was expected to rise to approximately 90 percent by September." The Southern Regional Council in December 1969 described actions being taken by HEW to effect immediate compliance but criticized the Department of Justice for deciding to seek compliance by September 1970 rather than immediately. Southern Regional Council, *The Federal Retreat in School Desegregation* (Atlanta, 1969), 38–41. See Norman, *Strange Career,* 986–88.

188. Richard Nixon, "Statement About Desegregation of Elementary and Secondary Schools," in *Public Papers of the Presidents of the United States: Richard Nixon, 1970* (Washington, D.C.: Government Printing Office, 1971), 305–6.

189. 402 U.S. 1 (1971).

190. Brief for the United States as amicus curiae at 7–8, *Swann v. Charlotte-Mecklenburg Bd. of Educ.,* 402 U.S. 1 (1971) (no. 281); Philip B. Kurland and Gerhard Casper, eds., *Landmark Briefs and Arguments of the Supreme Court of the United States: Constitutional Law,* vol. 70 (Arlington, Va.: University Publications of America, 1975), 381–82.

191. Id. at 16 (Kurland and Casper, *Landmark Briefs,* 70:390).

192. Id. at 17 (Kurland and Casper, *Landmark Briefs,* 70:391).

193. See *National Journal,* June 19, 1971, 1305–13. In spite of the Nixon administration's attitude toward busing, the enforcement policies of the 1960s and early 1970s were highly successful: "Segregation of African American students in the South declined dramatically from the mid-1960s through the early 1970s. . . . [T]he South has been the nation's most integrated region since 1970." Gary Orfield, *The Growth of Segregation in American Schools: Changing Patterns of Separation and Poverty Since 1968* (Alexandria, Va.: National School Boards, 1993), 1. "The changes were concentrated in the South, which was the only region to face a serious federal enforcement effort, and segregation is greatest where desegregation was never accomplished." Id. at 6.

194. See brief of the United States, in *United States v. Texas Educ. Agency (Austin Indep. School Dist.),* 467 F.2d 848 (5th Cir. 1972) (no. 71-2508) (filed September 3, 1971) (there is no page 54).

195. *United States v. Texas Educ. Agency (Austin Indep. School Dist.),* 467 F.2d 848, 873 (5th Cir. 1972) (en banc).

196. *School Bd. of City of Richmond v. State Bd. of Educ.,* 412 U.S. 92 (1973); *Milliken v. Bradley,* 418 U.S. 717 (1974).

197. *Board of Educ. of Oklahoma City Public Schools v. Dowell,* 498 U.S. 237 (1991).

198. See proposed constitutional amendment, H.R.J. Res. 56, 97th Cong., 2d Sess. (1982); Education Amendments of 1972, 20 U.S.C. §§1651–1656 (ban on federal funding of busing for racial balance); Equal Education Opportunities Act of 1974, 20 U.S.C. §1714 (ban on federal busing requirements); *Drummond v. Acree,* 409 U.S. 1228 (1972) (Powell, Circuit justice, denying stay of desegregation order) (1972 act only limits busing orders in de facto segregation cases); *Hart v. Community School Bd. of Educ.,* 512 F.2d 37 (2d Cir. 1975) (same ruling as to 1974 act).

199. William Bradford Reynolds, "The Role of the Federal Government in School Desegregation," in *Brown Plus Thirty: Perspectives on Desegregation,* ed. LaMar P. Miller (New York: New York University, Metropolitan Center for Educational Research, Development, and Training, 1986).

200. Stephen L. Wasby, *How Planned Is "Planned Litigation"?* 1984 Am. B. Found. Res. J. 83, 138.

201. See, e.g., *Local 28 of Sheet Metal Workers Int'l Ass'n v. EEOC,* 478 U.S. 421, 465 n.38, 470 n.42, 474 n.46 (1986), where the Court continually contrasts the current position of the department and the EEOC with their "contemporaneous interpretations" and their positions in prior cases.

202. See remarks of Rep. Kastenmeier, Chapter 4 n.78.

203. *Planned Parenthood of Southeastern Pennsylvania v. Casey,* 505 U.S. 833, 836 (1992).

204. Owen M. Fiss, *The Fate of an Idea Whose Time Has Come: Antidiscrimination Law in the Second Decade After* Brown v. Board of Education, 41 U. Chi. L. Rev. 742, 754 (1974).

205. See, e.g., Chapter 5 nn.16, 17.

206. Drew S. Days III, "The War Against Civil Rights," in NAACP Legal Defense and Educational Fund, "29 Years Since Brown" (Program for Annual Civil Rights Institute, New York, May 20, 1983), 7, reprinted from Northeast Magazine, *Hartford Courant,* May 1, 1983.

207. *Henslee v. Union Planters Nat'l Bank & Trust Co.,* 335 U.S. 595, 600 (1949) (Frankfurter, J., dissenting).

208. "Especially when one party is a governmental entity—an institution with public obligations—the litigant's 'interest' may change over time in response to debate and politics." William N. Eskridge, Jr., *Metaprocedure,* 98 Yale L. J. 945, 958 n.64 (1989) (reviewing Robert M. Cover, Owen M. Fiss, and Judith Resnik, *Procedure* [Westbury, N.Y.: Foundation Press, 1988]).

209. *United States v. Mendoza,* 464 U.S. 154, 161 (1984) (rejecting collateral estoppel of United States).

210. Senate Committee on the Judiciary, *Nomination of William Bradford Reynolds To Be Associate Attorney General of the United States: Hearings on the Confirmation of William Bradford Reynolds To Be Associate Attorney General of the United States,* 99th Cong., 1st sess., June 1985, serial no. J-99-29, 913–21.

211. Id. at 913.

212. Tim O'Brien, "Former Ally Charges Ethical Breach; Behind Justice's Flip-Flop in the N.J. Bias Suit," *Legal Times,* September 19, 1994, p. 2.

213. Clint Bolick, "Coronation of a Quota King at Justice," *Wall Street Journal,* August 31, 1994, sec. A, p. 13.

214. *City of Lockhart v. United States,* 460 U.S. 125 (1983). The Court noted, "The United States, which defended the suit below, now agrees with Lockhart that the changes have no retrogressive effect on the voting rights of Mexican-Americans. Cano continues

to defend the result below." Id. at 130. Note that had the matter not been in litigation, Cano would have had no recourse if the Reagan administration had simply reversed the prior denial of preclearance. See *Morris v. Gressette,* 432 U.S. 491 (1977).

215. Chandler Burr, "The Better Part of Valor," *California Lawyer* 15, no. 7 (July 1995): 44, 49.

216. Brief for the United States at 33, *Dayton Bd. of Educ. v. Brinkman,* 433 U.S. 406 (1977). See also *Dayton v. Bd. of Educ. v. Brinkman,* 443 U.S. 526 (1979).

217. Brief for the United States, *Dayton Bd. of Educ. v. Brinkman* at 16 and n.5.

218. Joel L. Selig, *Changing the Justice Department's Position in Pending Litigation,* 25 Land and Water L. Rev. 503, 504 (1990). This article provides a balanced and thorough account of the many different circumstances when the department might change position and the criteria that should be applied in deciding whether to do so. Several of the changes in position are described in Stephan L. Wasby, *Race Relations Litigation in an Age of Complexity* (Charlottesville: University Press of Virginia, 1995), 247–51.

219. Mark V. Tushnet, *Making Civil Rights Law: Thurgood Marshall and the Supreme Court, 1936–1961* (New York: Oxford University Press, 1994), 135–36, 139–40; Elman, *The Solicitor General's Office,* 821. See also *Henderson v. United States,* 339 U.S. 816 (1950).

220. *Mitchell v. United States,* 313 U.S. 80 (1941). See Tushnet, *Making Civil Rights Law,* 71–72.

221. *Henderson v. United States,* 339 U.S. 816 (1950).

222. Brief of Seattle intervenor plaintiffs/appellees at 68–70, *State of Washington v. Seattle School Dist. No. 1,* 458 U.S. 457 (9182) (no. 81-9) (arguing that the United States had intervened as a plaintiff under Sec. 902 of the Civil Rights Act of 1964, 42 U.S.C. §2000h-2 and that it is authorized to do so "only on behalf of civil rights plaintiffs").

223. Clifford Freed, comment, *Ethical Considerations for the Justice Department When It Switches Sides During Litigation,* 7 U. Puget Sound L. Rev. 405 (1984); note, *Professional Ethics in Government Side-Switching,* 96 Harv. L. Rev. 1914 (1983).

224. *General Telephone Company v. EEOC,* 446 U.S. 318 (1980), held that the EEOC acts on behalf of the public interest, not private interests, in suits under both 42 U.S.C.A. 2000e-5(f)(1) (general litigating authority) and 42 U.S.C.A. 2000e-6 (pattern or practice litigating authority) (Sections 706 and 707 of the Civil Rights Act of 1964 as amended). The Court reasoned largely from the attorney general's litigation authority, some of which had been transferred to the EEOC by the 1972 amendments to the act. It said that "the EEOC is not merely a proxy for the victims of discrimination and . . . the EEOC's enforcement suits should not be considered representative actions subject to Rule 23 [governing class actions]." Id. at 326.

225. 716 F.2d 1565, 1580 n.15 (11th Cir. 1983).

226. See also *Bratton v. City of Detroit,* no. 80-1837 (6th Cir. May 27, 1983), order denying the request of the United States to intervene on appeal to seek rehearing en banc in a fair employment case. The Court noted that "the Justice Department's claim . . . lacks much of the weight it might otherwise carry given the conflict between the position the Department has taken here and that taken by others vested with enforcement powers under Title VII, particularly the Equal Employment Opportunity Commission." Id. at 3 n.1.

227. See, e.g., *Liddell v. Caldwell,* 546 F.2d 768 (8th Cir. 1976), *cert. denied,* 433 U.S. 914 (1977) (intervention allowed after party had agreed to consent decree to which individuals objected); compare *Jones v. Caddo Parish School Bd.,* 735 F.2d 923 (5th Cir. 1984) (intervention untimely). Note that *Jones* relies in part on the ability of the complainants to file a separate action, since they are not bound by the judgment in a case between the United States and the school board. Id. at 937. See also *Martin v. Wilks,* 490 U.S. 755 (1989) (white individuals not bound by consent decree in fair employment litigation suit brought by African-American individuals and the United States against Jefferson County, Alabama).

228. Robert Pear, "Justice Dept. Challenges Its Civil Rights Division," *New York Times,* January 20, 1993, sec. A, p. 14, national edition.

229. Brief for the United States as amicus curiae supporting the respondents at 14 n. 7, *Holder v. Hall,* 114 S.Ct. 2581 (1994) (no. 91-2012) (May 19, 1993).

CHAPTER 9. THE ROLE OF CIVIL SERVANTS AND POLITICAL APPOINTEES

1. John Locke, *The Second Treatise of Civil Government and a Letter Concerning Toleration* (Oxford: Basil Blackwell, 1948), 72.

2. *Ex parte Curtis,* 106 U.S. 371, 373 (1882).

3. President Bush's nomination of William Lucas in 1989 and President Clinton's nomination of Lani Guinier in 1993 as assistant attorney general for civil rights both failed. In 1980, President Reagan had attempted to promote William Bradford Reynolds from assistant attorney general for civil rights to associate attorney general, and the nomination failed in the Senate.

4. 5 U.S.C.A. §§2301-2302.

5. Memorandum from Committee to Study and Make Recommendations About the Attorney General's Program for Honor Law Graduates, to Assistant Attorney General William Bradford Reynolds, Report on the Attorney General's Program for Honor Law Graduates, February 20, 1986, p. 3.

6. Leonard was one of three unsuccessful candidates for higher office who received appointments as assistant attorney general at the beginning of the Nixon administration. See Richard Harris, *Justice: The Crisis of Law, Order, and Freedom in America* (New York: E. P. Dutton and Company, 1970), 126.

7. John T. Elliff, *The United States Department of Justice and Individual Rights, 1937-1962* (New York: Garland Publishing, 1987), 785.

8. Victor S. Navasky, *Kennedy Justice* (New York: Atheneum, 1971), 162. See also the tributes to Burke Marshall by Judge Patricia M. Wald, Rep. John Lewis, and former Attorney General Nicholas de B. Katzenbach, 105 Yale L. J. 611, 621, 623 (1995).

9. See Chandler Burr, "The Better Part of Valor," *California Lawyer* 15, no. 7 (July 1995): 44, 47.

10. As Professor Burke Marshall, a former assistant attorney general for civil rights, told Congress: "Law enforcement in this area [civil rights] demands policy direction. It affects the lives of millions of people and the emotions and passions of millions of others. It seems right, not wrong, to me that an administration give policy direction on such matters as busing, employment quotas, school district consolidations, and private discrimination in places of public accommodations, as much as I disagree with the policy established by the present administration in most of these areas." Senate Committee on the Judiciary, Subcommittee on Separation of Powers, *Removing Politics from the Administration of Justice: Hearings on S. 2803, S. 2978, and S. 2615,* 93d Cong., 2d sess., March–April 1974, 114 (statement of Burke Marshall, deputy dean of the Yale Law School). See also id. at 204 (statement of Archibald Cox, Williston professor of law, Harvard University, and former special prosecutor in the Department of Justice). But see Joel L. Selig, *The Reagan Justice Department and Civil Rights: What Went Wrong,* 1985 U. Ill. L. Rev. 785, 793 ("Every enforcement decision the Department makes should depend solely on the relevant law and facts, and not on extraneous political or ideological considerations"). See Nancy V. Baker, *Conflicting Loyalties: Law and Politics in the Attorney General's Office, 1789-1990,* (Lawrence: University Press of Kansas, 1992), 28-36 (surveying views as to who is client

of the attorney general and noting the "dualism" of the office between loyalty to the president and loyalty to the law).

11. Senate Committee on the Judiciary, *Nomination of William Bradford Reynolds To Be Associate Attorney General of the United States: Hearings on the Confirmation of William Bradford Reynolds To Be Associate Attorney General of the United States,* 99th Cong., 1st sess., June 1985, serial no. J-99-29, 61.

12. Cornell W. Clayton, "Introduction: Politics and the Legal Bureaucracy," in *Government Lawyers: The Federal Legal Bureaucracy and Presidential Politics* (Lawrence: University Press of Kansas, 1995), 3.

13. See U.S. Department of Justice, Justice Management Division, *200th Anniversary of the Office of the Attorney General 1789–1989* (Washington, D.C., n.d.), ii. The fifteen are the attorneys general listed there, from William Rogers to Dick Thornburgh plus William Barr and Janet Reno, who are not listed.

14. Only one attorney general, William Wirt, served through two presidential terms (1817–1829).

15. Figures computed from memorandum from Stephen R. Colgate to Mark R. Disler, June 18, 1985, reproduced in Senate Committee on the Judiciary, *Nomination of William Bradford Reynolds To Be Associate Attorney General of the United States,* 947.

16. See Gary Orfield, *Must We Bus? Segregated Schools and National Policy* (Washington, D.C.: Brookings Institution, 1978), 326.

17. See Philip B. Heymann and Lance Liebman, *The Social Responsibilities of Lawyers* (Westbury, N.Y.: Foundation Press, 1988), 136. See also Lincoln Caplan, *The Tenth Justice: The Solicitor General and the Rule of Law* (New York: Knopf, 1987), 51–60.

18. Charles Fried, *Order and Law: Arguing the Reagan Revolution—A Firsthand Account* (New York: Simon and Schuster, 1991), 41. To his credit, Professor Fried has since expressed regret, acknowledging that he "saw little with my own eyes that would [justify my remark]." Letter from Charles Fried to Brian Landsberg, August 3, 1991.

19. Donald L. Horowitz, *The Jurocracy: Government Lawyers, Agency Programs, and Judicial Decisions* (Lexington, Mass.: Lexington Books, 1977).

20. Suzanne Weaver, *Decision to Prosecute: Organization and Public Policy in the Antitrust Division* (Cambridge, Mass.: MIT Press, 1977), 8–9.

21. My description of the civil service lawyers is not based primarily on examination of the records of the division, although such an examination might be revealing. Rather, I rely in large measure on my personal impressions formed during my twenty-two years there.

22. Honors program hiring has provided the majority of the department's new lawyers. Honors program attorneys are drawn from the top students graduating from law school each year and from judicial law clerks. The program is described in Weaver, *Decision to Prosecute,* 37–38.

23. See, e.g., Gerald M. Stern, *The Buffalo Creek Disaster* (New York: Random House, Vintage Books, 1976), 4.

24. Jonathan Yardley, "Two Good Men and True," *Washington Post,* June 15, 1987, sec. C, p. 2.

25. Federal Rules of Civil Procedure, 54. "The Division was not prepared to take the terrible risk of losing a single case because of lack of proof. We faced tough judges. We wanted the proof to be so overwhelming so as to lock up the trial judge . . . and to convince the country as well." John Doar and Dorothy Landsberg, "Performance of the FBI," 905–6, quoted in Arthur Schlesinger, Jr., *Robert Kennedy and His Times* (New York: Ballantine Books, 1978), 323–24.

26. *Rock Island, Ark. and La. R.R. v. United States,* 254 U.S. 141, 143 (1920) (Holmes, J.). See also John MacArthur Maguire and Philip Zimet, *Hobson's Choice and Similar*

Practices in Federal Taxation, 48 Harv. L. Rev. 1281, 1299 (1935) ("it is hard to see why the government should not be held to a like standard of rectangular rectitude when dealing with its citizens").

27. Douglas Letter, *Lawyering and Judging on Behalf of the United States: All I Ask for Is a Little Respect,* 61 Geo. Wash. L. Rev. 1295, 1300 (1993).

28. Most recently, President Bush recognized that tradition in his executive order concerning civil justice reform, which recites, "The United States sets an example for private litigation by adhering to higher standards than those required by the rules of procedure in the conduct of Government litigation in Federal court, and can continue to do so without impairing the effectiveness of its litigation efforts." President, Executive Order, "Civil Justice Reform, Executive Order 12778," *Federal Register* 56, no. 207 (October 23, 1991): 55195, microfiche.

29. Memorandum from John Doar to the deputy attorney general, September 11, 1967, p. 6.

30. Id.

31. Weaver, *Decision to Prosecute,* 49.

32. Untitled memorandum from Assistant Attorney General John Doar to section chiefs, Civil Rights Division, October 30, 1967, p. 2.

33. Navasky, *Kennedy Justice,* 109 (internal quotation marks omitted).

34. A congressional committee has noted that "since the Commission has no enforcement authority, the force of its work has come from its scholarly reports." House Committee on the Judiciary, *Civil Rights Commission Amendments Act of 1994,* 103d Cong., 2d sess., 1994, H. Rept. 775 (reproduced in 1994 U.S.C.C.A.N. [U.S. Code Congressional and Administrative News] 3532–33). Commission studies tend to be incomplete because "oversight agencies produce evaluations which reflect their policy mission as it is embodied in the oversight agency's enabling legislation," thus giving their work "a uni-dimensional thrust." Howard Ball, Dale Krane, and Thomas P. Lauth, *Compromised Compliance: Implementation of the 1965 Voting Rights Act* (Westport, Conn.: Greenwood Press, 1982), 182–83.

35. A study of the Antitrust Division concluded: "The Antitrust attorney seizes whatever is helpful, discards whatever might tell against him. . . . He gathers evidence instead of finding facts. . . . The attorneys develop zeal in their work, are persuaded of the guilt of the accused, bend every effort that the breach of the law shall be atoned." Walton Hamilton and Irene Till, *Antitrust in Action,* Monograph no. 16 of the U.S. Temporary National Economic Commission, Investigation of Concentration of Economic Power (Washington, D.C.: U.S. Government Printing Office, 1940), 27–30, quoted in Weaver, *Decision to Prosecute,* 34–35. This overstates the case because both the Antitrust Division and the Civil Rights Division—like all litigators—must take into account the weaknesses as well as the strengths of their case if they are to bring cases that are likely to succeed in court.

36. Quoted in Senate Committee on the Judiciary, *Nomination of William Bradford Reynolds To Be Associate Attorney General of the United States,* 86. Similarly, Suzanne Weaver's interviews with Antitrust Division attorneys yielded only rarely any "mention of a conscious trade-off between competing values." Weaver, *Decision to Prosecute,* 47. Of course, to the extent that the Constitution or laws of the United States have already resolved the competing values, it should lie beyond the province of the career attorneys to make their own trade-offs.

37. See Caplan, *Tenth Justice,* 42–43. Caplan himself perpetuates the error, saying that Wallace was hired in 1969.

38. Id. at 239.

39. *City of Rome v. United States,* 446 U.S. 156, 206 n.17 (1980) (Powell, J., dissenting).

40. Daniel J. Meador, *The President, the Attorney General, and the Department of Justice*

(Charlottesville: University of Virginia, White Burkett Miller Center of Public Affairs, 1980), 108.

41. Ronald G. Carr, *Mr. Levi at Justice,* 52 U. Chi. L. Rev. 300, 307 (1985).

42. U.S. Department of Justice, Civil Rights Division, *Case Management System Statistics Report,* October 16, 1992.

43. *United States v. City of Philadelphia,* 644 F.2d 187 (3rd Cir. 1980).

44. Senate Amendment no. 817 to H.R. 14765, 89th Cong., 2d sess., September 6, 1966.

45. E.g., requirement that the department first receive a citizen complaint before initiating a school desegregation action, 42 U.S.C. §2000c-6(a); requirement that the attorney general sign the complaint, 42 U.S.C. §§2000a-5(a), 2000b(a), 2000e-6(a).

46. See Meador, *The President, the Attorney General, and the Department of Justice,* 28–29.

47. "Report by the District of Columbia Bar Special Committee on Government Lawyers and the Model Rules of Professional Conduct," *Washington Lawyer* 3, no. 1 (September–October 1988): 53, 54 (internal quotation marks omitted). See also C. Normand Poirier, *The Federal Government Lawyer and Professional Ethics,* 60 A.B.A. J. 1541 (1974), citing Opinion 73-1 of the Committee on Professional Ethics of the Federal Bar Association, 32 F.B.J. 71 (1973) (the government lawyer "assumes a public trust . . . [which] requires him to observe in the performance of his professional responsibility the public interest sought to be served by the governmental organization of which he is a part").

48. Former Solicitor General Griswold states: "My client was the United States. I did not regard the President of the United States as my client, though he was my ultimate boss, and my tenure was at his will." Erwin N. Griswold, *Ould Fields, New Corne: The Personal Memoirs of a Twentieth Century Lawyer* (St. Paul, Minn.: West Publishing Company, 1992), 327. Other federal agencies are sometimes referred to as clients, but ultimate control over their litigating positions lies with the attorney general, not the "client agency." See 28 U.S.C. §516. Professor Selig argues that "the Department's client is the law and the public interest." Selig, *The Reagan Justice Department,* 793. Both the open-ended nature of the law and the public interest and their disembodied nature argue against such a characterization.

49. Quoted in Homer Cummings and Carl McFarland, *Federal Justice: Chapters in the History of Justice and the Federal Executive* (1937; reprint, New York: Da Capo Press, 1970), 500. In a similar vein, Abraham Lincoln's attorney general, Edward Bates, acknowledged, "It is my duty, above all other ministers of State, to uphold the Law, and resist all encroachments, from whatever quarter, of mere will and power." Id. at 499.

50. Michael Horowitz, quoted in *Wall Street Journal,* February 20, 1986, p. 24.

51. Cf. the Code of Ethics for Government Service, House Concurrent Res. 175, July 11, 1958, *U.S. Statutes at Large* 72 (1959): B12; 5 U.S.C.A. §7301 note: "Any person in Government service should: 1. Put loyalty to the highest moral principles and to country above loyalty to persons, party, or Government Department. 2. Uphold the Constitution, laws, and legal regulations of the United States and of all governments therein and never be a party to their evasion." The Code also appears as an appendix to the Department of Justice's Standards of Conduct, 28 C.F.R. Part 45.

52. Deval L. Patrick became assistant attorney general in April 1994, almost fifteen months after President Clinton's inauguration. See Pierre Thomas, "Justice Dept. Civil Rights Chief Pledges Activism," *Washington Post,* April 15, 1994, sec. A, p. 23. During the interim, a career attorney, James P. Turner, served as acting assistant attorney general (and I returned to serve as his chief deputy for seven months), but all major decisions had to be approved by Associate Attorney General Hubbell or Attorney General Janet Reno. After Patrick took office the division was allowed to engage in new initiatives, and by October 1994 the *Post* reported: "Patrick has taken the department in a '180-degree turn

contrary to the previous administrations,' said Charles J. Cooper, former Justice Department official who served in the Reagan administration. 'That's their right, that's what we did.' " Pierre Thomas, "Deval Patrick and the 'Great Moral Imperative,' " *Washington Post,* October 26, 1994, sec. A, p. 1. Some changes in position had occurred during the hiatus period, but only where the press of litigation schedules required decision. Thus, for fifteen months the division's civil service employees were forced into a holding pattern because of the lack of political leadership.

53. *Branti v. Finkel,* 445 U.S. 507, 530 (1980) (Powell, J., dissenting).

54. Roger C. Cramton, *On the Steadfastness and Courage of Government Lawyers,* 23 J. Marshall L. Rev. 165, 167 (1990). Professor Cramton served as assistant attorney general for the Office of Legal Counsel.

55. Carr, *Mr. Levi at Justice,* 313. See also, Weaver, *Decision to Prosecute,* 107–12, describing the process by which the assistant attorney general of the Antitrust Division typically reviews litigation recommendations from the staff.

56. *Morgan v. Kerrigan,* 509 F.2d 580 (1st Cir. 1974), *cert. denied,* 421 U.S. 963 (1975).

57. Meador, *The President, the Attorney General, and the Department of Justice,* 85. Rebecca Mae Salokar, *The Solicitor General: The Politics of Law* (Philadelphia: Temple University Press, 1992), 102–3. But see Bob Woodward and Scott Armstrong, *The Brethren: Inside the Supreme Court* (New York: Simon and Schuster, 1979), 427 ("there were reports that the Ford administration would come out against busing. But when these reports were followed by more violence, the White House decided not to intervene").

58. Carr, *Mr. Levi at Justice,* 316. See also Orfield, *Must We Bus?* 353–54.

59. See Navasky, *Kennedy Justice,* 99 (discussions regarding voter discrimination litigation) and 297–322 (discussions regarding the department's position in reapportionment cases); Schlesinger, *Robert Kennedy and His Times,* 258–60.

60. Leon E. Panetta and Peter Gall, *Bring Us Together: The Nixon Team and the Civil Rights Retreat* (Philadelphia: J. B. Lippincott Company, 1971), 111–14. These three attorneys general were in other respects quite dissimilar. One author categorizes Levi as "the Neutral Attorney General," Kennedy as "the Advocate Attorney General," and Mitchell as an attorney general with "no respect for rule of law." Baker, *Conflicting Loyalties,* 82, 122, and 140.

61. Barbara Allen Babcock, *Defending the Government: Justice and the Civil Division,* 23 J. Marshall L. Rev. 181, 193 (1990).

62. Cramton, *Steadfastness and Courage,* 167.

63. Brian K. Landsberg, "Remarks at Civil Rights Division Farewell Reception in His Honor," Washington, D.C., June 20, 1986, p. 1.

64. See *Whitney v. California,* 274 U.S. 357, 375 (1927) (Brandeis, J., concurring).

65. See Caplan, *Tenth Justice,* 51–64; Brian K. Landsberg, book review, 6 Const. Commentary 165, 177–79 (1989) (reviewing Caplan, *Tenth Justice*).

66. Senate Committee on the Judiciary, *Nomination of William Bradford Reynolds To Be Associate Attorney General of the United States,* 53.

67. I describe here two techniques of government by fiat: government by unilateral command from the political appointee to the civil service lawyer and government by end run.

68. *Davis v. Board of School Comm'rs,* 402 U.S. 33 (1971).

69. Orfield, *Must We Bus?* 336 (footnote omitted).

70. *Kelley v. Metropolitan County Bd. of Educ.,* 463 F.2d 732 (6th Cir. 1972), *cert. denied,* 409 U.S. 1001 (1972).

71. Griswold, *Ould Fields, New Corne,* 319. Dean Griswold misidentifies the case as involving Montgomery County, Maryland, schools. See memorandum of the United States, *Vaughns v. Board of Education,* 410 U.S. 918 (1973) (denying stay); see 468 F.2d 894 (4th

Cir. 1972). Griswold was fired by President Nixon, effective with the end of the Supreme Court's October 1972 term in the summer of 1973. Griswold, *Ould Fields, New Corne,* 317.

72. See Orfield, *Must We Bus?* 338–40, referring to me among others: "The head of the Civil Rights Division's education section, Brian Landsberg, found that he could not, in good conscience, sign a number of the briefs submitted in major school desegregation cases." Orfield cites a memorandum from me to Assistant Attorney General Pottinger, October 12, 1972. See also the description of the attorney protest in Harris, *Justice,* 218–21.

73. See Norman C. Amaker, *Civil Rights and the Reagan Administration* (Arlington, Va.: University Press of America, 1988), 124.

74. *Williams v. City of New Orleans,* 729 F.2d 1554 (5th Cir. 1984) (en banc). I was one of the persons not timely consulted. The Equal Employment Opportunities Commission prepared a brief supporting entry of the consent decree but was dissuaded by the administration from filing it. See id. at 1572 n.5 (Wisdom, J., concurring in part and dissenting in part). This encounter between the Department of Justice and the EEOC is described in Neal Devins, *Unitariness and Independence: Solicitor General Control over Independent Agency Litigation,* 82 Cal. L. Rev. 255, 298–99 (1994).

75. For another claim of government by fiat, see Robert D. Dinerstein, "Rights of Institutionalized Disabled Persons," in Citizens' Commission on Civil Rights, *One Nation, Indivisible: The Civil Rights Challenge for the 1980s* (Washington, D.C., 1989), 388, 393 (Assistant Attorney General Reynolds adopted a narrow interpretation of meaning of *Youngberg v. Romeo,* 457 U.S. 307 [1982], without consulting staff attorneys in or the leadership of the trial section responsible for enforcing the rights of institutionalized persons). This claim does not entirely conform with my own, possibly flawed, recollection, which is that Reynolds consulted with both the Trial Section and the Appellate Section, whose views were closer to, though not in complete accord with, his own.

76. Sissela Bok has well described the costs of secrecy: Secrecy "can debilitate judgment, first of all, whenever it shuts out criticism and feedback, leading people to become mired down in stereotyped, unexamined, often erroneous beliefs and ways of thinking. Neither their perception of a problem nor their reasoning about it then receives the benefit of challenge and exposure." Sissela Bok, *Secrets: On the Ethics of Concealment and Revelation* (New York: Pantheon Books, 1982), 25. She also points out the divisiveness of secrecy: "While secrecy may heighten a sense of equality and brotherhood among persons sharing the secret, it can fuel gross intolerance and hatred toward outsiders." Id. at 28.

77. Sissela Bok notes that "secrecy is as indispensable to human beings as fire." Id. at 18. Her explanation includes the following words, applicable to the Department of Justice: "Secrecy for plans is needed, not only to protect their formulation but also to develop them, perhaps to change them, at times to execute them, even to give them up." Id. at 23.

78. Navasky, *Kennedy Justice,* 183.

79. See Panetta and Gall, *Bring Us Together,* 296.

80. For example, the annual report for FY 1976 reports that the division filed thirty-five fair housing suits, of which twenty-one were against owners and operators of apartments and trailer parks; the report does not mention any suits involving discriminatory land-use rules. Attorney General, *Annual Report of the Attorney General of the United States for Fiscal Year Ended June 30, 1976,* 104–5. See also Joel L. Selig, *The Justice Department and Racially Exclusionary Municipal Practices: Creative Ventures in Fair Housing Act Enforcement,* 17 U. C. Davis L. Rev. 445, 447 (1984) ("Of the 285 suits the Division filed during its first decade of Fair Housing Act enforcement, only thirteen were against public sector defendants, and only three of these involved exclusionary land use practices").

81. Selig, *The Justice Department and Racially Exclusionary Municipal Practices,* 448 (Days "was dissatisfied with requests to approve routine lawsuits affecting small numbers

of units of housing, and with the absence of proposed lawsuits challenging exclusionary land use practices").

82. Letter from Hon. Frank E. Schwelb to Brian K. Landsberg, May 2, 1994.

83. Selig, *The Justice Department and Racially Exclusionary Municipal Practices,* 448.

84. Id. at 450.

85. Attributed to Thucydides. See Charles P. Curtis, Jr., and Ferris Greenslet, eds., *The Practical Cogitator,* 3d ed. (New York: Dell Publishing Company, 1975).

CHAPTER 10. THE FUTURE OF THE CIVIL RIGHTS DIVISION

1. Robert Doar, "Doar to Doar," *Dutchess Magazine* (winter 1996): 16, 21.

2. Id. at 20.

3. John Kaplan, *Comment on the Decade of School Desegregation—Progress and Prospects,* 64 Columbia L. Rev. 223, 229 (1964).

4. See *ICC Termination Act of 1995,* Public Law 88, 104th Cong., 1st sess. (December 29, 1995).

5. Linda R. Hirshman, *The Virtue of Liberality in American Communal Life,* 88 Mich. L. Rev. 983, 1021 (1990). Hirshman quotes from an article by Jennifer Hochschild, *Equal Opportunity and the Estranged Poor,* 501 Annals Am. Acad. Pol. and Soc. Sci. 143 (1989), who recommends programmatic solutions to joblessness, teen pregnancy, and high school dropouts and a broad range of social efforts to provide multidimensional aid.

6. For example, the department settled a suit against U.S. Steel Corporation for injunctive relief and $30 million in back pay. Although a large lump sum, the monetary settlement was criticized for providing too little to individual victims of discrimination. See Jack Greenberg, *Crusaders in the Courts: How a Dedicated Band of Lawyers Fought for the Civil Rights Revolution* (New York: Harper Collins, Basic Books, 1994), 424. In a private suit, litigants routinely settle for less than they might win after an expensive, time-consuming, and risky trial. They are guided by a cost-benefit–type analysis in deciding what is a fair settlement and have less incentive to follow such an analysis where the costs of litigation are borne by the government. The government must have the capacity to settle cases, but the cost-benefit analysis is more difficult where the principle costs accrue to the government while private individuals would reap the benefits. See *United States v. Allegheny-Ludlum Industries, Inc.,* 517 F.2d 826, 843 (5th Cir. 1975) (the suit by the United States is to "vindicate the broad public interest in eliminating unlawful practices, at a level which may or may not address the grievances of particular individuals").

7. Alexander M. Bickel, *The Least Dangerous Branch: The Supreme Court at the Bar of Politics,* 2d ed. (New Haven: Yale University Press, 1986), 251.

8. See *Guinn v. United States,* 238 U.S. 347 (1915) (upholding conviction under predecessors of §§241 and 242 for enforcing Oklahoma's grandfather clause).

9. Compare, e.g., Netherlands Penal Code Article 429 quater: "(1) Any person who in exercising a profession or a trade discriminates between persons on the ground of race is punishable by imprisonment not exceeding one month or a fine in the third category. (2) This provision shall not apply to actions which grant preferential treatment to persons belonging to certain ethnic or cultural minorities." Reproduced in Irene Asscher-Vonk, *Equality in Law Between Men and Women in the European Community: The Netherlands* (Dordrecht: Martinus Nijhoff Publishers, 1995), 77.

10. 42 U.S.C.A. §1973j(a) and (c). There are no reported cases of prosecution under that provision.

11. 18 U.S.C.A. §245(b)(2)(B).

12. See, e.g., California Assembly, A.B. 2468 (1996).

13. See, e.g., Sanford H. Kadish, *Comment: The Folly of Overfederalization,* 46 Hastings L. J. 1247 (1995).

14. See Franklin E. Zimring and Gordon Hawkins, *Toward a Principled Basis for Federal Criminal Legislation,* 543 Annals Am. Acad. Pol. and Soc. Sci. 15, 23 (1996), who mention some possible justifications for enacting federal criminal laws, including that "the federal interest is stronger and more direct than that of states" and that "agencies of state criminal justice are relatively inefficient in the detection, prosecution, or punishment of behavior as compared with the federal government." The criteria suggested by Zimring and Hawkins would lead to the conclusion that because of its responsibility to enforce the Reconstruction amendments, there is the requisite "significant nexus between the federal branch of government" and violations of the antidiscrimination laws. See also Kadish, *Comment: The Folly of Overfederalization,* 1250.

15. Renèe M. Landers, *Reporter's Draft for the Working Group on the Mission of the Federal Courts,* 46 Hastings L. J. 1255, 1263 (1995).

16. In 1967 more than 95 percent of attorneys in the United States were men. See Herma Hill Kay, *Sex-Based Discrimination,* 3d ed. (St. Paul, Minn.: West Publishing Company, 1988), 881 (4.7 percent of lawyers and judges in 1970 were women). Only a handful of women lawyers served in the division in 1967.

17. Memorandum from John Doar to the deputy attorney general, Sept. 11, 1967, p. 4.

18. For other anecdotes about learning from John Doar, see Gerald M. Stern, *The Buffalo Creek Disaster* (New York: Random House, Vintage Books, 1976), 129–34.

19. I base this statement on my experience from June 1993 to January 1994 as acting deputy assistant attorney general. As to one filing, I wrote a note observing that it "belongs to the gee whiz school of lawyering, containing few facts, plenty of colloquialisms . . . , word misuses . . . , non sequiturs . . . and precious little law." As to another, I questioned "how we got into a situation of filing on summary judgment without knowing what if any material facts are contested." See also Ana Puga, "Civil Rights Office Called Inefficient," *Boston Globe,* December 26, 1993, p. 18 ("some attorneys from civil rights organizations charged that the lack of leadership has translated into sloppy work").

20. *United States v. Lynd,* 301 F.2d 818, 821 (5th Cir. 1962) (Tuttle, C. J.).

21. *South Carolina v. Katzenbach,* 383 U.S. 301, 328 (1966), referring to the Voting Rights Act of 1965.

22. The existence of continued racial discrimination may no longer be clear to the American people. As Kimberlè Williams Crenshaw has explained, influential voices now claim that "the goal of the civil rights movement—the extension of formal equality to all Americans regardless of color—has already been achieved." Kimberlè Williams Crenshaw, *Race, Reform, and Retrenchment: Transformation and Legitimation in Antidiscrimination Law,* 101 Harv. L. Rev. 1331, 1334 (1988).

23. 42 U.S.C.A. §1973j(a) and (c).

24. Burke Marshall, *A Comment on the Nondiscrimination Principle in a "Nation of Minorities,"* 93 Yale L. J. 1006 (1984).

Glossary

AGE DISCRIMINATION ACT OF 1975: 42 U.S.C. §6101 et seq. Prohibits (with some exceptions) the use of any person's age as the basis of exclusion from participation in, denial of benefits of, or other discrimination under any program or activity that receives federal financial assistance.

AMERICANS WITH DISABILITIES ACT OF 1990: 42 U.S.C. §§12101–12213. Prohibits discrimination in employment, accommodations, public services, transportation, and telecommunications against any person disabled by a physical or mental impairment that substantially interferes with a major life activity.

BLACK CODES: Laws adopted by southern states after the Civil War to restrict the freedom of blacks and replace the institution of slavery. Harsh labor laws were instituted in many states limiting the employment opportunities that blacks could seek. Some states required blacks to contract for employment at the beginning of each year and carry evidence of such employment. In other states blacks were limited to employment as servants or farm workers. Other laws prescribed penalties to prevent whites from competing for black workers. Vagrancy laws were enacted, and violations were punishable by fine or plantation labor. In addition apprenticeship laws provided for plantation labor without compensation. The right to rent, inherit, own, and convey property was also severely restricted.

CIVIL LIBERTIES ACT OF 1988: 50 App. U.S.C. §1989b. Provides for restitution payments to Americans and permanent resident aliens of Japanese ancestry who were confined, relocated, or held in custody during World War II as part of the mass internment of Japanese Americans on the West Coast.

CIVIL RIGHTS ACT OF 1866: Provides that all citizens have the same rights to make and enforce contracts, to sue and give evidence in the courts, and to own, purchase, sell, rent, and inherit real and personal property as are enjoyed by white citizens. Now codified at 42 U.S.C. §§1981, 1982.

CIVIL RIGHTS ACT OF 1870: Also known as the Ku Klux Klan Act, this act made it a federal crime to conspire to injure, oppress, threaten, or intimidate any person in the free exercise of any right or privilege protected by the laws or Constitution of the United States. In addition, the act made it a crime for any person acting under color of law to willfully subject any person to the deprivation of any rights, privileges, or immunities protected by the Constitution or laws of the United States, or to different punishments, pains, or penalties on the basis of that person being an alien or based upon such person's color or race than were prescribed for the punishment of citizens. Now codified at 18 U.S.C. §§ 241, 242.

CIVIL RIGHTS ACT OF 1875: Prohibited the race-based denial of equal access to places of public accommodation. This act was invalidated by the Supreme Court in the *Civil Rights Cases,* 109 U.S. 3 (1883).

CIVIL RIGHTS ACT OF 1957: 42 U.S.C. §1971. Protects the right of any person otherwise qualified to vote without distinction of race, color, or previous condition of servitude. In addition the act prohibits the use of intimidation, threats, coercion, or the attempted intimidation, threat, or coercion of any person for the purpose of interfering with their Fifteenth Amendment right to vote. The attorney general has authority to institute a civil action on behalf of the United States for any violation of this act or where there are reasonable grounds to believe that any person is about to engage in conduct that would deprive any other person of any rights or privilege secured by this act.

CIVIL RIGHTS ACT OF 1960: 42 U.S.C. §1971(e). Requires the maintenance of certain records pertaining to voting and authorizes suits by the U.S. attorney general to find a pattern or practice of race discrimination in voting exists. Where a pattern or practice of race discrimination exists, the act provides for the appointment of federal referees to review applications to be declared qualified to vote and permits a person otherwise deemed unqualified to vote as a result of such practices to obtain a court order declaring that person to be a qualified voter. Additionally, the act prohibits the willful theft, destruction, concealment, mutilation, or alteration of election documents.

CIVIL RIGHTS ACT OF 1964:

TITLE II: 42 U.S.C. §2000a et seq. Prohibits discrimination on the basis of race, color, religion, or national origin in places of public accommodation including hotels, restaurants, and theaters. Private individuals may bring suits for relief. In addition the attorney general has authority to bring suit in pattern or practice cases.

TITLE III: 42 U.S.C. §2000b et seq. Upon receipt of a written complaint that an individual has been denied equal access to public facilities owned, operated, or managed by or on behalf of any state based upon race, the attorney general is authorized to institute a civil action where the complainant is unable to institute and maintain an action.

TITLE IV: 42 U.S.C. §2000c et seq. Upon receipt of a written complaint that an individual has been denied admission or attendance to a public school or college based upon race, color, religion, or national origin (or sex, under a 1972 amendment), the attorney general is authorized to institute a civil suit where the complainant is found unable to maintain an action.

TITLE VI: 42 U.S.C. §2000d et seq. Prohibits the exclusion from participation in or discriminatory denial of benefits of any program or activity receiving federal financial assistance based upon race, color, or national origin. The attorney general has enforcement authority upon referral from the federal agency.

TITLE VII: 42 U.S.C. §2000e et seq. Prohibits employment discrimination based upon race, color, religion, sex, or national origin.

TITLE IX: 42 U.S.C. §2000h-2. Authorizes the attorney general to intervene in cases of general public importance alleging denial of equal protection of the laws on account of race, religion, sex, or national origin.

CIVIL RIGHTS ACT OF 1991: *U.S. Statutes at Large* 105 (1992): 1071. Provides that an employment practice is unlawful if the complaining party can demonstrate that the particular practice has a disparate impact on the basis of race, color, religion, sex, or national origin, and the respondent fails to show that the practice in question is job-related and is required due to business necessity. The act does not allow the defense of business necessity for intentional discrimination in employment practices.

CIVIL RIGHTS ATTORNEY FEE AWARD ACT OF 1976: 42 U.S.C. §1988b. Authorizes a court in its discretion to award to the prevailing party a reasonable attorney's fee as part of the cost of any action or proceeding to enforce specified civil rights sections.

CIVIL RIGHTS OF INSTITUTIONALIZED PERSONS ACT OF 1980 (CRIPA): 42 U.S.C. §1997e. Authorizes the attorney general to institute a civil action whenever there is reasonable cause to believe that a pattern or practice of a state, political subdivision, or any person acting on behalf of a state is subjecting persons residing in or confined in an institution to egregious conditions that deprive such persons of any rights, privileges, or immunities protected by the Constitution or laws of the United States.

COMMERCE CLAUSE: Article I, Section 8, clause 3 of the U.S. Constitution. Section 8 enumerates Congress's powers. Clause 3 empowers Congress to enact legislation regulating interstate commerce.

COMMISSION ON CIVIL RIGHTS: 42 U.S.C. §1975. The Civil Rights Act of 1957 established the commission in order to investigate allegations of deprivations of the right to vote by reason of color, race, religion, or national origin. The commission's role is one of information gathering and not one of enforcement. Throughout its years in existence, the commission has conducted investigations in the areas of education, employment, housing, and justice as well as voting.

EQUAL CREDIT OPPORTUNITIES ACT: 15 U.S.C. §1691. Makes it unlawful for any creditor to discriminate against an applicant on the basis of race, color, religion, national origin, sex, marital status, age, because all or part of the applicant's income is derived from a public assistance program, or in retaliation for exercising any right under this act by taking adverse action on a credit application such as a denial or revocation of credit. The attorney general has authority to bring a civil action for violation of this act when there is reason to believe that a pattern or practice of discrimination exists or whenever the responsible enforcement agency requests attorney general assistance.

EQUAL EDUCATIONAL OPPORTUNITIES ACT: 20 U.S.C. §1701 et seq. Guarantees equal educational opportunity to all public school children without regard to race, color, sex, or national origin. The attorney general has authority to sue civilly to enforce equal educational guarantees.

FAIR HOUSING ACT OF 1968, AS AMENDED BY THE FAIR HOUSING AMENDMENTS ACT OF 1988: 42 U.S.C. §§3601–3619, 3631. Prohibits discrimination based upon race, color, religion, sex, or national origin in the sale, lease, rental, or financing of homes by licensed agents or brokers. The 1988 amendments added provisions prohibiting housing discrimination based upon disability and familial status. Aggrieved individuals may file private suits or request HUD to initiate administrative proceedings. If HUD finds probable cause to hold an administrative hearing, the attorney general is required to initiate a lawsuit on behalf of the victim if either party to the hearing requests that the action be heard in federal court; such suits are referred to as "election suits." Additionally, the attorney general is authorized to initiate a civil action upon referral from HUD or where a pattern or practice of housing discrimination exists.

FREEDOM OF ACCESS TO CLINIC ENTRANCES ACT OF 1994: 18 U.S.C. §248. Makes it a federal crime for any person to use or attempt to use force, threat of force, or by physical obstruction to intentionally injure or intimidate any other person or class of persons from obtaining or providing reproductive health services. The act also prohibits the intentional damage or destruction of such facilities. The U.S. attorney general and any state attorney general is permitted to institute civil actions for violations of the act when there is reasonable cause to believe that any person or group is being, has been, or may be injured by conduct violating the act.

INDIAN BILL OF RIGHTS ACT OF 1968: 25 U.S.C. §§1301–1303. Guarantees that Indian tribes in exercising the power of self-government will not violate rights protected by the Constitution and laws of the United States by codifying the principal provisions of the Bill of Rights and the equal protection clause of the Fourteenth Amendment to be binding on Indian tribes. There is no private or U.S. right of action under this act.

JIM CROW LAWS: Laws adopted after the *Civil Rights Cases* that required racial segregation of public facilities for blacks and whites including railroads, schools, parks, restaurants, and other places of public accommodation. Jim Crow was upheld by the Supreme Court in *Plessy v. Ferguson,* 163 U.S. 537 (1896), and later disapproved in *Brown v. Board of Education,* 347 U.S. 483 (1954).

NATIONAL LABOR RELATIONS ACT: 29 U.S.C. §151. Protects the rights of employees to organize unions and to engage in concerted activities for the purpose of collective bargaining or other mutual aid protection. This act served as a partial model for Title VII of the Civil Rights Act of 1964.

PART 3: Initially proposed by Attorney General Brownell, this approach to civil rights violations would have conferred authority on the attorney general to bring civil suits to enforce the equal protection clause.

SHERMAN ACT OF 1890: 15 U.S.C. §§1–7. Prohibits the formation of contracts, trusts, or conspiracies to restrain trade or commerce between the states, U.S. territories, the District of Columbia, and with foreign nations. In addition, the act prohibits monopolies, attempted monopolies, or conspiracies to monopolize any part of trade or commerce between the states or with foreign nations.

TITLE IX OF THE EDUCATION AMENDMENTS OF 1972: 20 U.S.C. §1681. Prohibits discrimination based upon sex in admissions to institutions of vocational and professional education, public graduate and undergraduate institutions of higher education, and any other form of sex discrimination in the provision of education-related programs or services. The attorney general may file suits upon referral from federal agencies alleging sex discrimination in federally assisted education programs.

VOTING RIGHTS ACT OF 1965: 42 U.S.C. §1973 (as amended). Adopted to eliminate racial discrimination in voting practices as provided by the Fifteenth Amendment. The act forbids the use of voting tests and authorizes the attorney general to assign federal voting registrars and poll watchers to specially covered jurisdictions, defined as any state or political subdivision in which fewer than 50 percent of the voting age population was registered to vote on November 1, 1964, 1968, and 1972. It also grants individuals and the attorney general the right to sue in federal court to challenge discrimination in state and local elections and prohibits the use of any voting qualification or prerequisite to voting or standard, practice, or procedure that results in the denial or abridgement of voting rights.

VOTING RIGHTS ACT §5: 42 U.S.C. §1973a. This section of the Voting Rights Act of 1965 prohibits the specially covered jurisdictions from implementing any changes in voting procedures or regulations without first satisfying the U.S. District Court for the District of Columbia or the Department of Justice that the change does not have the purpose and will not have the effect of discriminating based on race.

Bibliography

Amaker, Norman C. *Civil Rights and the Reagan Administration.* Arlington, Va.: University Press of America, 1988.

Anderson, John Weir. *Eisenhower, Brownell, and the Congress: The Tangled Origins of the Civil Rights Bill of 1956–1957.* University: Published for the Inter-University Case Program by the University of Alabama Press, 1964.

Asscher-Vonk, Irene. *Equality in Law Between Men and Women in the European Community: The Netherlands.* Dordrecht: Martinus Nijhoff Publishers, 1995.

Attorney General. *Annual Report of the Attorney General of the United States for Fiscal Year Ended June 30, 1984.*

——. *Annual Report of the Attorney General of the United States for Fiscal Year Ended June 30, 1982.*

——. *Annual Report of the Attorney General of the United States for Fiscal Year Ended June 30, 1980.*

——. *Annual Report of the Attorney General of the United States for Fiscal Year Ended June 30, 1979.*

——. *Annual Report of the Attorney General of the United States for Fiscal Year Ended June 30, 1976.*

——. *Annual Report of the Attorney General of the United States for Fiscal Year Ended June 30, 1974.*

——. *Annual Report of the Attorney General of the United States for Fiscal Year Ended June 30, 1973.*

——. *Annual Report of the Attorney General of the United States for Fiscal Year Ended June 30, 1970.*

——. *Annual Report of the Attorney General of the United States for Fiscal Year Ended June 30, 1968.*

——. *Annual Report of the Attorney General of the United States for Fiscal Year Ended June 30, 1967.*

——. *Annual Report of the Attorney General of the United States for Fiscal Year Ended June 30, 1966.*

——. *Annual Report of the Attorney General of the United States for Fiscal Year ended June 30, 1965.*

——. *Annual Report of the Attorney General of the United States for Fiscal Year Ended June 30, 1964.*

———. *Annual Report of the Attorney General of the United States for the Fiscal Year Ended June 30, 1962.*

———. *Annual Report of the Attorney General of the United States for the Fiscal Year Ended June 30, 1960.*

———. *Annual Report of the Attorney General of the United States for the Fiscal Year Ended June 30, 1959.*

———. *Annual Report of the Attorney General of the United States for the Fiscal Year Ended June 30, 1958.*

Babcock, Barbara Allen. *Defending the Government: Justice and the Civil Division.* 23 J. Marshall L. Rev. 181 (1990).

Baker, Nancy V. *Conflicting Loyalties: Law and Politics in the Attorney General's Office, 1789–1990.* Lawrence: University Press of Kansas, 1992.

Ball, Howard, Dale Krane, and Thomas P. Lauth. *Compromised Compliance: Implementation of the 1965 Voting Rights Act.* Westport, Conn.: Greenwood Press, 1982.

Bass, Jack. *Taming the Storm: The Life and Times of Judge Frank M. Johnson, Jr., and the South's Fight over Civil Rights.* New York: Doubleday, 1993.

———. *Unlikely Heroes: The Dramatic Story of the Southern Judges of the Fifth Circuit Who Translated the Supreme Court's* Brown *Decision into a Revolution for Equality.* New York: Simon and Schuster, 1981.

Belknap, Michal R. *Federal Law and Southern Order: Racial Violence and Constitutional Conflict in the Post-*Brown *South.* Athens: University of Georgia Press, 1987.

———. *The Vindication of Burke Marshall: The Southern Legal System and the Anti-Civil-Rights Violence of the 1960s.* 33 Emory L. J. 93 (1984).

Belknap, Michal R., ed. *Administrative History of the Civil Rights Division of the Department of Justice During the Johnson Administration.* Vol. 17 of *Civil Rights, the White House, and the Justice Department, 1945–1968.* New York: Garland Publishing, 1991.

———. *Justice Department Briefs in Crucial Civil Rights Cases: 1948–1968.* Vol. 18, pt. 1, of *Civil Rights, the White House, and the Justice Department, 1945–1968.* New York: Garland Publishing, 1991.

———. *Justice Department Civil Rights Policies Prior to 1960: Crucial Documents from the Files of Arthur Brann Caldwell.* Vol. 16 of *Civil Rights, the White House, and the Justice Department, 1945–1968.* New York: Garland Publishing, 1991.

Bell, Derrick A., Jr. Brown v. Board of Education *and the Interest-Convergence Dilemma.* 93 Harv. L. Rev. 518 (1980).

———. *Race, Racism, and American Law.* 3d ed. Boston: Little, Brown and Company. 1992.

———. *The Racism Is Permanent Thesis: Courageous Revelations or Unconscious Denial of Racial Genocide.* 22 Cap. U. L. Rev. 571 (1993).

———. *Serving Two Masters: Integration Ideals and Client Interests in School Desegregation Litigation.* 85 Yale L. J. 470 (1976).

Bell, Griffin B., with Ronald J. Ostrow. *Taking Care of the Law.* New York: William Morrow and Company, 1982.

Belton, Robert. *A Comparative Review of Public and Private Enforcement of Title VII of the Civil Rights Act of 1964.* 31 Vand. L. Rev. 905 (1978).

Bennett, Walter Hartwell. *American Theories of Federalism.* Kingsport, Tenn.: University of Alabama Press, 1964.

Berger, Morroe. *Equality by Statute.* Rev. ed. Garden City, N.Y.: Doubleday, 1967.

Berman, Daniel M. *A Bill Becomes Law: Congress Enacts Civil Rights Legislation.* 2d ed. New York: Macmillan, 1966.

Bestor, Arthur. "The American Civil War as a Constitutional Crisis." In *American Law and the Constitutional Order: Historical Perspectives,* edited by Lawrence M. Friedman and Harry N. Scheiber. Cambridge, Mass.: Harvard University Press, 1978.

Bickel, Alexander M. *The Decade of School Desegregation: Progress and Prospects.* 64 Colum. L. Rev. 193 (1964).

———. *The Least Dangerous Branch: The Supreme Court at the Bar of Politics.* 2d ed. New Haven: Yale University Press, 1986.

Bixby, David M. *The Roosevelt Court, Democratic Ideology, and Minority Rights: Another Look at* United States v. Classic. 90 Yale L. J. 741 (1981).

Blumrosen, Alfred W. *Modern Law: The Law Transmission System and Equal Employment Opportunity.* Madison: University of Wisconsin Press, 1993.

———. *Strangers in Paradise:* Griggs v. Duke Power Co. *and the Concept of Employment Discrimination.* 71 Mich. L. Rev. 59 (1972).

Bok, Sissela. *Secrets: On the Ethics of Concealment and Revelation.* New York: Pantheon Books, 1982.

Bolick, Clint. *Unfinished Business: A Civil Rights Strategy for America's Third Century.* San Francisco: Pacific Research Institute, 1990.

Branch, Taylor. *Parting the Waters: America in the King Years, 1954–1963.* New York: Simon and Schuster, 1988.

Brauer, Carl M. *John F. Kennedy and the Second Reconstruction.* New York: Columbia University Press, 1977.

Briffault, Richard. *Our Localism: Part I—The Structure of Local Government Law.* 90 Colum. L. Rev. 1 (1990).

Brownell, Herbert. *Civil Rights in the 1950s.* 69 Tul. L. Rev. 781 (1995).

Burk, Robert Fredrick. *The Eisenhower Administration and Black Civil Rights.* Knoxville: University of Tennessee Press, 1984.

Burns, Haywood. "The Federal Government and Civil Rights." In *Southern Justice,* edited by Leon Friedman. Westport, Conn.: Greenwood Press, 1965.

Burr, Chandler. "The Better Part of Valor." *California Lawyer* 15, no. 7 (July 1995).

Caplan, Lincoln. *The Tenth Justice: The Solicitor General and the Rule of Law.* New York: Knopf, 1987.

Cappelletti, Mauro. *Governmental and Private Advocates for the Public Interest in Civil Litigation: A Comparative Study.* 73 Mich. L. Rev. 793 (1975).

Carr, Robert K. *Federal Protection of Civil Rights: Quest for a Sword.* Ithaca, N.Y.: Cornell University Press, 1947.

Carr, Ronald G. *Mr. Levi at Justice.* 52 U. Chi. L. Rev. 300 (1985).

Chayes, Abram. *The Role of the Judge in Public Law Litigation.* 89 Harv. L. Rev. 1281 (1976).

Clayton, Cornell W. "Introduction: Politics and the Legal Bureaucracy." In *Government Lawyers: The Federal Legal Bureaucracy and Presidential Politics,* edited by C. W. Clayton. Lawrence: University Press of Kansas, 1995.

Cooter, Robert. *Market Affirmative Action.* 31 San Diego L. Rev. 133 (1994).

Council for Public Interest Law. *Balancing the Scales of Justice: Financing Public Interest Law in America.* N.p.: Council for Public Interest Law, 1976.

Cramton, Roger C. *On the Steadfastness and Courage of Government Lawyers.* 23 J. Marshall L. Rev. 165 (1990).

Crenshaw, Kimberlè Williams. *Race, Reform, and Retrenchment: Transformation and Legitimation in Antidiscrimination Law.* 101 Harv. L. Rev. 1331 (1988).

Cummings, Homer, and Carl McFarland. *Federal Justice: Chapters in the History of Justice and the Federal Executive.* 1937. Reprint. New York: Da Capo Press, 1970.

Curriden, Mark. *When Good Cops Go Bad.* 82 A.B.A. J. 62 (1996).

Curtis, Charles P., Jr., and Ferris Greenslet, eds. *The Practical Cogitator.* 3d ed. New York: Dell Publishing Company, 1975.

Days, Drew S., III. *Reality.* 31 San Diego L. Rev. 169 (1994).

de Tocqueville, Alexis. *Democracy in America.* Vol. 2. New York: Knopf, Vintage Books, 1954.

Devins, Neal. *The Civil Rights Hydra,* 89 Mich. L. Rev. 1723 (1991).

———. *Unitariness and Independence: Solicitor General Control over Independent Agency Litigation.* 82 Cal. L. Rev. 255 (1994).

Dinerstein, Robert D. "Rights of Institutionalized Disabled Persons." In Citizens' Commission on Civil Rights, *One Nation, Indivisible: The Civil Rights Challenge for the 1990s.* Washington, D.C., 1989.

Dixon, Robert G., Jr. "The Attorney General and Civil Rights, 1870–1964." In *Roles of the Attorney General of the United States.* Washington, D.C.: American Enterprise Institute, 1968.

Doar, John. "The Voting Rights Act: 25 Years Later." *Civil Rights Division Journal* (December 9, 1992).

Doar, John, and Dorothy Landsberg. "The Performance of the FBI in Investigating Violations of Federal Laws Protecting the Right to Vote, 1960–1967" (conference paper, 1971), 56. Reproduced in U.S. Senate, *Intelligence Activities, Senate Resolution 21: Hearings Before the Select Committee to Study Governmental Operations with Respect to Intelligence Activities,* 94th Cong., 1st sess., November–December 1975, vol. 6, 888.

Doar, Robert. "Doar to Doar." *Dutchess Magazine* (winter 1996).

Donohue, John J., III. *Prohibiting Sex Discrimination in the Workplace: An Economic Perspective.* 56 U. Chi. L. Rev. 1337 (1989).

Easterbrook, Frank H. *The State of Madison's Vision of the State: A Public Choice Perspective.* 107 Harv. L. Rev. 1328 (1994).

Eisenstein, James. *Counsel for the United States: U.S. Attorneys in the Political and Legal Systems.* Baltimore: Johns Hopkins University Press, 1978.

Eisenstein, Miriam R. "The Civil Rights Division at Thirty-Five: A Retrospective." *Civil Rights Division Journal* (December 9, 1992).

Elliff, John T. *The United States Department of Justice and Individual Rights, 1937–1962.* New York: Garland Publishing, 1987.

Elman, Philip. Interviewed by Norman Silber. *The Solicitor General's Office, Justice Frankfurter, and Civil Rights Litigation, 1946–1960: An Oral History.* 100 Harv. L. Rev. 817 (1987).

Ely, John Hart. *Democracy and Distrust: A Theory of Judicial Review.* Cambridge, Mass.: Harvard University Press, 1980.

Emerson, Thomas I., and David Haber. *Political and Civil Rights in the United States: A Collection of Legal and Related Materials.* Buffalo, N.Y.: Dennis and Company, 1952.

Epstein, Richard A. *Forbidden Grounds: The Case Against Employment Discrimination Laws.* Cambridge, Mass.: Harvard University Press, 1992.

Equal Employment Opportunity Commission. "Guidelines on Employment Testing Procedures." *U.S. Law Week* 35 (August 24, 1966).

Eskridge, William N., Jr. *Metaprocedure,* 98 Yale L. J. 945 (1989). Reviewing Robert M. Cover, Owen M. Fiss, and Judith Resnik, *Procedure* (Westbury, N.Y.: Foundation Press, 1988).

———. *Reneging on History? Playing the Court/Congress/President Civil Rights Game.* 79 Cal. L. Rev. 613 (1991).

Eskridge, William N., Jr., and Philip P. Frickey. *Foreword: Law As Equilibrium.* 108 Harv. L. Rev. 26 (1994).

Executive Office of the President, Office of Management and Budget. "Special Analysis J: Civil Rights Activities." In *Special Analysis: Budget of the United States Government, Fiscal Year 1984.* Washington, D.C.: Government Printing Office, 1984.

Farber, Daniel A., and Suzanna Sherry. *A History of the American Constitution.* St. Paul, Minn.: West Publishing Company, 1990.

Federal Courts Study Committee. *Report of the Federal Courts Study Committee.* N.p.: April 2, 1960.

Fiss, Owen M. *The Civil Rights Injunction.* Bloomington: Indiana University Press, 1978.

———. *The Fate of an Idea Whose Time Has Come: Antidiscrimination Law in the Second Decade After* Brown v. Board of Education. 41 U. Chi. L. Rev. 742 (1974).

———. *A Theory of Fair Employment Laws.* 38 U. Chi. L. Rev. 235 (1971).

———. *Troubled Beginnings of the Modern State, 1888–1910.* Vol. 8 of *History of the Supreme Court of the United States.* New York: Macmillan Company, 1993.

Foner, Eric. *Reconstruction: America's Unfinished Revolution, 1863–1877.* New York: Harper and Row, 1988.

Freed, Clifford. Comment, *Ethical Considerations for the Justice Department When It Switches Sides During Litigation.* 7 U. Puget Sound L. Rev. 405 (1984).

Fried, Charles. *Foreword: Revolutions?* 109 Harv. L. Rev. 13 (1995).

———. *Order and Law: Arguing the Reagan Revolution—A Firsthand Account.* New York: Simon and Schuster, 1991.

Friendly, Henry J. *Federal Jurisdiction: A General View.* New York: Columbia University Press, 1973.

Fuller, Lon L. *The Forms and Limits of Adjudication.* 92 Harv. L. Rev. 353 (1978).

Galanter, Marc. *Why the "Haves" Come Out Ahead: Speculations on the Limits of Legal Change.* 9 Law and Soc'y 98 (1974).

Garrow, David. *Protest at Selma: Martin Luther King, Jr., and the Voting Rights Act of 1965.* New Haven: Yale University Press, 1982.

Garth, Bryant. *Neighborhood Law Firms for the Poor: A Comparative Study of Recent Developments in Legal Aid and in the Legal Profession.* Rockville, Md.: Sijthoff and Noordhoff, 1980.

Gaylord, Clarice E., and Geraldine W. Twitty. *Protecting Endangered Communities.* 21 Fordham Urb. L. J. 771 (1994).

Gitter, Donna M. Comment, *French Criminalization of Racial Employment Discrimination Compared to the Imposition of Civil Penalties in the United States.* 15 Comp. Lab. L. J. 488 (1994).

Goldman, Eric F. *The Tragedy of Lyndon Johnson.* New York: Knopf, 1969.

Graham, Hugh Davis. *Civil Rights and the Presidency: Race and Gender in American Politics, 1960–1972.* New York: Oxford University Press, 1992.

———. *The Civil Rights Era: Origins and Development of National Policy, 1960–1972.* New York: Oxford University Press, 1990.

Greenberg, Jack. *Crusaders in the Courts: How a Dedicated Band of Lawyers Fought for the Civil Rights Revolution.* New York: Harper Collins, Basic Books, 1994.

Gressman, Eugene. *The Unhappy History of Civil Rights Legislation.* 50 Mich. L. Rev. 1323 (1952).

Griswold, Erwin N. *Ould Fields, New Corne: The Personal Memoirs of a Twentieth Century Lawyer.* St. Paul, Minn.: West Publishing Company, 1992.

Gunther, Gerald. *Constitutional Law.* 12th ed. Westbury, N.Y.: Foundation Press, 1991.

Hamilton, Alexander. "Federalist Paper No. 78." In *The Federalist Papers.* New York: New American Library, Mentor Books, 1961.

Harris, Richard. *Justice: The Crisis of Law, Order, and Freedom in America.* New York: E. P. Dutton and Company, 1970.

Hart, Henry M., Jr. *The Aims of the Criminal Law.* 23 Law and Contemp. Probs. 401 (1958).

Heymann Philip B., and Lance Liebman. *The Social Responsibilities of Lawyers.* Westbury, N.Y.: Foundation Press, 1988.

Higginbotham, A. Leon, Jr. *In the Matter of Color: Race and the American Legal Process, the Colonial Period.* New York: Oxford University Press, 1978.

Hirschman, Albert O. *The Rhetoric of Reaction: Perversity, Futility, Jeopardy.* Cambridge, Mass.: Harvard University Press, 1991.

Hirshman, Linda R. *The Virtue of Liberality in American Communal Life.* 88 Mich. L. Rev. 983 (1990).

Holmes, Oliver Wendell. *The Common Law.* Boston: Little, Brown and Company, 1881.

Horowitz, Donald L. *The Courts and Social Policy.* Washington, D.C.: Brookings Institution, 1977.

———. *The Jurocracy: Government Lawyers, Agency Programs, and Judicial Decisions.* Lexington, Mass.: Lexington Books, 1977.

Hurst, Willard. "The Law in United States History." In *American Law and the Constitutional Order: Historical Perspectives,* edited by Lawrence M. Friedman and Harry N. Scheiber. Cambridge, Mass.: Harvard University Press, 1978.

Jackson, Robert H. *The Supreme Court in the American System of Government.* Cambridge, Mass.: Harvard University Press, 1955.

Kaczorowski, Robert J. *The Politics of Judicial Interpretation: The Federal Courts, Department of Justice, and Civil Rights, 1866–1876.* New York: Oceana Publications, 1985.

Kadish, Sanford H. *Comment: The Folly of Overfederalization.* 46 Hastings L. J. 1247 (1995).

Kaplan, John. *Comment on the Decade of School Desegregation—Progress and Prospects.* 64 Colum. L. Rev. 223 (1964).

Kay, Herma Hill. *Sex-Based Discrimination.* 3d ed. St. Paul, Minn.: West Publishing Company, 1988.

Kelley, Michael. "Segregation Anxiety." *New Yorker* (November 20, 1995).

Kelso, R. Randall, and Charles D. Kelso. *Studying Law: An Introduction.* St. Paul, Minn.: West Publishing Company, 1984.

Kennedy, John F. "Annual Message to the Congress on the State of the Union." In *Public Papers of the Presidents of the United States: John F. Kennedy, 1961.* Washington, D.C.: Government Printing Office, 1962.

———. "Excerpts from Annual Message to the Congress: The Economic Report of the President." In *Public Papers of the Presidents of the United States: John F. Kennedy, 1963.* Washington, D.C.: Government Printing Office, 1964.

———. "Radio and Television Report to the American People on Civil Rights." In *Public Papers of the Presidents of the United States: John F. Kennedy, 1963.* Washington, D.C.: Government Printing Office, 1964.

———. "Special Message to the Congress on Civil Rights and Job Opportunities." In *Public Papers of the Presidents of the United States.* Washington, D.C.: Government Printing Office, 1964.

Kennedy, Randall. *Reconstruction and the Politics of Scholarship.* 98 Yale L. J. 521 (1989).

King, Martin Luther, Jr. "Letter from Birmingham Jail." In *Why We Can't Wait.* New York: New American Library, Signet Books, 1964.

Klarman, Michael J. *Brown. Racial Change, and the Civil Rights Movement.* 80 Va. L. Rev. 7 (1994).

Kluger, Richard. *Simple Justice: The History of Brown v. Board of Education and Black America's Struggle for Equality.* New York: Random House, 1975.

Kotkin, Minna J. *Public Remedies for Private Wrongs: Rethinking the Title VII Back Pay Remedy.* 41 Hastings L. J. 1301 (1990).

Krent, Harold J. *Executive Control over Criminal Law Enforcement: Some Lessons from History.* 38 Am. U. L. Rev. 275 (1989).

Kurland, Philip B., and Gerhard Casper, eds. *Landmark Briefs and Arguments of the Supreme Court of the United States: Constitutional Law.* Vol. 110. Arlington, Va.: University Publications of America, 1980.

———. *Landmark Briefs and Arguments of the Supreme Court of the United States: Constitutional Law.* Vol. 88. Arlington, Va.: University Publications of America, 1977.

———. *Landmark Briefs and Arguments of the Supreme Court of the United States: Constitutional Law.* Vol. 70. Arlington, Va.: University Publications of America, 1977.

———. *Landmark Briefs and Arguments of the Supreme Court of the United States: Constitutional Law.* Vol. 49. Arlington, Va.: University Publications of America, 1975.

———. *Landmark Briefs and Arguments of the Supreme Court of the United States: Constitutional Law.* Vol. 49A. Arlington, Va.: University Publications of America, 1975.

———. *Landmark Briefs and Arguments of the Supreme Court of the United States: Constitutional Law.* Vol. 46. Arlington, Va.: University Publications of America, 1975.

Kushner, James A. *The Fair Housing Amendments Act of 1988: The Second Generation of Fair Housing.* 42 Vand. L. Rev. 1049 (1989).

Lanctot, Catherine J. *The Duty of Zealous Advocacy and the Ethics of the Federal Government Lawyer: The Three Hardest Questions.* 64 S. Cal. L. Rev. 951 (1991).

Landers, Renèe M. *Reporter's Draft for the Working Group on the Mission of the Federal Courts.* 46 Hastings L. J. 1255 (1995).

Landes, William M., and Richard A. Posner. *The Private Enforcement of Law.* 4 J. Legal Stud. 1 (1975).

Landsberg, Brian K. Book Review. 6 Const. Commentary 165, 179 (1989). Reviewing Lincoln Caplan, *The Tenth Justice: The Solicitor General and the Rule of Law.* New York: Knopf, 1987.

———. *Race and the Rehnquist Court.* 66 Tul. L. Rev. 1267 (1992).

———. "Remarks at Civil Rights Division Farewell Reception in His Honor." Washington, D.C., June 20, 1986.

Letter, Douglas. *Lawyering and Judging on Behalf of the United States: All I Ask for Is a Little Respect.* 61 Geo. Wash. L. Rev. 1295 (1993).

Levinson, Sanford. *Identifying the Compelling State Interest: On "Due Process of Lawmaking" and the Professional Responsibility of the Public Lawyer.* 45 Hastings L. J. 1035 (1994).

Levinson, Sanford, and Paul Brest. *Processes of Constitutional Decisionmaking: Cases and Materials.* 3d ed. Boston: Little, Brown and Company, 1992.

Locke, John. *The Second Treatise of Civil Government and a Letter Concerning Toleration.* Oxford: Basil Blackwell, 1948.

Lowman, Michael K. Comment. *The Litigating Amicus Curiae: When Does the Party Begin After the Friends Leave?* 41 Am. U. L. Rev. 1243 (1992).

Madison, James. "Federalist Paper No. 39." In *The Federalist Papers.* New York: New American Library, Mentor Books, 1961.

Maguire, John MacArthur, and Philip Zimet. *Hobson's Choice and Similar Practices in Federal Taxation.* 48 Harv. L. Rev. 1281 (1935).

Maltz, Earl M. *The Civil Rights Act and the* Civil Rights Cases: *Congress, Court, and Constitution.* 44 Fla. L. Rev. 605 (1992).

Marshall, Burke. *A Comment on the Nondiscrimination Principle in a "Nation of Minorities."* 93 Yale L. J. 1006 (1984).

———. "The Control of the Public Lawyer." In *Law and the American Future,* edited by Murray L. Schwartz. Englewood Cliffs, N.J.: Prentice-Hall, Spectrum, 1976.

———. *Federalism and Civil Rights.* New York: Columbia University Press, 1964.

Maslow, Will, and Joseph B. Robison. *Civil Rights Legislation and the Fight for Equality, 1862–1952.* 20 U. Chi. L. Rev. 363 (1953).

Meador, Daniel J. *The President, the Attorney General, and the Department of Justice.* Charlottesville: University of Virginia, White Burkett Miller Center of Public Affairs, 1980.

Mikva, Abner J., and Eric Lane. *Legislative Process.* Boston: Little, Brown and Company, 1995.

Mitchell, Clarence. *Moods and Changes: The Civil Rights Record of the Nixon Administration.* 49 Notre Dame Law. 63 (1973).

Moss, Randolph D. Note. *Participation and Department of Justice School Desegregation Consent Decrees.* 95 Yale L. J. 1811 (1986).

Nathan, Richard P. "Jobs and Civil Rights." Prepared for Commission on Civil Rights by the Brookings Institution, Washington, D.C., 1969.

Navasky, Victor S. *Kennedy Justice.* New York: Atheneum, 1971.

Nixon, Richard. "Statement About Desegregation of Elementary and Secondary Schools." In *Public Papers of the Presidents of the United States: Richard Nixon, 1970.* Washington, D.C.: Government Printing Office, 1971.

Norman, David L. "The Civil Rights Division of the U.S. Department of Justice, 1954–1973." Unpublished manuscript, 1992.

———. *The Strange Career of the Civil Rights Division's Commitment to* Brown. 93 Yale L. J. 983 (1984).

Note. *Professional Ethics in Government Side-Switching.* 96 Harv. L. Rev. 1914 (1983).

Note. *The Scope of the Attorney General's Power Under Title VII: Appraisal and Reform.* 2 Rut.-Cam. L. J. 185 (1970).

Olson, Susan M. "Challenges to the Gatekeeper: The Debate over Federal Litigating Authority." *Judicature* 68, no. 1 (June–July 1984).

O'Neill, Timothy J. Bakke *and the Politics of Equality: Friends and Foes in the Classroom of Litigation.* Middletown, Conn.: Wesleyan University Press, 1985.

Orfield, Gary. *The Growth of Segregation in American Schools: Changing Patterns of Separation and Poverty Since 1968.* Alexandria, Va.: National School Boards, 1993.

———. *Must We Bus? Segregated Schools and National Policy.* Washington, D.C.: Brookings Institution, 1978.

Panetta, Leon E., and Peter Gall. *Bring Us Together: The Nixon Team and the Civil Rights Retreat.* Philadelphia: J. B. Lippincott Company, 1971.

Patrick, Deval L. Statement of Deval L. Patrick, assistant attorney general, Civil Rights Division, Before the Subcommittee on the Constitution, Committee on the Judiciary, U.S. House of Representatives, regarding H.R. 2128; the Equal Opportunity Act of 1995, December 7, 1995.

Peltason, J. W. *Fifty-Eight Lonely Men: Southern Federal Judges and School Desegregation.* New York: Harcourt, Brace and World, 1961.

Percy, Stephen L. *Disability, Civil Rights, and Public Policy: The Politics of Implementation.* Tuscaloosa: University of Alabama Press, 1989.

Poirier, C. Normand. *The Federal Government Lawyer and Professional Ethics.* 60 A.B.A. J. 1541 (1974).

Pollak, Stephen J. "Remarks to the Lawyers' Committee for Civil Rights Under Law on Receipt of Whitney North Seymour Award." New York, October 1994.

Posner, Richard A. *An Economic Analysis of Sex Discrimination Laws.* 56 U. Chi. L. Rev. 1311 (1989).

———. *The Economics of Justice.* Cambridge, Mass.: Harvard University Press, 1981.

President's Committee on Civil Rights. *To Secure These Rights.* Washington, D.C.: Government Printing Office, 1947.

Quade, Vicki. "Treating Civil Rights Law as a Business: Interview with Guy Saperstein." *Human Rights* 21, no. 2 (spring 1994).

Rabin, Robert L. *Federal Regulation in Historical Perspective.* 38 Stan. L. Rev. 1189 (1986).

Reinstein, Robert J. *Completing the Constitution: The Declaration of Independence, Bill of Rights and Fourteenth Amendment.* 66 Temp. L. Rev. 361 (1993).

"Report by the District of Columbia Bar Special Committee on Government Lawyers and the Model Rules of Professional Conduct." *Washington Lawyer* 3, no. 1 (September–October 1988).

Report of the National Advisory Commission on Civil Disorders. New York Times edition. New York: E. P. Dutton and Company, 1968.

Reynolds, William Bradford. "The Role of the Federal Government in School Desegregation." In *Brown Plus Thirty: Perspectives on Desegregation,* edited by LaMar P. Miller. New York: New York University, Metropolitan Center for Educational Research, Development, and Training, 1986.

———. Statement of William Bradford Reynolds, assistant attorney general, Civil Rights Division, Before the Subcommittee on Civil and Constitutional Rights, Committee on the Judiciary, and Subcommittee on Employment Opportunities, Committee on Education and Labor, House of Representatives, concerning affirmative action, July 11, 1985.

Rhode, Deborah L., and David Luban. *Legal Ethics.* Westbury, N.Y.: Foundation Press, 1992.

Rhodes, James Ford. *History of the United States, 1850–1877.* Vol. 7. New York: Macmillan Company, 1906.

Robinson, Jeffrey D. "Fair Housing Act Amendments of 1988." In Citizens' Commission on Civil Rights, *One Nation, Indivisible: The Civil Rights Challenge for the 1990s.* Washington, D.C., 1989.

Rodgers, Harrel R., Jr., and Charles S. Bullock III. *Law and Social Change: Civil Rights Laws and Their Consequences.* New York: McGraw-Hill, 1972.

Rose, David L. *Twenty-Five Years Later: Where Do We Stand on Equal Employment Opportunity Law Enforcement?* 42 Vand. L. Rev. 1121 (1989).

Rosenberg, John M. *Personal Reflections of a Life in Public Interest Law: From the Civil Rights Division of the United States Department of Justice to Appalred.* 96 W. Va. L. Rev. 317 (1993–1994).

Salokar, Rebecca Mae. *The Solicitor General: The Politics of Law.* Philadelphia: Temple University Press, 1992.

Sax, Joseph L. *Defending the Environment: A Strategy for Citizen Action.* New York: Knopf, 1971.

Schlesinger, Arthur, Jr. *Robert Kennedy and His Times.* New York: Ballantine Books, 1978.

Schwartz, Bernard, ed. *Statutory History of the United States: Civil Rights.* New York: Chelsea House Publishers, 1970.

Schwarzschild, Maimon. *Public Law by Private Bargain: Title VII Consent Decrees and the Fairness of Negotiated Institutional Reform.* 1984 Duke L. J. 887.

Schwelb, Frank E. "Promotion of Civil Liberties by the Department of Justice." N.p., n.d.

Schwemm, Robert G. *The Future of Fair Housing Litigation.* 26 J. Marshall L. Rev. 745 (1993).

Seldin, Richard. *Eradicating Racial Discrimination at Public Accommodations Not Covered by Title II.* 28 Rutgers L. Rev. 1 (1974).

Selig, Joel L. *Changing the Justice Department's Position in Pending Litigation.* 25 Land and Water L. Rev. 503 (1990).

———. *The Justice Department and Racially Exclusionary Municipal Practices: Creative Ventures in Fair Housing Act Enforcement.* 17 U. C. Davis L. Rev. 445 (1984).

———. *The Reagan Justice Department and Civil Rights: What Went Wrong.* 1985 U. Ill. L. Rev. 785.

Selmi, Michael. *The Value of the EEOC: Reexamining the Agency's Role in Employment Discrimination Law.* 57 Ohio St. L. J. 1 (1996).

Selznick, Philip. *The Moral Commonwealth: Social Theory and the Promise of Community.* Berkeley: University of California Press, 1992.

Sherry, Suzanna. *Selective Judicial Activism in the Equal Protection Context: Democracy, Distrust, and Deconstruction.* 73 Geo. L. J. 89 (1984).

Smith, William French. "Address of Attorney General William French Smith Before the American Law Institute." Philadelphia, May 22, 1981.

———. *Urging Judicial Restraint.* 68 A.B.A. J. 59 (1982).

Southern Regional Council. *The Federal Retreat in School Desegregation.* Atlanta, 1969.

Stein, Anne. "Race Relations in America: What We Really Think of Each Other." *Human Rights* 21, no. 3 (summer 1994).

Stern, Gerald M. *The Buffalo Creek Disaster.* New York: Random House, Vintage Books, 1976.

Sullivan, E. Thomas, ed. *The Political Economy of the Sherman Act: The First One Hundred Years.* Athens: Ohio University Press, 1991.

Symposium. *The Department of Justice and the Civil Rights Act of 1964.* 26 Pac. L. J. 765 (1995).

Truman, Harry S. "Special Message to Congress on Civil Rights." In *Public Papers of the Presidents of the United States: Harry S. Truman, 1948.* Washington, D.C.: Government Printing Office, 1964.

Tushnet, Mark V. *Making Civil Rights Law: Thurgood Marshall and the Supreme Court, 1936-1961.* New York: Oxford University Press, 1994.

Ungar, Sanford J. *FBI.* Boston: Little, Brown and Company, 1976.

U.S. Bureau of the Census. *1968 Statistical Abstract of the United States.* Washington, D.C.: Government Printing Office, 1968.

U.S. Commission on Civil Rights. "Education." Bk. 2. *1961 United States Commission on Civil Rights Report.* Washington, D.C.: Government Printing Office, 1961.

———. *Funding Federal Civil Rights Enforcement: A Report of the United States Commission on Civil Rights, June 1995.* Prepared by Conner Ball. Washington, D.C., n.d.

———. *Political Participation: A Report of the United States Commission on Civil Rights— 1968.* Washington, D.C.: Government Printing Office, 1968.

———. *Report of the United States Commission on Civil Rights, 1959.* Washington, D.C.: Government Printing Office, 1959.

———. *The Voting Rights Act: Ten Years After.* Washington, D.C., January 1975.

U.S. Congress, House. *Civil Rights of Institutionalized Persons Act: Conference Report to Accompany H.R. 10.* 96th Cong., 2d sess., 1980. H. Rept. 897.

———. *Equal Employment Opportunities Enforcement Act of 1971.* 92d Cong., 1st sess., 1971. H. Rept. 238. Reprinted in *Legislative History of the Equal Employment Opportunity Act of 1972,* 92d Cong., 2d sess., November 1972.

U.S. Congress, House, Committee on Appropriations, Subcommittee on Departments of State, Justice, Commerce, the Judiciary, and Related Agencies Appropriations. *Departments of State, Justice, and Commerce, the Judiciary, and Related Agencies Appropriations for 1968: Hearings Before a Subcommittee of the House Committee on Appropriations.* 90th Cong., 1st sess., 1967.

———. *Departments of State, Justice, and Commerce, the Judiciary, and Related Agencies Appropriations for 1965, Hearings: Department of Justice.* 88th Cong., 2d sess., 1965.

———. *Departments of State, Justice, and Commerce, the Judiciary, and Related Agencies Appropriations for 1964, Hearings: Department of Justice.* 88th Cong., 1st sess., 1964.

U.S. Congress, House, Committee on Banking and Currency, Subcommittee on Consumer

Affairs. *Credit Discrimination: Hearings on H.R. 14856 and H.R. 14908.* 93d Cong., 2d sess., June 1974.

——. *To Amend the Equal Credit Opportunity Act of 1974: Hearings on H.R. 3386.* 94th Cong., 1st sess., April 1975.

U.S. Congress, House, Committee on Rules. *Hearings on H.R. 826.* 89th Cong., 2d sess., 1966.

U.S. Congress, House, Committee on the Judiciary. *Civil Rights: Hearing on Legislation Regarding the Civil Rights of Persons Within the Jurisdiction of the United States.* 84th Cong., 2d sess., April 1956.

——. *Civil Rights: Hearings on H.R. 7152, as Amended by Subcommittee no. 5.* 88th Cong., 1st sess., October 1963.

——. *Civil Rights Act of 1966.* 89th Cong., 2d sess., 1966. H. Rept. 1678 (to accompany H.R. 14765).

——. *Civil Rights Act of 1957.* 85th Cong., 1st sess., 1957. H. Rept. 291. Reprinted in 1957 U.S.C.C.A.N. (U.S. Code Congressional and Administrative News) 1966, 1968.

——. *Civil Rights Commission Amendments Act of 1994.* 103d Cong., 2d sess., 1994. H. Rept. 775. Reproduced in 1994 U.S.C.C.A.N. 3532–33.

U.S. Congress, House, Committee on the Judiciary, Subcommittee no. 3. *Hearings on Antilynching and Protection of Civil Rights.* 81st Cong., 1st and 2d sess., 1950.

U.S. Congress, House, Committee on the Judiciary, Subcommittee no. 5. *Civil Rights: Hearings on H.R. 300, 351, 352, 353, 400, 430, 461, 617, 618, 619, 759, 913, 914, 1902, 2346, 2479, 2538, 2786, 3090, 3147, 3148, 3212, 3559, 4169, 4261, 4338, 4339, 4342, 4348, 4457, 5008, 5170, 5189, 5217, 5218, 5276, 5323, 6934, 6935.* 86th Cong., 1st sess., March 1959.

——. *Civil Rights: Hearings on H.R. 300, 351, 352, 353, 400, 430, 461, 617, 618, 619, 759, 913, 914, 1902, 2346, 2479, 2538, 2786, 3090, 3147, 3148, 3212, 3559, 4169, 4261, 4338, 4339, 4342, 4348, 4457, 5008, 5170, 5189, 5217, 5218, 5276, 5323, 6934, 6935.* 86th Cong., 1st sess., March-April-May 1959.

——. *Civil Rights: Hearings on H.R. 140, 142, 143, 159, 359, 360, 363, 374, 395, 424, 438, 439, 440, 441, 542, 548, 549, 550, 551, 552, 555, 887, 956, 957, 958, 959, 1097, 1099, 1100, 1101, 1102, 1134, 1151, 1254, 2145, 2153, 2375, 2835, 3088, 3481, 3613, 3616, 3617, 3618, 3793, 3945, 3946, 3951, 3955, 3956, 3957, 3959, 4121, 4126, 4269, 4420, 4496, 4782.* 85th Cong., 1st sess., February 1957.

——. *Civil Rights: Hearings on Miscellaneous Proposals Regarding the Civil Rights of Persons Within the Jurisdiction of the United States.* 88th Cong., 1st sess., June 1963.

——. *Voting Rights: Hearings on H.R. 6400.* 89th Cong., 1st sess., March-April 1965.

U.S. Congress, House, Committee on the Judiciary, Subcommittee on Courts, Civil Liberties, and the Administration of Justice. *Civil Rights of Institutionalized Persons: Hearings on H.R. 10.* 96th Cong., 1st sess., February 1979.

U.S. Congress, House, Committee on the Judiciary, Subcommittee on the Constitution. *Hearings on H.R. 2128, the Equal Opportunity Act of 1995.* 104th Cong., 1st sess., December 1995.

U.S. Congress, Senate. *Intelligence Activities, Senate Resolution 21: Hearings Before the Select Committee to Study Governmental Operations with Respect to Intelligence Activities.* 94th Cong., 1st sess., November–December 1975, vol. 6.

U.S. Congress, Senate, Committee on Banking, Housing, and Urban Affairs. *Comprehensive Deposit Insurance Reform and Taxpayer Protection Act of 1991.* 102d Cong., 1st sess., 1991. S. Rept. 167.

U.S. Congress, Senate, Committee on Banking, Housing, and Urban Affairs, Subcommittee on Consumer Affairs. *Equal Credit Opportunity Act Amendments and Consumer Leasing Act—1975, Hearings on S. 483, S. 1900, S. 1927, S. 1961, and H.R. 5616.* 94th Cong., 1st sess., July 1975.

U.S. Congress, Senate, Committee on Commerce. *Civil Rights—Public Accommodations: Hearings on S. 1732.* 88th Cong., 1st sess., July 1963, serial 26, pt. 1.

U.S. Congress, Senate, Committee on Labor and Public Welfare. *Equal Employment Opportunities Enforcement Act of 1971.* 92d Cong., 1st sess., October 1971. S. Rept. 415. Reproduced in *Legislative History of the Equal Employment Opportunity Act of 1972.* 92d Cong., 2d sess., November 1972.

U.S. Congress, Senate, Committee on Labor and Public Welfare, Subcommittee on Labor. *Legislative History of the Equal Employment Opportunity Act of 1972.* 92d Cong., 2d sess., November 1972.

U.S. Congress, Senate, Committee on the Judiciary. *Civil Rights—The President's Program, 1963: Hearings on S. 1731 and S. 1750.* 88th Cong., 1st sess., July-August-September 1963.

———. *Confirmation Hearings on Federal Appointments: Hearings on Confirmation Hearings on Appointments to the Federal Judiciary.* 101st Cong., 2d sess., 1990, serial no. J-101-6.

———. *Department of Justice Confirmations: Hearings Before the Committee on the Judiciary.* 97th Cong., 1st sess., 1989.

———. *Department of Justice Confirmations: Hearings on the Nominations of Rex E. Lee To Be Solicitor General of the United States, and William Bradford Reynolds To Be Assistant Attorney General, Civil Rights Division, Department of Justice.* 97th Cong., 1st sess., June–July 1981, serial no. J-97-7, pt. 2.

———. *Nomination of Burke Marshall: Hearings on the Nomination of Burke Marshall To Be an Assistant Attorney General.* 87th Cong., 1st sess., March 1961.

———. *Nomination of W. Wilson White: Hearings Before the Committee on the Judiciary on Nomination of W. Wilson White, of Pennsylvania, To Be an Assistant Attorney General, To Head the Civil Rights Division of the Department of Justice.* 85th Cong., 2d sess., February 1958.

———. *Nomination of William Bradford Reynolds To Be Associate Attorney General of the United States: Hearings on the Confirmation of William Bradford Reynolds To Be Associate Attorney General of the United States.* 99th Cong., 1st sess., June 1985, serial no. J-99-29.

———. *Senate Judiciary Committee Confirmation Hearing of Deval Patrick To Be Assistant Attorney General for Civil Rights.* March 10, 1994. Available in LEXIS, Legis Library, Fednew file.

———. *Voting Rights: Hearings on S. 1564.* 89th Cong., 1st sess., March–April 1965, pt. 2.

U.S. Congress, Senate, Committee on the Judiciary, Subcommittee on Constitutional Rights. *Civil Rights—1959: Hearings on S. 435, S. 456, S. 499, S. 810, S. 957, S. 958, S. 959, S. 960, S. 1084, S. 1199, S. 1277, S. 1848, S. 1998, S. 2001, S. 2002, S. 2003, and S. 2041.* 86th Cong., 1st sess., March 1959.

———. *Civil Rights—1957: Hearings on S. 83, an amendment to S. 83, S. 427, S. 428, S. 429, S. 468, S. 500, S. 501, S. 502, S. 504, S. 505, S. 508, S. 509, S. 510, S. Con. Res. 5.* 85th Cong., 1st sess., February–March 1957.

———. *Hearings on the Nomination of John Doar, of New Richmond, Wis., To Be Assistant Attorney General, Civil Rights Division, U.S. Department of Justice.* 89th Cong., 1st sess., February 1965.

U.S. Congress, Senate, Committee on the Judiciary, Subcommittee on Separation of Powers. *Removing Politics from the Administration of Justice: Hearings on S. 2803, S. 2978, and S. 2615.* 93d Cong., 2d sess., March–April 1974.

U.S. Department of Justice. *The Department of Justice Manual.* Vol. 6. Clifton, N.J.: Prentice-Hall, 1988.

———. *United States Department of Justice Legal Activities, 1993–94.* Washington, D.C.: Office of Attorney Personnel Management, n.d.

U.S. Department of Justice, Civil Rights Division. *Case Management System Statistics Report*. Washington, D.C., October 16, 1992.

U.S. Department of Justice, Justice Management Division. *200th Anniversary of the Office of the Attorney General 1789–1989*. Washington, D.C., n.d.

U.S. Department of Justice, Office of Legal Policy. *Redefining Discrimination: Disparate Impact and the Institutionalization of Affirmative Action*. Report to the Attorney General, Washington, D.C., November 4, 1987.

Walker, Samuel. *In Defense of American Liberties: The History of the ACLU*. New York: Oxford University Press, 1990.

Walton, Hanes, Jr. *When the Marching Stopped: The Politics of Civil Rights Regulatory Agencies*. New York: State University of New York Press, 1988.

Ware, Leland B. *New Weapons for an Old Battle: The Enforcement Provisions of the 1988 Amendments to the Fair Housing Act*. 7 Admin. L. J. Am. U. 59 (1993).

Wasby, Stephen L. "Civil Rights Litigation by Organizations: Constraints and Choices." *Judicature* 68, no. 9–10 (April–May 1985).

——. *How Planned Is "Planned Litigation"?* 1984 Am. B. Found. Res. J. 83.

——. *The Multi-Faceted Elephant: Litigator Perspectives on Planned Litigation for Social Change*. 15 Cap. U. L. Rev. 143 (1986).

——. *Race Relations Litigation in an Age of Complexity*. Charlottesville: University Press of Virginia, 1995.

Wasserstrom, Richard A. Book review. 33 U. Chi. L. Rev. 406 (1966) Reviewing Burke Marshall, *Federalism and Civil Rights*. New York: Columbia University Press, 1964.

Weaver, Suzanne. *Decision to Prosecute: Organization and Public Policy in the Antitrust Division*. Cambridge, Mass.: MIT Press, 1977.

Whalen, Charles, and Barbara Whalen. *The Longest Debate: A Legislative History of the 1964 Civil Rights Act*. Cabin John, Md.: Seven Locks Press, 1985.

Wilkinson, J. Harvie III. *From* Brown *to* Bakke. New York: Oxford University Press, 1979.

Witherspoon, Joseph P. *Civil Rights Policy in the Federal System: Proposals for a Better Use of Administrative Process*. 74 Yale L. J. 1171 (1965).

Woodward, Bob, and Scott Armstrong. *The Brethren: Inside the Supreme Court*. New York: Simon and Schuster, 1979.

Zimring, Franklin E., and Gordon Hawkins. *Toward a Principled Basis for Federal Criminal Legislation*. 543 Annals Am. Acad. Pol. and Soc. Sci. 15 (1996).